From
Gesture to
Language
in Hearing
and Deaf Children

From Gesture to Language

in Hearing and Deaf Children

Virginia Volterra and
Carol J. Erting, Editors

Gallaudet University Press
Washington, DC 20002

Gallaudet University Press, Washington, DC 20002
@1994 by Gallaudet University. All rights reserved
Published 1994
Printed in the United States of America
Originally published 1990 by Springer-Verlag, Berlin Heidelberg

Library of Congress Cataloging-in-Publication Data
From gesture to language in hearing and deaf children / Virginia
    Volterra, Carol J. Erting (eds.).
            p.   cm.
    Originally published: Berlin: New York: Springer, 1990 in series :
Springer series in language and communication : 27,
    Includes bibliographical references and index.
    ISBN 1-56368-029-7: $39.95
    1. Deaf—Means of communication. 2. Children, Deaf—Language.
3. Language acquisition. I. Volterra, Virginia. II. Erting, Carol.
HV2471.F76   1994
401'.93—dc20   93-43153
                                                  CIP

The paper used in this publication meets the minimum requirements of
American National Standard for Information Sciences—Permanence of
Paper for Printed Library Materials, ANSI Z39.48- 1984.   ∞

Foreword

Virginia Volterra and Carol Erting have made an important contribution to knowledge with this selection of studies on language acquisition. Collections of studies clustered more or less closely around a topic are plentiful, but this one is unique. Volterra and Erting had a clear plan in mind when making their selection. Taken together, the studies make the case that language is inseparable from human interaction and communication and, especially in infancy, as much a matter of gestural as of vocal behavior. The editors have arranged the papers in five coherent sections and written an introduction and conclusion. No introductory course in child and language development will be complete without this book.

Presenting successively studies of hearing children acquiring speech languages, of deaf children acquiring sign languages, of hearing children of deaf parents, of deaf children of hearing parents, and of hearing children compared with deaf children, Volterra and Erting give one a wider than usual view of language acquisition. It is a view that would have been impossible not many years ago – when the primary languages of deaf adults had received neither recognition nor respect. Yet such is the advance of knowledge that it has become impossible now to consider the processes involved in child development without looking at the progression from gestures to sign languages in addition to that from vocal noises to speech languages.

The problem for those unfamiliar with the different conditions imposed by deafness in child or parents or both is to find what of lasting significance has been done in this special area. The problem for those totally immersed in studies of sign languages and deafness is to relate their observations and findings to the body of knowledge developed by study of the majority, hearing, condition. Volterra and Erting have gone a long way to solving both these problems with this selection of studies and with their clear, no-nonsense commentaries.

The studies selected and the editors' overview of them raise another problem, however. There is wide variety in the studies in this volume: variety in method, from case studies to large subject populations, from short term to longitudinal observation; variety in theoretical foundations; and variety in terminology.

The editors recognize this – in fact it may have been one reason for their undertaking this collection in the first place; and they offer eminently sensible solutions. Based on Volterra's earlier work is their suggestion that a progression in both hearing and deaf children needs to be recognized and clearly denominated: at first, infantile *movements* and *sounds;* then, a clear attempt to communicate with *gestures* and *vocalizations;* later, a truly symbolic use of *signs* and *words;* and still later, genuinely linguistic combinations of symbols in *sign language* and *spoken language.* The papers in the collection amply justify this parallelism in word and sign acquisition and the conclusion that language is acquired by deaf and hearing children in comparable stages.

Volterra and Erting also see a deeper problem that must be addressed before their clear distinction of modalities and stages can be appreciated and their suggested terminology adopted. If greater understanding is to be gained about language acquisition, the central need (perhaps not sufficiently appreciated by some of the authors represented) is to establish strict and widely shared criteria for making the distinction between behavior that is only generally communicative and behavior that is truly symbolic, between behavior depending on context and behavior that transcends context, as language does.

Having selected papers that reflect the state of the art in assessing language acquisition (not just speech language acquisition) and pointed out ways that this state can most surely be advanced, Volterra and Erting continue as they began, looking always at real data and leading the advance.

May 1989   WILLIAM C. STOKOE

Preface

This book results from the ideas, encouragement, and cooperation of many people. Elizabeth Bates and Ursula Bellugi urged us to pursue the initial idea, and William Levelt responded enthusiastically when we approached him with the proposal. The authors all recognized the need to draw together the various lines of research on this subject and generously contributed their work. A NATO Postdoctoral Fellowship in Science awarded to Carol Erting made the early collaboration possible, and our institutions, the Istituto di Psicologia of the CNR and Gallaudet University, supported us throughout. Special thanks are due to Patrizia Valentini for secretarial assistance and to Paul Setzer for his production of the figures.

VIRGINIA VOLTERRA
CAROL J. ERTING

Preface to 1994 Gallaudet University Press Edition

The papers compiled for this volume report on research conducted between 1980 and 1990 on the transition from gesture to language in hearing and deaf children. During the past three years, new work on this topic has appeared, some a direct consequence of or influenced by this volume, the rest carried on independently. We briefly review some of that research below.

Bonvillian and his collaborators have continued the studies presented here in Chapter 17, analyzing data collected on young children with deaf parents for hand preference while signing and during nonsign actions (Bonvillian *et al.*, 1993). They also have examined the development of sign language phonology with particular attention to the acquisition of location, movement, and handshape (Siedlecki and Bonvillian, 1993).

Bonvillian's subjects are hearing and deaf children with deaf parents. A comparable corpus of data has been collected for several years by Elena Eisenina, a Russian researcher at the University of Ivanovo, on hearing and deaf infants with hearing parents. She has compared the development of "protosigns," actions with objects and gestures, performed by both groups. We only recently have become aware of her work (Eisenina, 1993) and find striking similarities between Eisenina's data and the results reported here.

The publication of this volume in 1990 brought attention to evidence that the timing of the achievement of milestones of sign language acquisition corresponds fairly well to the achievement of milestones of spoken language acquisition. In that same year, a paper by Meier and Newport (1990) appeared, suggesting that signing children actually experience a consistent *advantage* in the size and rate of early vocabulary development. Volterra and Iverson (in press), as a reply to Meier and Newport, have summarized evidence from various sources showing that the emergence of first recognizable lexical items is not earlier in signing children than in speaking children. Their conclusion is in accord with the final remarks of the present volume; that is, a possible advantage of the gestural modality for early communication does not imply any advantage in the acquisition of language per se. A similar conclusion was reached by Abrahamsen *et al.* (1991) in a study exploring the emergence of language in children with mental retardation or other developmental delays who are exposed to bimodal input. They state, "the sign advantage is a conditional phenomenon, for which *boundary conditions* must be specified to appropriately delimit its range of generalization" (p. 253).

Goodwyn and Acredolo (1993) conducted research on 22 hearing infants exposed to gestures as well as spoken language. The results of their study suggest, in their view, that there "both *is and is not* a gestural advantage for the onset of symbol use within communication" (p. 697). A small, reliable tendency for gestural symbols to appear earlier than vocal symbols existed in their data, but the size of the gestural advantage was much smaller than had been previously suggested. In fact, on average, their infants developed symbolic functioning about the same time in both modalities. Goodwyn and Acredolo, like others, state that their research supports the conclusion that symbolic language in both modalities only emerges after certain milestones of cognitive development have been achieved, usually around the first birthday.

A topic related to the question of sign advantage and more generally to the question of the gesture-to-language transition is manual babbling, a phenomenon recently addressed by several researchers holding differing perspectives. According to previous studies (Lenneberg, 1967), babbling is a phenomenon of speech development that does not depend on the availability of input. From this point of view, all children, including deaf infants, would begin vocal babbling between the ages of six to eight months. More recent research indicates that vocal babbling is delayed in deaf children (Oller and Eilers, 1988) because they lack auditory input or because they lack auditory feedback (Locke, 1990).

Petitto and Marentette (1991) analyzed what they described as a manual analogue of vocal babbling in deaf and hearing children and concluded that deaf children produced many more "manual babbles" than hearing children. In addition to the quantitative difference, the manual babbling of deaf children was also qualitatively different from that of hearing children in that it was more varied, showing a more diverse set of handshapes and movement types. The researchers interpreted these results as evidence that babbling is an early expression of a brain-based language capacity that is fundamentally amodal. Meier and Willerman (in press) present findings that suggest a different picture from the one presented by Petitto and Marentette. While they agree that meaningless sign-like gestures can be identified in the prelinguistic gestures of both deaf and hearing children, they do not find deaf infants producing a markedly greater number than their hearing counterparts. In fact, Meier and Willerman suggest that such prelinguistic gestures may be relatively frequent in children who have no sign input.

Locke (1993) points out that infants are preadapted to process facial-vocal and manual movements for the purpose of identifying individuals and their intentions. Since the face and the eyes play a significant role in signed languages, he argues, it is not surprising that signed languages are learned at about the same rate as spoken languages. Furthermore, since the infant is sensitive to these physical cues from birth, it is not unlikely that the first components of a language that relies upon facial and manual expression might be expressed earlier than corresponding components in a vocal language. While it is not surprising, then, that signs may be detected earlier than spoken words, Locke advises sign language researchers to adopt stringent criteria for the study of first signs in the same way that investigators of early spoken language acquisition have. In the same way that the words *dada* and *mama* are eliminated from those studies due to the frequency with which infants produce [dada] and [mama] sounds, perhaps there are manual configurations that should be routinely eliminated from sign data so that they are not falsely credited as linguistic productions. Likewise, Locke suggests that there may be manual or facial behaviors that look similar to signs but should be discarded because they occur in all prelinguistic infants.

Locke (1993), in his book *The Child's Path to Spoken Language*, presents his argument for a theory that posits a dual specialization for language: the specialization in social cognition (SSC) and the grammatical analysis module (GAM). The SSC is quasilinguistic and richly communicative and is shared with other species to some extent. It is responsible for collecting the linguistic data for analysis by the GAM which handles phonology, morphology, and syntax and begins to operate between approximately 22 and 34 months of age. According to this theory, first words as well as first signs are not necessarily linguistic. They precede the acquisition of phonology, which can only be acquired once the GAM begins to function. Thus, once children are using single words and stereotypic verbal routines to refer to things in restricted social contexts, they are "standing at the threshold of grammatical language" (p. 348). Locke's dual specialization hypothesis provides an explanation for a prephonological stage of speaking and signing as well as for the subsequent development of a phonological system. As Locke points out, the "presumption of a single specialization for language has made it hard to understand observed differences in the development of signed and spoken languages, but these differences at the early lexical stage, and the similarities at later stages, are handled easily by a conjoint system" (p. 371).

The issue addressed in Chapters 19 and 20 of this volume, the role of gestures in the transition to two-word speech and in particular to cross-modal combinations produced by hearing children who have not been exposed to a signed input, has received considerable attention in recent years (Iverson, Capirci and Caselli, 1992; Iverson et al., 1992; Morford and Goldin-Meadow, 1992). Combinations of elements from the vocal and gestural modalities are used by children in two very different ways: the first combinations are complementary, with spoken and gestural elements providing redundant information; supplementary combinations with vocal and gestural elements providing different pieces of information, appear later. Supplementary combinations, containing "mismatched" gestural and speech elements, were found to be a good index of children's readiness for a new stage of linguistic development, namely the two-word stage.

Most past and present work on the relation between words and gestures has concentrated on production. Much less is known about comprehension in either modality (for an extensive discussion of this issue, see Savage-Rumbaugh *et al.*, 1993). However, some recent work by researchers in San Diego suggests that gestural development from 8–16 months may actually correlate better with the child's current level of word comprehension than it does with word production (Bates *et al.*, 1989; Fenson *et al.*, 1993; Thal and Bates, 1989). These results include evidence from "late talkers" who are delayed only in expressive language. For these children, performance on most gestural measures is normal for their chronological age and their word comprehension level, showing that many gestural measures that are *correlated* with word production in the normal population can be *dissociated* from word production in children with an expressive language delay. In a review of these findings, Bates *et al.* (in press) suggest that gestural production may serve as a kind of developmental bridge, from what the child *knows* about symbols (evident in word comprehension) to what the child is able and willing to *do* with those symbols (evident in word production). The evidence in favor of this three-way relationship is certainly not decisive, and the case for the "gestural bridge" hypothesis would be clarified by solid evidence on the emergence of gestural comprehension. This issue is certainly one that deserves further investigation.

References

Abrahamsen, A., Maureen, L., Brown-Williams, J., & McCarthy, S. (1991).
> Boundary Conditions on Language Emergence: Contributions from atypical learners and input. P. Siples & S. C. Fischer (Eds.), *Theoretical issues in sign language research*, 2. 231-254.

Bates, E., Dale, P., & Thal, D. (in press)
> Individual differences and their implications for theories of language development. In P. Fletcher and B. MacWhinney (Eds.). *Handbook of Child Language*. Oxford: Basil Blackwell.

Bates, E., Thal, D., Whitesell, K., Oakes, L., & Fenson, L. (1989)
> Integrating language and gesture in infancy. *Developmental Psychology, 25*: 6, 1004–1019.

Bonvillian, J. D., Richards, H. C., Dooley, T. T., and Saah, M. I. (1993).
     Early Sign Language Acquisition and the Development of
     Hand Preference. Paper presented at the Sixth International
     Congress for the Study of Child Language. Trieste, Italy, July.

Eisenina, Y. (1993)
     Development of protolanguage and sensorimotor intelligence in
     hearing and deaf infants. Paper presented at the Sixth
     International Congress for the Study of Child Language.
     Trieste, Italy, July.

Fenson, L., Dale, P., Reznick, J. S., Thal, D., Bates, E., Hartung, J.,
Pethick, S. & Reilly, J. (1993)
     The MacAurthur Communicative Development Inventories:
     User's guide and technical manual. San Diego: Singular Press.

Iverson, J. M., Capirci, O., & Caselli, M. C. (1992).
     From communication to language in two modalities. Submitted
     for publication.

Iverson, J. M., Volterra, V., Pizzuto, E., & Capirci, O. (1922)
     The role of communicative gesture in the transition to the two-
     word stage. Submitted for publication.

Locke, J. L. (1990).
     Structure and stimulation in the ontogeny of spoken language.
     Developmental Psychobiology, 23, 621–643.

Locke, J. L. (1993).
     The child's path to spoken language. Cambridge, MA:
     Harvard University Press.

Meier, R. P. & Newport, E. L. (1990).
     Out of the hands of babes: On a possible sign advantage in lan-
     guage acquisition. *Language, 66,* 1–23.

Meier, R. P. & Willerman, R. (in press).
     Prelinguistic gesture in deaf and hearing infants. In K.
     Emmorey & J. Reilly (Eds.). *Language, gesture and space.*
     Hillsdale, NJ: Lawrence Erlbaum Associates.

Morford, M. & Goldin-Meadow, S. (1992).
     Comprehension and production of gestures in combination with
     speech in one-word speakers. *Journal of Child Language, 19,*
     559–580.

Oller, D. K. & Eilers, R. E. (1988).
     The role of audition in infant babbling. *Child Development,*
     59, 441–466.

Petitto, L. A. & Marentette, P. (1991).
     Babbling in the manual mode: Evidence from the ontogeny of
     language. *Science, 251,* 1493–1496.

Language comprehension in ape and child. *Monographs of the Society for Research in Child Development.*

Seidlecki, T., Jr., & Bonvillian, J. D. (1993).
Location, handshape, and movement: Young children's acquisition of the formational aspects of American Sign Language. *Sign Language Studies, 78,* 31–52.

Thal, D. & Bates, E. (1988).
Language and gesture in late talkers. *Journal of Speech and Hearing Research, 31,* 115–123.

Volterra, V., & Iverson, J. M. (1992).
When do modality factors affect the course of language acquisition? In K. Emmoray & J. Reilly (Eds.), *Language, gesture, and space.* Hillsdale, NJ: Lawrence Erlbaum Associates.

Contents

List of Contributors

Acredolo, Linda P., Department of Psychology, University of
    California, Davis, CA 95616, USA
Adamson, Lauren B., Department of Psychology, Georgia State
    University, University Plaza, Atlanta, GA 30303, USA
Bakeman, Roger, Department of Psychology, Georgia State
    University, University Plaza, Atlanta, GA 30303, USA
Bates, Elizabeth, Department of Psychology, University of
    California, San Diego, La Jolla, CA 92093, USA
Beeghly, Marjorie, Connecticut College, 270 Mohican Avenue,
    New London, CT 06320, USA
Bellugi, Ursula, Salk Institue, P.O. Box 85800, San Diego,
    CA 92138, USA
Beronesi, Sandra, CREA, Via Elea 8, 00183 Roma, Italy
Bonvillian, John D., Department of Psychology, University of
    Virginia, Gilmer Hall, Charlottesville, VA 22903, USA
Boyes Braem, Penny, Center for Sign Language Research,
    Lerchenstrasse 56, 4059 Basel, Switzerland
Bretherton, Inge, Department of Human Development and Family
    Studies, Colorado State University, Fort Collins, CO 80523, USA
Caselli, M. Cristina, Istituto di Psicologia, Consiglio Nazionale
    delle Ricecche (CNR), Viale Marx 15, 00137 Roma, Italy
Chandler, Penelope, Department of Psychology, University of
    Lancaster, Lancaster LA1 4YF, England
Corina, David, Salk Institute, P.O. Box 85800, San Diego,
    CA 92138, USA
Da Cunha Pereira, Maria Cristina, Area de Lingüistica,
    DERDIC/PUCSP, Rua Dra Neyde Apparecida Sollitto, 435,
    04022 San Paulo, Brazil
De Lemos, Claudia, Departamento de Lingüistica, Universidade
    Estadual de Campinas, (UNICAMP), Cidade Universitaria
    Zeferino Vaz, 13100 Campinas (SP), Brazil
D'Odorico, Laura, Dipartimento di Psicologia dello Sviluppo
    e della Socializzazione, Università di Padova, Via Beato
    Pellegrino 26, 35137 Padova, Italy
Erting, Carol J., Department of Linguistics and Director,
    Culture and Communication Studies Program, Gallaudet

Research Institute, College Hall 402, Gallaudet University, 800 Florida Ave., NE, Washington, DC 20002, USA

Folven, Raymond J., Department of Psychology, University of Virginia, Gilmer Hall, Charlottesville, VA 22903, USA

Goldin-Meadow, Susan, Department of Education, University of Chicago, 8535 South Kimbark Avenue, Chicago, IL 60637, USA

Goodwyn, Susan W., Department of Psychology, University of California, Davies, CA 95616, USA

Griffith, Penny L., 401 White Hall, Kent State University, Kent, OH 44224, USA

Levorato, M. Chiara, Istituto di Psicologia, Università di Verona, Vicolo San Francesco, 37122 Verona, Italy

Lillo-Martin, Diane, University of Connecticut, Department of Linguistics, U-145, 341 Mansfield Road, Storrs, CT 06269, USA

Lock, Andrew, Department of Psychology, University of Lancaster, Lancaster LA1 4YF, England

Massoni, Piera, CREA, Via Elea 8, 00183 Roma, Italy

Masur, Elise Frank, Department of Psychology, Northern Illinois University, DeKalb, IL 60115, USA

McIntire, Marina L., Department of Geography, California State University, 18111 Nordhoff Street, Northridge, CA 91330, USA

Mohay, Heather, Department of Child Health, Mater Children's Hospital, University of Queensland, South Brisbane, QLD 4101, Australia

Morford, Marolyn, 7 Lombardy Circle, Lewiston, PA 17044, USA

Mylander, Carolyn, Department of Education, University of Chicago, 8535 South Kimbark Avenue, Chicago, IL 60637, USA

O'Connell, Barbara, Department of Psychology, University of California, San Diego, La Jolla, CA 92093, USA

O'Grady, Lucinda, Salk Institute, P.O. Box 85800, San Diego, CA 92138, USA

O'Grady Hynes, Maureen, Red Willow, 13012 Martha's Choise Circle, Bowie, MD 20715, USA

Orlansky, Michael D., Department of Special Education and Nisonger Center, Ohio State University, Columbus, OH 43216, USA

Petitto, Laura A., Department of Psychology, McGill University, 1205 Docteur Penfield Avenue, Montreal, PQ, Canada H3A 1B1

Pizzuto, Elena, IAIF CNR-Palermo and Istituto di Psicologia CNR, Viale Marx 15, 00137 Roma, Italy

Prezioso, Carlene, Gallaudet Research Institute, Gallaudet University – Kendall Green, 800 Florida Ave., NE, Washington, DC 20002, USA

Service, Valerie, Department of Psychology, University of Lancaster, Lancaster LA1 4YF, England

Shore, Cecilia, Department of Psychology, Miami University of Ohio, Oxford, OH 45056, USA

Smith, Connie B., Department of Psychology, University of Lancaster, Lancaster LA1 4YF, England

Snitzer Reilly, Judy, Department of Psychology, San Diego State University, San Diego, CA 92182, USA

Van Hoek, Karen, Salk Institute, P.O. Box 85800, San Diego, CA 92138, USA

Volterra, Virginia, Istituto di Psicologia, Consiglio Nazionale delle Ricecche (CNR), Viale Marx 15, 00137 Roma, Italy

Young, Andrew, Department of Psychology, University of Lancaster, Lancaster LA1 4YF, England

Introduction

V. VOLTERRA and C. J. ERTING

The aim of this edited collection is to bring together recent research on the use of communicative gesturing in the first 2 years of life as an important step in the child's transition to a linguistic system. Ten years ago, *Action, Gesture and Symbol* (Lock, 1978) was published, reflecting the state of the art in research on the emergence of language with an emphasis on the transition from prespeech types of communication to a fully developed use of language. During the years between the publication of that volume and the present one, there was not only an increase in the number of studies examining this issue as it relates to hearing children acquiring spoken language, but there was an important new focus on the part of some researchers who began to examine the early communication of children acquiring sign language. This development was in large part due to the acceptance of sign language as a linguistic system and its entrance into the mainstream of linguistic study.

During the past decade, a number of researchers, including those whose work appears in this volume, have analyzed gestural communication, symbolic gesturing, sign language acquisition, and spoken language acquisition of deaf and hearing children. Their approaches to the investigation of early communicative gestures and their relationship to language acquisition have too often remained separate with different theoretical perspectives and questions resulting in a variety of populations studied and terminologies adopted. The intent of this collection is to provide the reader with research reports previously prepared for widely divergent audiences and representing different points of view in order to examine the possibility of outlining a theoretical position which can explain apparently different results. Our purpose is also to demonstrate that, at the present time, research on sign language acquisition and more generally on deaf children's communicative and linguistic development can shed new light on many of the basic questions regarding language acquisition in this early period. We will point out areas in which we believe this research is particularly relevant.

When hearing children acquiring a spoken language make the transition from prelinguistic gestural communication to language, a modality change occurs. Deaf children acquiring a sign language communicate prelinguistically and linguistically in the same visual-gestural modality. Thus, comparison between hearing children acquiring spoken language and deaf children acquiring sign language may help to clarify the relationship between prelinguistic communication and language. One question that can be addressed comes from the continuity/discontinuity argument, that is, whether language emerges from prelinguistic communication in a continuous manner or whether there is a discontinuity between the two such that language per se emerges when a specifically linguistic capacity of the child is called into play.

Other questions that can be addressed by comparative studies of speaking and signing children concern the sequence of language development. Models proposing states of language acquisition have been based primarily on studies of spoken languages. Studying the acquisition of language by deaf children exposed to sign languages may help to delineate those aspects of acquisition which are universal across languages and those aspects which may prove to be modality specific. It is possible that the sequence of the stages, the timing of them, or both may be influenced by the features of the modality in which the language occurs.

An interesting difference between the signed and the spoken modality is that iconicity is present in sign language to a greater degree than it is in spoken languages (Klima & Bellugi, 1979; Mandel, 1977). While iconic characteristics of sign languages have undergone significant historical modification and grammaticalization, it is often possible to perceive a relationship between a sign and its referent. At the same time, each sign language can chose to conventionalize a particular iconic relationship in an arbitrary way. In sign languages, then, a certain degree of iconicity coexists with one of the fundamental features of language: arbitrariness. The question that immediately arises concerns whether or not this type of iconicity plays a role in acquisition. If infants acquiring a sign language exploit the iconicity of a particular language, such a language-learning strategy could be taken as evidence of a facilitating effect of iconicity in the acquisition of languages in general.

Finally, it has been claimed that there is a critical period for the acquisition of language and that the timing of linguistic input has a clear effect on the child's acquisition of language. Research on language acquisition under conditions of no or limited input can be conducted very rarely since deprivation of the linguistic environment cannot be imposed deliberately. The case of Genie (Curtiss, 1977) is one of the few examples of such a situation, but in this circumstance language was only one of the many human factors missing from her early environment. In the case of deaf children, however, hearing loss can create atypical language learning conditions apart from other circumstances. Thus, deaf children can be seen as "experiments of nature" such that the study of their linguistic development affords an opportunity to understand better (a) language acquisition in the absence of adult linguistic input that is accessible to the child; and (b) the relationship between early exposure and native fluency in a language.

Often, perhaps usually, deaf individuals are not effectively exposed to a conventional language until school age or even later. The majority of deaf children learn sign language without input from their parents. Instead, they are first exposed to sign language whenever they happen to find themselves in settings where there are other signers. In the past, the first contact with sign language users tended to be at school age among their peers, a small minority of whom had learned sign language from their parents. Teachers did not usually sign, unless they themselves were deaf and taught older children, as was often the case in residential schools in the United States. In many countries outside of the United States and in strictly oral schools for deaf children, it was likely that the children received no adult sign language input at school. The question arises as to how these sign language users organize and process language in adulthood after having acquired it late and through exposure to limited input. The answer contributes to our understanding of the significance of linguistic input and age of acquisition. Newport and Supalla (1980) have observed important differences between native and non-native American Sign Language (ASL) signers: non-native signers do not achieve the same levels of fluency in ASL, especially in the use of complex morphology. Such differences might be due to age of exposure to the language, or to characteristics of the input, or both.

During the past 15-20 years, social and political environments have changed so that in many countries there is a growing tendency to expose children to both spoken and signed input from the time of the diagnosis of deafness. Here a distinction should be made between bilingual and bimodal exposure. The bilingual situation is one in which the deaf child is exposed to the two inputs in separate settings or from separate sources. In the bimodal situation, the deaf child is exposed to both inputs in the same setting and from the same source. In the case of the bilingual situation, the child is really exposed to two languages – one spoken language and one sign language. In the bimodal situation, the child is in fact exposed to only one language, either signed or spoken, and the communication that occurs in the other modality is used as support. When signing and speaking simultaneously, an individual uses one of the two languages or a kind of inter-language. Even in those cases in which the deaf child receives intensive and formal training in spoken language only, bimodal input prevails since in everyday communication, parents and teachers do, in fact, use gesturing unconsciously with deaf children.

An important question which remains unanswered then relates to the input available to the deaf child. Just how much of the spoken language and how much of the gestural input does a deaf child take in and how is it integrated? How does the input differ when the primary language is a sign language as compared with the situation where the primary language is spoken? Other related questions are: What is the child's contribution to language learning? How much is innate, how much depends on a model, and how much originates with the child? Human children are active and creative participants in the language acquisition process, going well beyond the data to construct a working theory of their language. Deaf children give us a unique opportunity to study this human capacity.

The book is organized into five sections based on the hearing status of the children (hearing or deaf) and the linguistic input they receive (spoken or signed). Part I includes studies of hearing children with spoken language input. The first chapters present studies that have built upon the seminal work conducted in the 1970s by Bruner (1975a, 1975b, 1978), Bates (1976a, 1976b), Bates, Benigni, Bretherton, Camaioni, and Volterra (1977, 1979), Bates, Camaioni, and Volterra (1975), and Lock (1978), focusing on gestures such as ritualized requests, showing, giving, and pointing. The remaining chapters examine a different type of gesture, that is, potentially symbolic gestures produced with or without objects. These latter gestures can be similar to first words not only because of their content and the fact that they can go through a comparable decontextualization process, but also because they function communicatively. In the past, studies of these two types of gestures have usually been considered separately. They are presented together in Part I so that similarities and differences between the two types of gestures might be more readily discerned.

Part II focuses on deaf children with sign language input. The studies reported here examine, in particular, the transition from communication to language which, in this case, occurs in the same modality. Part III presents research on deaf children of hearing parents who have not been exposed to a conventional sign language input. Some researchers emphasize the creative aspect of the gestures used by these children. Others focus on the emergence of these gestures within the interactional context established between the children and their hearing caregivers. The relationship between vocal and gestural communication is examined to some extent in all of these studies with all of the authors pointing out the delay and the limits of the linguistic development of these deaf children in both modalities.

Studies included in Part IV are concerned with hearing children of deaf parents exposed to both sign and spoken input. The first chapter concentrates only on sign language acquisition, comparing it with cognitive development. The second chapter examines the language development of these children from a bilingual perspective, describing the simultaneous acquisition of the two languages in the two modalities.

Part V provides the reader with three studies specifically designed to compare hearing and deaf children. While the hearing children had spoken language input, the deaf children were exposed to varying types of linguistic environments. The introduction to each section summarizes and discusses the results of the studies presented, identifying points of convergence as well as apparently disparate findings. The Conclusion suggests ways in which researchers might begin to reinterpret and compare some of the data on hearing and deaf children, asking a coherent set of questions, adopting uniform analytic criteria, and employing consistent terminology.

PART I

Hearing Children with Spoken Language Input

Overview

Chapters in this part are concerned with nonverbal activity by normally hearing infants and its relationship to communication and later language development. D'Odorico and Levorato discuss mutual gaze between two mothers and their 3- to 11-month-old infants as it relates to the development of eye contact as an early social schema. They describe the infants' increasing capacity for shifting interest spontaneously from object to mother, taking the initiative in establishing social contact themselves. Then, Masur, in her longitudinal study of four infants, considers three communicative gestures involving objects: open-handed reaching, pointing, and extending objects. She investigates the role that dual-directional signaling (a gesture involving an object accompanied by simultaneous gaze directed toward the mother when she is in a different visual field) may play in the transition from isolated gestures to gestures accompanied by conventional words (from about 8 to 18 months).

The problem for Adamson, Bakeman, and Smith was to study how infants coordinate attention to people and to objects as they develop referential communication. Using a sample of 28 infants in a longitudinal design, these researchers examined the infants' play with their mother, with a peer, and alone when the infants were 9, 12, and 15 months of age. They found that the typical progression was from the use of gestures only to the use of both words and gestures.

Lock, Young, Service, and Chandler present a cross-sectional study of 140 mother-infant pairs focusing exclusively on the pointing gesture. Their goal is to gather sufficient evidence to evaluate existing models of the development of this gesture by examining the origin of pointing, the function, and the role of the adult. According to their data, pointing is not established as part of the infant repertoire until after 10 months of age, with an increase in the frequency of gesturing up to 18 months followed by a decline to 24 months.

Caselli's longitudinal study of one infant from 10 to 20 months of age demonstrates that gestures which have been traditionally analyzed as symbolic play schemes can be used with communicative functions. She analyzes in great detail the progressive emergence of these gestures within communicative routines between child and caregiver and the relationship between early gestures and first words. Acredolo and Goodwyn focus on the same phenomenon using cross-sectional and longitudinal data from over 50 infants. They show that symbolic gestures are not rare events; on the contrary, they occur in the communication of a large proportion of normal infants between 10 and 24 months of age. The authors examine these gestures both within and outside of interactive routines, categorizing them according to content and communicative function and correlating the occurrence of symbolic gestures with spoken vocabulary. Shore, Bates, Bretherton, Beeghly, and O'Connell focus on the relationships between language and the type of object-specific, conventional, referential gestures referred to as enactive names and symbolic play. Summarizing the results of a number of studies conducted on a large sample of infants, they describe similarities and differences between gestural and vocal symbols in comprehension and production at three developmental junctures: 13, 20, and 28 months. They found that at each major transition point in language development, gesture and speech show parallel changes from the emergence of reference through the appearance of combinations to the increase in ordering elements according to conventional principles. From their results, these authors conclude that the relationship between gestural and vocal symbols changes over time. They argue for the importance of a time-dependent approach when measuring the complex relationship between symbolic production in the vocal and gestural channels.

While the authors in this part discuss similar phenomena, they do not do so within a common framework. They examine various developmental periods and employ differing terminologies. At one level of analysis, comparison of results is useful despite these differences. At a more detailed level of analysis, however, comparison is no longer fruitful or even possible since these researchers have asked different questions and have adopted disparate analytical criteria. Here we point out a few of the more important consistencies and inconsistencies evident in these chapters.

D'Odorico and Levorato as well as Masur are interested in the gaze behavior of infants during interaction with their mothers, but D'Odorico and Levorato consider the development of this behavior in the earlier stages while Masur studies a later period, up to 18 months. Masur is primarily concerned with the infant's gaze to the mother as it is coordinated with gestural behavior while D'Odorico and Levorato do not examine gestural behavior at all. Rather, they document the infant's developing ability to look from object to mother as a signal of readiness to engage in social interaction. This ability to integrate social and cognitive activity is necessary for the development of the interactive routines or joint engagement states discussed by other authors in this section.

Caselli et al., as well as Adamson et al., emphasize the importance of joint engagement of mothers and infants with objects as well as the interactive communicative routines between mother and child as the supportive context for the child's emerging capacity to use symbolic gestures. These authors agree that the gestures themselves derive from these contexts and that the typical developmental progression, as Masur also suggests, is from single or isolated gestures to the coordination of two or more simultaneous signals, including gesture accompanied by vocalization. While Adamson et al. are particularly interested in the special role of sophisticated partners in developing the supportive attentional context for the infant's early use of words and objects, Masur and Caselli attend more to the child's contribution. Similarly, Acredolo and Goodwyn, while acknowledging the importance of the parental role, argue that it is left to the infant to spontaneously generalize the gestures beyond the immediate context.

It is clear from several of these studies that pointing has a different status from other communicative gestures such as show/offer (Adamson et al.) or object extension (Masur), reaching, and referential gestures (Caselli), also referred to as symbolic gestures (Acredolo et al.) and symbolic play (Shore et al.). Lock and his colleagues suggest that pointing does not emerge from the immediate context – communicative routines – but is more spontaneous in origin. Masur, Adamson et al., Caselli, and Lock all provide evidence that pointing is often accompanied by vocalization and does not occur as a response as often as other gestures such as reaching and object extension; rather the infant uses pointing to initiate communication, often as a request for objects when accompanied by vocalization with a "request" intonation.

Lock et al. and Acredolo et al. report data for the largest number of subjects in their cross-sectional and longitudinal studies and find considerable variation as to the prevalence of gestural communication among infants. While Acredolo and her colleagues do not find symbolic gesturing to be rare in hearing children, they do highlight their finding that some infants are heavily involved in this kind of communication while others are not. They suggest an examination of parental behavior with these infants may provide some clues as to the reasons for the striking individual variation. It may be that some parents do not attend to the gestural communication of their children and reinforce it to the same extent that other parents do. Some support for this suggestion comes from Lock and his colleagues who present data showing maternal ignoring of infant points. They warn, however, that the view that infants develop communicative pointing through simple reinforcement is not supported. Another possible explanation advanced by Acredolo and Goodwyn relates to interactive routines: children who do more symbolic gesturing may have parents who frequently engage in routines of this sort, contexts which, according to Adamson et al. clearly elevate the rate of referential conventionalized acts.

In spite of individual variability in the quantity of symbolic gestures in infant repertoires, Caselli's case study material and the cross-sectional and longitudinal data of Acredolo and Goodwyn support the following conclusions regarding the symbolic or referential gestures of hearing infants up to 20 months of age:

1. Symbolic gestures are used by these infants to communicate.
2. They emerge out of interactive routines as well as out of the child's play with objects.
3. Symbolic gestures first appear alongside the first spoken words, with only a slight advantage for the gestural modality.
4. Many of the specific gestures described by these researchers are similar, despite the fact that they are drawn from different cultures.
5. Communicative gestures appear to be used earlier for requesting than for labeling.

6. For object gestures, the emphasis is usually on the function rather than the
    form of the object.
7. Both gestures and words follow a similar course of development from
    performance in context-bound routines to generalized use for an increasingly
    broad set of referents and situations.

The study by Shore and her colleagues bears out all of the above conclusions
with the exception of those relating to the communicative use of gestures since
they investigate symbolic play and object-related gestures exclusively. They also
examine these behaviors in older children — up to 28 months — analyzing the
relationship between gestural sequences and multiword combinations as well as
comprehension of gestures by the child.

The seven chapters in Part I provide information on the prelinguistic gestural
communication of hearing children from differing cultural and linguistic backgrounds who have been exposed to spoken language. They set the stage for the
subsequent parts which examine the same phenomena in children who differ with
respect to hearing status or linguistic input.

CHAPTER 1

Social and Cognitive Determinants of Mutual Gaze Between Mother and Infant

L. D'ODORICO and M.C. LEVORATO

Introduction

The value of eye contact in social communication is demonstrated by the great number of studies investigating the attractiveness of eyes for human infants (K. Bloom, 1974; Hainline, 1978; Robson, 1967; Samuels, 1985; Wolff, 1961). Mutual visual interaction is in effect the earliest opportunity the mother-infant dyad has for communication. From birth infants can control the flow of visual stimuli, maintaining visual fixation for interesting stimuli and diverting it from too familiar or too intense inputs (Cohen, 1973; Fantz, 1966). This capacity also applies to social contact; therefore, social exchanges between mother and infant by means of mutual gaze[1] create the first dyadic system in which the two individuals have similar control (Stern, 1971, 1974b).

Furthermore, especially in the early phase of development, eye contact is a very significant behavior for the caregiver, because it signals that the infant is really participating in the interactive exchange and is not simply a recipient of mother's solicitations.

Researchers in this field, however, have studied infants' gaze towards mothers, together with other communicative indices (smiling, vocalizations, particular postures) only in the perspective of identifying regularities in the early interactive structure (Herscherson, 1964; S. Friedman, 1972; Stern, 1971, 1974a); on the other hand, eye contact has been considered an important factor in the formation and maintenance of attachment (Brazelton, Tronick, Adamson, Als, & Wise, 1975; Hittelman & Dickes, 1979; Robson, 1967). In both cases the focus is on relational-affective aspects of eye contact or on its social value in the main-tenance of interaction. Our focus is different. We are interested in the cognitive determinants of the infant's capacity to interrupt active exploration of external reality to share the experience with the mother through eye contact.

In the 1st year of life, infants not only establish their first social relationships, but also make relevant steps in their knowledge of the physical external world:

A slightly different version of this paper was originally published in Italian in G. Attili and P. Ricci Bitti (Eds.) 1983, *Comunicare senza parole*, Roma: Bulzoni, pp. 49–62.
[1]The phenomenon by which both partners look into each other's eye has been referred to as "mu-tual glance," "mutual visual interaction," "eye contact" and "mutual gaze" (cf., Exline & Fehr, 1982). We use these terms interchangeably for indicating simultaneously exchanged looks between mother and infant.

they develop many skills for exploring objects, understand the first causal relationships between their actions and the consequences, and begin to search intentionally for the most suitable means of obtaining desired goals. It is necessary, therefore, to arrive at an integrated model of social and cognitive development, in which intentions towards objects are coordinated with intentions towards social agents. A first step in the construction of this model is to investigate how the communicative structures that infants develop in order to contact the social world and the cognitive structures they elaborate to interact with the physical world integrate with each other.

For vocal activity in the prelinguistic period, data have been reported elsewhere (Benelli, D'Odorico, Levorato, & Simion, 1980), showing that only at about 15 months of age are infants able to address intentional vocalizations to their mothers in order to make "comments" on their experience of the physical world. In this research, we investigate the ways in which this type of sharing occurs by means of an earlier type of communicative exchange: the mutual gaze. Although after birth eye contact is regulated in the infant by a homeostatic mechanism of attention/disattention, in our opinion it very soon becomes a real psychological behavior. More specifically, we hypothesize that:

— In the first months of life looking towards mother's eyes has the value of an answer to mother's solicitations, while in the following period the infant becomes more and more capable of initiating the exchange by her/himself.
— In the first months of life there is a sort of antagonism between the activity of interacting with a social partner and that of exploring objects; this fact makes it difficult for the infant to interrupt a sequence of explorations of an object in order to involve mother; if this occurs, loss of interest in the object is the result (for infants' incapacity to consider social and nonsocial objects at the same time, see also Nelson, 1979; Sugarman-Bell, 1978).
— The capacity to coordinate a social schema of communication and a cognitive schema of action is demonstrated when infants' experience of knowing becomes the "signified" of eye contact with mothers and the gaze becomes a real "significant."

Method

Subjects and Procedure

Two male infants, M and T, were videorecorded through a one-way mirror during interactions with their mother and an object in a laboratory equipped as a playroom. Each session lasted 30 min and different interactive situations were planned for each session: (a) mother-infant interaction; (b) mother-infant interaction with a toy; (c) experimenter-infant interaction with a toy; (d) infant alone with a toy. In each session every situation took place twice for a period of 2–3 min. The last 6 min were spent on informal observations. The first time situation b occurred mother and infant played with a toy the infant had already had some experience with (in previous sessions or, in the first session, taken from home) — henceforth *familiar object*. The second time, mother showed her baby an object never previously seen — henceforth *new object*.

At the time of the first session M was 3.19 months old and T 5.28. Sessions took place twice a month until M was 8.3 months old (eight sessions) and T was 11.7 months old (nine sessions). The infants were seated in a high chair in front of a small table and their mothers were seated at an angle of 90° to them. For this analysis, only mother-infant-toy interactions were used.

In the interaction in which an object is also involved, the shift of the infant's look from object to mother is more controllable than during face-to-face interactions when it is often difficult to distinguish casual eye contact from voluntary search for contact. There were 16 interactions for the first subject (M) (total time: 105.13 min) and 18 for the second (T) (total time: 110.26 min).

Analysis of Data

Both mothers attentively look at the infants during the entire interaction time, so it never happens that the infant, looking at mother, does not meet mother's eyes. The beginning of each episode of mutual visual interaction is thus the movement of infant's eyes towards mother, and the end is infant's diversion of eyes from mother's face. The transcription of videorecordings was performed considering: (a) duration of eye contact; (b) behavior of the infant immediately before and after the gaze at mother (e.g., baby looks at object, manipulates it, looks around); (c) mother's behavior immediately before infant's gaze (e.g., she speaks to the infant, acts on the object, looks at infant without performing any action). For some analyses, sessions were grouped into two age levels (see Table 1) for each subject in order to highlight the developmental characteristics of the phenomenon.

Table 1. Range of age of subjects in the two levels

	First age level months	Second age level months
Subject 1 (M)	3.19 — 6.5	6.19 — 8.3
Subject 2 (T)	5.28 — 8.20	9.0 — 11.7

Results

Tables 2 and 3 show the duration and frequency of eye contact during interactions with familiar and new objects for the two subjects in each session. Only for T (the older subject) does the duration of the episodes of eye contact increase with age in a significant way ($p < .02$ Mann test for trend). This result shows the increasing

Table 2. Duration and frequency of M's gazes

Session	Age	Duration (total)	Frequency	Duration		Frequency		Latency[a]	
				New object	Familiar object	New object	Familiar object	New object	Familiar object
1	3.19	1.99	3	2.55	–	3	–	600	–
2	4.2	5.51	9	1.5	9.38	3	6	900	700
3	5.14	5.0	7	1.1	11.3	2	5	350	1060
4	6. 5	1.78	5	2.7	1.33	2	3	550	290
5	6.19	1.14	2	2.68	–	2	–	1090	–
6	7.3	3.26	2	5.09	–	2	–	350	–
7	7.16	4.63	9	6.20	2.30	7	2	1490	530
8	8.3	2.31	6	3.18	1.11	4	2	890	270

Duration of eye contacts is calculated in percentages with respects to the interaction time (total, with new object, with familiar object).
[a] Latency refers to time spent from beginning of interaction and first eye contact, expressed in tenths of a second.

Table 3. Duration and frequency of T's gazes

Session	Age	Duration (total)	Frequency	Duration		Frequency		Latency[a]	
				New object	Familiar object	New object	Familiar object	New object	Familiar object
1	5.28	0.39	2	0.39	–	2	–	480	–
2	6.10	1.24	4	0.61	2.93	2	2	440	340
3	7.23	2.62	5	1.85	4.85	2	3	400	180
4	8.20	1.07	7	0.90	1.32	4	3	126	710
5	9.01	7.52	15	13.10	2.78	11	4	100	670
6	9.11	3.61	6	5.36	0	6	0	400	–
7	10.6	4.78	11	5.30	4.11	6	5	420	630
8	10.20	6.53	12	7.20	5.83	7	5	620	530
9	11.07	4.46	12	5.60	3.34	7	5	70	340

Duration of eye contacts is calculated in percentages with respect to the interaction time (total, with new object, with familiar object).
[a] Latency refers to time spent from beginning of interaction and first eye contact, expressed in tenths of a second.

capacity of the older subject to sustain eye contact with his mother for longer periods during situations of interaction with objects. The hypothesis that in this period eye contact becomes a means of "exchanging information" with mother is strengthened by analysis of the role played by the variable "familiarity of the object."

Tables 4 and 5, in which frequency of episodes of mutual visual interaction is summarized separately for familiar and new objects in the two age levels for each subject, show that in the first age level, for both subjects, familiar objects

Table 4. M's gazes in presence of new or familiar objects in the two age levels

	Familiar object (%)	New object (%)
First age level 3.19–6.15 months	58	42
Second age level 6.19–8.3 months	21	79

Table 5. T's gazes in presence of new or familiar objects in the two age levels

	Familiar object (%)	New object (%)
First age level 5.28–8.20 months	44	56
Second age level 9–11.7 months	33	67

elicit almost the same proportion of gaze towards mother, while in the second age level new objects elicit more gazes than familiar objects ($p < .01$)[2].

Considering that in M (the younger subject), shown in Table 1, the most impressive increase in the frequency of episodes of eye contact with new objects occurs in the last two sessions of the first age level (i.e., between 7.16 and 8.3 months) and that in T the shift occurs in the first session of the second age level (i.e., at 9 months), we may hypothesize that at about 8/9 months of age communicative exchanges by eye contact undergo an important change of strategy. Our results are consistent with the phenomena studied by Trevarthen and Hubley (1978), that is, the tendency to share the *new* experience with adults more and more systematically.

We believe that these data are difficult to interpret in the framework of the attachment model: if the search for eye contact only had the function of maintaining the affective bond, there would not be difference between familiar and new objects. On the other hand, according to the theory of optimal states of activation (Peery & Stern, 1975), the child would prefer to divert attention from familiar objects both at 5 months and 9 months. In our interpretation, our results may be explained by the fact that, at earlier ages, looking towards mother's face has the function of searching for a contact with the caregiver or of diverting attention from an annoying object, but the more sophisticated cognitive

---

[2]All comparisons between proportions of mutual gaze classified in different categories were carried out as proposed by Fleiss (1973).

capacities acquired during development transform this behavior so that it increasingly fulfills the need to share the significant experiences of the reality with others. The new object becomes a conversational "topic" which is more stimulating than the familiar object as the infant discovers its new properties and finds new ways of interacting with it.

Tables 6 and 7 show the relationship between mutual gaze and mother's behavior immediately before it. The basic partition regards the frequency of mutual gaze in the absence (category A) or presence (categories B,C,D) of mother's solicitations. For both subjects in the second age level the proportion of mutual visual interaction included in category A (mother only looks at her infant before he looks at her) increases, while the proportion of infant gazes when mother is speaking (category B) or acting on the object (category C) decreases. The comparison of proportions A and C in the second age level is significant for both subjects ($p < 01$)[3]. This result reveals the infants' increasing capacity for shifting their interest spontaneously from object to mother, taking the initiative

Table 6. M's gazes in relation to mother's preceding activity in the two age levels

	A (%)	B (%)	C (%)	D (%)
First age level 3.19–6.5 months	37.5	37.5	20.8	4.2
Second age level 6.19–8.3 months	57.9	31.5	5.3	5.3

Classification of mother's activities: A, she only looks at her baby; B, she only talks to him; C, she acts on the object, e.g., she touches it, moves it, etc.; D, she performs some meaningful action on the object, (e.g., she demonstrates its use, she makes some type of attractive noise, etc.).

Table 7. T's gazes in relation to mother's preceding activity in the two age levels

	A (%)	B (%)	C (%)	D (%)
First age level 5.28–8.20 months	27.8	50	22.2	0
Second age level 9–11.7 months	41	30.4	16	12.6

Classification of mother's activities: A, she only looks at her baby; B, she only talks to him; C, she acts on the object, e.g., she touches it, moves it, etc.; D, she performs some meaningful action on the object, (e.g., she demonstrates its use, she makes some type of attractive noise, etc.).

---

[3]Some problems might arise for this analogy of results in the two subjects who are of different ages. Other analyses performed on M, however, also showed this subject's precocity in the development of action and vocal schemas (Di Stefano, D'Odorico, Gobbo, Levorato, 1985; D'Odorico, 1984).

in establishing the contact themselves. Moreover, the proportion of gazes towards mother after she has performed some particularly relevant action on the object (e.g., presses a little pump so that a box opens and a doll appears), reaching 12% in T's second age level, can also be interpreted as a more advanced utilization of eye contact schema. In fact, in the earlier ages some interesting interactions with an object cause an increase of interest *for the object* and not for the adult. Now, however, the gaze towards mother seems to signify, "What did you do?! Let me see again!" and mothers almost always interpret eye contact in this situation as a request for repetition of the event.

Tables 8 and 9 summarize data on infants' behavior immediately before the search for eye contact. A distinction may be made between episodes before which the infant was not interested in the object (category A) and episodes before which the infant was involved in some activity with the object. In the second case, we further distinguish between mere visual observation (category B), generic manipulation (category C) and the application of action schema for obtaining specific effects (for the distinction between generic and specific manipulation of the object, see Benelli, D'Odorico, Levorato, & Simion, 1977).

The most interesting results concern the continuous decrease of category A eye contact from the first to the second age levels for both the younger subject and the older subject. After 9 months only 7% of the gazes stem from a situation in which the external object is not the focus of attention. On the contrary, the largest shift in the capacity to interrupt active exploration of an object to look at mother

Table 8. M's gazes in relation to preceding activity

	A (%)	B (%)	C (%)	D (%)
First age level 3.19–6.5 months	45.8	20.8	33.4	0
Second age level 6.19–8.3 months	26.3	10.5	63.2	0

Classification of infant's activity: A, not interested in object; B, visually explores object; C, manipulates object; D, has just obtained some meaningful effect by manipulation of object.

Table 9. T's gazes in relation to preceding activity

	A (%)	B (%)	C (%)	D (%)
First age level 5.28–8.20 months	27.8	22.2	50	0
Second age level 9–11.7 months	7.1	30.4	50	12.5

Classification of infant's activity: A, not interested in object; B, visually explores object; C, manipulates object; D, has just obtained some meaningful effect by manipulation of object.

(category C) occurs in M in the second age level (comparison of proportion in category C in the first and second age levels is significant at $p < .02$), while in T this capacity seems to be already consolidated at the beginning of observations.

Lastly, only in T's data are there some episodes of eye contact fulfilling the criteria of category D. This result is only partially due to the increasing capacity of the infant after 9 months to perform specific actions on the object; rather, the more engaging the action with the object is, the more it interferes with activation of social schema, and greater capacity for decentration is required.

The last analysis concerns behavior subsequent to the end of the episode of eye contact. We were interested in verifying if addressing mother by means of a gaze put an end to manipulation of the object, or if it was really a communicative act incorporated in the exploratory activity the infant was performing. Tables 10 and 11 therefore distinguish episodes of mutual visual interaction inserted in a continuum of interest for the object (categories B and C) from episodes in which there was a break in exploratory activity (before or after eye contact).

Again, from M's first age level to T's second age level there is a decrease in category A, while the other two categories (especially C) increase. In T's second age level, comparison between proportion of episodes in categories A and B + C is highly significant ($p < .001$).

Table 10. M's gazes incorporated or not in continuous sequences of object manipulation

	A (%)	B (%)	C (%)
First age level 3.19–6.5 months	54.17	41.67	4.16
Second age level 6.19–8.3 months	36.85	42.10	21.05

Classification of behavioral sequences in which gazes are incorporated: A, no interest in object either before or after; B, interest in object is maintained but type of manipulation changes; C, same type of action as before is performed after interruption of eye contact.

Table 11. T's gazes incorporated or not in continuous sequences of object manipulation

	A (%)	B (%)	C (%)
First age level 5.28–8.20 months	44.44	38.89	16.67
Second age level 9–11.7 months	12.50	57.14	30.36

Classification of behavioral sequences in which gazes are incorporated: A, no interest in object either before or after; B, interest in object is maintained but type of manipulation changes; C, same type of action as before is performed after interruption of eye contact.

Conclusion

Our research demonstrates the progressive integration of communicative and cognitive abilities in infants' utilization of an early social schema like eye contact. The most important phenomena in this respect are: (a) the increasing tendency with age to search for eye contact with mother during interactions with new objects; (b) infants' progressive capacity to take the initiative in establishing eye contact; (c) the increase in the incorporation of mutual visual interaction in sequences of object manipulation.

To summarize, the developmental progression in the functions fulfilled by the search for eye contact starts from a lack of integration between communicative and cognitive structures. In this phase, eye contact is a response to interactive exchanges initiated and solicited by mother, and its aim is the maintenance of interaction and proximity. Later, eye contact becomes a means of communicating infants' interest in the reality which they are discovering — something like the "referential look" of Newson (1978). A further step occurs when the search for eye contact assumes for infants the meaning of requesting approval about their actions or adult intervention. Lastly, with the completion of a more articulated structure of interaction and sharing, the infant utilizes eye contact for stressing the most salient passages of the joint action.

Our observations, although mostly at a qualitative level and dealing with only two subjects, seem to confirm this outline, showing the usefulness of studying the interaction of social and cognitive abilities for the construction of an integrated model of development.

CHAPTER 2

Gestural Development, Dual-Directional Signaling, and the Transition to Words

E.F. MASUR

Introduction

Although language researchers have often noted the frequency with which gestures accompany children's first words (e.g., Dore, 1974), only recently have they begun to explore the acquisition of these gestures and to inquire into the role they may play in children's transition to early verbal communication. Bruner (1975a) and Bates and her colleagues (Bates, Camaioni, & Volterra, 1975; Bates, Benigni, Bretherton, Camaioni, & Volterra, 1977; 1979) have emphasized the functional continuity between prelinguistic and initial linguistic signaling, suggesting that young children's early communicative intentions are expressed gesturally before they can be encoded in conventional verbal symbols. Thus, the pointing gesture has received particular attention since its object-distinguishing function may be a crucial precursor of verbal naming (Bates et al., 1979; Bruner, 1975a; Lempers, 1979; Lempers, Flavell, & Flavell, 1977; Leung & Rheingold, 1981; Murphy, 1978; Ninio & Bruner, 1978; Werner & Kaplan, 1963).

In addition to pointing, two other gestural forms, reaching toward objects and extending objects to others, have also been implicated in infants' transition to verbal communication. Open-handed reaching toward an object has been considered a "proto-imperative" (Bates et al., 1977) whose object-requesting function is later expressed in verbal directives. Extending objects toward others forms part of giving, showing, and exchanging rituals which come to include verbal elements (Bates et al., 1979; Bruner, 1975a) A.L. Carter (1975a) has traced the development of the lexical items *here* and *there* in the speech of one child to their origins in the vocal-gestural routines of reaching for objects and extending objects to others. In a longitudinal study of infants from 9.5 to 12.5 months, Bates et al. (1979) found the production of pointing, as well as ritualized requesting gestures such as open-handed reaching and two kinds of object extensions, giving and showing, to be significantly correlated with each other and with several measures of early language behavior, both receptive and productive. The infants' production of other gestures, such as headshaking and waving, however, was

Reprinted with permission from the *Journal of Psycholinguistic Research*, 1983, Vol. 12, No. 2, pp. 93–108. I would like to thank the many people who have participated in this longitudinal study, including Mathilda Holzman, Linda Ferrier, Joanne Morse, Kathleen O'Leary, Martha Davis, Stephanie Kalfayan, Deena Pavinato, Beverly Burton, and especially the four children and their mothers.

generally not significantly associated either with the three object-related gestural forms or with the measures of early verbal ability. The relationship between children's pointing, reaching, and object-extending gestures and their language acquisition past the 1st year has not yet been examined.

Communicative Pointing and Dual-Directional Signaling

Of all the gestures they studied in their longitudinal sample, Bates et al. (1979) found that communicative pointing was the best predictor of early linguistic performance. They defined "communicative pointing" in two quite distinct ways. First, they counted instances where children pointed toward an object while looking at their mothers or other conversational partners, either solely or in alternation with the object. In addition, they included instances of pointing that occurred within a "social context, e.g., sitting on an adult's lap while jointly looking at a book" (p. 135) whether or not they involved gaze toward the adult. Murphy (1978), in fact, reported that visual regard of an adult's face rarely occurred in that situation. Bates et al. (1979) discussed the child's ability to alternate his or her gaze between the object and the communicative partner as an indication of the child's intentionality in communicating, his or her awareness "of the effects that his signals will have as he emits them" (p. 35). The development of this capacity, they suggested, may be based on underlying cognitive development in the realm of means-ends relationships.

Another perspective on this issue is provided by experimental investigations of growth during the 2nd year in infants' abilities both to attend to and to produce two simultaneous nonverbal signals, one gestural and the other visual. For example, Macnamara (1977) found that 17-month-olds could take into account a simultaneously presented, but conflicting visual signal when responding to an experimenter's object-extending gesture, while 12-month-olds could not attend to both the experimenter's direction of gaze and his or her object-related gesture.

Murphy and Messer (1977) described a similar problem in young infants' comprehension of a pointing gesture which required coordination of two directions. They found that 9-month-olds were capable of following a point and looking at the object only when the mother's hand and the object were in the same visual field. However, the infants could not follow points directed across their midlines. That task would require attention toward two separate directions, the gesturing hand in front of the infant and the indicated object 90° away in the direction of the gesturer's finger and gaze. The majority of their sample of 14-month-old infants, however, had developed the ability to follow such points.

Generating two simultaneous but divergently directed signals seems to be equally difficult for infants at the end of their 1st or beginning of their 2nd year (Lempers, 1979). Murphy and Messer's (1977) 14-month-olds virtually never looked at their mothers while pointing or reaching toward objects. In a study of rudimentary perspective taking, Lempers et al. (1977) discovered a developmental progression from the age of 12–18 months in infants' abilities to produce coordinated dual-directional signals, pointing toward an object while simultaneously looking in a different direction at the experimenter. This productive capability appeared to develop in parallel with capacities to follow the experimenter's direction of gaze to an object and to orient objects toward another's point of view.

These studies all indicate that during the 2nd year infants are acquiring the capability both of sending and of interpreting messages involving two coordinated but divergent signals or directions. The relationship between the emergence of this dual-directional nonverbal signaling ability involving gesture and gaze and the appearance of dual signaling coordinating conventional linguistic signals with gestures has not previously been explored.

The present paper examines longitudinally the emergence and development of three communicative gestures involving objects, pointing, open-handed reaching, and extending objects, by four infants during natural interactions with their mothers from 9 to 18 months. As noted above, all three gestures, and especially pointing, have been theoretically and empirically linked to the emergence of early verbal communication. Analysis of these in particular, then, provides an opportunity to reveal any unique properties of pointing as well as to discover consistencies or discrepancies in developmental characteristics among three communicative gestures which all involve objects yet differ in structure and orientation. Previous studies of gestural development have been cross-sectional rather than longitudinal in design (e.g., Lempers, 1979; Leung & Rheingold, 1981), have examined gestural production in structured laboratory situations rather than the home (e.g., Leung & Rheingold, 1981; Murphy, 1978; Murphy & Messer, 1977), or have concentrated on an early, brief age span (e.g., Bates et al. 1979). Besides describing the changing characteristics of the gestures, this study investigates the infants' acquisition of conventional words in accompaniment. Furthermore, it examines the role that the capacity for dual-directional signaling may play in this transition.

Method

Subjects

Four first-born white middle-class infants, two girls and two boys, and their mothers who were their primary caretakers served as subjects. The infants were normal and healthy, and their parents were college-educated native speakers of English. The infants and their mothers were participants in a longitudinal naturalistic study of development that had involved bi-weekly 30-min video-taping sessions since the infants were approximately 3 months old. The study was presented as examining all aspects of infants' development and their relations with the people and objects in their environment. Neither communication nor language development was mentioned as being a special focus of study.

Procedure

The infants and their mothers were videotaped in their homes during a consistent set of behavioral episodes which centered around the infants' baths and usually included other caretaking activities and interactive play. Following its mention by Bruner (1975b), the behavioral context of the bath and accompanying activities was chosen because it was judged to be a situation that would remain substantially constant over time and across dyads, which proved to be the case. In addition, it was a familiar, relaxing, and playful experience for the mothers and infants which absorbed their attention and afforded numerous opportunities for interaction and object-related communication.

Each mother-infant pair was visited consistently by one of four female researchers. The observers began filming when the mothers commenced preparing the infants' baths and recorded continuously for the next 30 min. During the videotaping the observers were nonintrusive, positioning themselves a few feet behind and to the side of the mothers so that the infants were in three-quarters and the mothers in one-quarter view. In addition, the observers were trained to smile but not otherwise respond if addressed during the filming. For these reasons, the mothers had quickly learned to ignore their presence. The virtual absence on the videotapes of attempts by the mothers to prompt their infants to perform special behaviors or "show off" testifies to the success of this procedure in recording behaviors as naturally as possible.

For this study, the tapes of the infants closest to monthly intervals were analyzed, starting from 9 months for the children referred to as Carol, Joel, and Allen, and from 8 months for the child here called Jean and continuing through 18 months.

Gestural Analyses

All instances of the following three gestures involving three-dimensional objects were transcribed from the videotapes for analysis:

1. *Pointing at an object*, extensions of the index finger toward an object, excluding exploratory poking or manipulation.
2. *Extending an object toward the mother*, movements of the arm in the direction of the mother while holding an object.
3. *Open-handed reaching toward an object*, extensions of the arm with the hand open, excluding movements that were simply the first phase of grasping the object.

For each gesture the transcribers also recorded the following information:

1. The identity of the object involved.
2. Any action or speech by the mother in eliciting or responding to the gesture. Those gestures elicited by the mother's action or speech are hereafter referred to as responsive; those produced without such elicitation, spontaneous.

3. Whether the gesture was accompanied by a vocalization; conventional words and their lexical approximations which met criteria of both phonological and contextual appropriateness were transcribed.
4. The direction of the child's gaze, whether toward the object, the mother, the camera operator, or elsewhere.

Interobserver agreement computed on a randomly selected 20% of the transcripts for two researchers in independently identifying and transcribing these gestures and their characteristics averaged 92%. All disagreements were resolved by consensus.

Dual-Directional Signaling

Each gesture accompanied by gaze toward the mother, or in a few cases the camera operator, was reexamined on the videotape to determine whether it involved dual-directional signaling. "Dual-directional signaling" was defined as a gesture accompanied by simultaneous gaze directed toward the mother, or the camera operator, when she was not in the same visual field as the object involved in the gesture. To qualify as gaze toward a person not in the same visual field as the object, an instance on the videotape had to include the child's distinct head orientation or movement away from the object toward a person. In order to insure that the gaze was not simply drawn away from the object because of the mother's behavior, the head orientation or movement had to occur with the gesture and before, therefore not in response to, any maternal action or reply. In coding all gestures with gaze toward a person, two independent observers agreed 93% of the time in determining dual directionality. All disagreements were resolved by consensus.

Results

Tables 1–3 display the children's production of all three gestures and their characteristics by month. Since the sample is small, the findings will be presented descriptively with frequent recourse to the data in the tables.

Characteristics of Gestural Development

Despite individual variation in rate of acquisition and amount of production, the children's gestures exhibited consistent patterns of development. All the children acquired open-handed reaching early, by 8 or 9 months. Extending objects and pointing tended to appear somewhat later. Jean's performance was considerably in advance of the other three children's in this as in other aspects of development. She produced both gestures at 9 months, while the other children acquired object

Table 1. Characteristics and development of children's pointing gestures

	Total number	Age (months)										
Child		8	9	10	11	12	13	14	15	16	17	18
Jean												
Number	139	0	15	4	8	0	53	1	26	15	9	8
With vocalization (%)			73	100	75		89	100	81	93	78	88
Spontaneous (%)			93	100	100		72	100	69	67	67	88
Visual regard												
To mother (%)			33	0	12		19	0	12	47	67	50
Dual directional (%)			0	0	0		19	0	12	53	44	50
With words (%)			0	0	0		23	0	38	33	33	25
Carol												
Number	55		0	0	0	0	0	3	0	0	28	24
With vocalization (%)								100			71	83
Spontaneous (%)								100			78	75
Visual regard												
To mother (%)								67			64	25
Dual directional (%)								67			46	29
With words (%)								33			36	25
Joel												
Number	62		0	0	0	1	3	10	13	16	14	5
With vocalization (%)						100	100	50	92	88	100	100
Spontaneous (%)						100	100	80	100	81	50	80
Visual regard												
To mother (%)						0	33	80	23	62	21	80
Dual directional (%)						0	33	70	15	50	21	80
With words (%)						0	0	0	0	12	64	40
Allen												
Number	23		0	0	0	0	0	5	0	6	6	6
With vocalization (%)								60		67	67	67
Spontaneous (%)								80		100	67	0
Visual regard												
To mother (%)								0		0	17	0
Dual directional (%)								0		33	17	33
With words (%)								0		17	0	33

extending between 10 and 13 months and pointing between 12 and 14 months. The mean time of appearance of pointing for the four children was calculated as 12.25 months, in close agreement with Leung and Rheingold's (1981) estimate of 12.56 months based on cross-sectional data.

Early gestures frequently appeared first without vocal accompaniment. For all children vocal production was related to age. The differences in proportions of all gestures with vocalizations varied from an average of 37% at 9–12 months to 69% at 13–15 months and 72% at 16–18 months.

For Jean, vocal production was related to type of gesture as well Vocalization occurred with fewer than 40% of her nonpointing gestures until 11 or 12 months; pointing, however, was consistently accompanied by vocalization ($\geq$ 73%) from

Table 2. Characteristics and development of children's extending objects gestures

Child	Total number	8	9	10	11	12	13	14	15	16	17	18
Jean												
Number	162	0	4	7	11	43	30	23	8	6	17	13
With vocalization (%)			25	0	27	46	80	83	88	67	59	23
Spontaneous (%)			75	71	100	91	83	74	50	83	94	85
Visual regard												
To mother (%)			25	57	82	44	63	35	37	100	65	8
Dual directional (%)			0	0	0	7	0	4	25	0	0	0
With words (%)			0	0	0	0	47	30	37	67	18	15
Carol												
Number	78		0	2	0	2	4	7	51	7	5	0
With vocalization (%)				50		0	100	86	53	28	80	
Spontaneous (%)				100		100	75	71	90	57	40	
Visual regard												
To mother (%)				100		50	75	28	61	43	100	
Dual directional (%)				0		0	0	0'	0	0	0	
With words (%)				0		0	0	0	20	0	20	
Joel												
Number	26	0	0	0		0	8	4	0	8	3	3
With vocalization (%)							75	25		25	100	33
Spontaneous (%)							37	50		37	67	67
Visual regard												
To mother (%)							25	75		50	33	33
Dual directional (%)							0	0		0	0	0
With words (%)							0	0		0	67	0
Allen												
Number	26	0		0	0	4	6	0	9	6	1	0
With vocalization (%)						0	17		100	100	0	
Spontaneous (%)						25	83		67	67	100	
Visual regard												
To mother (%)						50	67		89	67	0	
Dual directional (%)						0	0		0	0	0	
With words (%)						0	0		0	50	0	

the outset. The other three children systematically began to include vocal accompaniments with all types of gestures at the same time. For Carol the transition occurred as early as 10 months, while Joel and Allen sharply increased vocal production with gestures at 12 and 14 months, respectively.

In contrast to the gestures of waving and headshaking which often first appeared in imitation games (Masur, 1980), none of these three object-related gestures emerged from an imitative context. Both object extensions and open-handed reaching did, however, frequently occur as responses to maternal behaviors, such as mothers' palm-up requesting gestures and their object manipulation or extensions, respectively. Pointing, on the other hand, developed

Table 3. Characteristics and development of children's open-handed reaching gestures

Child	Total number	Age (months) 8	9	10	11	12	13	14	15	16	17	18
Jean												
Number	86	4	11	15	9	3	5	5	19	4	4	7
With vocalization (%)		25	36	20	56	33	40	80	53	50	50	71
Spontaneous (%)		25	27	87	33	67	60	60	21	25	50	43
Visual regard												
To mother (%)		0	18	7	0	0	0	0	0	50	25	43
Dual directional (%)		0	0	0	0	0	0	0	0	50	25	14
With words (%)		0	0	0	0	0	0	0	5	25	25	28
Carol												
Number	37		5	6	0	0	6	6	1	4	5	4
With vocalization (%)			0	83			83	83	0	100	60	75
Spontaneous (%)			40	83			83	50	100	75	40	75
Visual regard												
To mother (%)			40	33			33	0	100	0	60	50
Dual directional (%)			0	0			17	0	100	0	20	50
With words (%)			0	0			0	0	0	0	20	0
Joel												
Number	106		2	9	11	7	11	18	16	10	7	15
With vocalization (%)			0	44	27	86	45	83	94	50	28	73
Spontaneous (%)			0	78	64	57	64	56	75	70	43	67
Visual regard												
To mother			0	11	18	0	0	22	31	20	14	13
Dual directional (%)			0	0	0	0	0	17	31	20	0	13
With words (%)			0	0	0	0	0	0	6	20	0	27
Allen												
Number	79		3	7	13	13	7	1	4	15	7	9
With vocalization (%)			33	0	23	15	14	100	100	80	71	100
Spontaneous (%)			67	0	23	46	43	100	75	53	57	67
Visual regard												
To mother (%)			0	0	0	0	0	0	50	13	0	11
Dual directional (%)			0	0	0	0	0	0	0	13	0	33
With words (%)			0	0	0	0	0	0	0	33	0	11

initially almost exclusively as a spontaneous rather than responsive gesture, appearing without any eliciting behaviors by the mother. On the average, 93% of all the children's first month points were spontaneous, while the corresponding percentages for open-handed reaching and extending objects 33% and 59%, respectively. This is in accord with suggestions by other authors of the self-directing attentional function of early pointing (Bates et al. 1979; Werner & Kaplan, 1963). Tables 1 and 3 demonstrate that pointing remained more spontaneous than reaching across time, especially for Jean and Joel whose rates of spontaneous pointing exceeded those of reaching for each month both gestures were recorded.

The Emergence of Dual-Directional Nonverbal Signaling

In Tables 1–3 all instances of gestures accompanied by visual gaze at the mother
are contrasted with those instances specifically involving dual-directional signaling, that is, gesturing toward an object in one direction while looking at a
person in a different visual field. Visual gaze toward the mother was present with
the children's earliest gestures, but *only* in those cases where the gesture was itself
directed toward the mother, such as extending objects toward the mother or
open-handed reaching or pointing toward objects held by the mother. This
parallels Murphy and Messer's (1977) report of young infants' receptive ability to
follow their mothers' points to objects only when both gesture and goal were in the
same visual field. The ability to send coordinated but divergently directed
gestural and gaze signals, however, emerged only at 12 months or later for all four
children.

When dual-directional signaling developed, it appeared within 1 month with
more than one type of gesture. Three (7%) of Jean's 43 object extensions to her
mother at 12 months were accompanied by gaze toward the camera operator. By
13 months, 10 (19%) of her 53 pointing gestures involved gaze in a direction
divergent from the gesture. Carol and Joel developed dual-directional signal
coordination starting at 13 months. For Carol it appeared first with open-handed
reaching and was evident at 14 months when pointing emerged. Joel displayed
dual-directional signaling first with pointing at 13 months, then with open-
handed reaching starting at 14 months. Allen demonstrated dual-directional
signaling beginning only at 16 months, where it occurred with both pointing and
open-handed reaching.

Although dual-directional signaling emerged with different kinds of gestures
approximately simultaneously, once it was well established for all children,
pointing was more likely than reaching to include such communicative gazing.
Divergent visual regard rarely occurred with object extensions since gaze and
gesture would normally both be oriented to the same goal, the mother. For the
period from 16 to 18 months, an average of 40% of the children's pointing gestures,
but only 20% of open-handed reaching included dual-directional signaling. The
differences for each of the children ranged from 12% to 32%, suggesting a
developing communicative preeminence for the pointing gesture.

Further examination comparing two-directional signaling with spontaneous
versus responsive pointing during this period revealed that for Jean, Carol, and
Joel, coordinated gesture and gaze characterized a greater percentage of spontaneous (average 51%) than of responsive points (average 30%; range of
differences 13%–28%). Three of the children, then, were consistently more likely
to monitor their mothers visually while initiating communicative interchanges
than while replying to them, when the mothers' attention could be assumed to be
already engaged. This accounts for Carol's apparent decline in dual-directional
signaling with pointing at 18 months, and Joel's at 17 months (see Table 1). Their
responsive points at those months did not involve visual monitoring at all
although coordinated signaling was displayed with 39% and 43% of their spontaneous points, respectively. This finding may explain Murphy's (1978) report

that during book reading sessions while seated on their mothers' laps children virtually never visually contacted their mothers. These children seemed to employ communicative gaze parsimoniously, omitting it when the mothers' attention to their gestures could be taken for granted.

The transcripts were also scanned for examples of another kind of dual signaling, that involving two simultaneous or immediately successive gestures. Such dual signaling occurred rarely, but first appeared with or shortly following the emergence of coordinated gesture-plus-gaze, a co-occurrence also noted by Bates et al. (1979). Joel exhibited successive gesturing, reaching then headshaking to an offered object, then reaching again, at 14 months, and simultaneous gesturing, reaching while headshaking, at 15 months. Jean also produced simultaneous gesturing, pointing plus nodding, at 15 months. Carol's only instances of successive gesturing involved pointing, reaching, and waving at 17 months. No examples of successive or simultaneous gesturing were observed on Allen's tapes. In addition, Joel and Jean each displayed evidence of visual perspective-taking at 14 months: Joel rotated a picture book 180° to face his mother, and Jean turned a mirror she had been looking into toward her mother's face.

Dual-Directional Signaling and the Emergence of Conventional Words with Gestures

Dual signaling involving a lexical component, pairing a conventional word or its recognizable approximation with a gesture, first appeared *only* when the children had demonstrated the coordination of gestural and gaze signals (refer to Tables 1–3). For Jean, Carol, and Allen, words appeared within 1 month of their first dual-directional nonverbal signaling; for Joel the interval was 2 months. For all children, words emerged when dual-directional signaling had been productively demonstrated with two different kinds of gestures.

Just as each child's dual-directional signaling appeared approximately simultaneously with different gestures, his or her conventional words generally emerged at the same time with more than one kind of gesture. Jean first produced words at 13 months with both points and object extensions, while Allen produced words with all three kinds of gestures at 16 months. Carol and Joel added words to different gestures slightly more gradually, at a rate of about one new gesture a month. For the period from 16 to 18 months, when all the children had become verbal, words tended more frequently to accompany points (29%) than object extensions (22%) or reaches (16%).

Categories of Words Accompanying Gestures

In order to examine more qualitatively the kinds of words accompanying different types of gestures, the children's verbalizations were classified into the following six categories: vocatives, such as *mommy*; nominals, encompassing

Table 4. Classification of children's words and the types of gestures they accompanied

Child	Age in months	Vocatives	Nominals	Performatives	Negatives	Requests	Demonstratives
				Word classes			
Jean	13	P E	P	P		E	
	14		E			E	
	15	E	P	P		E O	
	16		P	E O	P		
	17	E	P			E O	
	18		E O		E		P
Carol	14	P					
	15		E				E
	16						
	17		P	P O	P E		
	18		P				
Joel	15				O		
	16		P O				
	17		P E				
	18		P O				
Allen	16	P E O					
	17						
	18		P		P O		

P = Pointing; E = Extending objects; O = Open-handed reaching.

animate and inanimate object labels; performatives, including *hi, bye,* and *peekaboo*; negatives, like *no*; requests, such as *more*; and demonstratives, including *this* and *that*. Table 4 displays for each child by month the gestures these classes of words accompanied.

Individually, children varied in the extent to which they produced different classes of words. For example, Joel's range was restricted to nominals and a single negative, categories present in the repertoire of every child, while Jean's output encompassed all six verbal categories. For Jean, Carol, and Allen, the vocative *mommy* appeared with gestures the first month verbalizations occurred. For all three children *mommy* occurred with points, although not exclusively so for Jean and Allen. Thus, pointing at an object while calling the mother's attention was the first, or among the first, gestural-verbal combination to appear for these children, occurring before pointing while naming for two of them. This pattern, however, is at variance with Greenfield and Smith's (1976) finding in a case study of verbal development in two boys that the emergence of objects of reference, or "Indicative Objects," preceded the appearance of objects of demand, or "Volitional Objects," since they asserted that "the vocative may be defined as an animate Volitional Object" (p. 104). Thus, the sequential emergence of specific functions which Greenfield and Smith reported for words alone is not apparent in these children's gestural-verbal combinations.

Instead, it is evident from Table 4 that verbalizations and gestures rapidly became productively combined, making possible the generation of a variety of meaningful gestural-verbal expression. When all four children are considered together, it is clear that words in the first four of the six verbal categories accompanied all three kinds of gestures, while those in the two remaining categories appeared in conjunction with two gestural types each. No verbal class was specific to one particular gesture. On the average, words from 3.2 different verbal categories were produced with points, while words from 2.5 and 2.0 different classes accompanied extensions and reaches, respectively.

Furthermore, analysis of individual words disclosed that in many cases the same particular words appeared with more than one kind of gesture, a finding which contrasts with A.L. Carter's (1978) report of distinct prelinguistic vocalization-gesture pairs in her single subject. An average of 36% (range 13%–67%) of each child's words appeared in conjunction with more than one gesture; for all types of words except nominals the average was 53% (range 0%–100%), but among nominals the average percentage was only 11% (range 0%–33%). These results are consistent with previously reported findings that children produced nominals significantly more with points than with other gestures, illustrating the emerging referential emphasis of the pointing gesture (Masur, 1982).

Discussion

This study has followed the acquisition and development of three object-related communicative gestures in a longitudinal sample observed in natural interactions with their mothers. Because the sample size is small, conclusions must necessarily remain tentative until their generality can be verified with larger studies. However, this investigation has provided a detailed account of the pattern of development common to the gestural performance of four children. It has documented the elaboration of the children's rudimentary communicative skills from the emergence of simple gestures produced in isolation to their progressive mastery of the production and coordination of two or more simultaneous signals addressed to another person. This progression followed a sequence starting with gesture plus vocalization, continuing through gesture plus divergent gaze, and culminating in gesture plus gesture and gesture plus conventional verbalization.

Perhaps most importantly, the results of this study have served to highlight the distinction between children's gaze toward mother in general, frequently counted by itself as an indicator of communicative intent (Harding & Golinkoff, 1979; Leung & Rheingold, 1981), and specifically dual-directional gestural and visual signaling which involves the coordination of divergently directed signals. Although gaze toward mother in the same visual field was present even with very early gestures, only the emergence of truly dual-directional signaling had predictive value.

Dual-directional signaling appeared in the 2nd year approximately simultaneously with more than one type of gesture. The productive coordination of these two nonverbal signals of gesture and gaze preceded the appearance of other instances of dual nonverbal signaling, successive and simultaneous gesturing. In addition, the observation of examples of early visual perspective-taking at about the same time in two of the children argues for further inquiry into possible parallels in underlying cognitive functioning between dual-directional signaling and the development of a rudimentary receptive appreciation of another's direction of visual regard (cf., Lempers, 1979; Lempers et al., 1977). Each may represent a sensorimotor form of the cognitive ability to consider two things, means or perspectives, at the same time. Furthermore, the occurrence of dual-directional signaling in the 16–18-month period more often with pointing, and especially with spontaneous pointing where the mother's attention could not be taken for granted, indicates that the children were employing such signaling in a socially adjusted manner.

Finally, only when dual-directional signaling had been productively demonstrated with more than one kind of gesture did words appear for each child. This timing suggests that the capacity for dual nonverbal signaling may be a necessary, but not a sufficient prerequisite for the production of conventional linguistic signals with gestures. The additional role of the mother in promoting the acquisition of words with the gestures, especially pointing, merits attention as well (cf., Masur, 1982). Also striking was the appearance of a child's words at approximately the same time in conjunction with more than one kind of gesture. The nearly simultaneous onset of verbal accompaniment to all gestures and the rapidly formed multiple combinations of individual words or word classes with different gestures marked the transition to the new level of gestural-linguistic communication.

CHAPTER 3

Gestures, Words, and Early Object Sharing

L.B. ADAMSON, R. BAKEMAN, and C.B. SMITH

Introduction

An infant's first gestures and words are a developmental link between communication by "action" and communication by "symbol." Unlike literal acts, their meaning derives at least in part from social convention. Unlike truly symbolic acts, these conventionalized acts are not free from their context. Their referent is often so close at hand that, even if an act is poorly executed, its meaning is relatively clear.

The contextualization of first gestures and words has been stressed in several recent accounts of early communication development (e.g., Bruner, 1983a; Newson & Newson, 1975). Werner and Kaplan (1963), for example, argue that early exchanges "have the character of 'sharing' experiences *with* the Other rather than of 'communicating' messages *to* the Other" (p. 42). According to this view, acts of reference emerge in a social context as children and their communicative partners share concrete objects.

Several years ago, we began to examine systematically infants' conventionalized acts and the context in which they appear. We sought such empirical information because it may help explain how infants overcome a difficult attentional problem inherent in learning to communicate. Referential communication demands attention both to a shared topic (an object or event) and to a partner. Yet the skill of coordinating attention to people and to objects is typically not yet mastered as first words and gestures begin to be used at the end of the 1st year of life (Bakeman & Adamson, 1984; Nelson, 1979).

One way infants can learn to communicate without continually attending to both people and objects is to rely on more sophisticated partners for support. The baby essentially attends actively only to an object. The partner shares this object without demanding the infant's attention. In this way, the partner "socializes" the infant's attention, allowing the infant to experience objects in ways he or she might not yet be able to structure without assistance. Moreover, because infant and partner share attention to a common object, the partner is providing the attentional context for the communication of messages about objects.

In this chapter, we summarize research that documents how 9- to 15-month-old infants deploy their attention when they use gestures and words with

The work reported here was supported in part by the National Science Foundation (BNS-8012068 and BNS-8300716).

adult and peer partners. In addition, we discuss a study that examines the relationship between object sharing during the preverbal period and variations in early language acquisition. This work supports the view that sharing attention to objects with adults provides infants with a rich context for communication months before infants can routinely coordinate attention to both objects and people.

Background: The Socialization of Attention

Before reviewing our research, we need to "set the stage." Three fundamental psychological processes — attention, socialization, and coordination — play a central role. To introduce how we view each of them, we will assemble a cast of three grand theorists whose ideas have greatly influenced us.

The first character is William James. In a sense, he has played the role of "villain" in many contemporary considerations of infants since he is known to developmentalists best for his claim that newborns are "assailed by eyes, ears, nose, skin, and entrails at once" and so feel all is "one great blooming, buzzing confusion" (James, 1890, Vol. I, p. 488). It is unfortunate, we think, that he is not as well remembered for the reason that he came to this conclusion. His rationale is also presented in his 1890 *Principles of Psychology,* in a much reprinted chapter on attention.

To James, attention is an active psychological process whose function is selection. As an organism directs its attention, the nature of its experience is determined. James summarizes this idea in the following statement: *My experience is what I agree to attend to.* Only those items which I *notice* shape my mind — without selective interest, experience is an utter chaos (1890, Vol. I, p. 403).

But, how do young infants escape the experience of chaos? James did not think that they could until they could analyze the "bloom of confusion." But recent research suggests that even very young infants are "selective," that they have certain adaptive interests, particularly in people. These interests, in turn, suggest that infants do not have to select aspects of the environment on their own. Rather caregivers — more experienced in the ways of the world — can serve as guides who help them attend selectively.

Perhaps the most powerful statement of this view was made by Lev Vygotsky in his sociohistorical theory of the development of higher psychological processes. In his work, he repeatedly emphasized the importance of social mediation on a child's understanding of objects. He wrote, for example, that "the path from object to child and from child to object passes through another person" (Vygotsky, 1978, p. 30). We read this passage as an important reminder that a child experiences objects in a qualitatively different way when they are shared than when they are manipulated during solitary play.

Vygotsky provides a complicated view of socialization that meshes well with James' view of attention as an active process. Socialization is a process of guided learning that is timed to development. The opportunity for guidance is opened by development; when a new process emerges, its emergence is supported by (but not created by) others. This notion is captured by the now fashionable phrase "zone of proximal development" — the "region" between what is already developed, what a child can do alone, and what is emerging, what a child can do in concert with a more sophisticated partner.

While we find Vygotsky's general treatment of the relationship between socialization and development heuristic, we think he provides less guidance concerning the specific details of the socialization of attention in the months during the emergence of gestures and words. In short, Vygotsky's image of infants may prove less satisfying than his overall conception of development. Apparently, much to the chagrin of recent Soviet psychologists, Vygotsky characterized presymbolic babies as "unmediated" and so, "the development of attention in this period is based purely on the organic processes of growth, maturation, and development of the neurological apparatuses and functions of the child" (Vygotsky, quoted in van der Veer and van Ijzendoorn, 1985).

Like most Western psychologists, we have gained access to Vygotsky's work only gradually and so, in our ignorance, have been uninfluenced by his too sharp dichotomy between higher and lower processes. It is rather ironic, perhaps, that in this position Vygotsky sounds surprisingly like Jean Piaget, who is often presented as his opponent. But, it is Piaget who has provided us with guidance in our attempt to chart developmental changes in the ways infants are able to structure attention.

Piaget contends that the coordination of actions is a key achievement in infancy. To him, the coordination of two secondary circular reactions is particularly significant in that it permits intentional actions. Others (e.g., Bates, 1979; Harding & Golinkoff, 1979) have stressed that the coordination of actions also permits true communication by allowing the coordination of an act directed toward a person with one directed toward an object. Moreover, Piaget also implies that the coordination of actions opens up new possibilities for attention. In his words, "by coordinating the schemata which constitute the instruments of his intelligence, the child learns ipso facto to put things in relationship to each other" (Piaget, 1952, p. 211). The infant can now actively combine two previously separate aspects of the environment.

Piaget dates the emergence of coordinated actions around the last quarter of the 1st year of life. There is much support for this claim, including observations of the infant's coordination of acts related to objects and people (e.g., Leung & Rheingold, 1981; Murphy & Messer, 1977). Yet, as Nelson (1979) suggests, such coordination cannot be assumed as infants begin to use gestures and words. Rather, like conventionalized communicative acts, it too may have a long developmental course and it too may be a culminating skill of the preverbal period.

In summary, our work on the development of words and gestures blends · three lines of thought. We are indebted to James for a conceptualization that places the active process of attention at the heart of experience. From Vygotsky, we draw justification for highlighting the significance of sharing objects with partners. And, inspired by Piaget, we focus on the period of middle to late infancy when babies are developing the capacity to coordinate their actions in the object and the social realms.

First Gestures and Words in Context

The program of research we will now survey was designed to examine how infants' gestures and words are "contextualized." Given our emphasis on the "socialization of attention," we were especially interested in documenting the normative developmental relationship between conventionalized communicative acts and infants' attention to people and to objects. Moreover, we were interested in discerning what, if any, special role sophisticated partners might play in supporting the attentional context for an infant's first use of words and objects.

When we began this work, there was already considerable qualitative information about the subtle weaving of infants' and adults' acts during periods of shared object-focused play. Several detailed narrative reports (e.g., Bruner, 1975b; Ninio & Bruner, 1978; Ratner & Bruner, 1978; Trevarthen & Hubley, 1978) illustrated how adults simultaneously help infants share objects and communicate about them. Our first aim was to complement these reports by using systematic observational methods (Bakeman & Gottman, 1986) and a relatively large longitudinal sample of infants. There were also several recent reports that showed that interactive skills even for toddlers are few (e.g., Eckerman & Stein, 1982). Therefore, a second aim was to be able to compare infants' play with peers and mothers so that we might gain a better idea of why two infants often fail to sustain interactions.

Over the past several years, we have compiled an extensive library of videotapes of infants observed during semistructured play sessions. We will focus here primarily on observations made at 9, 12, and 15 months of 28 middle-class, healthy babies in their homes. We defined three conditions of infant play (with mother, with peer, and alone), and we videotaped about 10 min of each, varying their order systematically. During the mother condition, we suggested that the mother interact as she might if she had a few minutes to devote to spontaneous play. During the peer and alone conditions, we asked the mothers to remain in the room but to pay minimal attention to the infants, intervening only when necessary to calm or protect the infants. Mothers recruited a peer, an infant who played with her infant often and who was close in age. We provided toys, varying them systematically across conditions. (See Bakeman & Adamson, 1984, 1986 for more information.)

Our major empirical question was, to what or to whom is an infant most likely to be attending when using words and gestures. In order to answer this question, we needed to compile data concerning, first, when gestures and words were used and, second, when infants were attending to people and to objects.

The Occurrence of Words and Gestures

We defined words and gestures as acts that were at least partly "arbitrary," that is, acts that gained meaning through social understanding and not solely due to their physical or "natural" form or force. Coders noted every time an infant produced a point, a show/offer, a regulative gesture (such as a headshake "no" or a "wave" goodbye), a referential word (one that named or described an object, such as "dog" or "hot"), and a regulative word (such as "mine" or "bye").

The relationship between age and gestures and words was as expected (see Table 1). At 9 months of age, 15 of the 28 infants used gestures at least once but none used words. By 15 months, all gestured and 25 produced words. The typical developmental progression moved from the use of gestures only to the use of both words and gestures.

Mothers clearly promoted the use of conventionalized acts; all categories of words and gestures occurred significantly more often when the infant was observed in the mother condition as compared to either the peer or the alone condition. Given the clear effect of the mother on the use of words and gestures, it is not surprising that we also found that infants tended to use conventionalized acts at an earlier age when with their mothers instead of peers. This pattern is

Table 1. Number of infants observed using gestures and words and number of gestures and words observed per hour

Condition, act	Infants			Acts per hour		
	9-mo (n)	12-mo (n)	15-mo (n)	9-mo (n)	12-mo (n)	15-mo (n)
Mother						
Points	3	14	19	0.6	6.7	34.3
Show/offers	4	15	19	3.5	7.3	13.0
Regulative gestures	4	6	15	0.8	5.0	6.3
Regulative words	0	6	16	0	3.1	11.6
Referential words	0	7	18	0	4.6	28.4
Peer						
Points	0	9	12	0	2.1	5.1
Show/offers	6	13	10	1.6	6.4	8.3
Regulative gestures	2	9	7	0.6	2.8	2.2
Regulative words	0	3	4	0	1.1	2.2
Referential words	0	5	12	0	3.4	12.7
Alone						
Points	1	6	9	0.5	3.2	3.2
Show/offers	0	1	2	0	0.2	0.7
Regulative gestures	2	6	6	0.5	2.3	2.0
Regulative words	0	1	7	0	0.5	5.7
Referential words	0	4	8	0	3.4	16.2

Scores are based on pooled observations of 27 infants at 15 months in the peer condition, 28 infants otherwise.

consistent with the notion that infants first use an act during interaction with adults and then exercise it later during play with peers.

In striking contrast to mothers, peers appeared to promote words or gestures no more than no partner at all. The only exception to this generalization involved the show/offer gesture, which occurred in the peer condition at a rate midway between the rates recorded in the mother and the alone conditions. Interestingly, show/offers are the most "literal" conventional act we studied: while they contain a stylized component, the object referred to is actually in hand.

The results we have summarized so far suggest that mothers facilitate the use of newly developing, conventionalized acts. But they do not indicate whether this facilitation is selective or whether it simply reflects an overall tendency for infants to communicate more with mothers than with peers or while alone. The effect of condition on three nonconventionalized communicative acts — babbling, jargon (vocalizations that have the prosodic contour of a word or phrase but that could not be glossed), and positive affective expressions — supports the conclusion that mothers effect the production of conventionalized and nonconventionalized communicative acts differently. While mothers promoted the use of conventionalized acts, they were not always as essential for the use of nonconventionalized ones. Babies babbled quite a lot, particularly during the alone condition (4.1%), less with peers (2.2%), and least with mothers (1.6%). They also produced many jargon sounds without varying the rate (which reached almost one per minute at 15 months) across conditions. Only affective expressions were higher when infants were with mothers rather than with peers or alone (Adamson & Bakeman, 1985).

Engagement States

In setting up our observations, we manipulated the infant's access to social partners but we did not control the infant's involvement with them. We therefore needed a way to describe how infants deployed their attention to the people and objects we provided. To do this, we regarded the stream of the infant's activity in each of our conditions as a series of "engagement states." We selected the word "engagement" to emphasize that we were interested in the infant's active attention. The term "state" was used to tie our work conceptually to prior work on newborn state and on peer social interaction, and to suggest that relatively sustained engagement states might provide the context for specific acts such as affective expressions, gestures, and words (see Adamson & Bakeman, 1982).

Three engagement states are of particular interest here: person engagement, object engagement, and joint engagement. In joint engagement, the infant is sharing an object with a partner. Joint engagement can, we have found (Bakeman & Adamson, 1984), be differentiated reliably into two states. During the first, coordinated joint engagement, the infant actively integrates attention to objects and people. During the other, supported (or "passive") joint engagement, the baby shares an object with a partner but attends actively only to the object.

Toys clearly fascinated the infants, with well over 40% of each condition on the average being devoted to object engagement. People were must less likely to receive sole attention; by 15 months, less than 5% of the time was spent engaged only with the partner. So far, we do not need to qualify these statements by specifying whether the person is mother or peer. But for joint engagement, this qualification is necessary. Mothers — and not peers — supported joint engagement. This engagement state occupied about an average of 20% of the mother condition at each age. In contrast, it virtually did not occur with a peer. Coordinated joint engagement was very rare (less than 5% of the entire observation) with either partner at 9 and 12 months. At 15 months, babies had begun to coordinate attention to mothers and objects (11.2%) and to peers and objects (4.2%), a developmental trend that continued into later infancy (Bakeman & Adamson, 1984).

Conventionalized Acts and Engagement

We now have the data necessary to answer questions about the relationship between infants' engagement state and their production of communicative acts. We used the following strategy. For a given age and a given observational condition, we calculated the rate for a particular act. Then we asked, using a chi-square goodness-of-fit test, whether significantly more (or fewer) acts occurred in a particular context than might be expected given the act's base rate.

Gestures and words were clearly located more during some engagement states than others in the mother condition. Joint engagement clearly provided a favorable context while object engagement was not a time for words or gestures. At 15 months, all conventionalized acts occurred more often than expected by chance during periods of joint engagement with mothers. At 12 months, the rates of show/offers and regulative gestures (but not words or points) were elevated during these periods. At 9 months, the few conventionalized acts that were produced tended to occur during joint engagement although there were too few conventionalized acts noted to do formal analyses.

In contrast, there was no systematic influence of engagement state during the peer condition. The only exception was, once again, show/offers which seemed suppressed during periods of object engagement when infants were 15 months old.

We next applied the same strategy in order to determine if the effects noted for engagement state were specific only to conventionalized communicative acts. Jargon sounds appeared most like conventionalized acts in terms of their placement relative to infants' engagement. Infants at all ages tended to increase their use of jargon when they shared objects with their mothers. Their tie to engagement state was, however, less specific than conventionalized acts since at 12 months — but not at 15 months — jargon rates were elevated during both joint and object engagement in the peer condition. Affective expressions presented a different pattern than conventionalized acts in that, in addition to being more likely than expected during joint engagement with mothers, they were, not surprisingly, strongly related to person engagement. Finally, babbling presented a markedly different pattern from conventionalized acts. With mothers, it was elevated during object engagement at 15 months and person engagement at 12 months. With peers, at all ages, babbling was elevated during person engagement.

Action Formats and Joint Engagement

One explanation of how infants integrate conventionalized acts and joint engagement is that they share not only an object but also a "standard action format" with their partner. This is certainly a plausible idea. Sharing of games or repetitive rituals (Adamson & Bakeman, 1984) that support the placement of communicative acts has a history extending back into the first weeks of infancy (Stern, Beebe, Jaffe, & Bennett, 1977; Tronick, Als, & Adamson, 1979). Newson, for example, emphasizes that discrete signals are "repeatedly interwoven in familiar alternating sequences" within "well-worn rituals of interactions" (Newson, 1978, p. 33).

The infants often enacted a wide variety of formats (such as book reading, telephoning, playing puzzle, imaginary eating) when observed with their mothers. At 9 months, 23 of the 28 babies followed an action format during the mother condition and, at 15 months, all did for an average of almost 40% of the time. In contrast, formats rarely appeared with peers (0.8%, 5.9%, and 7.4% of the condition at 9, 12, and 15 months, respectively) or during the alone condition with the interesting exception of 15 months (1.2%, 4.7%, and 16.5% at 9, 12, and 15 months, respectively).

We found that there is a similar pattern for the effects of joint engagement and action formats on the rates of conventionalized acts, although fewer elevated rates were found during action formats than joint engagement, and those that were elevated — points and referential words at 15 months and for show/offers at 12 months when with mothers — were also elevated during joint engagement. This is hardly surprising since the two contexts often overlapped — 43% of the time that infants were jointly engaged in the mother condition they were also following an action format. This raises the question of whether the effects noted for both contexts are due primarily to one of these contexts or to their overlapping.

To answer this question, we looked separately at the occurrence of acts during times when babies were jointly engaged only, in action formats only, and in the period of their overlap. This analysis revealed that the apparent effect of action formats on show/offers at 12 months is really due to joint engagement. The effects on points and referential words at 15 months, however, seems to be due to both contexts operating jointly.

This pattern of findings suggests that the critical ingredient for the very early production of words and gestures at 9 and 12 months may well be joint engagement with an adult. Only at 15 months is there evidence that standard action formats clearly elevate the rate of referential (but not social-regulative) conventionalized acts, and then only when they are being enacted during joint engagement with the mother. Interestingly, it is also at this age that formats and, to a lesser degree, words and gestures began to appear quite frequently outside the mother condition. These findings suggest that a process of decontextualization (Werner and Kaplan, 1963) of words and gestures may have begun by 15 months.

Object Sharing and Later Language Development

The evidence we have reviewed indicates that when infants are actively attending to an object that they share with their mothers, they are most likely to produce their first words and gestures. This finding is consistent with the view that object sharing may play a critical role in early communication development. One way to explore this notion further is to ask whether variations in object sharing relate systematically to the striking variations evident in early language development (Nelson, 1981).

In a recent study (Smith, Adamson, & Bakeman, 1986), we tried to predict differences in the size of infants' vocabularies at 18 months using information about infant attention derived from our observations of play with mothers at 15 months. At 15 months, our subjects did not vary much in terms of vocabulary size; the range was from three to 39 words with a mean of 14.4. But when the mothers reported what words their 18-month-old infants said regularly, lists ranged from three words to 145.

While vocabulary sizes did not vary much at 15 months, the amount of time infants devoted to joint object play with their mothers did; the range was from 12% to 77% of the 10-min mother condition. If attending to objects with mothers supports early communication, then it is reasonable to expect that those infants who devote relatively more time to joint engagement might have larger vocabularies 3 months later.

To assess the predictive power of variation in infant joint engagement, we did a multiple regression analysis. First, we regressed the variable vocabulary size on the percentage of time infants spent unengaged. This step let us look at whether or not knowing just how much infants focused attention per se predicted later vocabulary. We found that it did not. In the second step, we entered the percentage of time spent in joint engagement during the 10-min play period to see if predictability improved over that obtained when considering only the engaged/unengaged distinction. It did so significantly ($p < 05$; adjusted $R^2 = .22$); the bulk of predictive power belonged to the second variable with the zero-order correlation between joint engagement and vocabulary size being $r = .46$.

We also asked whether or not 18-month vocabulary size could be predicted by what mothers did to focus their 15-month-old infants' attention on language and objects. We assessed this in two different ways. First, we categorized mothers' attention-directing acts toward objects in terms of their form (Adamson & Bakeman, 1984). An act was considered literal if it highlighted aspects of the environment by making them perceptually more salient (e.g., shaking a rattle). Mothers spent between 4% and 41% of the observation making literal attention-directing acts. An act was characterized as conventional if it derived its attention-influencing potential through shared meaning (e.g., a pointing gesture or a word). Mothers directed attention using conventional acts between 5% and 58% of the condition. A regression of infants' 18-month vocabulary size on mothers' literal and conventional object marking yielded an adjusted R^2 of .31 ($p < .01$) with the bulk of the predictive power attributed to the association between vocabulary size and mothers' conventional object marking (zero-order $r = .60$).

Secondly, we considered how differences in the way mothers used language might have affected their infants' vocabulary size. Using a coding scheme designed to classify the function of mother's speech (Jones & Adamson, 1987), coders reliably characterized each of the mothers' utterances as referential (referring to objects, e.g., "That's a cow"), social-regulative (focusing on the actions of the participants, e.g., "I like that" or "Look at me"), or metalingual (focusing on the linguistic code itself and its production, e.g., "Say, 'Hello!'"). Mothers produced per minute an average of 7.5 (range 2.5–13.2), 6.8 (2.1–13.2), and 4.0 (0.5–12.3) referential, social-regulative, and metalingual utterances, respectively.

Vocabulary size was predicted by the functions of mothers' utterances. In the regression analysis, we first entered mothers' verbalization rate to control for sheer level of talkativeness. Sheer talkativeness did not let us predict vocabulary size (adjusted $R^2 = 0$). The distribution of acts across the three utterance categories was entered next, producing an adjusted R^2 of .22 ($p < .05$). The partial correlations indicated that mothers who used more of their utterances to focus on language ($pr = .44$) and those who used fewer of their utterances to regulate the social interaction ($pr = -.43$) tended to have 18-month-olds with larger vocabularies.

Overall, we were able to account for 40% of the variance of infants' vocabulary size by knowing how often during 10 min of play 3 months earlier the infants engaged in joint object play with their mothers, how often their mothers used conventionalized acts to direct attention to objects, and how their mothers used language. These results are consistent with the view that adults may act as guides for infants just beginning to master conventionalized forms of communication.

Conclusion

By the middle of their 1st year, babies often turn away from people and attend with fascination to objects. New topics of communication are available. Yet, not until the first months of the 2nd year do babies begin to structure their own attention routinely so that these topics can be shared. As Nelson (1979) argues, the coordination of the social and the object worlds may occupy babies for the last months of infancy, and it may pave the way for the flowering of symbolic communication. The emergence of conventionalized communication is not, however, postponed. Words and gestures, just like objects, can be shared with a sophisticated and supportive partner before they are freed from the on-going interaction.

The mothers and infants observed in the studies reported here were no doubt motivated both by background and circumstance to display their "best" communicative activities. They showed us that infants' first words and gestures may truly be shared accomplishments embedded within an attentional context that is constructed by both the adult and the child. Now it is important to ask how infants who do not experience such supportive early object sharing negotiate the transition to symbolic communication.

CHAPTER 4

Some Observations on the Origins of the Pointing Gesture

A. LOCK, A. YOUNG, V. SERVICE, P. CHANDLER

Introduction

Piaget has observed that an acute observation is worth a thousand statistics. Recent studies of early prelinguistic and linguistic development bear this out. While experimental studies are being increasingly reported, work presenting interpretations of selected observations is still common. On the basis of such evidence, a number of claims have been made concerning the origin of the pointing gesture:

1. Bates (1976a) has proposed that the origins of pointing lie *outside* any communicative context: originally, the gesture is an orienting mechanism for the self. She supports this claim by alluding to one infant, and by appealing to the similar claim of Werner and Kaplan (1963), who themselves draw on anecdotes from two of the classical diary studies.
2. By contrast, Vygotsky (1966) saw pointing as originating in the failed reaching activities of the infant that are made successful through the intervention of an adult. The gesture thus develops *within* a communicative context. Vygotsky refers to no infants in making this claim.
3. Lock (1980), while claiming the actual origins of pointing are unimportant, adopted Vygotsky's line on the basis of a few observations of three infants: "pointing *appears* to arise from unsuccessful direct attempts. . .to grasp or reach for an object. . ." (p. 57).
4. In Bruner's (1983b) view, pointing "does not appear to be an extension or modification of reaching. . . It seems that pointing is part of a primitive marking system for singling out the noteworthy" (p. 75). This is on the basis of two children.
5. Leung and Rheingold (1981), on the basis of a more specific study of 32 children, report that pointing "eventually replaces reaching as a reference gesture" (p. 220) — without committing themselves to any developmental link — and note that pointing may have its origins in modelling: ". . . as children get older, the greater is their opportunity to observe older persons using the index finger. They then model their pointing after that of adults. . ." (p. 220).

This paper was presented at the biennial meeting of the Society for Research in Child Development, Toronto, April, 1985.

6. Kaye (1982) makes the same point:
    In pointing to an object in which the infant seems to be interested, the parent
    may only be asking for verification of the intention he or she attributes to the
    infant. Any time this attribution is correct, however, the parent will in effect
    have modelled a pointing gesture. After many such demonstrations, the
    infant will imitate (p. 179).

Three models of development have thus been proposed:

1. Spontaneous development followed by change of function from asocial to
    social.
2. Derived development from failed action within a social context.
3. Acquired development by imitation.

All these models are plausible, but none of them has sufficient evidence behind
it. We will present our data in an attempt to either distinguish between these
alternatives or establish whether they really are alternatives. These data come
from the following study.

Study Details

A total of 140 mother-infant pairs were videotaped in four different tasks in a
cross-sectional study. The groups in the investigation were determined by the
infants' age. There were 14 groups: 5–15 months, 18, 21, and 24 months. Each pair
spent 5 min playing with toys, looking at books, putting together jigsaws, and
looking at slides projected on a wall about 3 m from them. Pointing and indicative
gestures were scored for both mother and infant. Some of the dimensions on
which they were scored will become apparent as we progress. Inter-observer
reliability was good for the measures we are dealing with here. The total number
of gestures resulting from this study was over 7000.

Preliminary Remarks on Interpreting the Data

The data show a great deal of variance: in each group there are both mothers and
children who point a lot and a little. However, the overall patterns in the data are
interpretable. For example, Fig. 1 shows the mean frequency of infants' total
gesturing at each age. It appears as though gesturing is not really established as
part of the infant's repertoire until after 10 months of age, that there is an increase
in the frequency of gesturing up to 18 months, and then a decline to 24 months.
This seems reasonable, because:

1. Previous studies of early gesturing point to a time around 9–12 months for its
    onset.

2. The total amount of communication in fact continues to rise when one takes
    spoken language into account, even though the amount of gesturing is
    decreasing. This suggests language replaces gesture as the main commu-
    nicative channel, in line with the findings of Bates, Benigni, Bretherton,
    Camaiori and Volterra (1979).

If, though, we add the ranges to the graph in Fig. 1 (Fig. 2) and also the standard
deviations (Fig. 3), it would seem that we should place little confidence in this
pattern: it could be entirely spurious. However, if we rank the children in each
group in order of the amount of their gesturing and plot each rank across the
groups, we get an increase in the "rainbow" pattern already apparent in Fig. 3.
Thus, even though the variance is sufficient to give us little statistical confidence
in the group means, we have grounds for taking them as good indicators of the
course of development. Further:

1. A non-parametric analysis of variance on the data grouped into larger sets
    than monthly age yields a significant difference (Kruskal-Wallace, $H =$
    88.81, $df = 5, p > 0.001$) between the ages, indicating that there is develop-
    mental change occurring.
2. The children who define the floor of the range, i.e., children who show a low
    frequency of gesturing at any age, show consistent differences in their
    gesturing to other infants. Either their gesturing is ineffective, that is, their
    mothers respond to only a small percentage of their gestures, or they likewise
    act on only a small percentage of their mothers' gestures. In the early age
    range, these infants are characterized by both these factors. While the figures
    are small (14 dyads), they show a consistent pattern that changes at 13
    months. Prior to that time, both these infants and their mothers show the
    lowest level of responding to each other's gesturing in their group. After 13

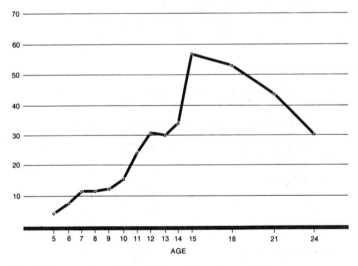

Fig. 1. Mean number of infant gestures for each age group

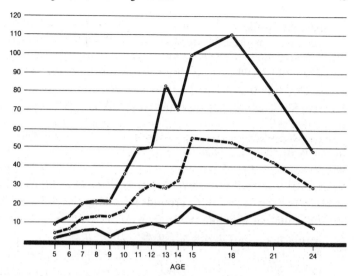

Fig. 2. Means (*broken line*) and ranges (*solid lines*) of infant gestures

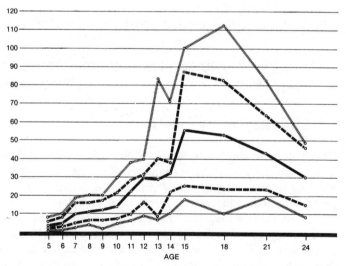

Fig. 3. Means (*solid line*), ranges (*dotted lines*), and standard deviations (*broken lines*) for infant gestures

months, while the mothers are acting on the majority of their infants' gestures, the infants are ignoring their mothers' gestures. Perhaps such infants are being socialized as low communicators.

3.   The children who define the ceiling of the range may be thought of as either early developers or highly communicative. Either way, the pattern shown by the ceiling infants parallels that shown by the mean frequency of gesturing in each group.

In what follows we outline our views on the developmental characteristics of the early stirrings of interpersonal communication. Because of the nature of the data these claims are open to other interpretations. These claims are in theory open to empirical testing, but it is probable that such testing will find itself bedevilled by:

1.   The inherent variability of mother-infant communication when it is sampled by the small snapshots such investigations take.
2.   The fact that in its early stages mother-infant communication is a fairly uncommon event, leading to low frequencies for "analysis."

Longitudinal studies may well prove profitable, and we recommend that these should be undertaken. We also suggest that more thought be given to the relation between large-scale and case studies in developmental research.

The Origins and Elaboration of Pointing

We will conduct a quick tour of some of our findings before offering an interpretation of them.

Indicative Gestures and Pointing Gestures

Childrens' gesturing was scored as either indicative or pointing, the two being distinguished by handshape, pointing requiring an extended index finger. If pointing were developed from the indicative gesture, we would expect to find points superseding indicatives over the course of development. As can be seen in Fig. 4, this is not the case. The frequency of indicative gesturing is fairly stable over the age range of the study. This suggests it has a constant function, and a function that differs from that of pointing. As was noted earlier, the decline in gesturing seen in the older children is compensated for by an increase in word usage, such that the total level of the child's communicative actions stays constant.

Postures Accompanying Gestures

Both these gestures were scored for their accompanying posture. Two postures were distinguished: "reaching," in which the child's body moved forward in the direction of the gesture; and "sitting back," where only the arm was extended. If

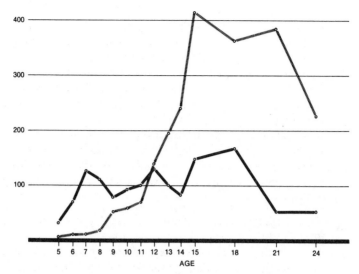

Fig. 4. Total pointing gestures (*dotted line*) and total indicative gestures (*solid line*)

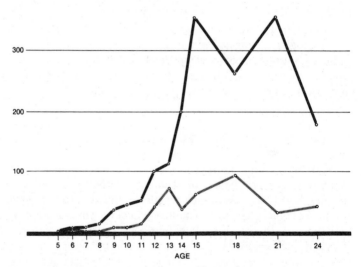

Fig. 5. Posture accompanying pointing. *Solid line,* indicative posture; *dotted line,* reaching posture

pointing were developed from failed reaching, we would expect to find early instances of it accompanied by the reaching posture. As can be seen in Fig. 5, there is little evidence for this. From the beginning, pointing is characteristically accompanied by the sitting back posture. Further, the indicative gesture does not show this differential association with one or the other posture. As can be seen in Fig. 6, indicatives occur equally with each posture. We will return to this later.

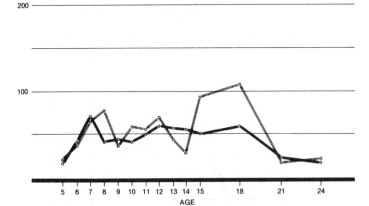

Fig. 6. Posture accompanying indicative gestures. *Solid line*, reaching posture; *dotted line*, indicative posture

Distance of Objects Invoked by Pointing

Both gestures were scored for the distance of the object they implicated from the child. Proximal gestures were those where the implicated object was within the child's reach, and distal ones where that was not the case. As can be seen in Fig. 7, proximal pointing is both more frequent and emerges earlier than distal pointing. Distal indicative gesturing is almost absent across the age range. This suggests that distal pointing is a developmental extension of proximal pointing and again has no relation to the indicative gesture.

The Developmental Course of Pointing

Looking at pointing alone, it can be seen that (Fig. 8) the greatest percentage increase in the production of pointing occurs at 9 months. The second peak increase is at 12 months, which is also the first age group in which all the infants produced pointing gestures. These indices of the onset of pointing are comparable with those of other studies. These findings suggest that pointing, when it emerges, does so quite rapidly.

Characteristics of Mothers' Communication

As we noted, claims have been made that imitation may play a role in the development of communicative gestures: maternal pointing activity is germane to this claim. Our graphs of maternal pointing are similar to those we have already presented for the child, with one major exception: the changes that occur in the frequency of maternal pointing occur 2 months before those of the infants. This is prima facie evidence that mothers are very sensitive to subtle cues from their

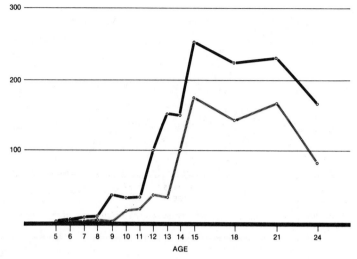

Fig. 7. Distance of object pointed at. *Solid line*, proximal; *dotted line*, distal

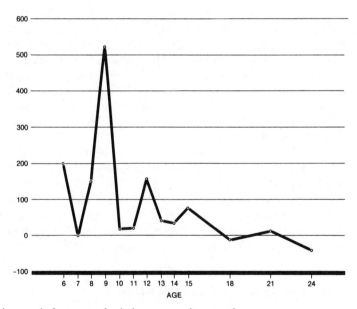

Fig. 8. Percentage increase in frequency of pointing over previous month

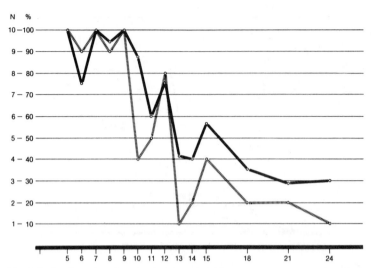

Fig. 9. Infant ignoring of mother's points. *Solid line,* mean percentage of mother's points ignored; *dotted line,* number of infants ignoring over 50% of mother's points

infants, and that they provide an excellent model of actions for the child to imitate. But do infants "perceive" mother's points? We ideally need information on two aspects of maternal pointing to have confidence in this interpretation. First, for infants to model pointing they need to have seen it. We cannot think of a reliable way of measuring this. But secondly, we can provide information on how infants responded to maternal pointing. This information unfortunately confounds whether infants actually saw a particular gesture with their comprehension of it if they did see it.

Figure 9 shows two things: first, the percentage of maternal points that we scored from the tapes which are not responded to by infants; and secondly, the number of infants who ignore over 50% of their mother's pointing. There are two extreme interpretations that can be put forward: either young infants see very few of their mother's points; or they in fact see all of them, but are incapable of perceiving them as meaningful, and hence are unable to fashion any response to them. We will return to this in our discussion.

Mother's "Responses" to Infant Points

We can ask a similar question with respect to the mothers: what do they do when their infants point? Figure 10 shows both the percentage of infant points ignored by mothers, and the number of mothers who ignore more than 50% of infant pointing. We are again faced with a similar dilemma between the two extreme interpretations. But whatever the reason, the view that infants develop pointing through simple reinforcement is given little support. We will return in our

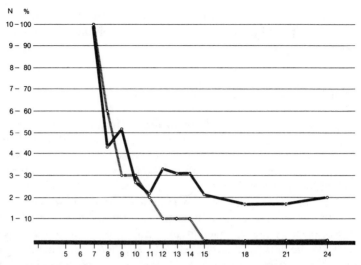

Fig. 10. Mother's ignoring of infant's points. *Solid line*, mean percentage of infant's points ignored; *dotted line*, number of mother's ignoring over 50% of infant's points

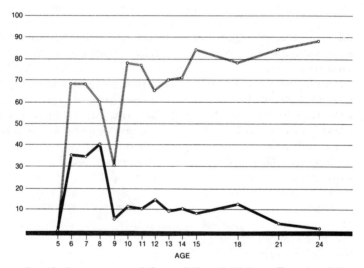

Fig. 11. Percentage of mother's responses to infant pointing. *Solid line*, offers; *dotted line*, "referential"

discussion to the mismatch between the sensitivity of our scoring system and that of mothers in "picking up" on infant pointing.

But, what do mothers do when they do make some response to infant points? Figure 11 plots the percentage of points responded to with offers of an object, and those responded to by providing a name for the object implicated in pointing, an expansion of naming (e.g. "Yes, it's a pretty one"), or asking a question (e.g.

"What's that, then?"). It is apparent that mothers do not interpret pointing as a demand for an object, suggesting again that pointing does not have its origins in failed attempts to obtain objects.

Other Related Gestures

The figures we gave before do not include all instances of pointing when it is solely defined by handshape. It was apparent in the younger infants that their hand often assumed the shape of pointing; that is, the index finger was extended, but the arm itself was not extended, nor did the index finger point in the direction of the child's gaze. While these occurrences may represent random hand manipulation, Fig. 12 suggests they may be of more significance.

We have termed these handshapes "point slips out." They are a common occurrence for the younger infants, but rare in the older ones (Fig. 12 only portrays the data for the younger children; there is nothing being hidden by our ignoring the older ones). Figure 12 shows the percentage of the infants' gestural communication contributed by pointing (the remainder being made up of indicatives), and the number of points slipping out as a percentage of the total number of points and indicative gestures produced. The third line on the graph plots the combined production of points and points slipping out. It is apparent that while the total number of events stays constant, the proportions contributed by the two categories change, such that as points slipping out declines, pointing increases.

Additionally, a second category of these pointing hand configurations was noticed: the use of the index finger and outstretched arm to "poke" or "scratch" proximal objects. This is probably an early form of object exploration. Such exploration appears to decline with age to 12 months, but we could not reliably distinguish this category from true points that culminated in touching the indicated object (a facet of the study we are not reporting here).

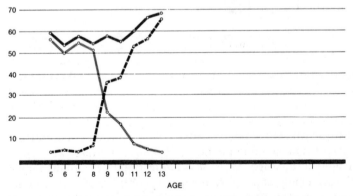

Fig. 12. Percentage of combined points and points slipping out (*solid line*), pointing as a percentage of total gesturing (*broken line*), and point slipping out as percentage of total gesturing (*dotted line*)

Table 1. Gestures Accompanied by Attention, Vocalization, or Attention and Vocalization

Age (months)	Attention (%)	Vocalization (%)	Attention and Vocalization (%)
5	0.0	15.6	0.0
6	0.0	20.6	0.0
7	0.9	22.6	0.9
8	2.5	28.0	1.7
9	0.8	21.0	1.6
10	7.9	15.8	2.0
11	0.0	40.7	3.7
12	3.4	49.8	2.0
13	0.7	41.0	3.1
14	2.7	50.0	4.8
15	1.3	60.0	3.4
18	1.2	52.0	6.5
21	4.1	68.3	6.2
24	0.7	85.8	3.4

The Communicative Status of Pointing

Finally, attention checking has often been taken as a measure of the communicative status of gestural communication. Table 1 shows the percentage of gestures accompanied by attention checking (looking at the mother while pointing) at each age. In addition, the percentage of vocalizations is given. Attention checking stays at a very low level throughout (mean = 2.18%). By contrast, gestures are accompanied by vocalizations from the earliest ages, with a fairly regular rise to 85.8% by 24 months. We suggest, then, that it is only under controlled experimental conditions, and not naturalistic ones, that attention checking can be used as an index of communicative capability.

The Development of Pointing

Our data do not lead us to conclude that pointing as a gesture has any single origin. We must distinguish between the origin of the form of pointing and the communicative intention that eventually animates it. Thus, we conclude that the form of the pointing gesture is not derived from either indicative gestures or failed reaches. However, the social consequences of these activities may well enable the infant to construct communicative schemas, which are then "borrowed" by pointing. This distinction has not been observed in the previous studies from which claims for the origin of pointing have been made. Further, we suspect clear-cut stage models of development are oversimple, and it is incorrect to argue that "pointing-for-the-self" is superseded by "pointing-for-others." One ability does not supplant another. Development occurs by an expansion of functions, not a simple replacement. The metaphor for development we favor is that of spinning wool. On the basis of our data, we suggest the metaphorical strands in the construction of pointing as an interpersonal activity contain the following:

The Action of Pointing Has to Be Constructed. We suggest that there are maturational factors behind the infant's employment of the index finger for early object exploration. This exploration not only involves the index finger, but involves it with objects. "Pointing" may well become part of the infant's repertoire exercised when opportunities for exploration arise and so has the apparent character of an attential orienting mechanism for the self in some of its uses.

Pointing Has to Be Coordinated in a Coherent Way into Interactions. Here Kaye's (1982) conception of "frames" is useful. For example, let us take the high level of ignoring of early infant pointing that we find in mothers. We could use this finding to rebut claims made for how attentive mothers are to infant activities and how they thus provide an "as if" environment of rich interpretation in which development is fostered. Instead, though, we suggest that mothers ignore many activities because they do not make sense. Laing (1970) concludes *Knots* thus:

a finger points at the moon . . .

What an interesting finger
let me suck it

It's not an interesting finger
take it away

The statement is pointless
The finger is speechless

Similarly, we suggest that the young infant's fingers are initially "speechless," and the actions they perform with them "pointless." Such infants are engaged in the process of coordinating their activities into "frames" of interaction in which those activities make intersubjective sense, and in which they only make intersubjective sense. We thus score more points from the youngest infants than mothers act upon because we are not trying to make sense of them, and mothers are: we are using objective criteria, whereas mothers are using the intersubjective criteria of active participants. Extended fingers are not points if they do not make sense: they have to occur in appropriate contexts.

We interpret our data on the relation between points slip out and pointing proper as an aspect of the infant's "getting appropriateness together." The child has the elements of pointing, but cannot coordinate them. The transition from point slips out to pointing proper reflects a change in the child's ability to construe frames. The same transition is apparent in the developing responsiveness to maternal pointing. It becomes attended to and acted on as it becomes comprehensible to the child.

To understand the origin and growth of pointing, then, we need to distinguish between its bodily posture and the coordination of different elements in the child's social perception. We can conclude that:

1. Pointing does not have its origins as an action in failed reaching, although an adult's action on perceiving a failed reach may well provide an infant with important information about how to influence the actions of another, i.e. how to communicate.
2. Pointing is not used for demanding objects.
3. Pointing does not appear to be an action that is acquired by imitation. Adults provide models of the frames within which pointing may be used, not models of the action itself.

Finally, all the theories proposed for the origins of pointing have an element of truth in them. Initially, pointing is not for others: but we would not describe it as asocial, rather unsocialized. Pointing is not socially constructed from failed action, rather it is socially constructed from inchoate object exploration. Pointing is not a modelled action, it is rather employed in ways that benefit from its demonstration in context. Its origins are not straightforward.

CHAPTER 5
Communicative Gestures and First Words

M.C. Caselli

Introduction

In recent years developmental psycholinguistics have taken into consideration the period preceding the acquisition of the verbal language, stressing the fundamental role of gestures used by infants in the process of acquisition (Camaioni, Volterra, & Bates, 1976; Dore, 1974; Lock, 1978, 1980). These studies, in particular the one by Bates, Benigni, Bretherton, Camaioni, and Volterra (1979), emphasized that, while the infant manifests from birth a series of both gestural (grimaces, smiles, reaching for objects) and vocal (different types of crying, vocalizations, babbling) behaviors which serve as communicative signals, one can only speak of really intentional communication towards 9 months of age. This intentional communication is initially expressed by gestures such as: ritualized REACHING (the infant reaches for an object, opening and closing the palm, looking alternately at the adult), GIVING objects (the infant gives an object towards the adult), SHOWING objects (the infant raises an object for the adult to see), and POINTING (the infant points the index finger towards an object or a person and looks alternately at the adult).

The authors emphasize three fundamental criteria for these gestures which serve to establish a continuum between them and the subsequent use of the verbal language:

1. They are used with the intention of communicating.
2. They are conventional.
3. They refer to some external object or event.

All of the above-mentioned studies are concerned with the communicative development of the child as it relates to cognitive development, using the framework of Piaget (1945) and his colleagues (Sinclair-de Zwart, 1967). However, systematic consideration of the social genesis of communication as well as careful analysis of the interactive process and dialogue between the adult and the child are missing in these works. This is the primary focus in the works of Bruner and his colleagues (Bruner, 1975b; Ninio & Bruner, 1978; Ratner & Bruner, 1978). These authors argue that the participation of the child in ritualized

---

A slightly different version of this paper was originally published in Italian as *Gesti Comunicativi e Prime Parole. Et à Evolutiva*, (1983), *16*, pp. 36–51.

exchanges within familiar contexts is the fundamental basis on which the child builds first communicative and then linguistic abilities.

Ninio and Bruner (1978) in particular demonstrate how the ". . . reference, then is dependent not only upon mastering a relationship between sign and significate, but upon an understanding of social rules for achieving dialogue in which that relationship can be realized" (p. 15). Bruner (1975b) considered it necessary to single out the various "aids" which allow the child to acquire the language. The first aid is represented by the dialogue and by the interaction with other human beings; the second by the awareness which the child has of reality; the third by what the child learns from its understanding of relationships present in the world.

In the present work, my goal has been to study the child's gestural communication and its relationship to language acquisition, trying to combine the two theoretical perspectives mentioned above, one which follows the cognitive hypothesis (using the terminology of Cromer, 1974) and one which follows the interactional approach. I propose to show in particular:

— It is possible to distinguish different types of gestures in the child's gestural communication.
— Some gestures which have been traditionally analyzed as symbolic play schemes can be used with communicative functions and denote specific referents.
— Gestures are created and acquire their communicative function within those interactive and communicative routines with the adult which Bruner considered fundamental for the emergence of the verbal language.

I will call gestures such as POINTING and GIVING objects "deictic gestures"(DG): they are conventional, refer to external objects and events, and clearly express communicative intention on the part of the child but the referent can only be understood through the extralinguistic context to which the child refers. On the other hand, I will call gestures such as MORE, EAT, and TELEPHONE "referential gestures." As well as expressing a communicative intention and being conventionalized by the child and his/her interlocutors (characteristics shared with DG), they denote a precise referent. In other words, they have a semantic content (a meaning) which does not change depending on the context.

Method

The data analyzed in this work refer to the author's son Luca who was followed longitudinally from the age of 10 to 20 months. They were primarily diary accounts which were supplemented with videotaped sessions. The daily diary served to record information necessary for the correct interpretation and classification of particular behaviors. Contextual information was systematically recorded together with the description of the child's behavior. It was noted if the behavior was imitative, occurred within a routine, was spontaneous, or was in response to adult prompting; in addition, notes were made regarding the probable communicative intention of the child when he produced the behavior. The diary records included a reconstruction of the nonverbal and verbal context in which the child's production occurred as well as a comment on the child's general attitude. The limitations and advantages of the diary have been highlighted by Jakobson (1969) and subsequently by Greenfield and Smith (1976). The greatest limitation is that no check exists on the interpretation and classification of the recorded data. The most obvious advantage is that it allows the exact time of occurrence of the child's behavior to be recorded and thus it preserves the chronology of development. The diary also records the uses the child makes of infrequent behavior patterns which do not appear in standardized observation sessions. Data collected in this way were integrated with those obtained in organized sessions, videotaped in an observation room through one-way mirrors so that the recording apparatus was out of the child's sight. One experimenter and the mother were present at the videorecorded sessions. The mother participated as observer, only taking active part if requested by the child or by the experimenter and collaborating if necessary in the interpretation of the child's behavior.

References to the gestures used by the child are written in capital letters, while the actual words used by the child are written in *lower case letters* between quotation marks.

Analysis and Discussion of the Results

The longitudinal data emphasize different stages in the child's communicative development. Attention is concentrated particularly on the period immediately after the transition from nonintentional communication through gestural and vocal signals such as crying, smiling, and babbling to intentional communication accomplished through gestures, sounds, or vocalizations, and first words. This transition happened in the child at about 10 months. At this age Luca started to master gestural and vocal signals in order to ask for something, to "name" an object or one of its characteristics, and to share his attention for objects and events with the adult. The gestures used in the first period under consideration were exclusively deictic gestures. For example:

1. (*Deictic gesture*) GIVING. Luca could not open a box so he gave it to his father, emitting the vocalizations which express the request.

2. (*Deictic gesture*) POINTING. Luca points the ball out to his mother, gurgling with joy.

The deictic gestures are consistently interpreted by the adult interlocutor on the basis of the overall behavior of the child (from his actions or movements), the particular vocalizations which accompany it, and from the context.

In the first example above, the father interprets the GIVING gesture as a request for action on the object which the child has offered him and so opens the box; in the second example, the POINTING gesture accompanied by vocalizations of joy and excitement is interpreted by the mother as a form of proto-statement, her reply is therefore, "*Si, è una palla*" (Yes, it is a ball). Exchanges of this sort between adult and child are comparable with others we observed in the subsequent periods in which the roles are exactly the opposite. When the child is 10 months old, he points at an object and the mother names the object indicated. This is a rich and stimulating communicative situation which lays the foundations for the developing structure of dialogue and which precedes the emergence of the child's naming capacity (Ninio & Bruner, 1978). Later, with the emergence of the first words, POINTING to an object or a figure will be used by the mother to stimulate and consolidate the child's capacity to denote a precise referent. The roles are therefore reversed and the routine is transformed into a precise question by the mother ("*cosa è questo?*" — what is this?) accompanied by POINTING and by the child's verbal reply [e.g., "*miaow*" (cat)].

The POINTING gesture, as opposed to the other deictic gestures, is used progressively by the child in ever more complex and developed ways. In fact, such a gesture is born in direct connection with its context and used to make reference to an object, event, or attribute. Subsequently, it is produced in various combinations with other gestures and words and it acquires a function totally different from the one of general and contextual reference: in fact, it can be used with a pronominal, possessive, locative, or other function (e.g., THIS MINE; THAT THERE, etc.) (see Pizzuto, this volume; Lock et al. this volume).

The deictic gestures analyzed here are, therefore, at the age of 10–11 months, gestures which do not denote a precise referent. The correct identification of the referent depends entirely on the quantity and quality of contextual information which the interlocutor is capable of gathering.

At 11–12 months, the second kind of gesture which I have called "referential gestures" appeared in Luca's communication.

It is interesting to note how these gestures seem to be the same as the ones used by the child in his symbolic play patterns. Starting from the age of 9 months and 28 days in fact, Luca began to show a capacity for "pretend behavior." The relationship between symbolic play and first words was emphasized by Bates et al. (1979). These authors found a similar progression in the development of the two domains: symbolic play and language production.

I will show that there is a continuity between symbolic play and gestural communication and then between the latter and spoken communication.

From the moment Luca started to carry out symbolic play patterns, his referential gestures gradually increased; the symbolic games referred to the same content expressed in his referential gestures. The first of Luca's referential gestures appeared at 11 months and 15 days:

3.   BRAVO (GOOD BOY). Luca has managed to fit a shape into the correct space on the board; he extends the board towards his mother appearing very satisfied with himself but she is intent on doing something else; then the child

claps his hands while holding out the game, alternating this behavior with request sounds.

This gesture derives from a routine that the child usually does with the adult. Luca uses a part of the familiar routine, clapping his hands, to request the same adult behavior. The communicative intention is drawn from the use of a particular tone of voice but the content is given by the particular gesture used.

Two days after this episode was recorded, a second example occurred in which the referential gesture was produced with a statement performative:

4.   BYE-BYE. Luca is sitting in the Kitchen eating; his father, who is going out, says, *"Ciao Luca"* (Bye-bye Luca) and leaves. Hearing the front door bang (which he could not see from where he was sitting) Luca turns to his mother and, very seriously, waves bye-bye with his hand. His mother interprets this gesture as an assertion regarding an event which has just happened and replies *"Si papà è uscito"* (Yes, daddy has gone out). The gesture was not a deferred imitation since the father made no gesture when saying good-bye. Another referential gesture appeared at 11 months and 27 days:

5.   DANCING. Luca is in his mother's arms; at a certain moment he points to the radio adopting a request attitude. The mother interprets this as a naming request and says: *"E' la radio"* (That's the radio); but she has obviously misunderstood because Luca continues to point at the radio with a request attitude. The child climbs down from the mother's arms and starts to dance still looking at the mother with a request attitude. The mother interprets the gesture correctly this time and when she says *"Ah, vuoi accendere la radio!"* (Ah, you want the radio on!). Luca seems very happy. It must be emphasized that even this gesture used now in a communicative way originated in a routine in which the child was asked to dance to the sound of music. And at 12 months and 9 days:

6.   HURTING ONESELF. The child wants to have an object but cannot be satisfied. The adult loses interest in the capricious child. Luca, to draw attention to himself, throws himself on the floor and pretends to hit his head on it; then he puts his hand to his head and pretends to cry. This is also an anticipation, this time of a habit: when the child hurts himself, the adults cuddle him and often try to give him what he wants to console him. The child therefore pretends to hurt himself in order to get something from the adult.

In these data, the referential gestures used communicatively are produced by the child in the same progression as the first referential words used in a decontextualized way (Volterra, Bates, Benigni, Bretherton, & Camaioni, 1979). The first referential gestures, then, are initially found as parts of routines from which they are progressively detached until they are used productively for communicating by referring to a specific referent. Generally, the first gestures used in this way are formally equal in their content to the first symbolic play patterns and are usually produced as replies (not spoken) in dialogue situations with the adult, as we shall see later. They are therefore produced in vertical constructions similar to those proposed by Scollon (1979) wherein the child's language is structured within interactive exchanges with the adult.

The first referential gestures are: GOOD BOY, BYE-BYE, DANCING, HURTING ONESELF, and NO (this gesture will be analyzed later). The similarity of these gestures lies in the fact that they are actions which the child performs with his own body and not with specific objects. The first and the last of these actions are usually performed by the other persons who are with the child (the child therefore assumes the role which is usually the adult's); the others are actions he normally carries out. These gestures originate, as we have said, within routines (games or habits) with the adult and are progressively detached to be used communicatively.

When the first gestures bound to actions with particular objects (EATING, DRINKING, TELEPHONING, OPENING, etc.) began to appear from 1 year and 12 days of age, they seemed to be reflections of recognition schemes for the objects themselves and appeared to be used, at least in some cases, with the same function as the POINTING FOR SELF gesture (Werner & Kaplan, 1963). I will refer to these kinds of gestures as "object recognition gestures." Around 13 months Luca began to use these gestures spontaneously (not only within routines) to ask for something, to assert something, and progressively also to amplify the adult's sentence.

As far as the request is concerned, two types can be distinguished. At first the child points to the desired object and then uses the appropriate gesture if the communication does not succeed. For example, at 13 months and 28 days:

7.   PACIFIER. The child asks for his pacifier by pretending to suck something.

8.   SHAMPOO. He ruffles his hair with his hand to ask for the bottle of shampoo which is in front of him. At 15 months and 13 days:

9.   DRINK. He asks for some water by pretending to drink and looking at the tap.

The second kind of request refers to some action that the child wants the adult to do or that he wants to do himself (see also examples 3 and 5). At 13 months and 15 days:

10. BYE-BYE. Luca waves bye-bye asking to go out.

11. SLEEP. He rests his cheek on his hand and closes his eyes to ask to go to bed.

As for assertion, we found the following examples: at 12 months and 10 days:

12. BYE-BYE. Luca uses the BYE-BYE gesture (see also example 4) to describe that someone or something (a car in the street for example) is going away from him.

13. NO. His aunt starts to play with some objects on the table. Luca, looking at her very seriously, reaches out his hand towards the plant on the table and then makes a NO gesture with the same hand.

The child obviously wants his aunt to understand that the plant on the table must not be touched remembering his mother's warning. It is interesting to observe how the child constructs a negative sentence, at the gestural level, by first asserting something (I touch the plant) then negating it (no). This type of construction agrees with the findings of Volterra and Antinucci (1979) for verbal language.

Finally, Luca used gestures to expand adult's utterances. Some examples of "expansion" are: at 13 months and 5 days:

14. HAT. An adult friend asks Luca, *"Dov'è nonno?"* (Where's grandad?), and the child replies by putting his hand on his head, referring to the fact that grandpa always wears a hat (a thing which impresses him very much). At 13 months and 15 days:

15. SLEEP. His mother says, *"Povero bimbo, sei stanco?"* (Poor little boy, are you tired?). Luca rests his cheek on his hand with a request attitude (I want to go to sleep). At 14 months and 1 day:

16. PHONE. Luca looks for his mother, his aunt tells him, *"Sta telefonando"* (She's on the phone). Luca makes the gesture of speaking on the telephone empty handed. It is interesting to note that while these gestures expand the adult's sentence by adding new elements, they are also clear anticipations of patterns very familiar to the child: the added element is an integral part of the pattern itself (e.g., "What is grandad wearing? His hat!" and "Let's go to sleep because you're tired").

After the child made these first expansions using elements of established routines, he progressively started to use gestures and/or words within long and complex dialogical interactions (quite long and complex) with the adult. For example at 14 months and 2 days:

17. Luca and his Mother are Playing on the bed. Luca (L) starts to push his mother with a request attitude.

Mother (M): *"Mi devo alzare?"* (Must I get up?).
L: POINTS to her shoes, still with the request attitude.
M: *"Mi devo mettere le scarpe?"* (Must I put my shoes on as well?).
L: POINTS to the door and waves BYE-BYE still with the same request attitude.
M: *"Ho capito, mi devo alzare e mettere le scarpe, cosi usciamo"* (I must get up, put on my shoes, and then take you out). Luca seems very pleased with her interpretation.

From this example we can infer that the child wants confirmation that the adult has understood his message before proceeding to point to the next element. If the adult does not understand, the child continues to gesture until his mother interprets his message correctly.

The same kind of construction is later produced by Luca through referential gestures and words and is similar to "vertical constructions" described by Scollon (1979) "... children at the single-word stage may specify an object in one utterance and another object related to the previous one in a subsequent utterance" (p. 225).

It is important to distinguish between object recognition gestures, symbolic play, and communicative gestures. In the following examples we can note some important differences and the different behaviors that the various spoken interventions by the adults provoke in the child. These occurred during videotaped sessions with the mother and the experimenter when the child was 16 months old.

18. STIRRING. The experimenter gives the child a plate and a teaspoon (both toys) and asks the child, *"Che cos'è questo?"* (What's this?); the child stirs the spoon in the plate. The gesture is performed in a very concise way and is immediately interrupted. The experimenter again intervenes: *"Ma che ci fai con questo?"* (But what do you do with it?). The child pretends to feed himself with the spoon, smiles, and turns to the adult, tries to feed his mother, and then says jokingly: *"Più, più!"* (There is no more).

The second part of the interaction was classified as "play": the child tries to establish an interactive relationship with the adult through and within the game; but the purpose remains the game itself.

19. PLAY PIANO. The experimenter gives a piano to the child. The child produces an object recognition gesture, pretends to play the piano. After a while he sits down and starts to play the piano for a game, playing for a long time and laughing, looking for the adult's approval. He then gets up and holds the piano towards his mother with a request attitude (imploring look, whining tone). His mother asks, "What must I do?". Luca replies by playing himself but only for an instant. His attitude is still one of request and the gesture is brief and concise; the child seems as though he is really answering his mother with: "I want you to do this: PLAY PIANO." The mother carries out her child's request. Later, the child is again playing with the piano and at a certain point he gives it towards his mother with a request attitude. She begins to play but has misunderstood because the child, still with his request attitude and looking his mother in the eyes, tries to open the piano.

The interpretation of the child's action is similar to the preceding one (the child wants the mother to open the piano); the only difference between the two PLAY PIANO gestures is that the first time it was a recognition gesture used without urging by the adult, the second time it was produced with a request attitude in response to his mother's question, replacing his previous showing gesture.

It is evident that it is not easy to distinguish object recognition gestures from the truly symbolic games that the child performs with those same objects; some fairly consistent indicators which allow the observer to recognize object recognition gestures are: the child is very serious (all the playful mimicry (smiles, etc.) which Piaget talks about (1945) with respect to the symbolic game is missing); the gestures are short and concise; they are manifestations of essential aspects, briefly hinted at and very often incomplete. They are also produced without the characteristic sounds which give unmistakable indications about the child's communicative intentions, even when the child interacts with the adult. Once again, it must be emphasized that the vocalization (in this case the request attitude is accompanied by a whining sound) produced by the child in these cases are not a structural part of the gesture, but rather a part of the performative expressed through the whole attitude. To summarize, it is possible to distinguish when a gesture is used as a pattern of symbolic play and when it is used as a communicative signal from the context of the situation and from the child's behavior and attitude. It should again be remembered that these examples refer to when the child was 16 months old and they have been analyzed here in detail to clarify the criteria adopted to identify the various types of gestures and their functions.

In the same period in which the child starts to use referential gestures in a decontextualized way and outside the original routines, he also starts to produce his first words to communicate. All of the first words Luca uses consist of:

— Accompaniments to action schemes that the child is applying to persons or objects.
— Names for persons or objects to which those schemes apply. Gradually the same terms (or new terms) are applied instead to "categorize" new persons, objects, and events within a much broader range of contexts.

From 10 months and 10 days to 15 months and 5 days the first 20 words appear. We can observe the decontextualization process through the following examples from Luca's diary. Let us consider the word "bam" (fall down). At 13 months and 8 days:

20. *"Bam".* Luca produces this word while falling down, and again, 10 days later, when throwing a ball and when knocking down a pile of building blocks. The word is produced 10 days later to anticipate the game of knocking down the pile of blocks and, then shortly thereafter it is used as a substantive to identify the blocks.

Luca's use of the word *"acqua"* (water) is particularly interesting because of the relationship between the word and the corresponding referential gesture. At 12 months and 11 days:

21. *"Amba" (Water).* Luca produces this word while standing in the kitchen and pointing to the water tap. He produces it again 3 or 4 days later, but then the word disappears and the child uses only the pointing gesture for a certain period. At 14 months:

22. DRINK. Luca asks to drink by opening and closing his mouth and pointing to the tap. At 15 months the word *"acqua"* reappears but is used to indicate "water" as an object and not as the action of drinking itself. The action is expressed by the gesture. The following example shows both gesture and word:

23. DRINK — *"aqua".* Luca is in the kitchen and, using the request attitude, he gestures that he wants to drink. His mother asks him what he wants. He repeats the gesture. His mother has understood but wants to stimulate the word production and asks: "And what's it called?" Luca replies: *"Attia."* In both cases the child has not used the pointing gestures.

A similar use is observed with the word *"pappa"* (food) and the corresponding EAT gesture. At 15 months and 8 days:

24. EATING — *"pappa"*. Luca asks to eat by POINTING to food and making a CHEWING gesture. The same day he describes the dog eating by using the same referential gesture and later on, pointing to what is inside the dog's bowl he says *"pappa."* The child uses the gesture requesting to eat and the word to refer to a particular food.

Luca tended to use referential gestures to request something or to describe some event and pointing to focalize an object whose name was not in his repertoire. When he knew the name for an object he used the word.

First words were not used simultaneously with the corresponding referential gesture: Luca's gestural and spoken productions tended to refer to different referents. These data are comparable to data from studies on early bilingualism. When children are exposed to two languages from birth, their first lexical system includes words from both languages but there are few equivalents (Volterra & Taeschner, 1978). In a similar way, in Luca's production of this period there are not many equivalents in the two modalities. Instead there is one lexicon constructed partially from gestures and partially from words.

The same "vertical construction" observed in the gestural modality (see example 17) are found in the spoken modality. For example, at 16 months and 20 days:

25. Luca's Father asks him: *"Sei stato al giardino?"* (Have you been to the garden?). Luca replies: *"Bimbi"* (Children) (meaning with the children). And similarly, at 17 months and 5 days:

26. Luca asks his Mother. *"Papa?"* (Daddy?). His mother replies, *"E' al lavoro"* (He's at work). Luca says, *"Gigi"* (the name of a colleague with whom his father works). Here, as was the case with referential gestures, the first expansions are related to routines. In fact the child anticipates affirmations or questions of the following types: "Have you been playing with the children in the garden?" and "Who does daddy work with? With Gigi."

When the child starts to produce the first combination of words (and this happens at about 16 months) it may be that he uses the gesture to expand his already more complex production. The expansion occurs first in vertical construction and is encouraged by the adult. At 17 months and 1 day:

27. *"Mamma ... più"*. (Mommy ... no more) produced using an intonation of request. His mother replies: *"Cosa non c'è più?"* The child makes the eating gestures (his cookie was just finished) (the word for cookie was already in his repertoire). Similarly at 17 months and 4 days:

28. *"Mamma ... dà"*. (Mommy gives) produced without any gesture by the child (he wants his pacifier). His mother asks: *"Cosa vuoi?"* (What do you want?). The child makes the sucking gesture (the word for pacifier was already in his repertoire).

Conclusion

Several conclusions can be drawn from these data. First, the child produces different types of gestures to communicate intentionally. Alongside deictic gestures (POINTING, GIVING, SHOWING) other gestures, denoting a precise referent, begin to appear around 11 months of age. These gestures have been defined as "referential": unlike deictic their semantic content does not change gestures depending on the situational context. Referential gestures (like deictic gestures and words) emerge from ritualized exchanges with caregivers and acquire their communicative function as a result of a decontextualization process.

Furthermore, while referential gestures can be traced back to symbolic play schemas produced by the child, they are used with communicative intention in such a way that they become a real communicative system. The developmental progression I have found in the use of referential gestures is the same that other authors have found for symbolic play. In fact, in symbolic play first the child performs an action he would produce in reality with his own body (e.g., he pretends to sleep) and only later does he perform actions related to objects or other persons (e.g., he pretends to telephone).

There is an important difference between referential gestures and words. The gestures described above are conventional and symbolic but they never reach the level of abstractness and arbitrariness of verbal language. Referential gestures often seem to refer to actions, mimicking and repeating the typical function of an object rather than tracing in space the object shape.

In the use of referential gestures I distinguished three stages. First, they are almost always used as a support or as a substitution for communicative non-referential gestures: the child spontaneously uses the pointing gesture. He substitutes or alternates this gesture with the appropriate referential gesture only if requested by the adults, when he is not understood, or when he wants to strengthen an element.

In the second stage, referential gestures are used productively by the child. For Luca, this stage occurs between the ages of 12 and 16 months. These gestures are more frequent and more complex than the first words and tend to express events or actions while words tend to refer to objects or people. During this stage words are context bound. They are produced especially in reply to questions like, "What's that?", "What's this?" in the presence of the person or object labeled. The spoken utterances are produced mainly with declarative performatives while referential gestures are used with a variety of performatives. First words are used by the child in order to establish or maintain social interaction with adults rather than to initiate communication or to express his immediate needs.

In the third and last stage the spoken system is consolidated and is used by the child to refer to absent objects or past events and to expand adult language creatively, with various performatives. By this stage the gestural system is progressively replaced by spoken language, and gestures continue to be used only in the following cases:

— As an alternative to the spoken system when communication is not successful;
— To expand one or two utterances so that they become a mixture of spoken and gestural elements.

While these conclusions are based on a single case study, recent longitudinal and cross-sectional studies (such as those appearing in this volume-eds.) have provided additional evidence concerning the use of communicative gestures by hearing children and their role in the early stages of language acquisition.

CHAPTER 6
Sign Language Among Hearing Infants:
The Spontaneous Development of Symbolic Gestures

L. P. ACREDOLO and S. W. GOODWYN

Introduction

A 15-month-old infant sees something in the corner, points to it, looks at her mother, and then rubs her index fingers together. Her mother smiles and says, "Yes, that is a spider." Another 15-month-old child sees a pattern on his grandmother's dress, points to it, and then wrinkles up his nose and loudly sniffs out three times. In this case the mother's response is, "Yes, that's a flower." Still a third infant comes to her mother and moves both hands up and down rapidly. The movements continue in bursts until the mother acquiesces to the "request" and places the baby on the piano bench.

What are we to make of these behaviors? Are these deaf children who have spontaneously developed gestural communication of the types noted by Goldin-Meadow and Feldman (1975, 1977)? Are they deaf or retarded children who have specifically been taught to communicate in this fashion? Or are they perhaps hearing children who for some reason have been systematically exposed to American Sign Language (ASL) during infancy as in cases reported by Holmes and Holmes (1980), Prinz and Prinz (1979) and Bonvillian, Orlansky, and Novack (1983)?

The answer is "no" to all of these. Instead, what has just been described is spontaneous behavior observed by parents of normal infants who, in the early stages of language development, seem to be intent on communicating with those around them through whatever means they have at their disposal. In these cases their choice is to use gestures which have become endowed with the same type of symbolic status typical of early verbal words. Based on data from over 50 infants, we are now firmly convinced that such behaviors are not the rare events some have assumed (Bates, Bretherton, Shore, & McNew, 1983). On the contrary, our data indicate that symbolic gestures occur in a large proportion of normal infants, generally precede their verbal counterparts, are used in a variety of contexts, occur quite frequently in the daily life of the child, and are routinely interpreted by parents as if they were words. In other words, they serve as an excellent example of the classic developmental dictum that old forms serve new functions. The new function in this case is "naming" and the "old form" is the sensorimotor

Portions of this paper were reported at the biennial meeting of the Society for Research in Child Development in Toronto, April, 1985, and the International Conference on Infant Studies, Beverly Hills, April 1986.

scheme. It is a natural marriage between the two which yields some of the earliest examples of symbolization in the service of naming.

Although ours is perhaps the most systematic attempt to document this phenomenon, we are not the first ones to have noticed its existence. In their classic book on symbol formation, Werner and Kaplan (1963) make a case for the probable existence of symbolic gestures as a natural transition between action and words. Moreover, they cite in support of their argument individual examples culled from diary and case studies as far back as Perez' (1911) report of an infant who developed a waving hand motion to symbolize "negation." More recently, Volterra and Caselli, two Italian co-workers, reported longitudinal data from several Italian infants who developed repertoires of symbolic gestures simultaneously with their development of early verbal words (Caselli, 1983a; Volterra, 1981a; Volterra & Caselli, 1985). These data led them completely independently to many of the same conclusions we have reached in regard to the role of symbolic gestures in early language development. In addition, Zinober and Martlew (1985b) have recently reported gestural behaviors in two children which, from their brief description, seem to correspond to the types of behaviors of interest here. Our own curiosity about the phenomenon also grew out of such case study data. The subject was a normal female infant whose language development was followed from birth through 2 years. Her spontaneous development of a repertoire of symbolic gestures first came as a surprise but quickly became our primary focus of attention (Acredolo & Goodwyn, 1985b).

Data Base

As instructive as such case study research can be, however, it obviously leaves unanswered questions about the prevalence of the phenomenon among infants in general. As a consequence we soon began to look at larger groups of infants. The results of two studies, one cross-sectional and one longitudinal, can now be reported. (See Acredolo & Goodwyn, 1988, for a more detailed report than is possible here.)

Cross-Sectional Study

The cross-sectional study involved lengthy interviews with 38 mother-infant pairs. These were conducted when the infants were 16–18 months old ($M = 16.89$). Subjects included 17 females (seven first born) and 21 males (nine first born), all of whom came from middle-class backgrounds. Mothers were alerted to the type of gestures under investigation by a letter received prior to the interview. During the interviews, all of which were audiotaped, discussion centered around any nonverbal behaviors the mothers thought might qualify, and specific information was sought in regard to the following: (a) the form the gesture routinely took; (b) the contexts in which the gesture was used; (c) the approximate age at which the behavior first appeared; (d) the way in which the gestures was thought to have been acquired; (e) the frequency with which the gesture was used; and (f) if appropriate, the point at which the gesture had been replaced by its verbal counterpart. In addition to these questions about nonverbal behavior, we also established an estimate of each infant's verbal vocabulary. To this end, specific categories were suggested to the mother (e.g., foods, toys, people), and she was asked to list any words within the categories which she felt occurred in a consistent form and under consistent circumstances. This rough measure was adequate for the types of correlational questions we were asking.

Longitudinal Study

The cross-sectional study was followed by a relatively large-scale longitudinal study of 16 middle-class families. In each case an infant in the family was followed from 11 to 24 months. Subjects included six males (three first born) and ten females (seven first born). The major source of data in each case was weekly diary records kept by the mothers until the infants were 20 months old. On specially designed diary sheets, mothers were asked to describe any potentially symbolic gestures they had witnessed during the week, along with details about the contexts in which they had occurred. Since we realized that despite a lengthy orientation session, mothers could not be expected to comprehend fully the criteria for categorizing a gesture as symbolic, we stressed that they should describe any gesturing that even remotely seemed to qualify as communicative and/or symbolic, and that it was up to us to determine which behaviors actually were of interest. In addition to this information about non-verbal behavior, we also asked on the diary sheets about any new verbal words occurring during the week. In doing so we were careful to stress a definition of "word" which involved a particular sound used consistently to refer to a particular referent or class of referents. Diary sheets were collected each month during a home visit.

In addition to the diary records, the study also included data from several formal testing sessions. At 17 months each child was videotaped as it reacted to gestures modelled by an adult. The purpose here was to assess the child's propensity to imitate the nonverbal behaviors provided in his/her environment. At 20 months each family was interviewed about the data gathered on the weekly sheets and asked to fill out a questionnaire designed to estimate the infant's verbal vocabulary at that point. Then finally, at 24 months, infants were again visited in their homes in order to assess mean length of utterance (MLU), verbal vocabulary, and performance on the Mental Development Inventory (MDI) portion of the Bayley Scales of Infant Development.

Criteria for Establishing Symbolic Status

The idea that gestures play a role in early communication is not new. Bates and her colleagues pointed out some time ago that performative gestures such as pointing, giving, and showing are some of the earliest signs of communicative intent in normal language development (Bates, Benigni, Bretherton, Camaioni & Volterra, 1979). These researchers have even documented a type of nonverbal behavior they call "gestural names" in 9–13-month-old infants. These latter behaviors, in contrast to ours however, are not used communicatively but rather appear to be akin to symbolic play in that they involve interactions with objects in stereotyped, object-appropriate ways (e.g., pretending to talk on a telephone, pretending to feed a doll). What differentiates the gestures upon which we are focusing from these other types of gestures is the contention that ours are operating as *symbolic* vehicles whose purpose is to represent in a communicative context a particular referent or class of referents. Thus, establishing that these gestures are truly symbolic is extremely important.

Attributing symbolic status to any behavior cannot be done cavalierly. Even within the domain of verbal behavior there is a good deal of controversy over what does and does not qualify as a true lexical symbol. In a recent review of the early-word stage of development, Nelson and Lucariello (1985) conclude that evidence exists to suggest that at least five types of "prelexical" utterances predate the onset of lexical symbols (or "denotative" symbols in Dore's, 1985, terminology). Although such utterances would appear to a naive observer to be words, they simply do not function in a way which indicates that the child truly understands the representative relation true words convey. Specifically, many of these forms of prelexical utterances can be characterized as "context bound," that is, tied exclusively to the context (game, routine, situation) in which they were originally encountered. For the child the use of such words may mean no more than the repetition of any well-rehearsed segment of a routine, and the child is unaware of the generalizability of the label to other circumstances.

With these and other potential nonsymbolic forms in mind, we established a conservative set of criteria for determining which gestures would and would not be called symbolic. In doing so, we also found it useful to categorize the gestures into a number of different classes depending upon their function for the child. These included OBJECT signs, REQUEST signs, and ATTRIBUTE signs as the major divisions, with the less frequent REPLY and EVENT signs collapsed under the OTHER category for some analyses. The criteria used to assign gestures to each classification follow.

OBJECT Signs

Included under OBJECT signs were gestures which seemed to function as labels for the child to denote specific objects, for example, sniffing for "flower" or rubbing the index fingers together for "spider." These gestures, which were often accompanied by pointing, had to meet three criteria. First, they had to occur repeatedly in the same, stereotyped, abbreviated form not physically involving the object itself. Thus, a one-time-only imitation of an object would not qualify, nor would the type of "gestural names" noted by Bates, since those included interactions with toy replicas of the objects themselves. Secondly, and perhaps most important, the gesture had to occur outside of the specific context in which it had originally been learned. For the majority of object signs this requirement was met by generalization of the gesture to pictures and other representations (e.g., toys, models, etc.) as well as to the real objects. In other cases, it was met by the use of the gesture to label multiple examples of the object. Thus, a child who learned a gesture for spider within the context of a song ("Eency Weency Spider") would not be given credit for a symbolic gesture unless the action also occurred outside this context for the purpose of communicating with those around him or her. A third requirement was that the behavior include a truly gestural component. Thus, onomatopoetic sounds alone were not included.

REQUEST Signs

To be included under REQUEST signs, a gesture had to function for the child as a means to evoke a particular response from the listener. The purpose for the child was to indicate something he or she wanted or needed. For example, a child might make a knob-turning gesture to indicate a desire to go out, or pump his or her fingers up and down to indicate a desire to play the piano. One important criterion here was the requirement that the gesture should not be directly instrumental itself in achieving the desired goal. Instead the gesture had to work exclusively through its communicative impact on the listener. For example, banging on the door was not counted as symbolic of a desire to go out because the action itself could have been undertaken by the child to achieve the goal without the mother. Likewise, raising of the arms to be lifted was not counted as symbolic because it could be considered part of the act of being lifted itself rather than being symbolic of it. Instead, a gesture such as opening and closing the fist as a request for being lifted would have qualified. These relatively strict guidelines meant the elimination of many useful non-verbal behaviors in the children's repertoires, but the criteria were considered essential to ensure that only symbolic gestures were included in our data base.

ATTRIBUTES

Gestures included under ATTRIBUTES were those used by the child to describe objects or situations, for example, the use of a blowing gesture to indicate something was "hot." Once again, care was taken to be sure that the gesture was being used communicatively, not instrumentally (e.g., to actually cool off the item).

REPLIES

Included under REPLIES were gestures other than "yes" and "no" which were used to respond to questions. The prime example was a shrug for "I don't know."

EVENTS

EVENTS included gestures which seemed to label whole events, such as the use by one child of a clapping gesture for "baseball game."

Prevalence of Symbolic Gestures

Having determined what should and should not be considered as part of our data base, the question is how prevalent those gestures were which we felt truly confident about calling symbolic. The results of both the cross-sectional and longitudinal studies indicated that the vast majority of infants had at least one symbolic gesture in their repertoire. In fact, as Tables 1 and 2 indicate, the mean number of signs for subjects in the cross-sectional study was 3.9 (range 0–16) and 5.1 (range 1–17) for subjects in the longitudinal study. Overall a total of 94 signs was documented among the 38 infants in the cross-sectional study and 81 among the 16 infants in the longitudinal study. (See Table 3 for examples of specific signs observed.) From these data, then, we feel it is safe to conclude that symbolic gesturing is not the rare phenomenon some have assumed (Bates et al., 1983).

Although most infants showed signs of the behaviour, we also found strong evidence of individual differences. Some groups, notably first-born females, were more reliant upon this type of communication than others, and some individuals stood out as particularly heavily involved in gesturing of this sort. The question of how to account for such differences among children naturally arises. A clue to at least part of the answer may be found in the manner through which many of the signs are acquired. As shall be discussed below, the establishment of ste- reotyped routines (e.g., "Eency Weency Spider" song) between parent and child seems to be one fertile ground for the acquisition of object gestures in particular. It may be, therefore, that children who develop a larger number of signs are among those who experience larger numbers of such routine interactions. What this really implies is that responsibility for sign development may lie in part with the parents, since it is they who usually provide the structured situations we are talking about. The parental role may also manifest itself in another way. In order to be successful, any communicative act must be interpreted correctly by the receiver. In other words, the development of a symbolic gesture is dependent not only on the infant's recognition of the representative relation between vehicle and referent but also the parent's recognition of the same. It may well be that infants experiment all the time with gestural symbols for objects and events but that only some parents under some circumstances interpret the infant's efforts correctly

Table 1. Subjects in cross-sectional study producing symbolic gestures and the mean number of gestures exhibited in five categories

Subjects	Total		Objects		Requests		Attributes		Replies		Events	
	(%)	(M)	(%)	(M)	(%)	(M)	(%)	(M)	(%)	(M)	(%)	(M)
Females												
Firstborns ($n = 7$)	86	7.1	86	3.9	57	2.6	71	1.0	29	0.3	29	0.3
Laterborns ($n = 10$)	80	3.8	20	0.9	60	2.6	50	1.0	00	0.0	20	0.2
Total ($n = 17$)	82	5.2	47	3.4	59	2.1	24	0.2	24	0.2	24	0.2
Males												
Firstborns ($n = 9$)	89	2.8	44	1.9	67	1.9	33	0.3	00	0.0	00	0.0
Laterborns ($n = 12$)	92	2.9	50	1.0	83	1.0	75	0.8	00	0.0	8	0.1
Total ($n = 21$)	90	2.9	48	1.4	76	1.1	57	0.6	00	0.0	5	0.1
Total												
Firstborns ($n = 16$)	88	4.7	63	2.4	63	1.4	50	0.6	13	0.1	13	0.1
Laterborns ($n = 22$)	86	3.3	36	1.0	73	1.3	64	1.0	00	0.0	14	0.1
Total ($n = 38$)	87	3.9	47	1.6	68	1.4	59	0.8	5	0.1	13	0.1

Table 2. Subjects exhibiting symbolic gestures and mean number of gestures exhibited by subjects in longitudinal study

Subjects	Gesture category									
	Object		Request		Attribute		Other		Total	
	(%)	(M)	(%)	(M)	(%)	(M)	(%)	(M)	(%)	(M)
Females ($n = 10$)	90	3.00	90	1.70	70	1.30	30	0.4	100	6.30
Males ($n = 6$)	50	1.33	50	0.67	67	0.83	17	0.16	100	3.00
Total ($n = 16$)	75	2.38	75	1.31	69	1.13	25	0.31	100	5.06

and provide appropriate reinforcement to fuel the behavior further. Of course, at the present time all this is pure conjecture, but it does at least provide an hypothesis for the follow-up research with which we are currently involved.

Where do They Come from?

As mentioned above, one important question is how the infants acquired their symbolic gestures, particularly those used to label objects or events. Analysis of the maternal reports suggests that the manner of acquisition of the OBJECT gestures seems to fall into one of two major categories: (a) WITHIN INTER-ACTIVE ROUTINES: or (b) OUTSIDE OF INTERACTIVE ROUTINES. Gestures falling into the first category were those which were part of some kind of frequently repeated game or behavior sequence initiated by adults, where the goal was consciously or *un*consciously to elicit a certain gesture from the child. In

Table 3. Examples from two studies of gestures observed in three major categories

Category	Examples	Symbolic gesture
OBJECT	"Flower"	Sniff
	"Dog"	Panting
	"Airplane"	Arms out
	"Wind"	Arms waving
	"Moon"	Cupped hand high
	"Lightswitch"	Wiggle finger
	"Ball"	Throwing motion
	"Horse"	Bounce body
	"Spider"	Rub index fingers together
	"Blinking lights"	Blinking eyes
	"Rabbit"	Hop
	"Telephone"	Fist side of face
REQUEST	"Out"	Knob-turning gesture
	"Out"	Knock on door
	"Play piano"	Hands up/down
	"Nurse"	Pat mother's chest
	"Food"	Smack lips
ATTRIBUTES	"Hot"	Blow
	"Hot"	Wave hand back/forth
	"All gone"	Palms up
	"Many"	Wave hand back/forth
	"Big"	Raise arms

contrast, those in the second category seemed more to be products of the child's own experience with the objects. Of the OBJECT signs in the cross-sectional study 59% fell into the first category and 41% fell into the second. For the longitudinal study the figures were 32% and 78%, respectively. Overall, then, it is safe to say that a sizeable number of gestural labels have their roots in interactive routines between parent and child. However, it is important to emphasize that even for these routinized gestures, the achievement of symbolic status depended upon the infants' spontaneous generalization of the gestures beyond the immediate context within which they were originally acquired. Thus, a good deal of the credit still belongs to the infant.

In some sense the gestural labels which were developed outside of interactive routines were the more interesting since they seemed to stem more directly from the infant's own interpretations of the objects and events being depicted. Thus, they seemed more likely to provide a window into the nature of the infant's concept of the individual object represented. For this reason, it is instructive to consider the various types of signs that fell into this category. The vast majority of these gestures consisted of an action which depicted either an action the child did with the object (e.g., fist to ear for "telephone," blow for "match," throwing motion for "ball") or an action inherent in the object itself (e.g., palm to mouth for "Cookie Monster," waving hands for "butterfly," panting for "dog"). The few remaining signs within this category were depictions of perceptual qualities of the object (e.g., cupped hand held high for "moon"). Thus, the emphasis seemed clearly to be on the FUNCTION rather than the FORM of the object, a priority which fits very well with Nelson's contention that actions of objects and inter- actions with objects provide the core of children's initial concepts about objects (Nelson, 1974; Nelson & Lucariello, 1985).

Relation to Verbal Language Development

Although interesting in their own right, the symbolic gestures we have documented are also important for the light they may shed on the development of language as it is typically defined, that is, in terms of verbal development. Questions raised in this regard include the relative timing of symbolization in the two modalities, the degree to which progress in one domain predicts progress in the other, and in general whether or not the two are representative of a common developmental mechanism or develop independently of one another.

Age of Onset

In general mothers report that these behaviors occur primarily between 10 and 20 months of age. This is, of course, the same age frame normally cited for the onset of verbal development. Thus, on this rough scale, the two modalities appear to be developing in parallel. One way of looking in more detail at the relative timing of development in the two domains is to assess for individual children the degree of verbal development evidenced when each symbolic gesture appeared on the scene. Such an analysis would help determine whether symbolic gesturing precedes, co-occurs with, or follows development of verbal vocabulary. The longitudinal study provided the data necessary for this assessment. The results were quite clear: for most subjects symbolic gesturing was a behavior which overlapped with the earliest stages of verbal vocabulary development. Specifically, 70% of the symbolic gestures reported had an age of onset during the period when verbal vocabulary was between one and 25 words in size. This relation generally held for the subcategories as well (i.e., 81% for REQUESTS, 63% for OBJECT signs, 72% for ATTRIBUTES). Only 10% of the gestures preced- ed verbal development altogether, thus fueling the argument that development within the two modalities is the result of some common underlying mechanism. It is instructive to note, moreover, that the subjects responsible for the 10% of symbolic gestures which preceded verbalization were the four subjects whose ver- bal development was the slowest. This fact carries some implications for speech clinicians since it suggests that the search for symbolic gesturing in language- delayed children might help determine whether the locus of a child's problem is specific to the verbal modality or symptomatic of more basic cognitive deficits.

Of the two studies, the longitudinal study provided by far the more accurate data about age of onset since mothers in this case were making weekly recordings rather than relying on memory. Therefore, it was to these data we looked to see if all subcategories of signs developed simultaneously. Comparison of the age of onset of symbolic REQUEST and OBJECT signs indicated that they did not. On the contrary there was a significant tendency for the REQUEST signs to appear earlier in an individual infant's repertoire than OBJECT signs. Comparison of the mean age of onset for the sample as a whole also confirmed this pattern (M = 14.16 months for REQUESTS and 15.39 months for OBJECTS). What is interesting about this finding is the way it parallels verbal development. Griffiths (1985), for example, reviews literature showing a similar course of development in the verbal sphere. An explanation for the relative ordering may lie in the degree to which REQUEST and OBJECT signs require the child to generalize the symbolic vehicle from context to context. By definition, a specific REQUEST sign is somewhat context bound: although still symbolic, it has developed to accomplish a specific goal such as getting outdoors, being lifted, being allowed to play the piano, etc. In contrast, by our criteria, all OBJECT signs had to show evidence of being quite widely generalizable. The infant had to demonstrate knowledge that the sign was a label for a whole class of referents, not just a single, situation-specific exemplar. Such wide generalizability – or decontextualization, in Werner and Kaplan's (1963) terminology – would be expected to develop later. Moreover, since similar distinctions are just as applicable to verbal utterances, it is not surprising that a comparable sequence has been found in that medium as well.

Correlations Between Gestures and Verbal Vocabulary

Recall that verbal vocabulary size was assessed at 17 months in the cross-sectional study and at 20 and 24 months in the longitudinal study. In addition, the diary records provided details of verbal vocabulary development on a weekly basis from 11 to 20 months. One purpose of gathering this information was to determine whether symbolic gesturing enhances, retards, or generally has no impact on development in the more traditional modality of speech. Overall, the results of the correlational analyses applied to the data from the two studies revealed either positive or no relation between the two. Let us take the cross-sectional study with its larger sample size first. In this case, analyses revealed a correlation of + .42 between vocabulary and TOTAL number of signs (p = .009), a correlation of + .53 between vocabulary and OBJECT signs (p = .001), and essentially a zero correlation between vocabulary and REQUEST signs. Thus, it appears that OBJECT signs are the kind of signs most predictive of verbal development. This relation, in fact, even held when sex, birth status (first- versus later-born), and mother's education were all partialled out.

Although the smaller sample size of the longitudinal study (n = 17 versus n = 38) was problematic, even here we found evidence suggestive of a positive relation between OBJECT signs and verbal vocabulary. Specifically, comparison of the number of OBJECT signs in an infant's repertoire and his or her age at reaching the ten-word point yielded a correlation of –.48 ($p <$ .10), indicative of a trend toward faster vocabulary development among those with more OBJECT signs.

Presuming this positive relation between OBJECT signing and verbal development continues to hold in future research, how might it be explained? Our contention will be that it indicates the existence of a common mechanism underlying development on these two communication fronts. For example, the advent of the "naming insight" (McShane, 1979), which is thought by some to spark the onset of the vocabulary explosion often seen in the middle of the 2nd year, may fuel development of both gestural and verbal labels. Or at a more general level, the common bond may be development of the symbolic function or mental representation skills which allow recall as well as recognition memory. Whatever the causative factor or factors, our data are certainly consonant with the view that language, at least before the onset of syntax, need not be strictly a verbal affair. What happens after the single-word stage is less clear. We have seen upon occasion the combining of two symbolic gestures into a form comparable to a two-word utterance. For example, a child in the cross-sectional study combined her signs for "dog" (panting) and "go out" (knob-turning gesture) to indicate to her mother that the dog wanted to go out. In addition, the subject of our own case study (Acredolo & Goodwyn, 1985b) produced her first two-word and two-gesture combinations on the same day. Thus, although not common, the combining of gestures does exist, thereby pointing even more strongly toward the conclusion that language is not modality specific for hearing infants.

The Demise of Symbolic Gestures

Despite their apparent usefulness in the early stages of language development, symbolic gestures eventually disappear and are replaced by their verbal counterparts. (The one exception in our studies is the shrug of the shoulders for "I don't know," a gesture which even adults use to augment verbal communication.) In fact, symbolic gesturing really has a relatively short lifespan, serving the infant for the few months between the onset of communication and the middle of the 2nd year. Why the rapid demise? There are many reasons, all of which boil down to the advantage of verbal communication over non-verbal communication. For example, these gestures are interpretable by only those few individuals closest to the baby. As the child's world expands, there is the need for a less idiosyncratic system. Secondly, as any ASL user can tell you, visual-gestural language has the disadvantage of requiring the "listener" not only to be present, but to be watching the "speaker." As babies begin to roam farther afield from those attending them, verbal language takes on new importance. Finally, parents are generally very encouraging of verbal development. Their goal is an infant who can talk, not an infant who manages to communicate non-verbally. In fact, we have seen real prejudice in some homes against the use of symbolic gestures by infants under the assumption (not upheld in our data) that the promotion of such behaviors will have an adverse effect on verbal language. Whatever the reasons, the fact is that symbolic gestures do tend to disappear in favor of verbal language sometime in the middle of the 2nd year, but not before they have played a significant part in the development of language for the hearing child.

CHAPTER 7

Vocal and Gestural Symbols:
Similarities and Differences from 13 to 28 Months

C. Shore, E. Bates, I. Bretherton, M. Beeghly, and B. O'Connell

Introduction

In this paper, we will describe some of the work we have conducted investigating the similarities and differences between symbol use in the vocal and gestural modalities by normal hearing children between 13 and 28 months of age. Interest in the relationship between vocal and gestural symbols follows from the hypothesis put forward by Piaget (1962) and Werner and Kaplan (1963) that symbols have their origins in actions with objects. Consequently, symbols can be either gestural or vocal in nature, and the processes which allow the discovery that things have names can be manifested in either modality. The definition of "symbols" which we have used follows from the Piaget/Werner position and emerges from these behaviors:

> The comprehension or use, inside or outside of communicative situations, of a relationship between a sign and its referent, such that the sign is treated as belonging to and/or substitutable for its referent in a variety of contexts; at the same time the user is aware that the sign is separable from its referent, that is, not the same thing. (Bates, Benigni, Bretherton, Camaioni, & Volterra, 1979, p. 43).

Similarly, we have defined "naming" as follows:

> The use of a symbol to recognize, categorize, identify, or otherwise label a referent as a member of a known class of entities, or as an instantiation of a known unique individual. This naming act may be carried out for the purpose of identifying that referent for an intended listener, or in a private act of recognition for oneself. When used communicatively, a naming act may be the major point of an utterance or it may be a subsidiary act in the service of making further points about that referent. Similarly, in private cognition, a naming act may be carried out in isolation, or as a subsidiary act within a higher relational or predicative construction. (Bates, Bretherton, Shore, & McNew, 1983, p. 60).

This work was supported by grants from the Spencer Foundation and the National Science Foundation to Elizabeth Bates and Inge Bretherton. We wish to thank the parents and infants who participated in the study. We are also grateful to Vicki Carlson, Karlana Carpen, Maxine Fischer, Ann-Claire France, Antony Gerard, Andrew Garrison, Kim Kirschenfeldt, Sandra McNew, Cynthia Rodacy, Lynn Snyder, Elizabeth Teas, and Carol Williamson for help with data collection and analysis.

Consequently, we will focus in this discussion on relationships between language and the type of object-specific, conventional, referential gestures referred to as "enactive names" and "symbolic play." We will not discuss here gestures which are communicative in nature but do not have the object specificity of symbols (e.g., giving, showing, pointing). Nor will we discuss conventional games or routines, e.g., "pat-a-cake," "so big" which are dependent on social-contextual support and which do not serve the function of reference. A number of investigators besides ourselves (e.g., Fein, 1975; Fenson & Ramsay, 1980; McCune-Nicolich, 1981) have been struck by the parallels between language and symbolic play. Some of these are:

1. Language is a tool for the representation of absent persons, objects, and actions. Symbolic play is a tool for the representation of events (including persons, objects, and actions) outside their everyday context.
2. In language, arbitrary sounds come to stand for objects, events, and persons. In symbolic play arbitrary objects are made to stand for other objects (a child may substitute a placeholder, such as a block or a counterconventional object such as a spoon, to represent a telephone).
3. In language and play the child begins by producing single units (vocal and enactive names) which are later combined into meaningful sequences (sentences and event schemata). (Bretherton & Bates, 1984, p. 233)

At the same time, however, these two domains are different from one another. Some of these differences are (adapted from Bretherton and Bates, p. 234):

1. In language temporal and spatial relations between agents and objects come to be expressed as separate morphemes indicating time, direction, and location grammaticization. In symbolic play these relations are implicit in the enactment itself.
2. In symbolic play realistic toys provide a measure of perceptual support as the child plans to enact an event outside its normal context. Some perceptual support is provided even by substitute objects used as placeholders or other objects. In language about absent persons, objects, or events such planning may be carried out with little or no perceptual support.
3. Language is much more highly conventionalized than symbolic play although partners may develop idiosyncratic play conventions in the course of repeated interactions.
4. Language is an obligatory form of representation for hearing and speaking children, whereas symbolic play is an optional form. The skills associated with the latter are therefore not so consistently and frequently practiced.

Given the similarities and differences between language and symbolic play, several possible relationships could obtain between these two domains. First, these two domains may be correlated because they both rely on the same general maturational factors. Hence the correlation between language and symbolic play might be no more illuminating than the correlation between age and shoe size. Data from our subjects indicates that this is not the case. For example, language and symbolic play are correlated, but neither correlates with combinatorial play. So the relationship between these two symbol domains seems to be more specific than "general maturation." Secondly, symbolic play and language could be correlated because both rely on the same underlying specific process — a process that they both share throughout the relevant stages of development. Thirdly, the two domains may be correlated only at specific points in time, when each draws on similar component processes. If the third model obtains, then the patterns of correlations at several points in time may be necessary to understand the component skills of the symbolic processes which underlie language and symbolic play.

We will describe similarities and differences between gestural and vocal symbols at three developmental junctures: 13 months, corresponding to the emergence of first words; 20 months, corresponding to the appearance of early multiword combinations; and 28 months, corresponding to the "grammaticization" process in language. This discussion will be drawn from a number of studies which we have conducted, as well as some relevant data from other investigations. We will also present some new data which are relevant to differences between vocal and gestural symbols.

Similarities and Differences in Vocal and Gestural Symbol Production

Vocal and Gestural Naming: 13 Months

Around the time that children produce their first words, there is a parallel shift taking place in the gestural modality. Toward the end of the 1st year, children frequently use a conventional gesture associated with an object (e.g., drinking from a cup, or combing with a comb) to recognize or classify members of that object class. Escalona (1973) and Werner and Kaplan (1963) were among the first to argue that these brief "I know what to do with this" gestures are enactive names. Volterra and Bates (1984) have summarized several lines of evidence in support of the idea that object-associated or "recognitory" gestures serve as a kind of naming (Acredolo & Goodwyn, 1985a, 1985b; Bates et al., 1979; McCune-Nicolich, 1981; McCune-Nicolich & Bruskin, 1982; Volterra & Caselli, 1985).

Onset Time. First words for objects and object-associated gestures both appear at approximately 11 to 13 months. If there is a difference in onset time, it is that gestures sometimes appear slightly before words (a difference that may reflect maturational schedules for the visual/manual versus acoustic/articulatory channels).

Correlations. In this initial phase of symbol use (i.e., from 11 to 16 months), there is a positive correlation between the number of recognitory gestures and the number of object names in a given child's repertoire. This is particularly true for recognitory gestures that involve some kind of object substitution or are carried out empty handed.

Content. During this phase, gestures and words tend to cover the same basic "vocabulary": eating, drinking, greeting, bathing, dressing, certain household activities, vehicles, appearance and disappearance of objects, etc. Interestingly, any one child typically initially has either a gesture or a word for a particular referent.

Form. Enactive gestures, like early names, are very brief and stylized in form. The child who touches cup to lip in object recognition seems to distinguish between this act and "real drinking," and shows no surprise or disappointment if there is nothing to drink.

Decontextualization. Both words and gestures show a similar course of development from context-bound routines to generalized use for an increasingly broad set of referents and situations. For example, the child may only put a brush to his or her ear at first in a reciprocal brushing game with mother. Later he or she may produce the same gesture to anything vaguely resembling a brush (e.g., a spaghetti lifter, a duster, or even a block), by him- or herself or with anyone interested enough to play the game. Words and gestures may also be used to refer to absent referents, and to past or future events (Acredolo & Goodwyn, 1985a, 1985b). There is considerable variation among children in the tendency to use gestures in this way (e.g., making a stirring gesture as a request for an absent spoon).

It appears, then, that the two modalities are developing in parallel during the first few months of symbol use. By the middle of the one-word stage, however, normal hearing children start to give much more priority to the vocal modality. For example, Bretherton, Bates, McNew, Shore, Williamson, and Beeghly-Smith (1981) attempted to elicit vocal and gestural names by presenting familiar objects one at a time to 13- and 20-month-olds. Although at 13 months the gestural and vocal vocabularies of the children were comparable, the children were significantly more likely to produce a recognitory gesture than a vocal label — as though the "threshold" for eliciting gestural schemes were somehow lower. By 20 months of age, these same children showed the opposite pattern: vocal naming had increased markedly, and the probability of producing a recognitory gesture was much lower than at 13 months.

Gestures and words, then, begin as apparently parallel expressions of reference. If one modality has an initial advantage, it appears to be the gestural one. By the end of the one-word period, however, the relative use of these two modalities for purposes of naming appears to have diverged in favor of the vocal channel. As we shall see, however, links between language and gesture will occur again on a completely different plane, in the passage from single units to planned combinations of symbols at 20 months of age.

First Sentences in Language and Gesture: 20 Months

A number of investigators have observed similarities of onset time between multigesture combinations and multiword utterances (Fenson & Ramsay, 1980; McCune-Nicolich, 1981; McCune-Nicolich & Bruskin, 1982). Shore, O'Connell and Bates (1984) followed up these suggestions in a longitudinal study of 30 children at 20 and 28 months of age. At both sessions, they extracted the usual measures of vocabulary and mean length of utterance from free speech records, and used elicited symbolic play scenarios to extract estimates of "vocabulary" and "mean length of sequence" in symbolic gesturing. At 20 months, the vocal and gestural modalities were strikingly similar in the average length of an unbroken sequence and in the longest chain of different elements that a child could produce (averaging two, with a range of one to four). They also found that combinations of content words and gestural sequences were correlated, and that these correlations held up even when size of vocabulary (in either modality) was partialled out. Hence, the common ability to combine elements in language and play was not simply a by-product of the developmentally earlier linkage between vocabularies of the two modalities.

Shore (1986) showed that the variance shared by gestural sequencing and word combinations was also shared with a measure of the range and flexibility of individual words. In other words, the ability to combine words and/or gestures seems to be tied to the efficiency and/or automaticity of individual items (see also Bloom, Lightbown, & Hood, 1975). This finding is compatible with arguments by Case (1985) and Case and Khanna (1981) that the transition to multiword speech is one manifestation of a general cognitive reorganization near the end of the 2nd year involving increases in "working memory." These changes result from greater efficiency in the planning and execution of individual cognitive schemes, so that more and more of these schemes can be packed into the same mental space. Many domains undergo a parallel shift during this age period, e.g., gestural imitation (McCall, Parke, & Kavanaugh, 1977), classification of objects (Sugarman, 1982a, 1982b), block building, and a variety of other behaviors (Case & Khanna, 1981). This lends plausibility to the proposal of a common underlying factor of some kind that permits increases in the efficiency of individual linguistic and nonlinguistic "chunks."

Yet another aspect of the word/gesture combinatorial transition has been studied by Shore and Bauer (1983) and Bauer (1985) who compared individual differences in language with individual differences in symbolic play. They found, among other things, that nominal/referential children show a different pattern of correlations between language and play than do pronominal/expressive children. For nominal/referential children, language measures are most highly correlated with play involving object substitution; for pronominal/expressive children, language measures are instead correlated more highly with play involving realistic objects. Like Wolf and Gardner's (1979) "patterner/dramatist" distinction, Shore and Bauer (1983) have proposed that some children emphasize the analysis of a symbol system into its component parts (yielding referential style in language and object substitution in symbolic play), while others are more interested in the reproduction of reality through symbols (resulting in a more imitative, expressive style in language and realistic approaches to symbolic play).

To summarize, symbolic play shows parallels to language in style as well as rate of transition to multisymbol combinations. This may be part of a more general cognitive reorganization. Now we will turn to the final phase of language development in infancy, the period of grammaticization.

Grammaticization: 28 Months

During this period of language development, children begin to conquer the rules of morphology (both affixes for modifying words and free morphemes such as articles and prepositions) and syntax (principles for ordering sentence elements). As we mentioned before, symbolic play has no real counterpart to the morphological component of grammar, but it does have parallels to the ordering principles of syntax.

Some recent studies of elicited symbolic play from 20 to 36 months suggest that children's ability to reproduce a conventional sequence may increase considerably during this period (McCune-Nicolich, 1981; McCune-Nicolich & Bruskin, 1982; O'Connell & Gerard, 1985; Shore et al., 1984). Before this point, even though the 20-month-old can produce sequences of two or three gestures, the sequence in which those gestures are produced does not always correspond to conventional adult "scripts." For example, a child may carry out a bath scenario by first soaping the teddy bear, then wrapping it in a towel, and only then placing it in the bath tub. To the extent, however, that they do reproduce conventional scenarios in canonical order, they are likely to show greater linguistic sophistication (C. Shore & P. Bauer, in preparation). By 28 months, in both spontaneous and imitative play, the child is much more likely to act out the script in order. Furthermore, if props are missing for the correct execution of a script, the child will try to make the necessary plans in advance (e.g., finding a wooden block that can serve as the soap). By 28 months, the child is much more proficient at utilizing the principles that hold an ordered sequence together (Gerard, 1984; O'Connell, 1984). Because the 20–28 month period is so important in the acquisition of grammar, this raises the interesting possibility that grammaticization and conventional sequencing in play are based on some common change in the capacity to order a series of units according to conventional principles.

To summarize so far, there are striking similarities between the vocal and gestural modalities in the development of symbolic production and combination. At each major transition point in language, gesture shows parallel changes: the emergence of reference, the appearance of combinations, the increase in ordering elements according to conventional principles.

There are differences, however, between these modalities in hearing children. In the one-word period, an initial slight advantage for the gestural modality gives way to an increasing reliance on the vocal channel for naming. Similarly, although the lengths of symbol combinations are comparable at 20 months, by 28 months children's vocal sequences (even when only content words are considered) are longer than those in gesture. It is likely that these discrepancies are related to the obligatory demand for symbolization in language for hearing/speaking children and the optional nature of symbolic play for these children. In other words, children are more frequently called on to utilize language for communicating with others than they are to use object-specific referential gestures for the same purpose. This same discrepancy in communicative press is likely to be operating in the comprehension of vocal and gestural symbols.

Comprehension of Gestural Symbols

Thus far, we have been describing a considerable body of work which points out similarities and differences in the production of vocal and gestural symbols. By contrast, very little is known about comprehension in the gestural modality (at least in hearing children), or how gestural comprehension relates to other forms of symbol use. Ideally, of course, one would like to have a completely crossed design: comprehension and production of vocal and gestural symbols. The Bretherton et al. (1981) study mentioned before covers three of these cells: vocal and gestural production, as well as vocal comprehension at 13 and 20 months. They presented infants with a "multiple choice" vocal comprehension task. In order to operationalize the concept of decontextualization which is so important to symbol development during this age period, they used two versions of each object: a realistic, perceptually detailed version, and an "abstract" version of wood or cloth which retained only the basic shape and one criterial feature. On a given trial, the child was presented with three either realistic or abstract toys and asked, for example, to "get the phone." When the child made his/her choice, spontaneous vocal and enactive names were scored. The fact that the fourth cell, gestural comprehension, was not included is informative: pilot work indicated that being asked to choose an object represented by an empty-handed gesture was too difficult for even the 20-month-olds.

Consequently, we attempted to elicit gestural comprehension at 28 months, and to relate it to the vocal modality. We thought that children might show comprehension of empty-handed gestures in their 3rd year for two reasons. First, a number of investigators have observed imitation of these gestures during this age period (Elder and Pederson, 1978; Jackowitz & Watson, 1980; Ungerer, Zelazo, Kearsley, & O'Leary, 1981). If imitation serves the purpose of helping the child understand information which is moderately discrepant from his/her current understanding (see review by Uzgiris, 1981), then imitation of empty-handed gestures in the 3rd year might be indicative of moderate comprehension by children in this age range. Secondly, observations of mother-child interactions suggest that these gestures are more commonly used by mothers with children in this age range than at either 2 years or 4–5 years (Bridges, 1979; Gutmann & Turnure, 1979), especially in object retrieval tasks when the verbal label is unfamiliar. We assume that mothers use these gestures at this point in time with some belief that their children understand them.

The suggestion that mothers use gestural symbols with 2.5-year-olds to supplement communication when verbal labels are unfamiliar, taken together with the hypothesis that imitation appears at the "frontier" of children's understanding, would predict an interesting relationship among word vocabulary, imitation of enactive gestures, and gestural comprehension. When the child's vocal vocabulary is low, the child's mother may rely heavily on deictic rather than enactive gestures (as did the mothers of 2-year-olds in Bridges' study). As the child's vocabulary increases, the mother may begin trying to involve the child more in the problem-solving aspect of object retrieval games, using gestural symbols along with other cues. These other cues may provide a background of partial comprehension for the enactive gestures, making them just novel enough for the child to begin to imitate them. Further increases in vocabulary, however, may make it less necessary for mothers to rely on enactive gestures for communication, and indeed, mothers of 4- to 5-year-olds in Gutmann and Turnure's study replaced "pantomime" with more abstract forms of gesture in their communications with their children. By the time the child has a fairly sophisticated vocabulary, he or she could have come to comprehend the enactive gestures used by others and so show a decrease in imitation. In short, one might expect an interaction of word vocabulary and imitation to predict gestural comprehension, as well as a curvilinear relationship between imitation and comprehension of gestural symbols.

Method

Subjects. Twenty-nine children from middle-class families in the Boulder, Colorado, area participated as part of a longitudinal study from 10 to 28 months. There were 14 males and 15 females. At the time of this session, all children were 28 months old. At the beginning of the longitudinal study, names were obtained through birth announcements in the local newspaper. After eliminating all infants with reported birth weights under 5.5 pounds, letters were sent to parents explaining the nature of the project. A follow-up telephone call yielded a consent rate of 70%.

Materials and Procedure: Gesture Comprehension. The materials and procedure for this study followed those used by Bretherton et al. (1981). The vocal comprehension task at 13 and 20 months included realistic and abstract objects for eight common nouns: doll, phone, cup, car, spoon, bottle, shoe, and bear. In the present study, we used the same realistic and abstract versions of the doll, phone, cup, car, and spoon. However, in place of the bottle, shoe, and bear, we used versions of a brush, book, and necklace. Hence, there were eight distinctive gestures for the gesture comprehension task. Materials also included a transparent plastic box divided into three compartments. The back was open to permit insertion of the target object and two distractor toys. The front was covered with a transparent door hinged at the top which could be closed while the objects were set in place and opened after the instructions were given. In the vocal comprehension test, the child was asked, for example, to "Get the phone." As a test of gestural comprehension in the present study, the experimenter asked the child to "Get the one that goes like this" (with an empty-handed gesture of putting phone receiver to ear). Children were so attracted by the toys in the box that they found it difficult to attend to the instruction when the objects were in view. We therefore found it necessary to use a cloth to cover the box during the instruction for each trial. The instruction was given twice before the cloth was lifted from the box and the door opened. For each object, a conventional gesture, performed with no object in hand, served as the visual part of the instruction.

In all other respects, the procedure was the same as in Bretherton et al. (1981). There were 16 multiple choice trials, each involving a target and two distractors. Items were presented in two randomly assigned quasi-random orders. Real and abstract trials were alternated, and no two trials with the same target followed one another. On each trial, after the children had selected an object, they were allowed to play with it for approximately 30 s while a new trial was set up.

Scoring and Reliabilities. On each trial, the child was given four yes/no scores: (a) correctness of object choice, using the first object touched and taken as the child's choice; (b) presence of vocal schemes, i.e., all recognizable words explicitly related to the referent object, including some which were not names for the object, such as "yum" or "juice" for cup; (c) presence of gestural schemes, conventional object-related gestures which were clearly distinguishable from exploratory manipulation, e.g., "drinking" from the cup; and (d) imitation of the experimenter's gesture command during the instruction. Since no objects were in view during the instruction, this last measure was different from the measure of gestural schemes produced after an object had been selected. The dependent variables were the number of trials on which correct choice, vocal schemes, gestural schemes, and imitation occurred. Each of these four measures could vary from 0 to 8 for both realistic and abstract trials.

Two raters independently scored four randomly selected videotapes. Reliabilities for yes/no coding were calculated separately for each of the dependent measures: correct choice; 100%; imitation of demonstration, 97%; vocal schemes, 89%; and gestural schemes, 95%. The remaining tapes were scored by only one rater.

Procedure: Peabody Picture Vocabulary Test. The children were administered the Peabody Picture Vocabulary Test (PPVT) in their homes prior to the laboratory session. The test was administered and scored in standard fashion, except that items at the highest age levels were not administered.

Results and Discussion

Figure 1 depicts a comparison of gestural comprehension, vocal production and gestural production in these data with those from Bretherton et al. (1981).

Object Choice. Each child was assigned a plus or a minus according to whether he or she chose the correct object at above-chance level (six or more correct out of 16). A sign test was used to determine whether more children performed at an above-chance level than one would expect in a random distribution. Eighteen children chose the correct object at above-chance level, and 11 did not. This distribution was not statistically different from chance (p = .267, two tailed). That is, the children as a group cannot be said to have comprehended the gestural command. However, some individual children did understand the point of this gesture comprehension game. For example, one child spontaneously named the target object while the gesture was being modeled a total of six times, e.g., saying "brush" while the experimenter made the gesture of brushing her hair.

In general, we can say that the ability to comprehend gestures is just emerging at 28 months and is well-established in only a few children. This is comparable to the performance noted by Bretherton et al. (1981) for the same children at 13 months, in comprehension of vocal names for objects. Children were not more likely to understand the gesture command when given realistic objects than when

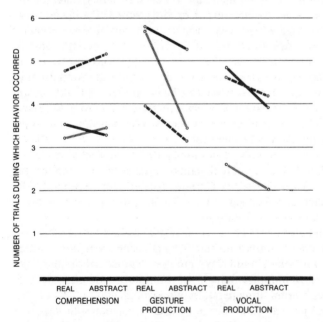

Fig. 1. Comparison of comprehension, vocal production, and gestural production at 13 (*dotted lines*), 20 (*broken lines*), and 28 months (*solid lines*). Real/abstract are discrete categories, but have been presented in histogram form for conciseness

they were given abstract objects (paired sample t test, t = .66). These results parallel those of the 13- and 20-month sessions.

Vocal and Gestural Production. Overall, the number of spontaneous vocal and gestural schemes produced in this task has not changed greatly, compared with performance at 13 and 20 months. Gestural output seems to have gone up — but after all, this was a gestural task, with the adult providing gestural models. The major insight offered by the spontaneous production data involves the effects of object realism: for gestures ($t = 2.05, p < 0.5$) and for words ($t = 2.60, p < .05$), more schemes were produced with realistic versions of the object. This is one more piece of evidence for a similarity between the modalities, similar to the findings at 13 and 20 months. Because the size of the abstractness effect at 28 months resembles the 20-month data, we can conclude that decontextualization has started to level off in both modalities.

Imitation During Demonstration. This variable was bimodal in its distribution. Fifteen children imitated on 0 or 1 of the 16 trials, 12 children imitated on 11–16 of the trials, and only two occupied the midrange of imitating on six to eight trials. In further analyses, these last two groups were counted as "imitators." What determined whether the child would imitate the model? What function did that imitation serve? As a *linear variable*, imitation did not correlate significantly with any of the within-experiment variables. Imitators and nonimitators were remarkably similar in terms of the number of correct choices they made ($M = 6.71$ versus 7.00), their gestural production ($M = 11.71$ versus 10.80), and their vocal production ($M = 8.64$ versus 8.40). Males and females were equally represented in the two groups (imitators: seven females, seven males; nonimitators: eight females, seven males).

However, if imitation appears at the frontier of children's understanding, and if the familiarity of enactive gestures is related to the vocabulary of the child, we should expect a *curvilinear relationship* between imitation and word vocabulary as measured by the PPVT. The children were divided into three equal-n groups corresponding to high, medium, and low PPVT scores. A one-way analysis of variance was performed with the PPVT as the independent variable and imitation as the dependent variable. There was a significant difference between the groups $F(2,26) = 3.93, p = .03$. The middle PPVT group imitated more frequently ($M = 10.9$) than did the high or low groups ($M = 3.5, 5.1$, respectively), demonstrating the expected curvilinear relationship.

Secondly, one would also predict a curvilinear relationship between size of vocabulary and the tendency to imitate during the gestural instruction. Imitators with relatively low vocabularies should show greater comprehension than low vocabulary nonimitators. Imitators with high vocabularies should comprehend fewer gestures than their nonimitating peers. In other words, imitation would be most likely at the mid-range of gestural comprehension. A median split was used to divide the sample into high and low PPVT groups. These were crossed with the high and low imitation classification to yield four groups. A 2 (PPVT) × 2 (imitation) analysis of variance with gestural comprehension as the dependent

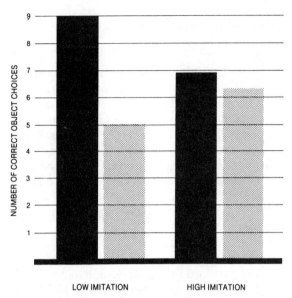

Fig. 2. Interaction of PPVT and imitation on gestural comprehension. *Solid columns,* high PPVT; *Shaded columns,* low PPVT

variable resulted in a main effect for PPVT, $F(1,25) = 6.53, p = .017$. Children who performed well on the PPVT had higher comprehension scores than those with lower PPVT scores. More interesting is the interaction between PPVT and imitation, $F(1,25) = 4.65, p = .04$. This interaction is illustrated in Fig. 2.

High imitators, regardless of their PPVT scores, performed at intermediate levels on gesture comprehension. Low imitators with high PPVT scores showed the highest degree of gesture comprehension, whereas low imitators with low PPVTs had the lowest gesture comprehension scores. In other words, gestural imitation bears a curvilinear relationship to the child's level of understanding.

Conclusions

This last experiment adds to our understanding of the similarities and differences between language and gestural symbols, in several ways. First, it is clear that the hearing child's comprehension of empty-handed gestural symbols for objects emerges much later — at least 15 months later — than comprehension of vocal labels for the same objects. Even though these children have been producing the same gestures themselves for rather a long time, most 28-month-olds have a hard time matching those gestures to the corresponding objects if the action is produced empty-handed by the adult (i.e., in a "sign-like" fashion). We suspect that this is due not to some inherent problem with the gestural channel, but to the fact that hearing children have very little opportunity to observe empty-handed pantomimes by adults — although this is certainly an empirical question, and one deserving further research.

Secondly, the curvilinear relationship between gestural imitation and comprehension has important implications for research on the development of symbolic play and language. Both of these modalities are often studied with elicited imitation procedures (particularly in clinical settings). And yet, if the underlying relationship between the child's understanding and his or her willingness to imitate is curvilinear in nature, we may come away with the mistaken conclusion that a very insightful child (who refuses to imitate the obvious) is behind in symbol development.

We may make even more serious mistakes at the group level in our efforts to understand the relationship between these two modalities. Correlations are by definition linear in nature. In this study, we found an interesting relationship between language comprehension (as measured by the PPVT) and gestural production (as measured by the child's propensity to imitate the adult's empty-handed pantomime) — but because that relationship is curvilinear rather than linear, it would never show up in a traditional correlational design. This lesson pertains not only to measures of imitation (where the rationale for the curvilinear relationship is clear), but also for longitudinal and cross-sectional studies of symbol development in general. As we obtain a deeper understanding of similarities and differences between language and gestural development, it becomes clear that the relationship between these two functionally and structurally distinct modalities is changing over time. For example, vocal names and recognitory gestures seem to appear around the same point (from 10 to 12 months), and they increase together for several weeks or months in both size and flexibility. However, we also know that these recognitory gestures drop off somewhere in the 2nd year as the vocal channel takes over. Depending on when we choose to measure the relationship between vocal and gestural symbols during the "single-word/single-scheme" stage, we may obtain a positive linear correlation, a negative linear correlation, or no significant correlation at all. The same inverted U will be repeated at the 20-month level: the two modalities first develop together (perhaps with a slight edge for gesture) in the passage from single schemes to combinations, but the vocal channel ultimately moves far ahead in the hearing child. Hence a linear correlation will hold only at the relevant point in development, i.e., when both modalities are affected by the "new" chunking ability. This time-dependent approach to the study of language and gesture is certainly complex, compared with Piaget's straightforward proposal that there is a "single" symbolic function. But we now have enough comparative information on symbol development across modalities to suggest that this is indeed the right approach.

PART II

Deaf Children with Sign Language Input

Overview

The five chapters that follow are concerned with deaf children who have deaf parents. American Sign Language (ASL) is the home language of all of the children studied by the researchers, and the infants' first communicative and linguistic experiences occur in the visual-gestural modality. Erting, Prezioso, and Hynes have analyzed the face-to-face interactions of eight deaf mothers and their deaf infants, 1–5 months of age. These authors describe the context of the infants' first interactional experiences with their mothers as one in which facial behaviors, eye gaze, and physical contact play major roles in facilitating and maintaining the interaction. Some of the earliest communicative routines enacted by these mothers are constructed around naming mother and infant and are carried out in a register of ASL analogous to baby talk in spoken languages. MOTHER signs produced by the deaf mothers during interaction with their infants were compared with MOTHER signs produced by these same mothers during conversation with a deaf adult. Analysis revealed baby talk modifications in sign production consistent with the conclusion based on studies of spoken languages that parents use special articulatory features in their communication with infants.

Reilly, McIntire, and Bellugi address two questions: how does a deaf infant learning ASL acquire the facial grammar and what role does the prelinguistic affective system play in this acquisition process? Data are drawn from videotapes of five deaf children, 1–4 years of age, interacting with their deaf caregivers and/or deaf siblings. The authors hypothesize that by analyzing children's first signs for affective states and behaviors and "emotionally-colored" signs, they will gain insight into the deaf child's developing mastery of facial expression for linguistic purposes. Microanalysis of their data lead them to the conclusion that deaf children's acquisition of grammatical facial behaviors is similar to the spoken language acquisition of hearing children. It is controlled by a linguistic mechanism that must reprocess the seemingly familiar information on the face and re-analyze it into linguistically relevant components. Reilly et al. suggest that the infants' early experiences with the facial expression of affect help them recognize the importance of the face in communication and eventually in the grammar of ASL.

The chapter by Boyes Braem focuses on the acquisition of handshape in ASL. The author first proposes a model of the stages of acquisition based on anatomical, developmental motor, and cognitive factors that might influence the course of handshape acquisition in the infant and young child. The model is described as the acquisition of eight features applied to the unmarked A handshape. Once the handshapes are acquired, production can be influenced by a set of secondary factors which the author outlines. Boyes Braem tests this developmental model by analyzing 1 h of data from a videotape of a congenitally deaf child (2.7 years of age) of deaf parents. The author cites other studies published since her own, in 1973, that support her proposed model.

Pizzuto reports on a longitudinal study of one deaf child acquiring ASL between the ages of 8 and 29 months. The author investigates the development of nonlinguistic deictic gestures and linguistic pronominal signs drawing her data from 12 videotaped samples of naturalistic interaction between the child and her deaf parents and older deaf sister. Results reported show a developmental pattern from no deictic gestures or deictic signs at 8 months to deictic gestures only at 12 months followed by deictic gestures and deictic signs from 15 months on. There is a gradual decrease in deictic gestures beginning at 18 months with a concomitant increase in deictic signs. Demonstrative deictic signs are the first to appear, at 15 months; locative and demonstrative-locative deictic signs are found at 18 months; person deictic signs do not appear until 20 months. After comparing these findings with those reported in the literature for hearing children acquiring deictic words, Pizzuto concludes that modality is not a significant influence on the appearance of deictic gestures or on the development of deictic signs and deictic words.

Petitto studied two deaf children between the ages of 6 and 35 months in order to examine their use of deictic pointing gestures and their comprehension and use of personal pronouns in ASL. She argues that because the form of pronouns is similar to the form of the prelinguistic gestures, this investigation is particularly relevant to the testing of two assumptions of current models of language acquisition: (a) that knowledge of linguistic structure is "mapped onto" earlier forms of nonlinguistic knowledge; and (b) that language acquisition is a continuous learning sequence from early gestural communication to linguistic communication. Results of the analysis corroborate the developmental progression reported by Pizzuto from deictic gestures to deictic signs for pronominal reference. Petitto argues that one of the children's pronoun reversal errors wherein she treated the indexical YOU point as a frozen lexical item for her own name reflects the child's over-application of an abstract linguistic principle. The author claims that these data provide strong support for the argument that the child brings a specifically linguistic, perhaps biologically given, type of knowledge to the language acquisition process.

These five chapters report on data involving 17 deaf children ranging in age from 1 month to 4 years. They are all children who are acquiring ASL; no other sign language or cultural group is represented. Furthermore, data for four of the studies were collected by researchers at The Salk Institute and the fifth study, examining maternal input rather than infant behaviors, was done by a team at Gallaudet University. Naturalistic interactions videotaped in the home or the laboratory provided the data for all of the studies. Petitto also used an elicitation task with one of her subjects, and Erting et al. employed a standardized face-to-face format.

The findings reported by Pizzuto and Petitto are basically in agreement. Both authors relate interesting anecdotes concerning pronoun use by the children they studied. Pizzuto's child makes a reversal error: she responds with ME when she should have responded with YOU to the question WHERE (or WHO) is MOTHER. Petitto reports that her child substitutes YOU for ME, arguing that the error is essentially a linguistic one. While these errors are intriguing, they are only single examples. It is clear from the chapters in this section that the study of deaf children of deaf signing parents is fertile ground for the study of the transition from gesture to language. It is also clear that we need more data, drawn from different sign languages and cultural groups, collected so that they are comparable, before we can begin to draw conclusions about this important stage of language acquisition.

CHAPTER 8

The Interactional Context of Deaf Mother-Infant Communication

C. J. ERTING, C. PREZIOSO, and M. O'GRADY HYNES

Introduction

Early parent-infant interaction has been studied from a variety of perspectives during the past 15 years. Developmental psychologists, pediatricians, and child psychiatrists have been concerned to elucidate the role of face-to-face interaction in the social, emotional and cognitive development of the infant (Brazelton, Koslowski, & Main, 1974; Cohn & Tronick, 1987; Field & Fogel, 1982; Kaye, 1982; Murray & Trevarthen, 1985; Stern, 1974a; Tronick, 1982). Researchers have also been interested in the communicative interaction of the mother-infant dyad (Bretherton, 1988; Bruner, 1975b; Chappell & Sander, 1979; Freedle & Lewis, 1977; Jaffe, Stern, & Peery, 1973; Kozak-Mayer & Tronick, 1985; Stevenson, Ver Hoeve, Roach, & Leavitt, 1986; Trevarthen, 1980). Especially relevant to the study described in this chapter are the investigations of baby talk or "motherese," that is, modifications adults make in their talk when interacting with infants (Ferguson, 1977; Furrow & Nelson, 1986; Gleitman, Newport, & Gleitman, 1984; Papousek, Papousek, & Haekel, 1987; Penman, Cross, Milgrom-Friedman, & Meares, 1983; Snow & Ferguson, 1977; Trevarthen & Marwick, 1986). These studies have described this simplified speech register as differing systematically from speech to adults on a variety of dimensions including phonological complexity, pitch, syntactic complexity, lexicon, repetition, intonation, and rate.

Mother-infant interaction and baby talk has been studied in a wide variety of cultures (Blount, 1982; Field, Sostek, Vietze, & Leiderman, 1981; Fernald, 1987; Ochs & Schieffelin, 1984; Papousek, 1987; Snow & Ferguson, 1977). Cross-cultural comparison of baby talk is, however, not a simple undertaking as Schieffelin and Ochs (1986) have demonstrated. It requires a detailed analysis of the "formal organization of discourse and the interpretation of sociocultural meanings which that organization may convey to infants and young children over developmental time" (Schieffelin & Ochs, 1986, p. 174). From this ethnographic perspective, Schieffelin and Ochs question the universality of simplification, seen as the hallmark of baby talk since the register was first described, noting that

Portions of this paper were first presented at the Fourth International Symposium on Sign Language Research, Lappeenranta, Finland, July, 1987. We thank the families who participated in this study as well as our colleagues Kathryn Meadow-Orlans, Pat Spencer Day, and Robert MacTurk. We express special thanks to Edward Z. Tronick and Hanus and Mechthild Papousek for their encouragement and advice. This work was supported in part by a NATO Postdoctoral Fellowship in Science awarded to the first author.

conclusions have been drawn based on data from only a limited number of speech communities. They refer to the more recent research on working class Blacks (Heath, 1983), Athapaskan Indians (Scollon & Scollon, 1981), Samoans (Ochs, 1982), and Kaluli (Schieffelin, 1979), illustrating the cultural embeddedness of baby talk and its multiplicity of forms and functions across cultures as well as within cultures across contexts and developmental time.

We have recently begun a study of deaf mother-deaf infant interaction in an effort to document the nature of early communicative interactions in the visual-gestural modality. The mothers in our study use sign language as their first and preferred language. Furthermore, they identify themselves and their children as members of the deaf community and expect them to acquire the language and culture of the deaf sociocultural group. Like Schieffelin and Ochs (1986), we believe that language socialization begins with the first social contact during infancy. The long-term goal of our research is to document the course of this language socialization from the first months of life through the deaf child's transition from gestural to symbolic communication. The analysis we report here is the beginning of our effort to understand the nature of the maternal input in the first months of face-to-face interaction when both mother and infant are deaf and American Sign Language is the language of the home.

Previous Research

During the last decade, there have been only a few studies of deaf mothers interacting with infants under 12 months of age. Maestas y Moores (1980) examined the interaction of seven infants with their deaf parents. Some of the infants had normal hearing and others were hearing impaired; most of the data were collected on four of the infants when they were between 1 and 6 months of age. (The hearing status of these four infants was not indicated in the published report.) The researcher, who is hearing, videotaped the parents and infants in their homes during feeding, bathing, and play situations. She describes the communication of these deaf parents as relying heavily on physical and visual contact with the infants, incorporating a variety of strategies to gain and maintain the infants' attention. Maestas y Moores suggests that "touch may well be the fundamental modality for parent-infant communication" (p. 5), noting that the deaf parents sign while they hold their infants, physically orient the infants so that they may attend to visual-gestural communication, tap and pat the infant's body, often sign on the infant's face or torso, physically mold the infant's fingers and hands into the shapes of signs, and guide the hands and arms in sign movements.

Maestas y Moores emphasizes the variety of communicative strategies employed by the deaf parents. They sign, fingerspell, and speak to their infants, often moving their hands into the infant's line of vision. Frequently parents position themselves behind or beside the infant with their signing hands moving in front of the infant's body. Furthermore, their signing may be modified through repetition, holding a sign in location, and producing a sign very slowly.

Recently, Harris, Clibbens, Tibbitts, and Chasin (1987) have reported on a study of two British deaf mothers interacting with their deaf infants at 7 and 10 months of age. The mothers were described as native users of British Sign Language. Video-recordings were made by one deaf and one hearing researcher in a laboratory setting arranged as a playroom. The authors note that the total number of signed utterances increased noticeably across the two recording sessions; most frequently these utterances consisted of single signs, and all signs had accompanying lip movement. The mothers managed to produce two-thirds of these utterances within the infants' visual field, primarily by moving their hands into the infant's line of vision. It was not often the case that these deaf mothers actively sought and achieved the infant's attention before signing, and it was quite infrequent to see the mother physically orient the infant's head or body in her direction before signing.

These researchers describe the ways in which the deaf mothers ensured that the sign as well as the context were presented to the child. First, as mentioned above, they signed "within the child's pre-existing focus of attention" (p. 9). The resulting sign productions were located in some cases in the usual place of articulation for adult-directed signs, but in other cases they were made on the child rather than on the mother or in the child's signing space rather than in the mother's signing space. A second strategy was to move the object of the child's attention into a position where both object and mother's signing could be seen simultaneously by the infant. Harris and her colleagues argue that the two deaf mothers they studied employed these strategies to a very important end – they provided their infants with "opportunities to observe the relationship between signs and the social-interactional context in which the signs occur" (p. 11). Furthermore, they did so most frequently by signing within the child's pre-existing focus of attention rather than trying to change the infant's focus of attention before signing. The authors compare this finding with a similar one for hearing mothers interacting with their hearing infants: these mothers also most frequently talk about their infants' focus of attention (Harris, Jones, & Grant, 1983, 1984).

Kyle and Ackerman (1987) present data on the interactions of three deaf mothers and their infants at 12, 26, and 40 weeks of age. Video-recordings were made in a laboratory setting with mother and infant in the face-to-face position. The mothers were given two toys, a duck and a rattle, and told to interest the child in the toys but not to give the toys to the infant. The hearing status of the three infants was not reported. Like Harris and her colleagues, Kyle and Ackerman find a considerable increase in the number of signed utterances over time. Notably, between 24.8% and 38.6% of these utterances are in the "naming" category with the most common form being the single word or single sign used to designate an object. This finding, too, is in agreement with Harris and her colleagues who indicate that single sign utterances are most frequent in the signing of the two deaf mothers they studied.

In their discussion of the deaf mothers' sign utterances, Kyle and Ackerman observe that they appear to be less complex and shorter than utterances produced by three hearing mothers with hearing infants. They caution, however, that the deaf mothers are doing something during these interactions which appears quite different from the behavior of hearing mothers — they are "engaging in a whole range of movement behaviors" (p. 14). The authors note that they have not yet developed a way of analyzing these movements and their role in deaf mother-infant interaction.

Launer (1982a, b) investigated the nature of motherese in American Sign Language in her study of four deaf mother-child pairs, the youngest subject being 9 months old when the research began. One-hour videotapes were collected, primarily in the homes by deaf experimenters, and included play with toys or picture books in addition to interaction during snack or meal times. All of the children were congenitally deaf, and American Sign Language was the language of the home. Launer, like Maestas y Moores (1980), finds that the communicative strategies used by deaf parents include "positioning the body to maximize attention, interspersing nonvocal affective acts with language acts, and using alternate or simultaneous sensory modalities to communicate to a young child" (Launer, 1982b, p. 1). Launer states that when addressing children under 2 years of age, deaf mothers "accentuated their sign production in a variety of ways, especially via large sign size and extreme amounts of repetition. For any given sign appearing in the earliest tapes, movement might be repeated up to 12 times" (1982a, p. 134). She describes this early input as highly redundant and simple in structure, usually comprising only one or two signs per string. Her observations support Maestas y Moores' (1980) descriptions of deaf parents' input, including signing on the child's face or body, molding the child's hands into sign configurations and movement shapes, signing on the referent object, and, when using the pointing gesture, touching the referent person or object. Unlike Maestas y Moores, Launer rarely observes the mothers fingerspelling to their infants. She interprets this finding as suggestive of a "considerable difference in input to infants under and over six months of age" (1982a, p. 137). Launer proposes that input to younger infants may be more complex because less comprehension is expected in general.

Launer concludes that these features of sign motherese "represent efforts to increase the clarity of sign production for young children" (1982a, p. 140), with mothers focusing on a root form consisting of handshape, location, and basic movement shape of the sign. While deaf mothers repeat movement within sign forms, they do not appear to use repetition for making morphological distinctions. Furthermore, "the number of movement repetitions, the size of the sign and the manner of movement are often distorted, not highlighted, in the interest of exaggeration" (Launer, 1982b, p. 5).

Kantor (1982) collected data on two profoundly deaf infants interacting with their deaf mothers at 3-week intervals over a 10-month period of time. The youngest child was 12 months of age at the beginning of the study. Dyads were videotaped in their homes by a team of one deaf and one hearing researcher; each videotape was 1 hour in length and consisted of both free and structured play episodes. Kantor reports that these mothers modify their sign language during interaction with their infants so that it is simplified and more linear. She states that the mothers "do not use the rich modulation system of adult ASL with their young deaf children but instead offer a model of ASL that separates out these highly analytic units into their simple components" (p. 234).

Kantor also suggests that the deaf mothers' signing is modified in ways that serve to help their infants acquire the complex system of referencing which is accomplished in ASL by indexic reference and verb modulation. They do so by employing the following strategies: (a) they bring the object to which they are referring directly into the infant's visual field; (b) they use POINTing extensively, often replacing the handshape normally used in a particular lexical item with a POINT; and (c) they do not modulate verbs unless they can incorporate present objects, persons, and locations. Instead, these deaf mothers use the POINT to mark semantic and grammatical roles.

The Study

Since 1985, as part of a larger study, we have been collecting videotapes of deaf mothers interacting with their deaf babies. All of these mothers are from the Washington, DC, area and are either students, graduates, or employees of Gallaudet University. We have been interested in the interaction that occurs between these mothers and infants in face-to-face situations. Our first questions about the earliest interactions, when the infant is younger than 6 months old, have focused on the mothers' strategies for gaining and maintaining the infants' visual attention, alerting the infant, and the mothers' linguistic communication through sign language. Our observations support previous researchers' findings cited above that deaf mothers are in physical contact with their deaf infants throughout much of their interaction, engaging in a variety of touching behaviors such as tapping, stroking, tickling, and movement of the infant's limbs. They vary the type of movement, location on the infant's body, intensity and speed of movement, and rhythmic patterning of the tactile behaviors as they seek to get and maintain the infant's attention (Marlborough, 1986).

Preliminary analysis of videotapes collected in the face-to-face laboratory setting at 3 1/2 and 6 months of age suggests that these deaf mothers spend the major proportion of their interaction time (70%–80%) with a positive affective expression on their faces, compared with less than 50% for normally hearing mothers with their normally hearing infants (Meadow-Orlans, MacTurk, Prezioso, Erting, & Day, 1987). They also use their faces to engage in dialogues with their infants as well as for coactional duetting wherein mother and infant perform the same facial expressions simultaneously. The term- "-coactional duetting-" -usually refers to vocal matching in pitch and prosodic contours in the case of normally hearing mothers and infants (Papousek & Papousek, 1987). Finally, deaf mothers modify the sign language they use with their infants, producing signing that appears slower, formationally different, and grammatically less complex than the signing produced during adult-directed discourse. As reported in the studies reviewed above, the signing space is usually related to the infant's direction of gaze: if the infant is looking at the mother, she usually signs near her face rather than making use of the full signing space available in adult-directed discourse; if the infant is looking away or at an object, the mother will often sign near or on the object or reach into the infant's visual field to sign. As in baby-talk varieties of spoken language, the content is related to the immediate context, the baby's behavior, or the mother's interpretation of the infant's feelings.

Here we present an analysis of some baby-talk productions of eight deaf American mothers. We have focused on the American sign for MOTHER produced by these mothers during interaction with their deaf infants when the infants were between 5 and 23 weeks of age. Some of the videotapes were made in a laboratory at Gallaudet University and some were collected during visits to the homes.

Two deaf researchers viewed the videotapes and isolated those MOTHER signs that they judged to be qualitatively different from everyday adult-talk MOTHER signs. These 27 MOTHER signs were then analyzed along nine dimensions: distance of the mother from the infant, handshape, location, orientation of the palm, type of movement, number of movements, accompanying nonmanual behaviors, maternal affect, and duration of the sign. In addition, we located 27 MOTHER signs produced by these same deaf mothers during a videotaped interview with a deaf researcher and analyzed them along the same dimensions.

The citation forms for the two most frequently used variants of the sign MOTHER are shown in Fig. 1. Both variants are produced with a 5 hand-shape, thumb tip on the chin, and palm oriented to the right or left. They differ along the parameter of movement, however, with variant A produced by touching the chin with the thumb twice and variant B produced with a wiggling of the fingers while the thumb remains in contact with the chin. Both MOTHER sign variants, in citation form, partially block the signer's face.

When we analyzed the deaf mothers' productions of the MOTHER signs with their babies, we saw that they were not using the citation forms of these signs. Formationally, the baby-talk signs differed most noticeably on the parameter of orientation of the palm. For the purposes of our analysis, we imagined an arc, or half-circle, in front of the signer and extending from one shoulder to the other. By locating five points along the arc, from 0° to 180°, we could code five different orientations of the signer's palm as shown in Fig. 2. For example, if the MOTHER sign were produced with the thumb touching the chin and the little finger oriented toward the 0 degree point, the palm of the hand would be fully visible to the infant. If, on the other hand, the sign were made with the thumb touching the chin and the little finger oriented toward the 180° point, the back of the 5 hand would be fully visible to the infant, not the palm. At 90°, the infant would be unable to see either the palm or the back of the hand if mother were squarely in front of the infant in the face-to-face position.

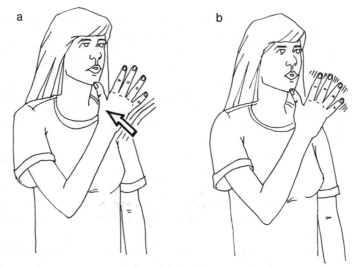

Fig. 1a,b. Citation forms for the two most frequently used variants of the American Sign Language sign MOTHER

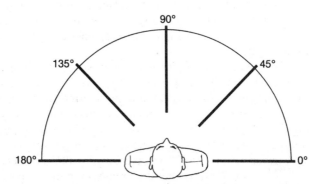

Fig. 2. Points on an arc representing five different orientations of the signer's palm

The baby-talk variants of MOTHER differed from the adult talk forms on seven of the nine dimensions analyzed as shown on Table 1. The deaf mothers produced the baby-talk MOTHER signs so that they were visible to the infants longer than the MOTHER signs that appeared during adult talk. They also showed the full palm or back of the 5 hand to the infant, making their own faces fully available for the infants to see. These mothers looked at the infant during every baby-talk MOTHER sign and expressed positive affect on their faces in every instance in which the infants were attending to them. In addition, they accompanied the manual sign with mouth movements for the English words "mother" or "mommy," with or without voice: The adult-talk MOTHER signs differed on these nonmanual dimensions: during

Table 1. Comparison of baby-talk and adult-talk MOTHER signs

	Baby-talk signs	Adult-talk signs
Distance from infant/adult	Close	No modification
Handshape	5	5
Orientation	25/27 show full palm or back of hand to infant	20/27 — palm faces right or left or slants at angle to floor
Location	11 on chin 15 to side of chin 1 not visible	19 on chin 8 to side of chin
Type of movement	27 — touch	17 — touch 8 — FW 2 — touch + FW
Number of movements	27 — 2 or more (10/27 — more than 2)	Not more than 2 (9 — 2 touches 8 — 1 touch 8 — FW)
Face/head	Face fully visible Eye gaze on infant 26/27 — mouth move- ment for word "mother" or "mommy" 12 without voice 14 with voice	9 — eyes away 8 — no mouth movement 26 — without voice 1 — with voice
Affect as expressed on the face	24/27 — positive 3/27 — neutral or negative (infant not attending)	23/27 — neutral
Duration: Range Mean	9–92 frames 24.3 frames[a]	4–25 frames 12.3 frames

Thirty frames per second. FW, fingers wiggle.
[a] $Z = 5.50, p < .001.$

nine of the 27 adult-talk productions the mothers' eyes were not on the conversational partner, facial expressions were neutral during most of these MOTHER signs, eight of the adult-talk MOTHER signs were not accompanied by mouth movements, and only one sign was produced simultaneously with voice.

While all of the 54 MOTHER signs were made with the same handshape and in the same location on or near the chin, the deaf mothers moved in close to the infant while they were signing the 27 baby-talk signs but maintained a constant distance from the interviewer during the adult-talk signing. In addition, even though both the "touch" and the "finger wiggle" variants were produced by these mothers

Table 2. Linguistic context of baby-talk signs

	(*n*)	Mothers
1. MOTHER LOVE (you)	4	B,B,C,G
2. D-O (you) LOVE (your) MOTHER	2	B,G
3. MOTHER ALWAYS WITH (you)	1	G
4. PULL-MOTHER'S-HAIR (your) MOTHER + S H-A-I-R	1	G
5. (Me) (your) MOTHER	5	C,C,S,S,S
6. (Me) MOTHER HERE	4	G,W,M,Sh
7. (Me) MOTHER	4	W,M,M,M
8. MOTHER	4	Be,Be,Be,Be
9. 2-LOOK-AT-1 (me) MOTHER	2	M,Sh

during conversation with the adult, only the "touch" variant was used with the infant. More than one-third of these baby-talk signs were executed with more than two movements (touches to the chin) while the majority of the adult talk MOTHER signs were made with only one touch or the finger wiggle movement.

In addition to the formational differences between baby-talk and adult-talk variants of MOTHERsigns, we can see in Table 2 that the linguistic context in which the baby-talk signs occur is quite specific. All of these signs are found in nine types of sentences. In fact, if we collapse sentence numbers 5–9 into one type of sentence, one which names the signer as MOTHER, we find that 19 of the 27 baby-talk signs occur in this kind of linguistic context. The adult-talk MOTHER signs, however, appear in a variety of linguistic contexts.

Conclusion

We have presented some evidence that these American deaf mothers modify the sign language they use with their deaf infants under the age of 6 months at least some of the time. When producing the sign MOTHER in baby talk, they (a) place the sign closer to the infant, perhaps the optimal signing distance for visual processing; (b) orient the hand so that the full 5 handshape is visible to the infant; (c) the face, too, is fully available for the infant to see; (d) eye gaze is directed at the infant; (e) the expression on the face is positive and inviting, possibly serving to maintain the infant's interest and engagement while the sign is displayed; (f) the sign is lengthened by repeating the movement, allowing the infant more time to see the sign.

This study adds support to the claim that parents use special articulatory features in their communication with infants (Blount, 1982) including parents from a visual culture whose primary means of communication is visual-gestural rather than auditory-vocal. These deaf mothers have the cultural knowledge about how to interact with their infants in this special environment in order to get and maintain their attention, to focus their attention on signing as an activity, and to begin to relate the interaction to the environment in a meaningful way. We see, then, that during the first months of life, deaf infants who have deaf, signing parents are acquiring the necessary foundation for further language socialization through interaction which is structured according to the requirements of a visual-gestural language.

CHAPTER 9

Acquisition of the Handshape in American Sign Language: A Preliminary Analysis

P. BOYES BRAEM

Introduction

This is a report of an unpublished pilot study (Boyes Braem, 1973) in which hypotheses about stages of acquisition of the handshapes of American Sign Language (ASL) are proposed and are tested against data from one deaf child. The data come from a videotape made by Dr. Ursula Bellugi at Salk Institute (San Diego, Ca.) of a congenitally deaf daughter of deaf parents fluent in ASL. The child was 2; 7 years old at the time of this taping and is called Pola in this study.

Due to the lengthy transcription time necessary to note the details of the handshapes, the data for this pilot study is based on a 1-h tape. All the data reported upon here are based on the observations and judgements of the author of this study. The combination of these factors — one child, 1 h of taped data, one transcriber — result in the preliminary and tentative nature of the hypotheses proposed about the nature of handshape acquisition. In the last section of this report, other studies on handshape acquisition, made after 1973, will be briefly discussed in light of the hypotheses of this study.

Hypotheses on the Acquisition of the Handshape

Primary Factors Involved in the Developmental Control of the Handshapes

The published studies on finger differentiation do not discuss specific factors which might determine the order of finger differentiation, but only suggest general influences such as the development of a body schema (Lefford cited in Connolly & Jones, 1970) and the ability to analyze external space (Kinsbourne & Warrington, 1963).

Two other factors present themselves as logical candidates for primary influences on the order of the differentiation and control of the fingers: (a) the anatomy of the hand; and (b) the complication of the image that the handshape represents (primarily whether the same features are applied to adjacent digits or to digits out of serial order).

Anatomical Factors and Handshape Control

The question posed here is to what extent does the anatomy of the hand determine independent movement and control of the digits? The thumb is the most independent of the digits having a highly mobile and independently articulated carpometacarpal saddle joint unlike the fingers whose carpometacarpal joints allow only a limited amount of freedom. This unique joint allows the opposition of the thumb. In addition, the muscles to the thumb are all completely independent of the muscles branching to the other digits.

The first finger is extended by a tendon from the long extensor digitorum muscle which has tendons going to all four fingers. In addition, however, the first finger has a separate extensor, the *extensor indicus*. The flexor muscle for the index finger originates in the forearm in the common flexor muscle for all the fingers. However, the part of this long muscle that flexes the index finger branches off in the forearm, whereas the tendons going to the second, third, and fourth fingers do not branch apart until the level of the wrist.

The little finger shares some of the advantages of the thumb and first finger. It has a carpometacarpal joint similar to the thumb's saddle joint although not with the same degree of mobility that the thumb has. The little finger cannot achieve true opposition, but its joint does allow more rotation than the other fingers are capable of. While the little finger has a tendon from the common *extensor digitorum*, it — like the index finger — also has an additional and separate extensor muscle (*extensor indicus*).

The least independent fingers, the middle and ring, have fairly immobile joints and no separate extensors or flexors. They are extended by tendons from the common long *extensor digitorum* but their movement is limited by intertendinous connections which bind together the middle and ring fingers and, to some extent, the ring and little fingers.

The nature of the musculature and joints of the hand indicate that independent movement of the digits may be conceived of as illustrated in Fig. 1: beginning in the inner rectangle one finds the anatomically most *inter*dependent digits, moving out to the most *in*dependent digit, the thumb, in the outer rectangle. Because the thumb and first finger are the most independently articulated, they will be treated as a group called the "radial group," being on the same side of the arm as the radius bone. The more interdependent second, third, and fourth fingers are referred to as the "ulnar" group, being on the ulnar bone side of the arm.

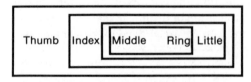

Fig. 1. Anatomical interdependency of the digits

Developmental studies have shown (Swan, 1936) that the index finger is the first digit to show independent movement (at 4 weeks) followed by the thumb (8 weeks), and little finger. The second and third fingers are the last to show independent movement. Thus, the first fingers to be moved and controlled independently by the infant are also those which are anatomically most independent.

It is proposed that the same anatomical interrelatedness of the digits which seems to influence which handshapes are independently controlled first by infants could also influence the order of handshape acquisition in sign language. Thus, one would expect the child first to learn handshapes which require the manipulation of the hand as a whole. Then one would expect the child to master the independent manipulation of the index finger and thumb, with the other three ulnar digits acting together as a group (as they do in the infant's early "palmar grasps"). The little finger is liberated next from the ulnar group followed, finally, by independent manipulation of the middle and ring fingers.

The anatomical interdependence of the digits means that the child must learn not only to extend specific fingers, but also to inhibit the fingers connected to the ones he or she wishes to extend. This is not much of a problem with the independent thumb and index finger but is a factor when the child is trying to operate independently the anatomically interdependent ulnar group of fingers. A further prediction would therefore be that the handshapes which require the *inhibition* of the digits in the inner circles of the rectangle (Fig. 1) will be more difficult and are acquired at later stages.

Cognitive Factors: The Idea of Finger Order

The child can usually oppose fingers serially before differentially (Lefford, cited in Connolly & Jones, 1970). That is, he or she can begin with opposition with the first finger, go on to the second, etc. However, he or she cannot begin directly with the third finger. To oppose a finger out of this serial order successfully requires the beginning of the idea of positional ordination among the fingers. Thus, one would predict that a handshape such as ASL 8 would be acquired fairly late, since in order to oppose the thumb to the required middle digit, the child must have some ordered image of his or her fingers.

This concept of order is not only necessary for finger-thumb oppositions, but for any of the handshapes which involve the manipulation of nonadjacent digits. Thus, one would predict that the extension of the relatively independent but nonadjacent thumb and little finger (the Y handshape) will be acquired later than the extension of the also independent but adjacent thumb and index finger (handshapes L, bO).

Of the two primary factors influencing individual finger differentiation and control mentioned in this section, one would predict the purely anatomical factors to be the major limiting influence in the early stages of acquisition, while in the later stages the more important restraints will become the cognitive factors of positional ordination.

Proposed Model of Stages of Handshape Acquisition

Descriptive Feature System

The feature system proposed here is based primarily on the anatomical factors described in the previous section. The A handshape, in which the fingers are flexed against the palm and the thumb flexed loosely against the side of the forefinger, is considered to be the most unmarked handform as it is most similar to the resting position of the adult hand in which all the muscles are in tonic balance (Jones, 1942). This resting position of the adult hand differs slightly from the A handshape in sign language in that the index finger is slightly extended and the other fingers are not completely flexed into the palm. In the infant, however, the fingers are usually held more flexed and more closely resemble the A handshape. Halverson (1937) reports that the infant's hand often has to be pried open for an object to be inserted. Even the early swiping movements are done with the A handshape (Twitchell, cited in Connolly & Jones, 1970). The proximity of the thumb to the first finger occurs not only in the child's resting position but is characteristic of all handshapes in early infancy, even those used for grasping [a kind of "palmar grasp" (handshape B closes to A) cf., Gesell & Halverson, 1936].

The acquisition of handshapes will be described here as the acquisition of features which are applied to the unmarked A handshape. Eight features are proposed for this developmental model: *+Opposition; +Full Extension; +Partial Extension; +Close; + Contact of fingertip(s) with opposed thumb; +Contact of knuckle with thumb; +Insertion of thumb between two fingers; +Crossing of adjacent fingers.*

For notation purposes, the index finger is labelled finger 1, the middle finger is finger 2, the ring finger is finger 3, and the little finger is finger 4. When the features are written out, the finger(s) to which the feature is applied appears as a superscript, (e.g., $+ Ext^1$ means only the index finger is extended; $+ Ext^{all}$ means all fingers plus the thumb are extended). See the Appendix for more information on the notation system.

Predicted Stages of Acquisition of Handshapes

Most studies of motor development are on a level far too general to be of much use in the study of handshape acquisition (a typical example of generality is from Illingworth's study: "At 3.0 the child can help to set the table, not dropping china" (1966). The early studies of grasping, however, are useful in indicating when the handshapes which are found in the first stage of sign language acquisition come under voluntary control, Gesell and Halverson (1936) report that the infant disassociates the thumb from the forefinger for the first time at 28 weeks. The infant, given a rod to grasp, originally puts his thumb in front of the rod, grasping it with what is essentially an A handshape. At 28 weeks, the child begins to put the thumb behind the rod. This means he can put the thumb in the position of opposition required for the S handshape.

The L, baby O (bO), and G handshapes probably come under voluntary control between the 32nd and 52nd weeks when the infant shows a shift of preference from using the ulnar group of digits (fingers 2, 3 and 4) to using the radial digits (index and thumb). Before 32 weeks, the infant's grasp reflex involves pressing the ulnar fingers against the ulnar side of the palm (this is, again, essentially a palmar grasp with an A handshape). The true voluntary grasp response begins when the infant opposes the thumb to the ulnar digits but soon switches (at about 32 weeks) to opposition with the more independent radial digits. At the same time, the child learns to use the sensitive fingertips instead of the palm for grasping in what may be called a proximal-distal shift.

The result of these ulnar-radial and proximal-distal shifts in the last half of the 1st year is that the child can now extend the thumb and forefinger independently of the other fingers (corresponding roughly to handshapes L and G) and achieve contact between the first finger and opposed (bO handshape). If one does measurements on Flory's 1935 photographs of the osseous development of the hand, one finds that the child at 2;0 years has a thumb that is slightly longer in proportion to the second and fourth fingers than is true of an 8;0-year-old. This proportionally longer thumb would mean that contact with the finger at 2 years requires less flexion at the phalangial joints of the fingers than at 8 years. Thus, the early bO and O handshapes are more likely to be "flat" — as in the adult ASL handshape in BIRD.

The 5 handshape requires full extension and the C handshape, partial extension of all the digits. Halverson (1937) points out that the flexors are the dominant muscles of infancy and the fingers only gradually extend as the child develops. The infant almost never voluntarily releases an object he or she has grasped before 24 weeks. The voluntary release usually appears between 36 and 48 weeks. Until he or she is almost 1 year old, then, the child can voluntarily flex his or her fingers quite easily but cannot freely extend them. One would expect, therefore, that the fully extended 5 handshape would be one of the last of this first group of handshapes to come under control. As the C handshape requires only partial extension of all the fingers, the fingers are also still involuntarily adducted due to the associated movement of adduction with flexion. The C handshape does not require the feature of + Close, this being redundant with partial extension.

Stage I: S,L,bO,G,5,C

The handshapes mastered in this first stage (Fig. 2) involve the manipulation of the hand as a whole and of the radial group of fingers. Hence, little or no inhibition of movement is necessary. The child is probably able to perform all these handshapes before he or she is ready to begin symbolic communication. Throughout the 1st year of life, the infant initially uses these handshapes for pointing, picking up and grasping objects, probing, and generally exploring his or her environment. For example, the child is able to pick up objects in a pincer grasp (similar to a bO handshape) by 8 months (Twitchell, cited in Cannolly & Jones, 1970). By 10 months, he or she is fully extending the index finger for pointing

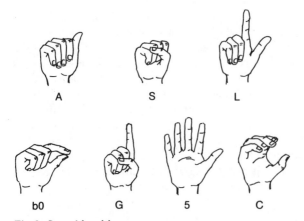

Fig. 2. Stage 1 handshapes

(Shinn, cited in Werner & Kaplan, 1963), as well as being able to fully extend all the digits in order to voluntarily release objects he or she has grasped. The ability to extend the first finger in a pointing gesture is also a preliminary stage in the child's development of visually directed reaching (Halverson, 1933). The handshapes of this first stage are thus firmly embedded in other behaviors before the child uses them for the new function of linguistic communication.

By the end of the 1st year, then, all children, no matter what language they are exposed to, have the physical control of the following handshapes for nonlinguistic as well as linguistic purposes: A, S, L, G, bO, C and 5. These handshapes involve combinations of the following features applied either to all the digits as a group, or to the most independent radial digits, the thumb and index finger:

+ Full extension of all the digits (as in 5) as well as the independent index and thumb (as in G and L)
+ Partial extension of all the digits (as in C) and of the index and thumb (bO)
+ Opposition (applied to the unmarked A handshape as in S; opposing the thumb to the most independent finger, as in bO)
+ Contact of the index finger with the thumb (as in bO).

Stage II: B,F,O

Most of the handshapes acquired after Stage I, except perhaps for the B handshape, are not ones that are as frequently used in the young child's normal exploration of his or her environment. Thus, after Stage I, the child can no longer rely on adapting handshapes he or she already uses often in his or her daily life to the function of linguistic communication. The least complicated of all the handshapes beyond Stage I are the B, F and O handshapes (Fig. 3). These

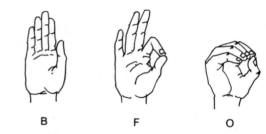

Fig. 3. Stage II handshapes   B   F   O

handshapes involve the acquisition of the following features applied to specific digits:

+ Close (for the B handshape)
+ Extension of the ulnar fingers as a group (2 + 3 + 4) in the F handshape
+ Contact of the opposed thumb with all the fingers (as in O).

One would expect the handshapes of stage II to be fully mastered about the time the child is cognitively ready to begin symbolic communication, probably corresponding to the hearing child's age of initial language acquisition.

Stage III: (I, Y) (D, P, 3, V, H) W

In stages I and II, only the highly independent thumb and index finger are manipulated separately; the three ulnar fingers are treated as a unit. In stage III (Fig. 4), the child begins to differentiate the individual fingers beyond what is

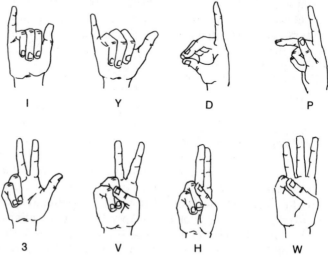

Fig. 4. Stage III handshapes

required for the early and highly functional bO pincer grasp handshape. This means that groups of fingers are inhibited as well as activated. In terms of inhibition, there are three subgroups in this stage: inhibition of fingers $1+2+3$ (in handshapes I and Y), inhibition of fingers $3+4$(in D,P,3,V,H), and inhibition of finger 4(W). The handshapes in this stage seem to fall into three subgroups (I,Y), (D,P,3,V,H) (W) which are probably mastered at slightly different times:

— The fourth finger is probably the first of the ulnar group to be used independently as its articulation makes it the most freely moveable. Consequently, handshapes I and Y are probably performed correctly by the child early in stage III, when not influenced by the movement of the sign.
— The D handshape is more complicated than the I or Y handshape in that it involves extension and manipulation of three separate groups of digits: the index finger must be fully extended at the same time as the thumb is put into opposition to the second finger which is partially extended. One would expect the child initially to simplify this handshape by partially extending all the ulnar fingers which then contact the opposed thumb (resulting in the O handshape with extended index finger).
— The P handshape is even more complicated in that the full extension of the second finger brings it into more acute opposition with the other ulnar fingers which are flexed into the palm. In addition, the opposed thumb makes contact with the knuckle of the second finger rather than the fingertip, thus requiring an accurate sense of finger ordination.
— The 3, V, and H handshapes all involve the breaking away of the middle finger from the ulnar group, thus implicating inhibition of the two other ulnar fingers.
— The W handshape involves the inhibition of the fourth finger and thumb.

In stage III, the child learns to apply the following features:
+ Extension to individual fingers of the ulnar group with accompanying inhibition of unextended fingers (fingers which are inhibited are shown in parentheses):

$+ \text{Ext-Full}^{4\,(2,3)} = \text{I,Y}$

$+ \text{Ext-Full}^{2\,(3,4)} = \text{3,V,H,D}$

$+ \text{Ext-Full}^{2,3\,(4)} = \text{W}.$

Stage IV: (8, 7), X, R, (T,M,N)

In this last stage (Fig. 5), the child learns to activate and inhibit independently and out of serial order the weakest of the ulnar group, fingers 2 and 3. He or she also learns to apply the features of + Cross and + Insertion. The difficulty of the 8 and 7 handshapes is not so much the independent manipulation of the middle finger (this was already being done in stage II for the D,P, and 3 handshapes), but the contact of the thumb with a finger which is in the middle of the series of fingers. Thus, 7 and 8 handshapes require an idea of finger order.

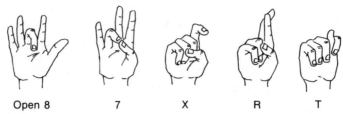

Open 8   7   X   R   T

Fig. 5. Stage IV handshapes

Handshape T also requires some notion of finger position in order to determine between which fingers the thumb is to be inserted (insertion between fingers 2 and 3 will result in an N handshape, between 3 and 4 = M). As discussed earlier, the crossing of the fingers in the R handshape is physically difficult to produce.

The X handshape involves the partial extension of the index finger. While this feature applied to the index finger has already been mastered in earlier stages in the bO handshape, here the combination of features does not involve any contact with the thumb, making the X more difficult to produce for the young child. (See the next section for a discussion of the preference for tactile over perceptual feedback as a factor in handshape production.)

Secondary Factors Influencing the Production of the Handshape

A child can often perform the routine of going through the fingerspelled alphabet (or copy the parent's model) but cannot correctly use these hand configurations during spontaneous signing. In contrast to fingerspelling, spontaneous signing requires that handshapes be combined with different movements, orientations, and positions. Some combinations are very likely to be physically and/or cognitively more difficult for the child than others. Furthermore, a child can often perform a skill or task quite accurately if there is no time constraint, but performance often deteriorates once the child is under time pressure. The pressures of communicating a proposition impose such a time constraint for the child.

In this section, I will discuss six secondary factors which seem to influence how the child produces handshapes in the context of spontaneous signing. These factors are proposed as explanations of many of the handshape substitutions which are found in the data of this study.

—   Preference for fingertip contact
—   Nature of the feedback
—   Nature of the movement
—   Pantomime/classifiers
—   Anticipation and retention of the adjacent handshape
—   Sympathetic thumb extension.

The handshape substitutions caused by these factors are always handshapes already within the child's repertoire. The first three factors force a substitution to an equally simple handshape or a more simple form; that is, to forms from the child's current stage of acquisition or from earlier stages. For example, an 8 handshape is not substituted for a Y handshape; rather, the easier and previously acquired 5 handshape would be substituted.

Preference for Fingertip Contact

Preference for fingertip contact means the child will substitute contact with the tip of the finger, particularly the index finger, for contact with other parts of the hand. For example, for the sign SHOE, whose citation form requires two S hands which make contact at the side of the hand, the child in this study substitutes two bO handshapes and then brings the two hands together to contact at the fingertips. There are also frequent substitutions of the bO handshapes in signs requiring the O handshape.

The preference for fingertip contact over contact with other parts of the hand is readily understandable as the papillary ridges of the fingertips are richly supplied with sensors. That the child prefers first fingertip contact over that of the other digits is explained by the early independence of the index and its long history of pointing, touching, and exploring functions for the child. Berges and Lezine (1965) found the same preference for index contact in their studies of gesture imitation with much older hearing children.

Influence of the Nature of the Feedback

In situations where visual feedback of the child's own signs is not possible, he or she can rely on two other forms of feedback: (1) tactile (cutaneous and surface impressions received from simple contact and pressure with another object); and (b) kinesthetic (information received from sensors in the muscles and joints). Haptic feedback refers to the combination of tactile plus kinesthetic feedback.

If the sign is made in a place which the child cannot visually monitor (i.e., the head or face), the handshape is often reduced to a more simple form. For example, the sign BLACK, normally made with a G hand drawn across the forehead, is made by the child with a 5 handshape (with a change in the orientation of the palm to away from the body). Instead of making the sign HORSE with the required H handshape on the head, he or she substitutes a G. WATER is made on the mouth with a 5 handshape instead of the required W.

Several studies indicate that, especially for young children, visual cues dominate kinesthetic and tactile cues in recognition and performance tasks. Lefford cited in Connoly & Jones (1970) found that until the child is 4 years old, the removal of visual cues in thumb-finger opposition tasks makes the task considerably more difficult. Millar (1964) found in a recognition task testing intersensory integration that 3-year-olds could make no use of haptic feedback even for haptic recognition of objects. When cues were presented haptically and visually, there was no improvement in haptic recognition over cues presented only visually. This seems to indicate that there is a visual cue dominance at this age level and no intersensory transfer of information. By the age of 4, there is some indication of cross-modal transfer as the addition of visual to haptic cues does improve haptic recognition over that from haptic cues alone. In another recognition study, Birch and Lefford (1963) found that by age 5, visual-haptic intersensory functioning was well developed. For the child to perform correctly a sign which he or she is not able to monitor visually requires, then, a prior establishment of an intersensory integration between visual and haptic systems.

Adults also rely on visual over haptic cues when learning a new skill. Fleishman and Rich (1963) found that spatial and visual cues were more helpful early in the learning of a new skill while proprioceptive feedback was relied upon more in later learning. One possible explanation for this early dominance of visual feedback in learning is that while rehearsal or attention aids retention for visual data, rehearsal of kinesthetic data does not aid retention (Posner, 1967).

There are many indications that the child in this study relies more on tactile than kinesthetic information. In her substitutions of a 5 handshape for G in BLACK, for instance, she ignores the kinesthetic information that five fingers are being extended but maintains the appropriate contact between her first finger and her forehead. Similarly when making HORSE on her head, she maintains the required contact of the tip of the thumb with the head, but substitutes a G handshape for the required H.

Studies of hearing children have indicated a general early reliance on tactile over kinesthetic information, Birch and Lefford (1967) found that 5-year-old hearing children in visual recognition tasks had overall increases in errors when cues were presented kinesthetically rather than haptically. They concluded that while 5-year-old children have cross-modal transfer between visual and haptic systems, the integration of visual and kinesthetic systems does not occur until several years later.

Influence of the Movement Component of the Sign

There are some cases in which a complicated movement seems to force a simplification of the handshape. For example, the sign PRETTY requires a 5 handshape held in front of the face, with the fingers successively closing, while the hand simultaneously twists inwards. The child in this study simplifies all this by maintaining a B handshape throughout the sign and only twisting the wrist.

Pantomime/Classifiers

The kinds of signs under discussion here are illustrated by an example in which the child in this study substitutes the handshape bO for B in a sign glossed as OFF. This substitution indicates exactly how the tail of the toy she was describing was probably grasped and torn off. In the 1973 version of this paper, these handshapes were described as a kind of pantomimic conflation of the verb, manner, patient, and agent into one sign, PINCH-OFF-TAIL. It was noted that in such substitutions the child never substitutes a handshape which is not already in her phonological system. Since that time, linguists have begun using the term "classifier" handshapes for such cases (e.g., Kegl & Wilbur, 1976; Supalla, 1982). The acquisition study by Kantor (1980) indicates that handshapes used as classifiers are not acquired as lexical items but as a complex syntactic process and must be analyzed as subject to more than the physical and cognitive constraints proposed here.

Anticipation and Retention

Many substitutions in child as well as adult signing are motivated by an anticipation or retention of an adjacent handshape in the string of signs. For instance, in the string URSIE (H) EAT (flat O), the child retained the H handshape of URSIE for the following sign EAT. All substitutions for deictic pronouns requiring the G handshape (THIS, HER, THERE, etc.) were due to either anticipation or retention. Both anticipation and retention are used about equally often; substitutions however, were never made from other than adjacent handshapes.

Sympathetic Thumb Extension

When the sign requires that the first finger alone is extended, the other radial digit, the thumb, is often also extended by the child in several signs. Termed here "sympathetic thumb extension," this is probably a failure of the child in early stages to inhibit extension of the most independent digit (the thumb) while extending the second most independent digit (the index).

Analysis of the Data in Terms of the Proposed Model

The handshape data from the 1-h tape of Pola's signing at age 2;7 is discussed in terms of the acquisition stages described in the previous section. Each handshape is analyzed in terms of

- The percentage of time it was used correctly when required by the adult sign
- The number of times it was used for substitutions by the child
- Its frequency (i.e., its percentage of all occurrences of all handshapes in the data)
- The percentage of the child's vocabulary that it represents
- The percentage of the adult vocabulary that it represents.

The percentage of correct use when required by the adult sign was arrived at in the following way: the number of *adult forms actually used* = total occurrences minus occurrences not required; the number of *required adult forms* = number of adult forms used plus the number required but for which substitutions were made; *percentage correct* = the number of adult forms used divided by the number of adult forms required; *percentage of substitutions* = number of forms which occurred but were not required divided by the total number of substitutions.

The percentage of handshapes used correctly does not give much information unless the errors are also investigated. Errors are divided into two groups: (a) those that are motivated by the secondary factors described earlier; and (b) all other errors.

The second group of errors almost aways results in substitutions of a handshape from an earlier stage. This is a strong argument for the reality of the stages proposed, as it indicates that this group of errors require handshapes which the child has not yet acquired at the time of observation. Not only are these substitutions from an earlier stage, but they are also handshapes that are related phonologically to the more difficult handshape. For example, if the difficult handshape involves extension of only two fingers, as in handshape Y, the child will apply the feature of extension to the hand as a whole, resulting in the 5 handshape.

Another way of getting at the same information about the validity of the stages is to note the number of times the handshape is used for substitutions. The handshapes from stages I and II are extremely popular substitutes, while substitutes from the more difficult groups of stages III rarely occur in this data and handshapes from stage IV never occur.

Frequency of use of the handshape on the tape is also some indication of validity of the stages. However, comparing the percentage of Pola's vocabulary that each handshape represents with the frequency of the handshape in the adult vocabulary, calculated by the signs listed in the *Dictionary of American Sign Language* (Stokoe, Casterline, & Croneberg, 1965), one finds that in most cases frequency of appearance in the child data equals frequency of appearance in the adult vocabulary. This makes the frequency of appearance in the lexicon a rather slippery argument to use in support of the proposed stages of acquisition. The child might use an overwhelming number of handshapes from stage I not only because they are physically easier, but because that is what is seen most often. There is, of course, a highly probable connection between the fact that the most physically and cognitively difficult handshapes are also those which are rare in adult sign languages.

Stage I Data: A, S, L, bO, G, 5, C

Stage I, illustrated in Table 1, begins with the unmarked A handshape and then develops extension of the hand as a whole (5 and C handshapes) and independent manipulation of the radial finger group (S, L, bO, and G handshapes). This group of handshapes represents 49% of Pola's vocabulary and 44% of the adult vocabulary. Pola also uses this group of handshapes very often for substitutions (76% of all substitutions come from stage I handshapes).

Table 1. Stage I handshape data (A, S, L, bO, G, 5, C)

Hand	Required Correct (2)	Correct (%)	Used for substitution (1)	Percentage of all substitutions (n = 124) (%)	Occurences (1)	Percentage of all occurrences (n = 593) (%)	Percentage of child vocabulary (%)	Percentage of adult vocabulary (%)
A	15/15	100	8	6	23	4	2	14?
S	15/31	48	1		16	3	7	?
L	7/8	88	14	11	24	4	1	3
bO	8/8	100	38	31	46	8	3	?
G	234/251	93	12	9	246	41	17	12
5	30/32	94	15	12	45	8	116	17
5	28/44	64	3	2	31	5		
C	9/9	100	8	6	17	3	3	8

Handshape A. Pola made no errors with the A handshape when it was required by the adult sign. It is a relatively frequent handshape for substitution purposes, but not as popular as the G and bO handshapes. This could be because the latter two handshapes, unlike A, also allow the child to use the preferred forefinger contact.

Handshape S. The S handshape does not seem to be a very well acquired handshape if one looks at its rate of successful production when required (48%). However, all but four errors in S were due to secondary factors – either incorporation of an intense manner (E and 5 handshapes are both substituted for S in BREAK) or preference for forefinger contact (in substitutions of bO for S in BREAK and SHOE). Of the four substitutions not influenced by secondary factors, two were to the primitive A handshape in the sign ORANGE. The A and S handshapes are very closely related phonologically and are possibly allophones. In two occurrences of ICE CREAM, the required S is changed into a 3 handshape, substitutions which are inexplicable by any of the factors previously proposed.

Handshape L. Pola made only one mistake when an L handshape was required in which she substituted G for L in WHO. Stokoe et al. (1965) note that G is an accepted form in some dialects for WHO; perhaps Pola was exposed to this form in adult signing. The L handshape is one of the most frequent forms for substitutions (11%). All substitutions but one to the L handshape were made from the G handshape in sympathetic thumb extension. What this probably indicates is that the L is perhaps a more primitive form than G. (It would be interesting to observe closely all early infant pointing gestures to see if their form is actually more of a loose L than a pure G handshape.) L was once substituted for H in the sign BUTTER, which might again have been influenced by a preference for forefinger contact, combined with a sympathetic thumb extension.

Handshape G. The G handshape is by far the most frequently seen handshape on the tape (occurring 234 times), largely because it is used for all deictic references. Very few errors are made with the use of G in nondeictic signs, and most of these errors can be accounted for by reliance on tactile over kinesthetic feedback. For example, the 5 handshape is substituted for G in BLACK, a sign made on the forehead. The sympathetic thumb extension converts some G handshapes into L. All deictic G errors but one are due to anticipation or retention of an adjacent handshape. The one exception to this is an error in which the right hand mirrors the left hand handshape.

Handshape bO. Baby O, essentially a pincer grasp, is a typical child handshape and accounts for 31% of all substitutions made. Most of these bO substitutions are for a required O handshape in signs which children frequently use (e.g., MORE, SHOE, EAT, HOME). The use of the bO means that the index fingertip is the point of contact, in contrast to the O handshape, in which all the fingertips form the contact.

Handshape 5. Pola makes only two mistakes in her use of the 5 handshape. She substitutes a C in WANT, which could be a way of incorporating the meaning "a lesser degree of wanting." For PRETTY, a B handshape was substituted for the required 5, which might be an example of a difficult movement (closing of fingers combined with hand rotation) influencing the handshape produced. By using the B handshape, the child has reduced the required movement to simple hand rotation. An A handshape was substituted for 5 in WHITE. The substitution would not be predicted if preference for forefinger contact were the influential factor here, as the adult version of the sign requires index (or all) fingertip contact of the 5 hand with the chest, followed by moving the arm straight out in front of the signer, simultaneously closing the 5 into an O handshape. What Pola might be doing in her substitution of A for 5 in this sign is again reducing a rather complex movement (movement of arm plus simultaneous movement of fingers) into the movement of the arm alone. This is also an example of substitution of large muscle for small muscle movement. At the same time, she is simplifying her handshape by using the primitive A form. The 5 handshape was used fairly often as a substitute (12%). These were all from more marked handshapes from later stages and often influenced by the movement (as in PLAY), by reliance on tactile over kinesthetic feedback (as in the substitution of 5 for S in CRACKER, made on the elbow), or by incorporation of a manner (as for intensity in BREAK).

Handshape C. The C handshape was used correctly all the time. It was often (seven times) used as a substitute for the more fully extended 5 handshape. Once, the C handshape was substituted for the open 8 handshape in the sign LIKE, which again might be an example of the substitution of an earlier and less marked form for a more marked later form.

Stage II Data: B, F, O

In stage II (Table 2), the child learns the feature + Close (for handshape B), learns to apply extension to the ulnar finger group (for handshape F), learns to overcome preference for forefinger contact, and learns to apply contact with the thumb to all the fingers simultaneously (O).

Handshape B. All five errors in the use of the B handshape were due to secondary factors (anticipation and retention, pantomime, influence from the movement). The B handshape is not a particularly popular substitute probably because if the child is going to regress to the very early forms, he or she will choose a 5 rather than B, perhaps as 5 does not require the feature of + Close. For instance, most signs requiring the Y handshape are made by Pola with a 5. In one rendering of YELLOW, however, she does use a B handshape.

Handshape F. The F handshape is never required by the signs on this tape. This is probably because F represents only 4% of the adult vocabulary and Pola does not see or know many signs requiring this as an initial handshape. The four occurrences of F are as a final handshape of a sign in which a finger opening movement is involved. What F might represent to the child at this stage is the result of a partial opening of the hand (extension of the ulnar group) from a bO or an O handshape. For example, Pola does ELEPHANT with an initial O handshape, moving the arm in an arc up from the face and partially opening up the fingers at the end of the arc (or trunk) into an F. The extension of the arm might contribute to a kind of sympathetic partial extension of the fingers. In another place, when making the sign BOY, she begins with the O handshape and flicks it partially open into an F. A more complicated occurrence is in the sign string, THAT-OFF, where she is showing that the tail of a toy has been torn off. In the immediately preceding string, she has signed the same thing, using a 5 handshape as an intense rendering of OFF. In the next string, then, she points at the tail, then imitates grasping of the tail (bO) and − still holding the imaginary tail − goes into a partial sign for OFF. The F handshape here is essentially a grasp hand used in classificatory way (BREAK-OFF-SMALL-OBJECT). In any case, the F hand-shape does not seem physically difficult for the child at this stage. While the ulnar fingers must be manipulated, they are manipulated as a unit and only the feature of extension is applied to them.

Table 2. Stage II handshape data (B, F, O)

Hand	Required Correct (2)	Correct (%)	Used for substitution (1)	Percentage of all substitutions ($n = 124$) (%)	Occurences (1)	Percentage of all occurrences ($n = 593$) (%)	Percentage of child vocabulary (%)	Percentage of adult vocabulary (%)
B	61/66	95	2	2	63	10	20	21
F	0/0	0	3	2	3	< 1	< 1	4
O	16/48	33	5	4	21	4	16	7

Handshape O. The O handshape is correctly performed only 33% of the time. This is due primarily to bO substitutions for O. Not only does bO allow the child forefinger contact but it is probably somewhat easier to control physically. The anatomy of the hand allows simple partial extension of the first finger to result in thumb contact while simple partial extension of the ulnar fingers results in no contact with the thumb. To achieve an O, the ulnar fingers must adduct more than what is naturally associated with flexion in order to make contact with the tip of the thumb. In only one instance is bO not substituted for O. In the string, URSIE EAT, Pola retains the H from the name sign URSIE and uses it for the handshape in EAT. Pola uses signs requiring O for 16% of the signs in this tape, as compared with 7% O handshape signs in the ASL dictionary. Perhaps this is influenced by the fact that many of the concepts which a child of this age tries to talk about (eat, food, home, more) require an O handshape.

Stage III Data: I, Y, D, P, 3, V, H, W

The handshapes in stage III (Table 3) all involve manipulation of individual fingers in the ulnar group. This means that some digits are inhibited while others are activated. The feature of + Contact with knuckle is also added in this stage.

Subgroup: I, Y (Inhibition of Fingers 2 and 3). There is no required I handshape on the tape and Pola never uses this handshape for substitution purposes. The Y handshape is required seven times, and Pola never gets it right. When combined with a difficult movement (such as twisting of the hand) the Y goes to 5 or B (PLAY, YELLOW). When made on a part of her body which she cannot see, she relies on tactile feedback and the Y becomes an A (TELEPHONE, done on the cheek, contact made with the knuckles) or a 5 (COW done on the side of the head).

Table 3. Stage III handshape data (I, Y, D, P, 3, V, H, W)

Hand	Required Correct (2)	Correct (%)	Used for substitution (1)	Percentage of all substitutions (n = 124) (%)	Occurences (1)	Percentage of all occurrences (n = 593) (%)	Percentage of child vocabulary (%)	Percentage of adult vocabulary (%)
I	0/0	0	0	0	0	0	0	1
Y	0/7	0	0	0	0	0	3	5
D	13/13	100	0	0	13	2	7	5
P	2/4	50	0	0	2	1	2	2
3	11/11	100	12	9	23	4	<1	1
V	0/4	0	1	<1	1	<1	3	5
H	18/27	66	1	<1	19	3	7	3
W	0/1	0	0	0	1	<1	1	1

Subgroup: (D, P) (3, V, H) (Inhibition of Fingers 3 and 4). Pola executes D correctly 100% of the time, but all these are instances of one sign – the name sign DARLENE, which requires contact of the tips 2,3,4, and thumb with the face. In one occurrence, Pola substitutes first fingertip contact for the required contact. D is never used as a substitute for other handshapes. How often P is done correctly is difficult to assess as the hand is usually held in such a way that + Contact is hard to determine from the tape. It is usually substituted for by a 3 handshape, but there are a couple of occurrences in which a true P could have been used. P is never used as a substitute for another handshape. It accounts for less than 2% of both child and adult vocabulary. The 3 handshape is always correct when required, but also provides 9% of all substitutions. All but two of these substitutions are from handshapes in the phonologically related subgroup (H,V,P). What could be happening is a failure to restrain extension of the thumb with the extension of the other fingers (sympathetic thumb extension). This occurs both in places where the child cannot visually monitor her sign (e.g., near the eye in SEE) and in places where she can monitor her handshape (TRAIN, CHAIR, or POTATO done in neutral space). Another explanation for the substitution of the 3 handshape in these signs is that the 3 hand is a variant form in the adult models to which the child is exposed. In the V handshape, Pola never seems to be able to inhibit the extension of her thumb. In all four signs requiring V, she substitutes either a 3 or a 5 handshape. The same failure to inhibit the thumb accounts for five of the nine errors in the H handshape. Three other errors are accounted for by reliance on tactile over kinesthetic feedback (HORSE and RABBIT, both done on the side of the head, are done by Pola with a G handshape), and preference for first fingertip contact (READ, which requires an H handshape goes to G). The final error, substituting a V for an H in TRAIN, is the failure to apply the feature of + Close.

Subgroup: W (Inhibition of Finger 4). The W handshape is required only once, for WATER, made on the mouth. A combination of two factors might have influenced the substitution of 5: reliance on tactile over kinesthetic feedback and difficulty in inhibiting the fourth finger. W is never used as a substitution. Inhibition of nonextended ulnar fingers does seem to be a problem for Pola at this age. The data on the P and D handshapes are not too enlightening in terms of inhibition as the ulnar finger involved is only partially extended and so does not exert much pressure on the other ulnar fingers also to extend. The I, Y, and W handshapes should present inhibition problems and they do – Pola invariably substitutes either 5 or B handshapes for them. The 3 handshape is puzzling as Pola always performs this handshape correctly and uses it fairly often for substitutions. A citation form of 3 would require full extensions of thumb and fingers 1 and 2. However, in the transcription of Pola's data, a more relaxed rendering, in which fingers 1 and 2 are only partially extended, was also coded as handshape 3. This relaxed form would not put as much antagonistic pull on the ulnar fingers and be easier to perform. Also, the idea of finger order is not as necessary for the correct performance of the 3 handshape as it is for the Y handshape, for example, where nonadjacent fingers are extended. The frequency with which handshapes V and H went to 3 seems to be an example of sympathetic thumb extension. The thumb is so mobile that Pola seems simply not to be conscious that it is extended. An adult V or H handshape requires very deliberate inhibition and opposition of the thumb. Stage III seems to be the stage which Pola has achieved at the time of the taping of the data, age 2; 7. She still has some trouble with some of the handshapes of this stage, and all substitutions go back to either easier handshapes of this or of earlier stages.

Stage IV Data: Open 8, 7, X, R, T

Stage IV handshapes (Table 4) account for a very small percentage of both child and adult vocabulary. None of these handshapes is never used for substitutions. Handshapes 7 and R are never required and never used. Handshape Open 8 (the open 5 hand with the middle finger bent downward) is required twice, both times for the sign LIKE. The phonologically related C and 5 handshapes are substituted, neither of which requires the inhibition of any fingers or an idea of finger order.

Table 4. Stage IV handshape data (open 8, 7, X, R, T)

Hand	Required Correct (2)	Correct (%)	Used for substitution (1)	Percentage of all substitutions (n = 124) (%)	Occurences (1)	Percentage of all occurrences (n = 593) (%)	Percentage of child vocabulary (%)	Percentage of adult vocabulary (%)
Op-8	0/2	0	0	0	0	0	2	2
7	0/0	0	0	0	0	0	0	?
X	1/10	10	0	0	1	< 1	3	5
R	0/0	0	0	0	0	0	0	1
T	0/1	0	0	0	0	0	2	?

Handshape X is performed correctly only once out of the ten times it is required. Most substitutions are to the G handshape, which is not only a phonologically related earlier handshape, but also allows the child to have forefingertip contact in signs in which this is not required (WITCH, DOLL). The preference for tactile over kinesthetic feedback seems to be operating in cases where A or S is substituted (DOLL, DRY) and the required knuckle point of contact is maintained.

Handshape T is required once, in the fingerspelled TV. Pola substitutes a 3 for this fingerspelling. What might be occurring here is her attempt to produce only the last part of the sign, V, with a sympathetic thumb extension yielding a 3 handshape.

Summary

In the analysis of these data on the handshapes produced by a young deaf child, a feature system has been proposed which is built around considerations of the anatomy of the hand and the motor development of the child. Handshape A has been designated the most unmarked form in this system, being anatomically the most relaxed and ontogenetically the earliest form.

Stages of acquisition of the handshape in ASL are proposed, determined primarily by the anatomy of the hand and the child's idea of finger order. These factors affect both the selection of features and the groups of digits to which the features may be applied at any given stage. Once handshapes are acquired, their production can be influenced by secondary factors such as anticipation and retention of adjacent handshapes, sympathetic extension of the thumb, preference for fingertip contact, whether, the handshape is used for pantomime or as a classifier, the nature of the movement parameter, and the nature of the feedback.

Since the study reported above was done in 1973, other studies have been published whose results bear on the proposed hypotheses. Concerning the grouping into stages from unmarked to more marked handshapes, Woodward (1978) did find some evidence that the handshapes 8, X, R, T, and 7 from stage IV of this model (plus handshape E) were marked, in that they occurred very infrequently across nine sign languages, some of which were not historically related.

Battison (1974) refers to the group of handshapes S, B, 5, G, C, and O as unmarked as these handshapes are found in all sign languages which have been studied to date and constitute 69% of all entries in the Stokoe et al. (1965) ASL dictionary. These unmarked handshapes are in stages I and II of the proposed acquisition model.

McIntire (1977) studied the handshapes of a deaf child of deaf parents, videotaped at ages 13, 15, 18, and 21 months. Her analysis of these data confirmed the basic hypotheses proposed in the Boyes Braem 1973 study, with some suggestions for slightly different descriptive features.

M. Carter (1981) studied a 25-month-old British child of deaf parents. Although British Sign Language is different from ASL, Carter found that the range of handshapes used by her subject was very similar to the first stage of the Boyes Braem 1973 model.

Von Tetzchner (1984) reported a study of a Norwegian deaf child of hearing parents, exposed to signed Norwegian. Based on notes kept by the mother, by 20 months the child used almost entirely handshapes from stages I and II of the acquisition model. Unlike the American children reported in the Boyes Braem and McIntire studies, however, the Norwegian child used more B than 5 handshapes at earlier stages.

Von Tetzchner also points out that the first stage handshapes proposed in the Boyes Braem model are very similar to early infant hand configurations reported by Fogel (1981). This is an extremely important point and underscores the anatomical base of the model. In other words, the handshapes acquired in the early stages by children learning sign languages are those which are available to any child, hearing or deaf, exposed to sign or spoken language. The production of stages I and II handshapes is, by itself, not to be taken as an indication that signs are being produced. Any small child can physically produce these handshapes, often quite early. Only when these handshapes are produced for recognizable symbolic communication purposes can one incorporate them into a description of a language acquisition process.

Appendix

Opposition (Opp) is applied only to the thumb. It is the abduction, rotation, and flexion of the thumb at the carpometacarpal joint resulting in the turning of the thumb inwards so that its volar surface can face that of an opposing finger. Application of the feature of opposition alone to the unmarked A handshape results in the S handshape (S: $+$Opp).

Full extension (Ext-Full) can be applied to any of the digits (when applied to all digits, the result is the 5 handshape which would be described as unmarked. A hand plus the feature Ext^{a11}).

Partial extension (Ext-Pt) – the digits may also be extended only partially, as in the C handshape ($+Ext\text{-}Pt^{a11}$) or the G handshape ($+Ext^{-1}$).

When the hand is opened (all digits fully extended), the fingers involuntarily spread. If an imaginary line is drawn through the center of the middle finger, this spread of the fingers can be described as abduction away from the central axis. Because of this involuntary spread of the fingers with extension, a feature such as $+$Spread is not necessary.

Close (Cl) can be applied to all digits. It is the moving together, or adduction, of the digits toward the axis running through the middle finger. Adduction usually accompanies flexion, or bending of the digits, in the same way that abduction is associated with extension. The closing together of the extended fingers *without* the associated flexion (as for handshape B) is thus considered here a physically more difficult task, therefore, than the normal adduction plus flexion (as in handshape A) and is notated with a separate feature (B: $+Ext^{a11} + Cl^{a11}$).

Contact of the fingertip with the opposed thumb (Ct) can be applied to any of the fingers. The volar surface of the opposed thumb contacts the volar surface of the partially extended finger(s). Thus, a pincer grasp (bO) would be notated $+Ext\text{-}pt^1 + Opp + Ct^1$.

Contact of the knuckle with the thumb (Ck) can also be applied to any of the fingers. The volar surface of the opposed thumb makes contact with the finger on the palmar or lateral side of the second joint of the finger. Handshape P, for example, would be notated $+Ext^{1,2} + Opp + Ck^2$.

Insertion of the thumb between two fingers (In) can be applied between any adjacent fingers: handshape T: $+In^{1\text{-}2}$; handshape N: $+n^{2\text{-}3}$; handshape M: $+In^{3\text{-}4}$.

Crossing of adjacent fingers (Cr) occurs in ASL only with the first and second fingers. The second finger, being longer, crosses over the top of the first finger. It is physically uncomfortable to cross the other fingers. Handshape R, therefore, is the only handshape requiring this feature (R; $+Ext^{1,2} + Cr^{1,2}$).

CHAPTER 10

Faces: The Relationship Between Language and Affect

J. SNITZER REILLY, M.L. MCINTIRE, and U. BELLUGI

Introduction

It has often been remarked that a signer's face behaves very differently from that of a person who is speaking. For many first-time observers, signers' faces appear to pass through a rapid series of grimaces and contortions. Why should this be so? In American Sign Language (ASL), facial behaviors function in two distinct ways: to convey emotion (as with spoken languages) and to mark certain specific grammatical structures. This dual functioning in ASL of similar facial behaviors presents a natural test case to explore the relationship between language and affect. Research on affect and its development suggests that certain specific facial expressions for basic emotions are universal and that children consistently use them by the age of 1 year. The subsequent acquisition of grammatical facial behaviors in ASL, then, provides a unique opportunity to examine how presumable innate behaviors, affective facial displays, come under voluntary control and are reorganized for linguistic purposes. Two logical questions which arise are: (a) how does a deaf baby learning ASL acquire these grammatical facial markings; and (b) what role, if any, do prelinguistically productive affective facial expressions play in their acquisition? Before we look at the acquisition data, it might be helpful to review aspects of the structure of a signed language, describe the role of facial expression in ASL, and then to present some background on affective facial expression and its development.

The Structure of ASL in the Hands

ASL is a visual-gestural language passed down from one generation of deaf to the next. It has been forged into an autonomous language, not derived from spoken

This research has been supported by the John D. and Catherine MacArthur Foundation Research Network on "The Transition from Infancy to Early Childhood"; by National Institutes of Health Grants NS 15175, NS 19096, NS 22343, HD 13249 to the Salk Institute for Biological Studies; and by the California State University Foundation, Northridge. We are grateful to the deaf parents and their children in our studies as well as the staff of the California School for the Deaf in Fremont, California, for their lively participation in our studies. We would also like to thank Diane Lillo-Martin, David Corina, Elizabeth Bates, Maureen O'Grady Hynes, and Lucinda O'Grady for their helpful comments. This chapter was originally presented as a paper at the Tenth Annual BostonUniversity Conference on Language Development, October, 1985.

languages, with its own formal devices for relating visual form with meaning. Like spoken languages, ASL exhibits formal structuring at two levels: sign or word internally (equivalent to phonology in spoken language) and at the sentence level, which specifies the way signs are bound grammatically in sentences. ASL (as well as other signed languages) has complex organizational properties shared by the spoken languages of the world, but also has grammatical devices of its own which are unlike those of spoken languages.

At all structural levels, the surface forms of a signed language are deeply influenced by the modality in which they develop. This is displayed most distinctively in two ways: (a) in the pervasive use of spatial contrasts and spatial manipulations at all linguistic levels; and (b) in the tendency of the language to rely on co-occurring simultaneous layers of organization.

At the lexical level, space is used to differentiate signs: for example, ONION, APPLE, and KEY differ only in the place of articulation (forehead, cheek, and hand). Furthermore, the parameters that distinguish signs co-occur throughout the sign. At the morphological level, space is used distinctively to differentiate operations on signs: verb signs, for example, undergo a wide variety of morphological markings, as demonstrated by Klima and Bellugi (1979), thus adding a co-occurring layer of structure to the signs. The most distinctive use of space is at the level of syntax and discourse in ASL. Nouns are associated with arbitrary points in signing space, pronoun signs are directed toward those points for anaphoric reference, and verb signs move between them in specifying grammatical relations. Thus, a grammatical function served in many spoken languages by case marking or by linear ordering of words is fulfilled in ASL by essentially spatial mechanisms, adding another layer of structure to the linguistic signal. In the basic lexical items, the morphological processes, and the sentences of ASL, the multilayering of linguistic elements is a pervasive structural principle (Bellugi, 1980; Klima and Bellugi, 1979). An additonal layer of structure — the grammaticized use of facial expression — will be discussed below.

Despite the radical differences in surface organization of signed and spoken languages, research with deaf children of deaf parents has shown striking similarities in the process of acquiring ASL and the process of acquiring a spoken language (Bellugi and Klima, 1982a; Launer, 1982a; Lillo-Martin, 1986b; Loew, 1981; Newport and Meier, 1985; Petitto, 1983a; Supalla, 1982; among others). The body of research to date has focused primarily on the layers of structure in the hands (lexical, morphological, and syntactic contrasts). However, there is another area of research that had not been addressed at all until very recently, and that affords a special perspective on issues in the acquisition of language by young children, namely, the nonmanual (facial) signals. The multichannel, multilayered nature of ASL is shown dramatically in the concurrent use of facial signals with manual signs, allowing us to examine the acquisition of these separable layers of structure. The dual purpose exhibited by facial signals in ASL (affective and linguistic) permits one to examine the intersection and separability of these cognitive functions in the developing child.

Linguistic Facial Expression in ASL

Recent research by Baker and Padden (1978), Baker-Shenk (1983), Liddell (1977, 1980), and Coulter (1979) has suggested that nonmanual behaviors are critical in marking certain grammatical structures in ASL. These findings indicate that facial signals in ASL function in basically two grammaticized ways: first, they mark specific syntactic structures, and secondly, they function as adverbials. A variety of syntactic structures are signalled with facial morphology; for example, relative clauses. Compare examples 1 and 2:

1.   WOLF CHASE PIG, COME HOME
     "The wolf chased the pig and [then] came home".
2.   _____ rel cl.
     WOLF CHASE PIG, COME HOME
     "The wolf that chased the pig came home".
(Conventions for transcription of ASL are in concord with standard usage in ASL linguistics; see appendix A, and Baker and Cokely (1980) for a complete description.)
     Baker and Padden (1978) describe a nonmanual marker as the obligatory conditional marker:
3.   _____ cond blink
     TODAY SNOW TRIP CANCEL
     "If it snows today, the trip will be cancelled".
In example 3, if the nonmanual marker were absent, the sentence would not be a conditional sentence, but rather a conjoined sentence as in example 4:
4.   TODAY SNOW TRIP CANCEL
     "It's snowing today; the trip is cancelled".
It is the presence and scope of the facial marker that make example 3 a complex sentence with a subordinate clause rather than simply two juxtaposed propositions.

     It has been suggested that grammatical facial behaviors in ASL share some characteristics with intonation in spoken languages. Similarly to facial expression, intonation plays a variety of grammatical and paralinguistic roles and, although there are some overlapping functions, they are clearly not identical. For example, in hearing children, sentence intonation contours are acquired before the one-word stage (Weir, 1962), whereas, in our data, nonmanual markers for topics and wh-questions initially appear at about the age of 3 years, but without full mastery of timing and scope. Further, conditional nonmanual marking still poses problems at the age of 7 years, 3½ years after the first conditionals appear.
     As their second syntactic function, certain facial behaviors represent adverbs which appear with a variety of predicates and carry with them specific meanings, as in examples 5 and 6. The two sentences use exactly the same signs, produced identically. They differ only in the nonmanual adverbials which co-occur with the signs. In example 5, the facial configuration called "mm" means "effortlessly," "easily" "regularly":

5.   —————————————— mm
   LAST YEAR MY C-P-A TAX FIGURE-OUT
   "Last year my CPA figured out the taxes really smoothly"
   (and we got a refund).

In example 6, the facial configuration called "th" means "awkwardly" or "carelessly," so that the same string of manual signs takes on a different meaning:

6.   —————————————— th
   LAST-YEAR MY C-P-A TAX FIGURE-OUT
   "Last year my CPA figured out the taxes carelessly"
   (and we had to pay an unnecessary $100).

A third type of nonmanual gesture in ASL accompanies particular lexical items, e.g., NOT-YET (which requires a protruding tongue) and RECENT (which is accompanied by a raised shoulder and a unilateral lip extension). This category includes those lexical items representing affective states and behaviors, such as SAD, SURPRISE, and HAPPY. The manual signs for affective states co-occur with the appropriate affective facial behavior, in these cases, a down-turned mouth, raised brows and widened eyes, and a smile, respectively.

Some of the facial expressions which are linguistically required in ASL thus appear to be isomorphic with aspects of affective facial expressions. Let us now look at those affective facial expressions.

Affective Facial Expressions

As we mentioned earlier, cross-cultural research on affect (Ekman, 1972; Izard, 1971) suggests that specific facial expressions for the basic emotions (joy, sadness, fear, anger, disgust, and surprise) are universal. Although there is some disagreement regarding the age at which one can attribute true emotions to a child, Hiatt, Campos, and Emde (1979) have found that in 10–12-month-olds there is specific facial patterning for the internal states of happiness and surprise. Stenberg, Campos, and Emde (1983) have also shown that 7-month-olds express anger with predictable facial expressions. In summary, studies on the development of affective facial expressions have demonstrated that children consistently use specific facial expressions both to express and to interpret emotional states of fear, surprise, and happiness by the end of their 1st year (Campos, Barrett, Lamb, Goldsmith, & Stenberg, 1983). Aspects of these affective facial behaviors, impressionistically labeled as brow raises, widened eyes, "knitted brows," and "frowning" mouth, appear to be similar in form to the obligatory grammatical markers in ASL. From this point on, our concern with affective facial expression is limited to those contexts in which it intersects with language.

Distinguishing Between Linguistic and Affective Faces

We should note here that Liddell (1977, 1980) and Baker-Shenk (1983) have both emphasized the importance of the timing and scope of the linguistic facial behaviors. Despite their apparent similarity, affective and linguistic facial behaviors differ significantly in their scope and timing in ASL. That is, grammatical facial behaviors have a clear and specific onset and offset pattern, and their coordination with manual signs is crucial in indicating the scope of such linguistic signals (whether syntactic or lexical/adverbial). In fact, Ekman (personal communication) has noted that the grammatical facial behavior which is part of the linguistic system of ASL is markedly different from the use of facial muscles displayed in emotional states. He singled out the rapid onset and rapid offset in firing of individual facial muscles in ASL grammaticized expressions, individual muscles which are rarely, if ever, isolated in affective displays. The linguistic onset/offset pattern is suggested in the "mesa"-like figure of example 7:

7.

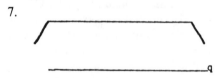

YOU LIKE CHOCOLATE ICE-CREAM
"Do you like chocolate ice cream?"

Affective facial actions, by contrast, are global, inconsistent, and inconstant in their onset/offset patterns and in their apex shapes. The shape represented in example 8 is but one possible pattern for affective nonmanual behaviors:

8.

TRUE [+ +] ME EXCITE SEE-YOU
"I'm really excited to see you!"
(c.f. Bakes-Shenk, 1983)

Given the apparent homeomorphy of affective and grammatical facial behaviors, we can see one obvious route to the acquisition of grammatical facial signals. The child could extend and generalize his or her prelinguistic affective communicative abilities to the appropriate linguistic contexts, thereby channeling his or her presumably innate affective displays into the service of the linguistic system. To evaluate this possibility, we have chosen to focus on those specific areas where affect and language intersect; such data offer us the best possible examples of facial expressions serving dual functions.

Methodology: Microanalysis of Facial Behaviors

In investigating the role of a baby's affective knowledge in the subsequent acquisition of the nonmanual aspects of ASL grammar, we have used Ekman and Friesen's (1978) Facial Action Coding System (FACS), a comprehensive, anatomically based system for coding facial expression. FACS uses 46 numbered "action units" to transcribe the firing of each muscle of the face. For example, facial expressions occurring with the affective signs mentioned earlier have the following configurations of action units:

SURPRISE: AU 1 + 2 + 5 (raised brows, widened eyes)
SMILE: AU 6 + 12 (raised cheeks, smile)
MAD: AU 4 + 7 (furrowed brows, squints)

Some of these can be described briefly as follows:

AU 1 = inner brow raise
AU 2 = outer brow raise
AU 4 = brow lower
AU 5 = widened eyes
AU 6 = cheek raise
AU 7 = lids tight
AU 12 = lip corner pull
AU 15 = lip corner depress
AU 17 = chin raise
AU 43 = eyes closed

For example, in example 9, the nonmanual topic marker, raised brows (AU 1 + 2) and widened eyes (AU 5), co-occurs with the manual sign WOLF; it is transcribed in the following way:
_____ AU 1 + 2 + 5

9. WOLF   BLOW HOUSE FALL-DOWN
"The wolf blew and the house fell down".

(See Appendix B for a complete list and description of action units which are discussed in this paper.)

We have examined 27 h of naturalistic videotaped data of five deaf children (1;0–4;0) who are learning ASL as a first language. We have concentrated on this particular age range because we anticipated finding here the first indications of language and affect interacting and diverging. The data are all interactive, involving deaf caregivers and/or deaf siblings. These children have participated in a variety of studies at the Laboratory for Language and Cognitive Studies at the Salk Institute, and many of these videotapes have been used in previous studies, including, Launer (1982a), Loew (1981), Meier (1981), and Petitto (1983a).

Our procedure was first to view a tape and select those portions where both the child's hands and face were visible, the interlocuter's hands were visible, and the participants were conversing. Once interactive sequences were selected, we transcribed the manually signed interaction and made contextual notes. Finally, using FACS, we transcribed the facial behaviors, their scope and timing. In this final stage of analysis, we focused on the child's face, transcribing the scope and timing of both affective and grammatical signals, as well as those contexts where we would expect linguistic facial markers, such as wh- and yes/no questions, negative structures, and those specific lexical items which require particular co-occurring eye gaze or nonmanual behaviors, for example, ANGRY,

SEARCH, and IMAGINE. This microanalytic method is extremely slow and time consuming. It requires multiple viewing at regular speed and slow motion as well as frame-by-frame analysis.

Results: The Intersection of Language and Affect

In discussing our findings, which include a variety of nonmanual facial behaviors, we focus primarily on two areas where affect and language intersect: (a) manual signs for affective states and behaviors; and (b) emotionally colored signs. Affective states and behaviors, as mentioned before, may involve a specific facial signal co-occurring with the manual sign. In contrast, emotionally colored signs are instances when the signer is attributing some quality to a character, or coloring a response, by layering a noncompulsory, descriptive affective face onto the linguistic signal. For example, the witch in "Hansel and Gretel" and the wolf in the "Three Little Pigs" have different characters than a possible good witch or a picture of a wolf in an animal book. We have called these "emotionally colored signs." In the following sections, we will describe a difference in the acquisition of these two types: signs for affective states and behaviors, and emotionally colored signs. We begin with signs for affect and their facial expressions.

Our findings indicate that, as predicted, deaf 1-year-olds have command of basic affective facial displays. In addition, they demonstrate modality-specific prelinguistic behaviors such as sign babbling, sign imitation, and culturally appropriate attention-getting devices.

The Acquisition of Grammaticized Facial Expression

Signs for Affective States. The first signs to be consistently accompanied by the canonical linguistic facial marker are those for affective states, and they appear at 1;6. This is consonant with Kagan's (1981) theory of developing self-awareness and with findings from Bretherton, McNew and Beeghly-Smith (1981) and Lewis and Michalson (1983) in hearing children. From this point until 2;3, in our data, signs for affective states and behaviors invariably appear with the appropriate facial expression, for example, HAPPY with AU 12 (smile), SAD with AU 15 + 17 (depressed mouth), and MAD with AU 4 + 7 (furrowed brows and tensed lower eyelids). Because of this noticeable consistency, we suggest that deaf children are learning these signs for affective states and behaviors as whole unanalyzed pieces or "gestalts," which entail both manual and nonmanual gestures. These structures appear to be much like the amalgams MacWhinney (1978) found in children learning spoken languages.

Supporting evidence that the child has applied this gestalt strategy to other areas of the facial grammar appears in a variety of contexts. First, specific lexical items where, similarly to affective signs, the canonical facial behavior is stable and unvarying appear regularly with the necessary facial behaviors, for example:

10.   _____ AU 5
    Corinne (2;0):   WAKE-UP
11.   _____ AU 19 + 26
    Corinne (2;0):   THROW-UP
12.   _____ gaze
    Corinne (2;0):   SEARCH

(We should note here that all examples are self-generated utterances, not imitations, unless specifically stated).

Secondly, between 1;6 and 2;0, we see gestalts in WHERE and WHAT questions. Rather than the obligatory AU 4 (furrowed brows), which marks wh-questions, the child adds a linguistically irrelevant head shake as in example 13 and 14.

13.   _____ AU 51,52
    Corinne (1;6):   WHERE
14.   _____ AU 51,52
    Kate (2;0):   WHAT

This head shake appears to stem from the adult model in which the caregiver typically adds a "searching" eyegaze and head movement as she signs wh-questions. The head shake is not part of the adult's linguistic signal, but rather a communicative gesture often used by caregivers with where questions.

A third piece of evidence for the gestalt strategy is in certain nonlinguistic articulation movements. In this instance, Corinne, who does not yet attend school, imitates English articulation movements with particular manual signs:

15.   _____ tongue flap
    Corinne (2;0):   LIGHT
16.   _____ AU 22 (funneled lips)
    Corinne (2;3):   SHARE
17.   _____ AU 18 (puckered lips)
    Corinne (2;3):   HOME

These examples are instances where the child has learned both the mother's face and hand movements. Although the mother uses no voice, she does intermittently mouth English words.

Fourth and finally, when the three babies under 2;0 imitated their mother's signs, they also consistently imitated her co-occurring facial expressions. Instances include single and stable lexical facial markings as in example 18, adverbials (example 19), and the emotional coloring or response the mother had given a certain proposition (example 20):

18.   _____ AU 12 (smile)
    Mother: EXCITED
                           _____ AU 12
    Kate (2;3):   EXCITED
19.   _____ AU 22 + 33 (funneled lips + blow)
    Mother: SCADS
                           _____ AU 18 + 44 (puckered lips + squint)
    Kate (2;3):   SCADS

20.   ____ AU 10 + 25 (upper lip raise + parted lips)
    Mother: NOISY
                                 ____ AU 10 + 25
    Corinne (2;0):   NOISY

All these examples suggest that the child is attending to both face and hands as articulators and recognizes both as contributing to the linguistic signal. More to the point, it suggests that signs are being acquired as whole and unanalyzed pieces.

At this point, one might be tempted to suggest that in fact the baby's "knowledge" of facial expression for affect has simply "spread" across to the linguistic system. But at 2;5, there is a noticeable change in the data. The signs for affective states and behaviors, which had previously been consistently accompanied by the linguistically required facial signal, began to appear sometimes with appropriate facial marking, as before, or with no facial marking whatever, as in example 21:

21. Corinne (2;9): CRY [no facial expression]

Additionally, these signs sometimes appeared with incongruent facial expressions, as in examples 22 and 23:

22.   ____ AU 12 (smile)
    Corinne (2;5):   SAD YOU
23.   ____ AU 12
    Corinne (2;5):   CRY

Initially, this seemed puzzling. On closer inspection, these instances bore a striking similarity to the reanalysis process discussed by MacWhinney (1978), Peters (1983), Reilly, Leaper, Baker and Greenfield (1985). In this period of reanalysis, it appears that the child is separating and learning to manipulate the individual components of the linguistic signal. Examples such as 24 support this interpretation:

24.   ____ AU 15 + 17 ____ (downturned mouth)
    Corinne (2;9):   CRY   CRY

Here, it appears that Corinne has separated the facial and manual signals and is trying to recombine them. Her timing, however, is wrong. The action units 15 + 17 should co-occur with the manual sign CRY.

By the age of 4 years, the children in our study show that the signs for affect are once again regularly co-occurring with the appropriate facial expression. So, not only has the child matched facial and manual signs, but he or she is also beginning to develop a new flexibility: he or she can manipulate them separately and recombine them for special situations. For example, at 5;1, Jane is playing dolls with her younger sister. When Jane signs CRY, she pretends to be sad. Her facial signal combines the expressions for happiness and sadness as she glances conspiratorially at her mother:

25.   ____ AU 12 + 15 + 17
    Jane (5;1):   CRY

To evaluate the acquisition of facial gestures for affective signs, it might be helpful to see them in the broader context of other linguistic developments of the same period. Between the ages of 2;0 and 4;0, deaf children are mastering the complex morphology and syntax of ASL, as has been detailed in many papers (Bellugi & Klima, 1982a; Launer, 1982a; Lillo-Martin, 1986b; Lillo-Martin, Bellugi, Struxness, & O'Grady, 1985; Newport & Meier, 1985; Newport & Supalla, 1980; Supalla, 1982). During this period, deaf children master pronominal reference, the spatial marking for verb agreement, derivational processes such as the formal distinction between related nouns and verbs, as well as many aspects of the spatial underpinnings of the syntax of ASL. Thus, at the same time that deaf children are analyzing out the morphemes in the multilayered linguistic signal in the hands (lexicon, morphology, and syntax), they are analyzing out the morphemes involved in grammaticalized facial expression as well.

Facial Adverbials. Another facet of ASL morphology, and pertinent to our study, is the acquisition of facial adverbials. These follow a developmental pattern similar to that of affective signs, but at a slightly later stage. Facial adverbials differ because they are morphemic and can be used in conjunction with any number of different predicates; they are not specific to any particular lexical item. Facial adverbials first appear in the data at age 2;0 and these early examples primarily represent imitations of the caregiver's previous utterance, as we saw in example 19. In this instance, the child's rendition imperfectly replicates the model. At 2;8 (during the middle period for affect signs), the first self-initiated facial adverbials occur:

26.   ___ AU 22 (lip funnel)
    Kate (2;8):   VACATION
27.   ___ AU 22
    Kate (2;8):   LIGHT-GO-ON-OFF

At 3;6, when affective signs are reuniting with their appropriate facial expression, the children are separating facial adverbials from their predicates, and experimenting with the timing and scope of the nonmanual adverbials with respect to the co-occurring manual signs. For example, in examples 28–30, which occurred within 3 min of each other, Jason struggles to approximate (not imitate) the adult timing for 'mm' (AU 17 + 22), the required adverbial on the modulated predicate, WORK. Modulated verbs often require specific co-occurring facial signals. In this particular example, WORK [+ + +] requires the facial adverbial 'mm' [FACS AU 22 (funneled lips) with an optimal AU 17 (raised chin)].

28.   ___ AU 17 + 22 ___
    Jason (3;10):   WORK [+ + + + +]
29.   ___ AU 17 + 22
    Jason (3;10):   WORK [+ + + +]
30.   ___ AU 22 + 25 ___
    Jason (3;10):   WORK [+ + +] INDEX WORK

It is his third attempt that most closely approximates the adult model with respect to the scope and timing of the facial adverbial.

We have now seen two instances of grammatical facial expression, nonmanuals co-occurring with affective signs and facial adverbials; both appear to follow similar patterns of separation and linguistic reanalysis.

Affect as a Complement to Language

The second broad area where language and affect intersect is in the use of facial expression to convey optional affective information as a complement to discourse. The child's increasing ability to modify manually signed utterances using optional affective facial expression undergoes gradual decontextualization in two dimensions: (a) present versus nonpresent states; and (b) the child's own state as opposed to another's emotional state or character. Initially, these affective signals appear on single morphemes and reflect the child's own present state. Remember also that utterances at this early stage of development, 1;0–2;0, are generally short, averaging one to two manual signs in length. In example 31, Kate is extremely upset and repeats herself 28 times before someone responds to her distress:

31.   _____ AU 7 + 9 + 20 + 26 ___ (tensed bottom lids, wrin-
                                                                   kled nose, square open mouth)
       Kate (1;6):   WRONG + + + + + (× 28)

Kate's mother commented that typically, when Kate is upset, she uses the sign WRONG.

Gradually, decontextualization begins and children are able to extend their use of paralinguistic facial expression to convey affective information about nonpresent states and behaviors. In example 32, Kate describes her reaction to a witch she had seen at Halloween:

32.   _____ AU 1 + 2 + 5 (raised brows, widened eyes)
       Kate (2;3):   SCARED

In example 33, Corinne tells about a past event, when she fell from a swing in the park.

33.   _____ AU 4 (furrowed brows)
       Corinne (2;3): BONK-ON-HEAD

Rather than any confusion or reanalysis, as we saw in the acquisition of affective states and adverbials, emotionally colored signs appear to be appropriately marked in increasing number and variety. In example 34, Corinne is describing the witch in "Hansel and Gretel" by accompanying the manual sign with a "mean" expression:

34.   _____ AU 4 + 9 (furrowed brows + nose wrinkle)
       Corinne (2;5): WITCH

In example 35, Corinne describes the wicked stepmother in "Hansel and Gretel" with an expression of distaste:

35.   _____ AU 9 (nose wrinkle)
       Corinne (3;0): FALSE (meaning the stepmother)

Then at 3;0, in a self-generated narrative about a "strict" bus driver, Corinne characterizes the bus driver using a configuration of action units 4 + 15 + 22B + 54 (furrowed brows, depressed mouth, protruding lower lip, chin in). This configuration is maintained over Corinne's entire narrative, a portion of which follows:

36.   _____ Au 4 + 15 + 22 + 54
       Corinne (3;0): BUS SAY-#NO-TO-ME LOOK STRAIGHT AHEAD
       "The bus driver said, 'No!' and told me to look straight ahead!"

Utterances like Corinne's have led us to explore the possibility that deaf children use affective facial expression to complement the linguistic message in a manner somewhat comparable to hearing children's use of paralinguistic intonation. Voice tone and intonation are often used to convey affective and character information in spoken discourse. We are currently exploring this notion by comparing hearing and deaf children's use of affective facial expression as a complement to language in their spoken and signed narratives.

In addition to attributing characteristics to an imaginary or nonpresent character by accompanying manual signs with affective facial expressions, the children can soon infer a character's response to a situation. In example 37, Corinne (3;4) tells about the pigs in "The Three Little Pigs"; she accompanies the sign PIG with AU 1+4 (raised furrowed brows/fearful expression).

37.   ____ AU 1+4   ____ AU 4
    Corinne (3;4):   PIG   SCARED

At 3;6 (in example 38), she incorporates the bears' surprised reaction upon finding a broken chair (in "The Three Bears"):

38.   ____ AU 1+2+5 (raised brows + widened eyes)
    Corinne (3;6): SEE BREAK

In summary, when nonmanual behaviors are used to affectively modify manual signs, there appears to be no reanalysis process comparable to that occurring in affective signs and adverbials. Rather, the developmental sequence in this case appears to be one of increasing complexity and decontextualization, suggesting the parallel development of these two communicative systems: language and affect.

Conclusions: Two Paths to Mastery of Faces

Why are there two paths of development in acquiring facial expression for linguistic purposes? We suggest that the first path we described is linguistic: previous affective knowledge has assisted the child in entering the linguistic system by encouraging him or her to recognize that the face plays a significant role in the linguistic signal. The affective "knowledge" begins as a gestalt; the pieces are separated and then re-analyzed by the linguistic system.

The second path is that of affect accompanying language — where neither system dominates, but rather they complement each other in the process of development. If this interpretation of two paths is correct, it suggests that the linguistic mechanism is fairly rigid and inflexible. It is incapable of using the affective information directly, even though, to the naive onlooker, it appears to be pertinent. Rather, the information must be reprocessed, analyzed, and separated into components that are linguistically meaningful before it can be integrated into the language. This is consonant with research on the acquisition of classifiers by Newport (1984), and that on deictic pronouns by Petitto (1983a). Like theirs, our research suggests that language functions, to a certain extent, independently of other communicative systems.

To return to our initial questions then: how does a baby acquire nonmanual facial signals in ASL? We have found that he or she uses analytic processes common to any natural first language acquisition situation. Deaf children's acquisition of grammatical facial behaviors bears a striking resemblance to early language acquisition processes in hearing children, as cited by MacWhinney (1978), Peters (1983), Greenfield et al. (1985) and Slobin (1985).

As to our second question regarding the role of a child's prior knowledge of affective facial expression in the acquisition of these grammatical facial signals: because signs for affective states and behaviors are the first to be consistently marked on the face, we propose that affect serves as the entry point into the facial grammar. This suggests that in some way, the baby's prior "knowledge" of facial expression for affective purposes has helped him or her to enter the facial grammar, or at least to recognize that facial expression plays a significant role in the linguistic system. The research on the acquisition of manual signals of ASL and the acquisition of nonmanual signals (linguistic facial expressions) taken together show that for the child, language functions as a separable domain and is acquired in a specifically linguistically driven manner. The deaf child, as does his or her hearing counterpart, analyzes out discrete components of the linguistic system presented despite radical differences in the form of the linguistic signal.

Appendix A

Notation Conventions

SIGN	Words in capital letters represent English glosses for ASL signs. A gloss is chosen on the basis of common usage among deaf researchers and informants in giving an English translation for the sign. The gloss represents the meaning of the unmarked, unmodulated, basic form of a sign out of context.
SIGN-SIGN	Multiword glosses connected by hyphens are used where more than one English word is required to translate a single sign, e.g., LOOK-AT.
"meaning"	Words within quotation marks indicate the meaning or referent of the words or signs.
W-O-R-D	Fingerspelled words are represented in italic letters with hyphens between letters.
SIGN^SIGN	Sign glosses joined by a circumflex indicate compound signs in ASL.
SIGN [Modulation]	A bracketed symbol following a sign gloss indicates that the sign is made with some change in form associated with

	a change in meaning from its basic, uninflected form and thus has undergone a morphological process. The particular specifications of inflectional or derivational processes in ASL (e.g., reciprocal, iterative, continuative, apportionative external, allocative indeterminate) are spelled out in Klima and Bellugi (1979).
SIGN[+ + +]	Indicates repetition of the sign.
neg SIGN	A line over a sign or signs indicates a particular facial expression occurring simultaneously with the sign(s), which adds to the grammatical meaning. The particular meaning of the facial expression indicated by the gloss, is written in lower case letters on the line, and by action units (see Appendix B).

Appendix B

Selected Action Units (From Ekman & Friesen, 1978)

AU	1	Inner brow raise
AU	2	Outer brow raise
AU	4	Brow lower
AU	5	Upper lid raise
AU	6	Cheek raise
AU	7	Lids tight
AU	9	Nose wrinkle
AU	10	Upper lip raise
AU	12	Lip corner pull
AU	15	Lip corner depress
AU	17	Chin raise
AU	18	Lip pucker
AU	19	Tongue show
AU	20	Lip stretch
AU	22	Lip funnel
AU	25	Lips part
AU	26	Jaw drop
AU	33	Blow
AU	44	Squint
AU	51	(Head) turn left
AU	52	(Head) turn right
AU	54	Head down

CHAPTER 11
The Early Development of Deixis in American Sign Language: What Is the Point?

E. PIZZUTO

Introduction

The purpose of this chapter is to provide evidence on the early development of deictic or "pointing" expressions in children exposed to a gestural-visual or signed language, and to compare this information with analogous information available on hearing children exposed to vocal-auditory or spoken language. This will hopefully contribute to the understanding of both universal and particular factors underlying the process of development in the signed and in the spoken modalities.

The paper explores the development of nonlinguistic deictic gestures (DG) and linguistic pronominal signs in the communicative and linguistic productive repertoire of one deaf child who is learning American Sign Language (ASL), the signed language of the deaf community in the United States. Previous studies on the acquisition of corresponding deictic expressions in hearing children have evidenced specific, seemingly universal developmental patterns at both the gestural (Bates, Benigni, Bretherton, Camaioni, & Volterra, 1979; Bruner, 1975a; Caselli, Ossella, & Volterra, 1983; E.V. Clark, 1978) and the linguistic levels

This paper is based on a study conducted by the author at the Salk Institute, Laboratory for Language and Cognitive Studies, and supported in part by a Fulbright Fellowship and by National Institutes of Health Grant No. NS15175 to Dr. Ursula Bellugi at the Salk Institute for Biological Studies, La Jolla, CA.

The author gratefully acknowledges the multifaceted and substantial help received from the whole staff during her stay at the Laboratory for Language and Cognitive Studies of the Salk Institute. Ursula Bellugi and Ed Klima provided their rich and experienced advice and criticism. Ben Bahan and Venita Driscoll gave invaluable help for the transcription and analysis of the data. I am indebted to Laura Petitto for many stimulating discussions over the ideas expressed in the present work. Special thanks to Dr. Michele Migliore of the Istituto per le Applicazioni Interdisciplinari della Fisica, Consiglio Nazionale delle Ricerche, Palermo, and to Gianni Crivello for their help in preparing the graphs shown in Figs. 1–4.

A preliminary version of this paper was prepared for the 1980 Boston University Conference on Language Development; an extended summary containing the data sets, the major conclusions and the interpretational framework appeared in the conference handbook (Pizzuto, 1980b). A modified version was submitted to Sign Language Studies in December 1982 and accepted for publication, pending referees' suggested revisions, in February 1983; but the work was never completed for publication. The paper in its present form adheres substantially to this earlier version improved by the suggestions of one unknown referee, to whom the author wishes to express her thanks. One important methodological question regarding the distinction between deictic "gestures" and "signs," also raised by the careful referee, is not addressed in the present work as being more appropriate, in the author's opinion, for a separate investigation which should be undertaken along with a critical review of other, related studies.

(Charney, 1980; E.V. Clark, 1978; Huxley, 1970; Strayer, 1977). In particular, as regards the patterns of acquisition of deictic pronominal expressions it has been suggested that they reveal the existence of what Bruner (1975, p. 273) has called a "locution dependent reciprocal concept"; this allows hearing children to overcome the major difficulty posed by such requirements as that of shifting reference according to the shifting of the basic discourse roles in ordinary conversation.

The question arises whether the above patterns can be extended to ASL, and can thus be characterized as truly universal, independent from both language-related and modality-related features, or whether they are limited to one or the other developmental modality and must thus be characterized as modality-dependent patterns. The evidence that is currently available is not sufficient to answer this question: some studies of deaf ASL children have explored a rather advanced stage of development, when deictic expressions have already appeared in the child's language (Hoffmeister, 1978a, 1978b), while others have provided preliminary, suggestive evidence that some patterns identifiable in the early stages are modality free. But this evidence is limited either to the earliest stages of communicative and linguistic development (Petitto, 1980; Pizzuto, 1980a), or to the comprehension of a few pronominal signs at one point in time (Pizzuto & Williams, 1980). Longitudinal evidence on the development of the child's communicative and linguistic productive skills is much needed.

A brief description of the DG and pronominal signs under investigation is necessary. The present study is restricted to (a) the most typical kind of DG, produced with the index finger extended, closed fist, to draw someone's attention toward objects, points in space or events in the environment; and (b) a subset of person, possessive, demonstrative, and locative pronominal signs. The signs to be considered are primarily manual signs, produced with the hand configurations known as "1" or "G" (for demonstrative, locative and several person signs), "A", "B", "V", "3", and "4" (for reflexive, possessive, dual, triple, and quadruple pronouns, respectively). Note that neither case nor gender is morphologically marked on these pronouns. Different movements and orientations imposed upon the signs convey relevant intracategory distinctions such as those between singular and plural, or between distal and proximal forms, as well as inter-category distinctions such as those between demonstrative, locative, and person forms (Baker & Cokely, 1980; Wilbur, 1979).

The signs specified above fulfill in ASL the same two interrelated functions that pronouns and pronominals play in spoken languages (see Lyons, 1977): (a) the *deictic* function, which allows the identification and/or the first introduction in discourse of referents by specifying their roles as discourse participants, or their relationship with respect to discourse participants; and (b) the *anaphoric* function, which allows the reintroduction in discourse of referents previously specified in the context of utterance (see, among others: Kegl, 1977; Klima & Bellugi, 1979; Pizzuto, 1978; Wilbur, 1979). The present study is concerned only with the deictic function of the ASL deictic signs (DS).

The interest of the investigation is enhanced by the following considerations. From a functional and conceptual point of view the DS are fully comparable to their corresponding spoken forms or deictic words (DW). However, they also exhibit unique, seemingly modality-specific formal features that distinguish them from DW. DS are produced directing the handshapes toward the referent they specify. Thus, for example, for first and second person reference the signer directs the "1" handshape inward, toward his or her own torso ("I"/"me") or outward toward the addressee ("you"). Since DS are produced taking into account the referents' actual physical locations, in the context of the utterance they are related to their referents in an apparently direct, nonarbitrary or entirely context-dependent fashion. In addition, person, demonstrative, and locative DS are produced with the same handshape used for producing DG: the "1" handshape is in fact a closed fist, with the index finger extended.

Considered from the perspective of spoken communication, DS thus resemble (in one or more morphological and especially functional aspects) seemingly simple "pointing gestures" that are assumed to be easily and universally understood across languages and cultures, and that are usually classified as nonlinguistic or, at most, paralinguistic devices.

The features mentioned above cannot be found in DW; although DW depend in part for their interpretation on the physical context of utterance (see Lyons, 1977), DW are also language-specific symbols. Thus, like all other vocal-auditory signals used in spoken language, DW are related to their referents via indirect, arbitrary linguistic conventions that establish specific sound-meaning correspondences. Furthermore, DW do not morphologically resemble DG. The question to be explored is whether the unique, seemingly modality-specific features of the ASL DS are relevant to the acquisition process.

Data and Procedure

Data were taken from a broader longitudinal study of ASL acquisition undertaken at the Salk Institute (Bellugi & Klima, 1982a, 1982b). For the present study one subject was investigated: a congenitally deaf girl who was acquiring ASL as her first language from her deaf parents and an older deaf sister. The child was videotaped in her home while she interacted with one or more deaf adults (usually the child's mother) and occasionally with her sister. Twelve videotaped samples of the child's spontaneous production were used for this study covering the age range 8–29 months. The length of the different samples varied from 30 (seven samples) to 60 min (six samples) (see Table 1). A part of these data has also been discussed in Bellugi and Klima (1982a, 1982b) and Pizzuto (1980a, 1980b, 1980c, 1982b, 1983).

All the communicative and linguistic utterances produced by the child and by the adult were interpreted and transcribed into English glosses in part by ASL native signers and in part by the author, with deaf signers being consulted as needed. The analysis was conducted by the author and it was focused upon the child's production of DG and DS. In addition, observations of the child's overall linguistic development across the recorded corpus were made by considering, for each sample: (a) the type, number, and frequency of occurrence of the lexical, nondeictic items produced by the child; and (b) the utterance patterns, and in particular the frequency of one- versus two- and multi-sign utterances, and the various combinations of lexical and deictic items exploited by the child.

The analysis of the child's corpus presented one major methodological problem: that of distinguishing DG directed to objects or points in space from linguistic demonstrative and locative DS. It must be underscored that even in adult ASL production it is often very difficult to draw a clear distinction between these DG and subcategories of DS (Coulter, 1980). In order to solve this problem the following arbitrary criteria were used:

1. All deictic utterances that consisted of one or more deictic elements were classified as DG. This criterion was based on the consideration that unlike DS, and much like prelinguistic or nonlinguistic DG, these utterances *suggested* but did not specify some kind of referent or referential relationship among people and objects. For example, in sample 4 the child produced a sequence of three pointings: the first was directed toward a point in the surrounding space, the second toward another point in space *or* toward an object (contextual information was not sufficient to interpret this pointing), the third toward a cup the child was holding in her hands. These three pointings were all classified as DG and further distinguished in the subcategories of: DG directed toward a place (the first one), an object or place (the second, unclear DG), and an object (the third DG).

2. All the deictic utterances that occurred together with lexical signs in elementary sentence patterns were classified as DS and further categorized as demonstrative or locative DS depending upon the linguistic and extralinguistic context in which they occurred. Unlike DG, these deictic utterances specified some precise referent and/or relationship. For example, in the same sample 4 the child produced a sequence composed of the lexical sign for "candy" and a pointing directed toward a bowl containing candies. This pointing was classified as a locative DS, and the utterance was interpreted as meaning "candy there." In another sequence the child produced a pointing toward a picture of a cat and the sign for "cat." This pointing was classified as a demonstrative DS, and the utterance was interpreted as meaning "that cat." Note that no attempt was made in the analysis to distinguish the proximal and distal forms of the locative and demonstrative DS.

Results

The major results are summarized in Table 1 and in Figs. 1–4. The raw data in Table 1 show a pattern of development from no DG nor DS (at 8 months) to DG only (at 12 months) to DG and DS (from 15 months on). It is interesting to observe the complementary developmental pattern followed by DG and DS, illustrated in Fig. 1. It can be seen that from 18 months DG gradually decrease, whereas DS increase. By 28 and 29 months of age the proportion of DG is insignificant (6%), whereas DS, initially very poorly represented, constitute 94% of the total.

Table 1. Number of deictic gestures and deictic signs in the different samples

Sample	1	2	3	4	5	6	7	8	9	10	11	12	1–12
Age (months)	8	12	15	18	20	21	24	25	26	27	28	29	
Sample duration (min)	30	30	30	60	60	60	60	60	30	30	30	30	510
DG	–	4	11	48	32	41	37	32	6	21	6	2	240
DS	–	–	2	68	41	68	108	157	51	50	93	32	670
	0	4	13	116	73	109	145	189	57	71	99	34	910

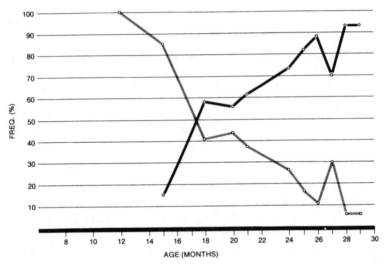

Fig. 1. Child's production of deictic gestures (*dotted line*) vs. deictic signs (*solid line*) as a function of age

Figure 2 describes the different categories of DG produced by the child and their relative proportion with respect to each other. It can be observed that DG are initially restricted to objects (at 12 and 15 months), and only later, from 18 months, are extended to places. Unclear DG, that could be classified equally well as being directed toward objects or places, were found from 18 to 25 months.

The most interesting findings are those on the development of DS. Figure 3 compares the acquisition of demonstrative and locative DS, and of forms that could be classified equally well as demonstrative or locative DS, with the acquisition of all types of person reference DS, grouped in one category. The data show that demonstrative DS are the first to appear, at 15 months of age, followed by locative and demonstrative-locative DS at 18 months, whereas person DS begin to appear only at 20 months. Note that demonstrative and locative DS are very largely represented in all samples; however, they are significantly more frequent in the early samples, from 20 to 24 months, and less frequent in four out

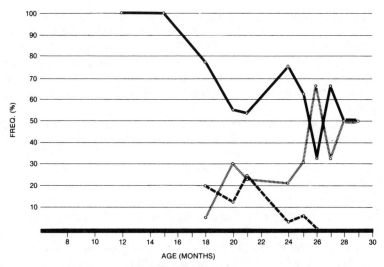

Fig. 2. Child's production of different types of DG as a function of age. *Solid line*, DG directed toward present objects; *dotted line*, DG directed toward points in space; *broken line*, DG that could be classified equally well as being directed toward objects or points in space

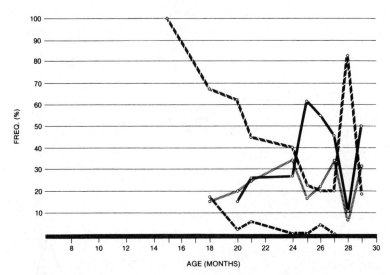

Fig. 3. Child's production of demonstrative (*diagonally broken line*), locative (*dotted line*), demonstrative-locative (*broken line*), and person (*solid line*) DS as a function of age. The demonstrative-locative category includes DS that could be classified equally well as demonstrative or locative DS. The person category includes all types of person and possessive DS grouped together

of five of the last samples, from 25 to 29 months. The sample taken at 28 months constitutes an exception to this pattern. Person DS, not surprisingly, follow a complementary developmental pattern: disregarding the sample taken at 28 months, where they constitute only 10% of all DS, we see that person DS increase rather systematically from the period between 20 and 24 months to that between 25 and 29 months of age. All but one of the DS found in the corpus were singular forms.

Figure 4 focuses on the acquisition of different classes of person DS. It must be underscored that the child's repertoire was limited to a subset of ASL person DS, namely: the first, second, and third person and possessive singular forms. There was only one occurrence of a dual DS (not included in the present analysis), and there were no reflexive forms.

The person DS found in the corpus were grouped in three major classes: the I-class (first person and possessive), the you-class (second person and possessive) and the s/he-class [third persons and possessive, corresponding in meaning to such English pronouns as "he" or "she" and "his" or "her(s)"]. Note that the person and possessive forms comprised within each class appeared in the child's repertoire either at the same point in time (e.g., first person and possessive of the I-class, and second person and possessive of the you-class), or within a short time interval (e.g., the third person possessive of the s/he-class appeared 1 month before the corresponding person forms). Within each class person DS were in general more frequently produced than possessive DS.

Looking at Fig. 4 we find that the forms produced appear in a different order and in different proportions: I-class DS appear first, at 20 months of age, and are

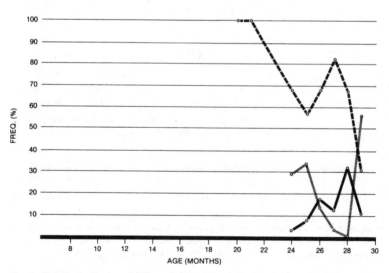

Fig. 4. Child's production of different types of person DS as a function of age. *Broken line*, I-class: first person and possessive DS; *dotted line*, you-class: second person and possessive DS; *solid line*, s/he-class: third person and possessive DS

the most frequently produced person DS across all age samples but the last; you-class DS appear next, beginning at 24 months. S/he-class DS are found at a significant frequency from 25 months on.

The person and possessive DS reported above include all forms that the child produced spontaneously and appropriately (total $n = 224$). In addition to these, in the early stages of DS acquisition (samples 3–8) the child produced a small number of person reference expressions that were not comparable to adult forms. These included: (a) elicited forms ($n = 18$); (b) spontaneously produced but unclear DS ($n = 13$); (c) nominal expressions used in substitution of first and second person DS ($n = 29$).

Since the purpose of this paper is to outline the major developmental trends in the child's spontaneous production of the standard, adult-like ASL DS, these nonstandard forms are not considered here in detail (see Pizzuto, 1980a, 1980c). It is worth noting, however, that most of the elicited forms mentioned above occurred within the context of a particular "language routine" in which the mother asked the child, in ASL, either one of the following questions: (a) "Where (or who) is mother?"; "Where (or who) is (child's name)?". Following these questions the child pointed to her mother (addressee) ($n = 5$) or to herself ($n = 10$), thereby producing forms that were phonologically and in part also semantically comparable with, respectively, second and first person DS. Interestingly, three of these forms, produced at 15 ($n = 2$) and 20 months ($n = 1$) were incorrect: in reply to the first question the child pointed to herself rather than to her mother, and thus apparently produced what are commonly known as "reversal errors": "I" forms instead of the required "you" forms. It must be observed, however, that unlike the person DS spontaneously produced by the child, all these elicited forms appeared to fulfill a "locative" or "demonstrative" function: they seemed to evidence the child's understanding of specific name-referent relationships rather than her knowledge of first and second person DS.

The development of DG and DS in the recorded corpus took place along with several important changes in the child's growing linguistic skills. These are reported elsewhere (Pizzuto, 1980a, 1980c) and are not described here in detail. For the present purposes, it suffices to mention the following: in samples 1–3 the child's corpus included only four different nondeictic or lexical signs (LS). In only two cases, at 15 months (sample 3), were these LS combined with the first DS produced by the child (demonstrative DS), thereby providing the first, elementary two-sign utterances (one LS + one DS). A rather dramatic change was observed in sample 4, at 18 months: the child employed a significantly larger number of LS ($n = 17$) and, at the same time, began combining LS not only together with DS but also, though in a smaller number of cases, with other LS. In addition to one-LS utterances ($n = 18$ or 23%) the child thus produced two types of two-sign utterances: (a) one LS + one DS ($n = 50$ or 63%); and (b) one LS + one LS ($n = 11$ or 14%).

While the child continued to produce one-LS utterances through the whole corpus, these gradually diminished from one sample to the next. As might have been expected, both types of two-sign utterances mentioned above gradually increased, along with a parallel, systematic increase of the number of different LS used by the child. In addition, from 26 months on the child began producing multi-sign utterances. It is worth noting that I-class DS were produced at 20 months of age (see Fig. 4), that is, only after the child had begun producing two-LS utterances.

Discussion

In order to clarify the issue addressed by this study, it is first necessary to compare the data discussed thus far with corresponding data on hearing children. Unfortunately, an exact comparison cannot be performed due to the differences in focus, data sets, and methodology between this and other studies. In particular it must be observed that the data on hearing children include very little, or no detailed information on the development of all forms of pointing behavior as related with "corresponding" DW (e.g., most notably, on the development of "pointing to self" or "pointing to addressee" as compared with first and second person DW). We shall thus compare only the major developmental trends that have been identified in the acquisition of some DG, DS and DW. The relevant findings are summarized in Table 2.

For the sake of comparison, four common developmental stages were identified, according to the following criteria:

Stage I. Transition from the prelinguistic to the earliest linguistic stage of development; beginning of intentional communication and appearance of the first few word- or sign-like utterances.

Stage II. Early stage of linguistic development characterized by a limited vocabulary (10–50 words or signs) and by the production of one-word/sign utterances.

Stage IIIA. Rapid vocabulary growth along with the appearance and, later, the establishment of two-word/sign utterances.

Stage IIIB. Advanced stage III, characterized by the production of multi-word/sign utterances.

Disregarding for the moment the category of general demonstrative-locative DW (G DE-LO in the Table), the data in Table 2 show substantial similarities in the patterns followed by the deaf and the hearing child: DG as well as the DS and DW considered are acquired at approximately the same age, at the same stage of communicative or linguistic development and, it is important to note, in the same order. Consistent correspondences in patterns emerge if we also consider other observations that are not given in Table 2. Thus it is known that demonstratives and locatives are very largely represented in hearing children's repertoires throughout the one- and two-word stage of linguistic development (E.V. Clark,

Table 2. DG, DS, and DW in the acquisition of signed and spoken languages

Category	Age		Stage		References	
	ASL (months)	SpL (months)	ASL	SpL	ASL	SpL
DG	10–12	10–12	I	I	Petitto (1980), present work	Bruner (1975a), Bates et al. (1979), Caselli et al. (1983), E.V. Clark (1978)
G DE-LO	–	12 +	–	II	–	E.V. Clark (1978), Gopnik (1981)
DE & LO	18 +	18 +	III	III	Present work	E.V. Clark (1978)
1P/1PO	20	19–23	III	III	Present work	Charney (1980), E.V. Clark (1978), Huxley (1970), Strayer (1977)
2P/2PO	24	24–26	III	III	Present work	Charney (1980), E.V. Clark (1978), Huxley (1970), Strayer (1977)
3P/3PO	24–25	25–28	III A	III A	Present work	Charney (1980), Strayer (1977)
PPF	30 +	27–35	III B	III B	Hoffmeister (1978b)	Huxley (1970), Strayer (1977)

SpL, spoken language; DG, DG directed towards present objects or points in space; G DE-LO, general DW with a demonstrative or locative meaning; DE & LO, demonstrative and locative DS and DW; 1P/1PO, 2P/2PO, and 3P/3PO: first, second, and third person and possessive singular DS and DW; PPF, plural person forms of DS and DW.

1978; Gopnik, 1981). It is also known that I-class forms are initially the most frequently produced person DW, followed in frequency by you-class and then by s/he-class forms (Charney, 1980; Strayer, 1977). This is what we have also observed and shown in Figs. 3 and 4. A small number of nonstandard person reference forms, including a few reversal errors that are in part similar to those observed in the course of the present study (see above), have also been noted in hearing children's early use of person reference expressions (Charney, 1980; E.V. Clark, 1978; Strayer, 1977).

Finally, it is worth mentioning what has been observed by Caselli et al. (1983) in two hearing subjects. These authors found that although their subjects used DG to objects or points in space from the age of 11–12 months, they produced pointing gestures to themselves considerably later, at 20–24 months, when they also produced first person reference DW. Interestingly, this is the age at which both first person DS and DW begin to be consistently found in other subjects (see Table 2).

One category of DW (C DE-LO) has been reported in Table 2 for hearing children only, at stage II. In the deaf child's corpus G DE-LO DS at the one-sign stage of development (stage II) were not singled out, since according to our classificatory criteria all utterances composed of only one deictic element were classified as DG, not as DS.

The information summarized above is clearly insufficient to draw definite conclusions about the development of deictic expressions in deaf and hearing children: the evidence on deaf children is in fact limited to the data on one subject reported in the present work, and data on another subject studied by Petitto (1980) (see also Bellugi & Klima, 1982a). More accurate information on the use of all types of pointing gestures by hearing children is also needed.

Although certainly further research is necessary, the comparative data in Table 2 provide a few major indications. These can be summarized as follows: neither the appearance of DG nor the development of DS and DW seems to be significantly influenced by the modality in which communication and language take place. In particular, with respect to the development of DS and DW, the similarities in the acquisition patterns seem to indicate the presence of a common perceptual and cognitive background and suggest that, in the deaf-signing as in the hearing-speaking child, this may be a major factor which overrides the formal differences distinguishing DS from DW. These results corroborate and extend those provided by Bellugi and Klima (1982a, 1982b), Petitto (1980), Pizzuto (1980a, 1980b, 1980c, 1982b, 1983), Pizzuto and Williams (1980) and support the theoretical points of view previously expressed by the author (Pizzuto, 1978, 1980a).

It is of particular interest that first person DS are virtually identical to self-referential gestures that seem to be universally known across cultures. It could have been plausible therefore to assume that the use of first person DS would not require symbolic-linguistic skills. On the contrary, it was found that first person DS are not used until stage III, just as are first person DW. It was also noted that, according to some recent observations, self-referential pointing gestures appear considerably late in hearing children's gestural repertoires. These considerations suggest that even signs (or gestures) which might superficially appear simple and nonarbitrary, and very different from spoken words, may possess the same underlying formal properties that characterize their corresponding spoken forms.

CHAPTER 12
The Transition from Gesture to Symbol in American Sign Language

L. A. PETITTO

Introduction

Research on sign languages over the past 20 years has revealed that they exhibit formal linguistic organization at the same levels found in spoken languages (e.g., phonological, morphological, syntactic, discourse). The structure of one sign language, American Sign Language (ASL), which is used by most deaf people in the United States, has been most thoroughly studied (e.g., Klima & Bellugi, 1979; Padden, 1981; Stokoe, 1960; Supalla, 1982; Wilbur, 1979; Wilbur & Petitto, 1983). This research yields the surprising conclusion that human languages are not restricted to the speech channel.

While signed and spoken languages share fundamental properties, it is also clear that they differ in important respects. First, space and movement (including facial expressions) are the key means for conveying morphological and syntactic information in signed languages, while in spoken language they are not. The continuous, analogue, nondiscrete properties of space and movement are used in ASL in systematic, rule-governed ways. These abstract spatial and movement units are analogous in function to discrete morphemes found in spoken language. In addition, the forms of some signs bear nonarbitrary relations to their meanings. In particular, indexical signs point to their referents while the forms of iconic signs physically resemble aspects of their meanings. The greater potential for nonarbitrary form-meaning correspondences afforded by the visual-gestural modality is in fact exploited in sign languages.

These modality differences allow us to address fundamental issues in language acquisition. Studies of ASL provide a way to resolve a major theoretical controversy concerning the role of prelinguistic gestures in the acquisition of linguistic symbols. Both deaf and hearing children rely upon gestural communication prior to language. For the hearing child, the transition from prelinguistic communication to spoken language involves a change in modality, while for the deaf child, the transition to signed language does not. That is, for the deaf child, gestures and symbols reside in the same modality. In evaluating the

This research was funded by a fellowship from the John D. and Catherine MacArthur Foundation's Network on the "Transition from Zero to Three," San Diego Node (Dr. Elizabeth Bates, Director), and grants from the Natural Sciences and Engineering Research Council of Canada, and, FCAR, Quebec, Canada; I am extremely grateful for this support. Some of this material appears in somewhat different form in Petitto, 1983a.

importance of prelinguistic gestures in early language acquisition, sign languages provide a unique methodological advantage. With a single modality, and external articulators, certain developmental processes in language can be observed directly over time. In spoken language, of course, this is not the case; there appears to be a transition from the primary use of prelinguistic manual gestures to the primary use of linguistic (vis-à-vis spoken) communication; however, this could be an artifactual consequence of the shift in modality, rather than reflecting a deeper discontinuity between prelinguistic and linguistic knowledge. The basic questions, then, are whether the acquisition of linguistic forms will (a) be facilitated by; (b) be continuous with; or (c) share important symbolic properties with the deaf child's knowledge of their extralinguistic communicative functions?

The study described in this chapter is concerned with the young child's transition from prelinguistic gestural communication to linguistic expression. Specifically, I examined the young deaf child's use of deictic pointing gestures and comprehension and production of personal pronouns. Two central assumptions of current models of language acquisition were addressed: (a) knowledge of linguistic structure is "mapped onto" earlier forms of nonlinguistic knowledge; and (b) acquiring a language involves a continuous learning sequence from early gestural communication to linguistic expression.

Background

Personal pronouns are found in all languages and have both a lexical and deictic (or indexical) function. Lexically, they can be marked for case and have other morphological and syntactic functions; deictically, they point to actual relations in the speech context (Ingram, 1971). In this respect, personal pronouns differ from most words because their meanings are generally interpreted with regard to the speech event. That is, the meanings of the pronouns *I* and *you* shift depending upon who is actually speaking at a given time. The same holds for other deictic terms denoting, for example, time (*now* or *yesterday*), and place (*here* or *there*), which can be understood by the listener only by understanding the perspective of the speaker at the time of the utterance. In contrast, the meanings of most other words do not shift with a change in speaker. For example, proper names such as *Sara*, or category names, such as *table*, do not change their meaning within a particular context with every change in speaker turn. For this reason, personal pronouns have been said to have "unstable" or "shifting" referencing properties, while most other words are "stable" (Jakobson, 1957; Jespersen, 1924; Lyons, 1977).

Three noteworthy features characterize the hearing child's acquisition of pronouns. First, they are acquired in a particular order. Beginning around 16–20 months the pronoun *me* enters, followed by *you* around 22 months, and then third person pronouns (e.g., Charney, 1978; Macnamara, 1982). Secondly, prior to this process children use full proper nouns (e.g., "Jane do X" instead of "I do X"), rather than use the pronoun *me*. Thirdly, around the time when *you* enters the lexicon, all children exhibit some form of unstable knowledge and use of pronouns (i.e., inconsistent and partial pronoun reversal errors), with some children engaging in systematic pronoun reversal errors. For example, mother might say to the child, "Do *you* want to go to the store?" and the child's reply would be, "Yes, *you* want go store." Here the child uses *you* incorrectly to refer to him- or herself rather than to mother. Similarly, the child may understand and produce *me* to refer to the adult rather than to him- or herself, although it is uncommon for symmetrical *you-me* error pairs to co-occur.

Two related proposals have been offered to account for the hearing child's knowledge underlying pronoun reversal errors. Pronoun-reversing children have been thought to regard pronouns as having fixed or stable referents like names (i.e., *you* = child's name, or *me* = adult's name) rather than having changing or "unstable" referents depending upon the speaker role (Chiat, 1981, 1982; E.V. Clark, 1978). In a similar vein, pronoun-reversing children have been regarded as being "egocentric," failing to shift pronouns because they are not yet able to take on the perspective of another person (i.e., errors are due to a cognitively based perspective-shifting problem; e.g., Charney, 1978; E.V. Clark, 1978; Piaget, 1955).

Although personal pronouns in ASL are constrained by the grammar of the language, they are not formed by arbitrary symbols. Rather, they are represented by pointing directly to the addressee (to intend YOU), or self (to intend I or ME) (cf., Lillo-Martin, 1985b, 1986a; Lillo-Martin & Klima, 1986). Thus, the formational aspects of these personal pronouns in ASL resemble extralinguistic pointing gestures which commonly accompany speech and are used prelinguistically by hearing and deaf children. This provides a means for investigating the deaf child's transition from prelinguistic gestural communication to linguistic-symbolic communication where both gestures and symbols are virtually identical in form.

Discussions of the role of pointing in language development have received considerable attention. E.V. Clark (1978) has proposed that the child's knowledge of the meanings of verbal deictic words, or context-bound indicating terms such as *here* and *there* and *you* and *me*, emerges directly out of early deictic pointing gestures in a natural and continuous progression (see also Bates, 1976a; Bates, Camaioni, & Volterra, 1975; Bruner, 1975b; Leopold, 1939–1949; Werner & Kaplan, 1963). A hallmark of human development is said to be the onset of pointing gestures at around 9 months. Pointing is thought to be a complex behavior, itself built up from earlier gestures in roughly the following manner: the child reaches and grasps (taking objects "inward"), "shows off" (e.g., imitative clapping in the pat-a-cake game), shows objects, gives objects (extending objects "outward"), points to objects without communicative intention (i.e., exploratory "pointing-for-self", does not visually seek adult to share gaze), and finally points to objects with communicative intention (i.e., visually seeks adult to share gaze and involves checks for feedback; Bates et al., 1975; Werner & Kaplan, 1963). That pointing develops in this way has been used to infer changes in the organization of internal mental "schemes" (Bates et al., 1975). For example, early noncommunicative pointing is said to represent the child's emerging ability to recognize and distinguish self from external, distant objects (Werner and

Kaplan's Gestalt-based concepts of emergence and distancing). By contrast, the later-emerging communicative pointing serves as the foundation for referential behavior and the concept of reciprocity arising from mother and child's joint actions and shared visual regard (Werner & Kaplan, 1963). Bates et al. (1975) further analyze the illocutionary (intentional) function of pointing gestures as protodeclaratives and protoimperatives because they function to direct the adult's attention to objects, events, or people, and to convey requests. Finally, E.V. Clark (1978) analyzes pointing gestures as nascent markers of definite and indefinite reference (i.e., the precursors of "the" and "a").

Given that the forms of personal pronouns in ASL are of the same form as prelinguistic pointing gesture common to hearing and deaf children, the following questions arise:

1. How does the deaf child move from the early biologically given, unconstrained, and communicative use of pointing gestures to the use of pronominal pointing constrained by the grammatical conventions of the language?
2. Is the acquisition of linguistically governed pointing facilitated by the child's knowledge of its extralinguistic communicative functions?
3. Finally, given the seemingly transparent meaning of YOU and ME pronouns in ASL, will deaf children learn these relations at an accelerated rate and in a relatively error-free manner?

Methods

The subjects were two, third-generation profoundly and congenitally deaf girls (called Child 1 and Child 2). The children were learning ASL as a first language from their deaf parents; they were of normal intelligence and free of other neurological or physical handicaps. Two types of data were obtained in this study: naturalistic and experimental. For Child 1, naturalistic data were obtained from ages 6 months to 3;7 and experimental data from two pronoun elicitation tasks — one at age 1;11 and one at 2;11 (for a detailed description of the elicitation tasks and overall procedures see Petitto, 1983a). Data between 6 months and 2;3 are summarized in this chapter. For Child 2, naturalistic data were obtained from ages 8 months to 4;9. Data between ages 8 months and 2;3 are summarized here.

One-hour videotaping sessions occurred approximately once a month for each child within the time period specified above (6 and 8 months to 2;3). The tapes were transcribed for adult and child signing with special attention to contextual information. Reliability checks on the transcriptions of four videotapes were done by two native deaf signers; their judgement showed 95% agreement with my own.

Results

The results indicated that deaf children acquire knowledge of personal pronouns over a period of time, displaying errors similar to those of hearing children despite the transparency of the pointing gestures. Although deaf children first begin using the deictic pointing gesture to objects and locations in a rich and varied way around 9 months, they do not use the pointing form to express the pronouns YOU and ME until around 17–20 months, within the precise age range that hearing children first begin to use verbal pronouns systematically. Soon after ME has been established, deaf children gain productive control over the YOU pronoun (around 22–23 months), followed by third person pronouns (see also Bellugi & Klima, 1982a, 1982b; Hoffmeister, 1978a; Kantor, 1982a; Lillo-Martin, 1986a, 1986b; Loew, 1983; Meier, 1982; Petitto, 1977, 1980, 1981, 1983a, 1988; Pizzuto, 1982a). Like hearing children they, too, use full proper nouns prior to the productive use of pronouns despite the fact that they use the pointing form in a fully communicative fashion. Surprisingly, the children used the pointing form to refer to aspects of their care giver's body, but seemed to avoid the use of the pointing form to indicate the adult, per se. For example, Child 1 (age 1;11) used the pointing form to refer to a spot on her mother's bathing suit, but did not use it to indicate her mother as in YOU, not even in an experimental task that was specifically designed to elicit this and other pronouns. Instead, the children used full proper names to refer to people around them. A critical fact is that the children were able to articulate the pointing form; they appeared to *avoid* a particular function of its use because of, I will argue, the complex role points play in the grammar of ASL.

Although the phenomenon of "avoidance" has been noted previously in child language literature (e.g., Ferguson & Farwell, 1975), this case is especially intriguing because the children avoided a particular function of a form rather than the form itself. Slobin (1982), for example, suggests that hearing children are biased towards relating one meaning (or concept) to one word-like surface form. In ASL, pointing enters into the language in a number of ways: (a) as a primary phonological unit; (b) as a primary component of the anaphoric referencing system; (c) as comprising one subset of the class of morphological forms called classifiers; (d) as personal pronouns; (e) as full deictic terms within the grammatical system of ASL, and (f) as paralinguistic gestures. Thus, pointing in ASL represents a single surface form with complex underlying grammatical functions and can be viewed as similar to linguistic forms in languages with fusional morphological units

On this basis, one might expect the child to avoid the use of the pointing form entirely, until its various meanings and functions can be understood. The obvious explanation for the selective avoidance, however, is simply that pointing has such a pervasive function in the language that its use cannot be avoided entirely (especially in light of its paralinguistic functions). But why, among the various linguistic functions of pointing, does the child specifically avoid first and second person pronominal pointing? In contrast to the other lexical items in the child's vocabulary, the referent of a pronoun shifts depending upon the speaker. In addition, the use of pronouns is constrained by other grammatical processes (e.g., strict co-referencing rules). Finally, the child has an alternate means for communicating the same information, namely through the use of full lexical nouns. Thus, when confronted with the grammatical pluri-functionality of pointing in the language, and the conceptual complexity of pronominal referencing, the child avoids YOU and ME pointing in favor of simpler lexical items. In this sense, the child can be said to be "avoiding" indexical pointing in favor of forms which remove any ambiguity.

Finally, like hearing children, the deaf children initially exhibited confusion over which pronouns were appropriate given a particular linguistic context, and both children produced pronoun reversal errors. The single noteworthy difference between the two girls' performance was that Child 1's pronoun reversal errors were consistent while Child 2's errors were not. Given the seemingly transparent meaning of personal pronouns in ASL, Child 1's error is especially intriguing and warrants further discussion.

Pronoun Reversals and the Nontransparent Point

Between ages 1;10–1;11 one child (Child 1) pointed to people occupying second person role as in YOU, but the sense of the pointing sign appeared to mean ME. After conducting several extensive analyses of the child's comprehension and production of pronouns, it soon appeared as if she regarded this form not as YOU, but as a nonreciprocal, nondeictic, "frozen" lexical sign that stood for her, and her alone. In short, she appeared to regard the form as her NAME. Other indices of this child's language development appeared quite normal: measures of her vocabulary growth (MLU), discourse skills, and even her symbolic play were all comparable to that of other age-matched hearing and deaf children. Moreover, the error was not attributable to imitation of adults' utterances. Surprisingly, the child's error was totally impervious to mother's modelling and especially resistent to mother's explicit correction. During the period when the child was producing the YOU pointing form to intend ME, the mother attempted to correct her daughter's error by molding her child's hand into the correct ME configuration. Such physical manipulation of the language articulators in spoken language is, of course, impossible. Consequently, it might be thought that deaf children would be at a distinct advantage over hearing children in this regard. However, the young girl's error persisted despite mother's physical manipulations.

Discussion

Child 1's pronoun reversal errors present an immediate question: given that the form of the linguistic symbol for expressing pronouns in ASL is very transparent relative to its meaning, why does the child make consistent pronoun errors?

The Basis of the Pronoun Reversal Error

I suggest that the child regarded the YOU form as a symbol which represented herself. Further, she did not have pronouns in her productive lexicon at the time of this error. This analysis shares with E.V. Clark (1978) the notion that the child has formed the erroneous hypothesis that the YOU pronoun is her name. Recall that Clark also suggests that children produce these errors because they fail to take on the perspective of the adult. From this view the hearing child's difficulties in learning the pronominal system of a language are seen as derived from a general problem in learning to distinguish self from other, a problem that is manifested in language and in other, nonlinguistic domains. The case of deaf children acquiring sign languages provides the basis for a stronger test of this perspective-shifting hypothesis than is possible in spoken language. In spoken language, a relatively small class of words requires perspective shifting, whereas in ASL, the specific nature of its transmission requires that all signs be acquired by first taking on the perspective of the signer.

The fact is that the mirror-image transformation required in order to learn signs presupposes that the child is nonegocentric. If the child's problem derives from a failure to shift perspective as a consequence of egocentrism, the child should exhibit pervasive reversals, with errors occurring for a wide range of lexical items; essentially, the child should sign backwards. In fact, this kind of pervasive reversal error does occur in the sign imitations, sign babbling, and "baby signs" of very young deaf children (ages 8–12 months) but rapidly disappears. The error seen in this study is selective, however, in that it is specific to a particular lexical item in a particular grammatical class. I propose that the child had to shift to the adults' perspective to have produced the YOU = ME error.

Moreover, on the perspective shifting hypothesis we would expect symmetrical errors (i.e., both YOU = ME and ME = YOU), but this did not occur as the child never signed ME. It appears, then, that the incorrect meaning that the child attached to the YOU form was a specific problem related to learning the structural properties of the lexicon, not the by-product of a general cognitive deficit.

The derivation of this error appears to be the following: the child's error occurs at a time when she has clearly begun to understand the symbolic relationship between a sign and its referent, when her vocabulary is growing rapidly and her MLU is steadily increasing. At the same time, the frequency and distribution of her deictic points have begun to decline, replaced by full lexical nouns. The child observes other people using the YOU form to refer to her. Regardless of who is signing, the referent is the same (i.e., her). Thus, drawing upon her knowledge of sign-symbol correspondences, she hypothesizes that the YOU point is a symbol referring to herself, that is, a name sign. In effect, she is applying the sign-symbol schema that works for other nouns to the YOU point. That is, she has over-symbolized the indexical YOU point, treating it as a frozen lexical item with a stable referent, herself.

This analysis makes clear the fundamentally linguistic nature of the error. Child 1 has grasped a basic fact about linguistic systems, namely the abstract relation between linguistic forms and their meanings. Rather than indexing particular objects in the world, these linguistic forms have intentional content; that is, they denote meanings or concepts rather than particular objects. The sign CUP, for example, does not index a particular object, but rather stands in an abstract relation to a class of items. The child's initial hypothesis about the meaning of YOU is that it is a symbol of this type: YOU refers to herself in the manner that CUP refers to cups. She consistently observes people using this form to refer to herself. Unfortunately, the correct, adult use of the sign in ASL, is in fact indexical. In hypothesizing that YOU is the lexical item referring to herself, the child ignores the indexical information provided by the form of the sign. Thus, the symbolization principle takes precedence, resulting in an error when applied to indexical signs.

Rather than reflecting a general cognitive deficit related to perspective-shifting, the YOU = ME error derives from the overapplication of an abstract linguistic principle. The error is striking because the child ignores transparent, perceptually salient information which she used to communicate prelinguistically, and which she continued to use deictically. This information is ignored in favor of a symbolization process that increases the abstractness of the relationship between form and meaning.

Two facts would count as evidence against the hypothesis that the child regards YOU as her name for the reasons specified above: (a) if during the error period the child produced the YOU form to refer to someone other than herself; or (b) if she comprehended the YOU form as referring to another person when she was not the addressee but an onlooker in a conversation between two adults. Both of these points cannot be supported by these data.

A final puzzle concerns the asymmetrical nature of the child's production error. The explanation appears to be as follows: when the child signs YOU to intend ME, YOU always has a single referent, the child. She does not sign ME, because she already has a form to represent this — the YOU sign. In addition, ME always means other people (but not their names). Since her YOU sign seems to function as a noun denoting herself, it might be expected that she would fail to use ME simply because pronouns are not part of her productive lexicon at this time.

Conclusions

In summary, the deaf children's performance was strikingly similar to that reported for hearing children acquiring pronouns. The major milestones in the deaf children's acquisition occurred at times that correspond closely to those reported for hearing children: (a) the early occurrence of proper nouns to refer to people; (b) the first occurrence of pronouns around 18–22 months; (c) a period of unstable knowledge and use of pronouns; and (d) correct use of pronouns by around 27 months. Between the ages of 12 and 18 months, both deaf children used only proper nouns to refer to people. Pronouns first appeared around 21–22 months, and correct usage was accomplished by 25 months for Child 2 and 27 months for Child 1. As with hearing children, the deaf children's initial production and comprehension of pronouns was not error free.

Thus, the study indicates that despite differences between the modalities that might be relevant to acquisition, both deaf and hearing children showed remarkably similar performance. Although it has been suggested by some that the transparent nature of the pointing gesture might make it possible for deaf children to acquire the use of these pronouns earlier than hearing children, this was clearly not the case. Such similarities between hearing and deaf children are strongly suggestive of the existence of universal processes in language acquisition, those that hold despite radical difference in modality that would otherwise be expected to facilitate the sign process compared to spoken language.

With respect to language acquisition models which propose a "direct mapping" and a strong continuity between the child's cognitive and linguistic representations, this study demonstrates that the deaf child's transition from gestural pointing to the linguistic use of YOU and ME pointing symbols is not smooth and effortless. The assumption that linguistic capacity is built up from (or mapped onto) pre-existing cognitive and communicative competence in a direct and continuous fashion cannot be supported by these data. On the contrary, the present study provides evidence for a discontinuity in the child's transition from prelinguistic to linguistic communicative systems, even when they share a single channel of expression and the forms are transparent. Further, the data from this study (including both the phenomenon of "avoidance" and the existence of pronoun-reversing errors) compel us to consider aspects of grammatical structure and its acquisition process to involve a relatively specific — linguistic — rather than general — cognitive — type of knowledge which the child brings to the language acquisition process, whose structure and organization may be biologically endowed.

The present study demonstrates how experimental research on sign language acquisition can provide a source of information bearing on theoretical issues in human cognition. The unique properties of sign languages (e.g., the fact that they make use of visual-gestural information expressed using external articulators, the hands) were exploited to provide a clear test of a current hypothesis concerning language learning. The results clarified aspects of the acquisition process that were obscured by the nature of speech.

PART III

Deaf Children Without Sign Language Input

Overview

The communicative and linguistic development of deaf children of hearing parents is the subject of chapters included in this part. In previously published studies, Goldin-Meadow and her colleagues reported on the home signs of ten deaf children of hearing parents, arguing that all of the children developed sign systems with a number of lexical and syntactic-semantic properties comparable to those found in early child language. In the study reported here, Goldin-Meadow and Mylander analyze the production of one of their subjects in greater detail in order to determine whether aspects of morphological structure can be developed by a child who has not been exposed to a sign language model.

Mohay's longitudinal study focuses on both gestural and vocal utterances of two profoundly deaf children between the ages of 18 months and about 3 years. Looking in particular at the interaction between gesture and speech, she concludes that deaf children acquire spoken language more slowly than hearing children and follow a different pattern. They can, however, express nonverbally the same range of semantic functions and pragmatic intents as those expressed verbally by younger hearing children.

The focus of Pereira's and De Lemos's study is on the communicative interaction between hearing mother and deaf child. The authors followed three deaf children between the ages of 2;7 and approximately 5 years longitudinally and concluded that the same processes observed in hearing mother-hearing child interaction are also found in their dyads. In their discussion, they underline the importance of interactional processes in the negotiation of meaning between the conversational partners. In this way, speech and gesture come to acquire symbolic status.

The aim of the single case study by Volterra, Beronesi, and Massoni is to analyze the gestural production of one deaf child from 6 to 7 years of age. The data, originally collected to observe the child's spoken communication, revealed almost casually the important role that gesturing played in the deaf child's communicative interaction and consequently in his linguistic development. The relationship between gestural and spoken production was analyzed and a first comparison between the deaf child's and the therapist's use of gestures was carried out.

Since the studies described in this part were conducted in the United States, Australia, Brazil, and Italy, the children came from differing cultural and linguistic environments. All of the deaf children described had hearing parents but they were not a homogeneous group in terms of family and educational background. Furthermore, the researchers did not focus on the same aspects of communicative and linguistic development in these four chapters. Nevertheless, all of the authors agree that despite their impoverished language-learning conditions, these deaf children develop gestural communication that serves many of the communicative functions of young children learning language in linguistic environments typically studied by students of child language. In particular, Goldin-Meadow and Mylander as well as Mohay emphasize that the deaf children they studied could express the same range of semantic functions and pragmatic intents nonverbally as those expressed verbally by hearing children.

There are important differences among these authors, however, in their explanations of the gestural behaviors of the deaf children. On the one hand, Goldin-Meadow and Mylander emphasize the creativity of the children in their use of symbolic gestures, finding no evidence that the communicative input of the hearing parents influenced the gestural production of their children. On the other hand, the remaining three chapters point out the relevance of the communicative environment created by the hearing adults – they do not participate in the interaction only through what they say or hear but also through the gestures they make or interpret. Pereira and De Lemos especially reexamine the concept of input, arguing for the point of view that sees interactive processes occurring between child and adult as constitutive of language acquisition in deaf as well as hearing children.

As an indirect consequence of these different perspectives, Goldin-Meadow and Mylander do not consider the spoken production of the deaf children while the other authors observe both gestural and spoken communication as well as the interaction between the two. These latter researchers agree that gestures tend to appear alone or simultaneously with the corresponding spoken productions, but as the deaf children become more confident in their use of words, the gestural accompaniment appears less frequently.

Another important difference between the first chapter in this section and those which follow concerns the morphological and syntactic properties of the deaf child's sign system. While Goldin-Meadow and Mylander find that all of the deaf children with hearing parents they studied developed gestural communication with complex syntactic properties comparable to those found in early child language, the other authors do not find such complexity. Instead, their position is that the deaf child's gestural production appears to be impoverished and unsystematic, differing markedly in structural complexity from early spoken and sign language. These contradictory viewpoints could result from a difference in the data collected by these investigators or from differing theoretical positions and criteria of interpretation. For example, the pointing gesture was considered by Goldin-Meadow and her colleagues as a deictic sign and classified as a nominal. This fact alone significantly affects the analysis and interpretation of the data and explains, in part, the marked differences between their conclusions and the conclusions of the other researchers.

CHAPTER 13
The Development of Morphology Without a Conventional Language Model

S. GOLDIN-MEADOW and C. MYLANDER

Introduction

The language-learning child in all cultures is exposed to a model of a particular language and, not surprisingly, acquires that language. Thus, linguistic input clearly has an effect on the child's acquisition of language. Nevertheless, it is possible that linguistic input does not affect all aspects of language development uniformly, and that variations in linguistic input will alter the course of development of some properties of language but not of others. In our own work, we have focused on isolating the properties of language whose development can withstand wide variations in learning conditions — the "resilient" properties of language. We have observed children who have not been exposed to conventional linguistic input in order to determine which properties of language can be developed by a child under one set of degraded input conditions. The children we study are deaf with hearing losses so severe that they cannot naturally acquire oral language, and born to hearing parents who have not yet exposed them to a manual language. Despite their impoverished language learning conditions, these deaf children develop a gestural communication system which is structured in many ways like the communication systems of young children learning language in traditional linguistic environments (Feldman, Goldin-Meadow, & Gleitman, 1978; Goldin-Meadow, 1979, 1982; Goldin-Meadow & Mylander, 1983, 1984b).

In our previous work we have shown that the gesture systems our deaf subjects develop are structured at the sentence level of analysis, i.e., there are patterns identifiable *across* gestures in a string. However, natural languages, both signed and spoken, are known to be structured at many different levels of analysis. If a hierarchy of structured levels is common to natural languages, it becomes important to ask whether the deaf children in our studies display such hierarchical structure as well (i.e., is hierarchical structure a resilient property of language?). Consequently, the primary objective of this study is to determine whether the deaf children's gesture systems are also structured at a second level of analysis, the level of the morpheme. Thus, we ask whether structure exists *within* gestures as well as across them, and consequently whether aspects of morphological structure can be developed by a child without the benefit of a conventional language model.

This chapter is reprinted from *Chicago Linguistic Society*, 1984, *20*, 119–135. We thank R.B. Church for her help in coding and analyzing the data, and our subject and his family for their continued cooperation and friendship. This work was supported by a grant from the Spencer Foundation.

Background

Sign languages of the deaf are autonomous languages which are not derivative from the spoken languages of hearing cultures (Klima & Bellugi, 1979). A sign language such as American Sign Language (ASL) is a primary linguistic system passed down from one generation of deaf people to the next and is a language in the full linguistic sense of the word – it has structural properties (as does a spoken language) at syntactic (Fischer, 1975; Liddell, 1980), morphological (Fischer, 1973; Klima & Bellugi, 1979; McDonald, 1982; Newport, 1981; Supalla, 1982), and "phonological" (Battison, 1974; Lane, Boyes Braem, & Bellugi, 1976) levels of analysis.

Deaf children born to deaf parents and exposed from birth to a conventional sign language (e.g., *ASL*) have been found to acquire language naturally, i.e., these children progress through stages in acquiring a conventional sign language similar to those of hearing children acquiring a conventional spoken language (Hoffmeister & Wilbur, 1980). Thus, in the appropriate linguistic environment (a signing environment), deaf children are not at all handicapped with respect to language learning.

However, 90% of deaf children are not born to deaf parents who could provide early exposure to a sign language. Rather, they are born to hearing parents who quite naturally expose their children to speech (Hoffmeister & Wilbur, 1980). It is extremely uncommon for deaf children with severe to profound hearing losses to acquire the spoken language of their hearing parents naturally, that is, without intensive instruction. Even with instruction, the children's acquisition of speech is markedly delayed when compared either to the signs of deaf children of deaf parents or the speech of hearing children of hearing parents. By the age of 5 or 6, and despite intensive early training programs, the average profoundly deaf child has only a very reduced oral linguistic capacity at his or her disposal (Conrad, 1979).

In addition, unless hearing parents send their deaf children to a school in which sign language is taught, these deaf children will not be exposed to conventional sign input. Under such nonpropitious circumstances, these deaf children might be expected to fail to communicate at all, or perhaps to communicate only in nonsymbolic ways. This turns out not to be the case.

Previous studies of deaf children of hearing parents have shown that these children spontaneously use symbols (gestures) to communicate even if they are not exposed to a conventional manual language model (e.g., Tervoort, 1961). These gestures are referred to as "home signs." Early studies, however, did not ask whether home sign systems are structured as human languages are. As a result, we have focused particularly on the *structural* aspects of deaf children's home signs and have attempted to determine which linguistic properties found in natural child language can also be found in home signs.

The Spontaneous Sign Systems of Deaf Children: Syntactic Properties[1]

We observed the home signs of six deaf children of hearing parents in Philadelphia and four in Chicago. We found that all ten children developed systems with a number of lexical and syntactic-semantic properties comparable to early child language (Feldman et al., 1978; Goldin-Meadow, 1979, 1982). In addition, we investigated the possibility that the deaf children might have learned their home sign systems from their hearing parents. In particular, we asked whether the parents, in an effort to communicate with their children, might not have generated a structured gesture system which their children then imitated, or whether the parents might not have shaped the structure of their children's gestures by patterning their responses to those gestures. We found no evidence for either of these hypotheses (Goldin-Meadow & Mylander, 1983, 1984b).

The children developed two major types of lexical signs: (a) deictic signs used to refer to people, places, and things (e.g., pointing gestures which rely on context for interpretation); and (b) characterizing signs used to refer to actions and attributes [e.g., a fist held at the mouth accompanied by chewing (EAT), or the index finger and thumb forming a circle in the air (ROUND)].

In addition, the children concatenated these lexical items into sign sentences expressing the semantic relations typically found in child language. We use linguistic terms such as "sentence" loosely and only to suggest that the deaf children's gesture strings share certain elemental properties with early sentences in child language. As an example of a sign sentence, one deaf child pointed at a block tower and then signed HIT (fist swat in air) to indicate that he had just hit the tower. In another example, the same child signed HIT, then pointed at his mother to request her to perform the hitting. These sign sentences were found to conform to regularities of two types: (a) construction order regularities which describe where a particular case or predicate tends to appear in a sign sentence (e.g., the sign for the patient, apple, tends to precede the sign for the act, EAT); (b) deletion regularities which describe the likelihood of a particular case or predicate to be omitted in a sign sentence (e.g., a sign for the patient, apple, would be less likely to be omitted in a sentence about eating than would a sign for the actor, boy).

Finally, the children were able to generate novel complex sentences (containing at least two propositions) from combinations of simple, one-proposition sentences. For example, one child pointed at a tower, produced the HIT sign and then the FALL sign (flat palm flops over in air) to comment on the fact that he had hit (act 1) the tower and that the tower had fallen (act 2).

---

[1] "Spontaneous" here is not meant as a developmental statement: undoubtedly, the development of the deaf child's sign system is influenced by both internal and external factors. We use "spontaneous" only to distinguish our subjects' individualistic sign systems from conventional sign language systems (e.g., ASL, Signed English).

Morphological Properties of the Deaf Child's Sign System

As described above, our previous work focused on the structural regularities across signs in our deaf subjects' gesture sentences. For the purposes of this "syntactic" analysis, we treated each sign as the minimal meaning-bearing unit. However, in examining the corpus of signs produced by each child, we began to notice certain sub-sign forms (e.g., handshape and motion) which seemed to be associated with consistent meanings, and which seemed to recur across different signs. For example, one child used the same motion form (moving the hand forward in a straight line) to mean "movement along a linear path" in at least two different signs, once with a fist handshape (resembling a person's hand moving a lawnmower in a straight line) and a second time with a flat palm handshape (resembling the lawnmower itself moving in a straight line). In addition to suggesting that the child can focus either on a person acting on an object or on the object itself in generating a sign, this example also suggests that handshape and motion might be separable sub-sign components within the child's gesture system.

A second type of example further reinforces the hypothesis that the deaf child's signs are divisible into components. Several children produced signs composed of two conflated motions, and at other times produced these same motions in one-motion signs. For example, one child produced a conflated two-motion sign to describe snow falling: a palm with the fingers spread hand-shape (representing particles of snow) was moved downward in a linear path (motion 1) while the fingers were wiggled (motion 2) ("snow-FALL + FLUT-TER"). The same child at other times produced each of these motions in separate one-motion signs: the finger wiggle motion was combined with the spread palm handshape to mean "snow-FLUTTER" and the linear path motion was combined with the spread palm handshape to mean "snow-FALL."

These examples suggest that at least some of the deaf children's signs are decomposable into smaller morpheme-like components. Nevertheless, these examples do not by themselves provide evidence of *systematic* hand and motion morphemes, as these selected cases may not be representative of the child's entire lexicon. In order to argue that the deaf child's signs are consistently divisible into hand and motion morphemes, we must review the corpus of signs as a whole and show: (a) that the child has a limited set of discrete hand and motion forms which comprise his or her lexical items; (b) that a particular hand or motion form is consistently associated with a particular meaning (or set of meanings) throughout the child's lexicon; and (c) that a particular hand or motion form recurs across different lexical items and thus is not limited to a single and (for the child) potentially unanalyzed lexical item.

Recent research on the signs of ASL that are highly mimetic in form has shown these signs to be composed of combinations of a limited set of discrete morphemes (McDonald, 1982; Newport, 1981; Supalla, 1982). These signs appear to be constructed from handshape, movement, and placement morphemes which combine with one another in a rule-governed fashion. To determine whether our deaf subjects' gestures can also be characterized by systematic combinations of meaningful forms, we selected one of our original subjects (David) and analyzed all of the characterizing signs the child produced during a 2-h naturalistic play session videotaped in his home when he was 3;11, an age at which both deaf and hearing children learning conventional languages have typically already begun to acquire certain morphemic distinctions (e.g., Mac-Whinney, 1976; Supalla, 1982). Following the ASL literature on morphological structure in mimetic signs, we coded each sign produced during this session in terms of its handshape, motion, and place of articulation.[2] Reliability between two independent coders was 85%-95% agreement for handshape, 83%-93% for motion, and 88% for place of articulation.

Handshape Morphemes

Handshape Forms. Following Supalla (1982) and McDonald (1982), we coded each handshape according to four dimensions: the shape of the palm, the distance between the fingers and the thumb, the number of fingers extended, and the presence or absence of spread between the fingers. We began by coding hand-shapes without any pre-established categories along these dimensions. Thus, for example, we wrote down the distance (in inches) between the fingers and thumb of a particular handshape and did not try to force that handshape into a limited set of thumb-finger distances. We found, however, that David used only a restricted number of values on each of the four dimensions (Table 1 displays the handshapes David used on these tapes described in terms of the four dimensions).[3] In fact, David used fewer values on certain of the dimensions than are used in ASL (e.g., David used three values for thumb-finger distance; Supalla lists five values for ASL) and he used them in a more restricted way than is typical of ASL (e.g., David used two fingers extended only with a straight palm and + Spread ; in ASL Supalla finds that two fingers can be used with a straight or round palm and with or without spread).

The handshapes we found in David's signs turn out to be, for the most part, the unmarked handshapes of ASL (cf., Klima & Bellugi, 1979) and the hand-shapes deaf children learning ASL from their deaf parents produce in their initial stages of acquisition (McIntire, 1977). Moreover, the most frequent of David's handshapes, the Fist, O, C, Palm, Spread Palm, and Point, also turn out to be just those handshapes found in the spontaneous gestures accompanying the speech of hearing children asked to explain conservation during a Piagetian task (Church & Goldin-Meadow, 1986). These handshapes thus appear to be common in the

---

[2]Place of articulation will not be discussed in this report.
[3]Numbers reported for handshape (Tables 1 and 2) reflect signs in which handshape was codable regardless of whether the corresponding motion could be seen and coded. Similarly, numbers reported for motions (Tables 3 and 4) reflect signs in which motion was codable, again independently of whether the corresponding handshape could be coded. Numbers reported for hand and motion combinations (Table 5) reflect signs in which both handshape and motion were codable.

Table 1. Description of handshapes used by David at age 3;11

	Shape of palm	Thumb-finger distance	Number of fingers	Spread between fingers	Times used (n)	(%)
Fist	Round	Fingers curled into palm	4	–	55	27
O	Round	Touch or < 1/2″	4	–	62	30
C	Round	3″	4	–	11	5
Palm	Straight	NA	4 +/– thumb	–	36	18
Spread Palm	Straight	NA	4 + thumb	+	14	7
Point	Straight	NA	1	NA	14	7
V	Straight	NA	2	+	7	3
L	Straight	NA	1 + thumb	+	1	1
Thumb	Straight	NA	thumb	NA	1	1
F	Round	Touch	1	NA	3	1

Both one-motion and two-motion signs are included in this table; NA, not applicable.

communications of both deaf and hearing individuals, and it is therefore not surprising that they appear in David's lexicon.

Handshape Form-Meaning Mapping. We saw above that David used a limited set of discrete handshapes in his signs. We next determined whether those hand-shapes mapped in any systematic way onto categories of meanings. We found that David used his handshapes in three ways (Table 2): to represent the way a hand is shaped as it HANDLES an object, to represent the shape of an OBJECT itself, or to function like a pencil TRACE of the extent of a static object or the path of a moving object. David's OBJECT and HANDLE handshapes are reminiscent of the classifier and instrumental handshapes, respectively, described for ASL (cf., Frishberg, 1975; Kegl & Wilbur, 1976; McDonald, 1982; Supalla, 1982) and his TRACE handshape resembles those handshapes Mandel (1977) cites in his descriptions of sketching in ASL. Within the TRACE category, note that the O hand is used to trace the extent of static objects and is thus distinguished from the Point hand, which is used to trace the path of moving objects.

Table 2 displays the handshapes David produced in one-motion signs, classified according to form and type of representation. Listed in each category are all of the objects David chose to represent with that form. For each group of objects, we were able to abstract a common attribute shared by all objects in that group. That common core we take to be the meaning of the handshape mor-pheme. All of David's 181 handshapes in one-motion signs could be classified into categories defined by particular hand forms and object meanings. In addition, 22

Table 2. Handshapes in one-motion signs

	Handle X-type of object	Type of object	Trace path or trace extent of object
Fist	Grasp small (< 2″ diameter) and long (> 5″ length) object: 10 (39) balloon string (3), drumstick (15), handlebar (2), hat brim (2), reins (10), shirt (3), spoon (1), steering wheel (1), trapeze ring (1), umbrella handle (1)		
O	Grasp small (< 2″ diameter) object of any length: 8 (42) banana (2), crank (1), drumstick (19), piece of food (1), shoe laces (1), spoon (1), straw (11), trapeze ring (6)	Round compact object: 2 (11) round hat (4), round nose (77)	Trace extent of object: 4 (9) beard (3), mustache (1), tie (1), straw (4)
C	Grasp large (> 2″ diameter) object of any length: 5 (7) cup (2), guitar neck (2), length of straw (1), wide knob (1), salt shaker (1)	Curved object: 1 (4) turtle (4)	
Palm	Contact large surface: 6 (13) top of push-down toy (1), stomach (4), mouth (1), sides of toy bag (2), back of turtle (1), front of guitar (4)	Flat, wide object: 7 (15) fish (2), flag (1), bird wings (4), butterfly wings (5), wheel (1), beard (1), hat (1) Vehicle or animate object: 4 (6) soldier in car (2), skate (2), Katie (1), Santa (1)	
Spread Palm	contact many small surfaces: 1 (2) piano keys (2)	Many small particles or object with individuated parts: 5 (7) snow (2), toes (1), spokes of umbrella (1), veins of bird wings (2), veins of butterfly wings (1)	
Point		Thin, straight object: 2 (6) straw (1), flat penny (2)	Trace path of object: 5 (8) bear (1), penny (1), Susan, (3), toy bag (2), wheel (1)
V		Scissors (7)	
L		Gun (1)	
F		Coin (3)	
Thumb	Contact press-button (1)		

The number in parenthesis next to each object represents the number of times the handshape was used for that object.

(92%) of the 24 handshapes in David's two-motion signs (now shown in Table 2) were found to conform to the form/meaning criteria established on the basis of the one-motion signs. It is worth noting that only two handshape categories were represented in the set of two-motion signs David produced – the Fist form meaning "grasp small and long object" and the Palm form meaning "vehicle or animate object" – suggesting that in David's system there may be additional constraints on the types of handshapes that can be used in two-motion signs.

Although most of the handshapes in Table 2 were used to represent a set of (more than one) objects, four were used for single exemplars only. The Thumb was used once to represent pushing a button. The other three handshapes, V, L, and F (all of which are marked handshapes in ASL), are conventional gestures within our hearing culture, representing scissors, a gun, and a coin, respectively.

It is important to note that the handshape David used in his signs was not necessarily a literal representation of the way a hand grasps a particular object in the real world. For example, the same form (the Fist) was used to represent grasping a balloon string, drumstick, and handlebars, objects which vary in diameter. Thus, David did not appear to distinguish objects with varying diameters within the Fist category. However, he did distinguish objects with small diameters *as a set* from objects with large diameters (e.g., a cup, a guitar neck, the length of a straw) which were represented by a C hand. Overall, David's handshapes appeared to be discrete categories rather than analog representations of "real world" actions.

Motion Morphemes

Motion Form. L.A. Friedman (1977) isolated manner of motion as a fundamental aspect of movement in ASL. In analyzing David's signs, we similarly focused on manner of motion, i.e., the way in which the arm and/or hand moved. We found four types of hand movements (open/close, bend, wiggle, finger revolve) and four types of arm movements (pivot, partial-revolve, full-revolve, rotate) in David's signs. We noted that arm movements, either alone or in combination, perforce create different trajectories traced by the hand. The shape of a trajectory is determined (a) by the type or types of arm movements used (e.g., a single wrist pivot results in a small arced trajectory; an elbow full-revolve combined with a shoulder pivot results in a circular trajectory); and (b) in instances of pivot combinations, by how those movements are combined (e.g., if two pivots in a combination move in opposing directions, the resulting hand trajectory is linear).[4] We also found that movements (or combinations of

---

[4] For combinations of pivots, the trajectory depends on how the movements are combined. If each pivot moves in the same direction (– Opposition), the trajectory produced appears arced in shape, e.g., an arm flap in which the arm pivots up from the shoulder as it also pivots up from the elbow. In contrast, if the two pivots in a combination move in opposing directions (+ Opposition), the trajectory produced appears linear, e.g., an arm push from the chest straight forward in which the shoulder pivots from right to left (counter-clockwise) as the elbow pivots from left to right (clockwise).

Table 3. Description of motions used by David at age 3;11

	Type of motion	Directionality	Times used (n)	(%)
Linear	Combination of pivots, + Opposition	Uni	26	12
Long arc	1. Combination of Pivots, − Opposition	Uni	21	11
	2. Combination of pivots and partial revolves	Uni		
Short arc	One pivot	Uni	16	8
Arc to and fro	1. Combination of pivots, − Opposition	Bi	58	31
	2. One pivot	Bi		
Circular	1. Combination of full revolves	Uni	15	8
	2. Combination of full revolves and pivots	Uni or Bi		
	3. Wrist rotates	Bi		
	4. Fingers revolve	Uni		
Open/close	Hand or fingers open or close	Uni	10	5
Bend	Hand or fingers bend	Uni or Bi	5	3
Wiggle	Fingers wiggle	Bi	3	2
No motion	Hand held in place	NA	36	19

Both one-motion and two-motion signs are included in this table; *Uni*, unidirectional; *Bi*, bidirectional; *NA*, not applicable.

movements) in David's signs varied in directionality — some were unidirectional and others were bidirectional.

Table 3 displays the different motion forms plus a "no motion" category found in David's signs. Each motion form was defined in terms of types of movements (alone or in combination) and directionality. The resulting nine motion forms are reminiscent of (but not identical to) the motion morphemes Newport (1981) and Supalla (1982) isolated in their descriptions of ASL.

Motion Form-Meaning Mapping. We next determined whether each of the nine motion forms was associated with a particular class of meanings. We found that David used most of his motion forms to represent actions but also used some to represent descriptive traits. Table 4 displays the motions David produced in his one-motion signs, classified according to form and type of representation. Listed in each category are all of the actions or traits David chose to represent with that motion form. As we did for the handshape analysis, we were able to abstract a common action or description meaning for each category. Of David's 171 motions in one-motion signs 92% could be classified into these categories (the 13 excep-

Table 4. Motions in one-motion signs

	Action	Description
Linear	Change of location along a straight path: 4 (7) snow fall (1), skate glide (1), turtle go (4), penny go (1)	Extent or outline of object: 7 (14) tall hat (2), long nose (1), wide hat (1), long beard (4), long tie (1), long straw (4), outline mustache (1)
Long arc	Change of location to or from a particular endpoint: 6 (11) penny go to (1), scoop spoon to (2), wheel tip to (1), Susan move to (3), move surface to (1), remove shirt from (3)	
Short arc	Reorientation at the beginning or endpoint of a change of location: 7 (7) don hat (1), Katie sit (1), jab food (1), lift bag (1), put straw (1), put bear (1), remove hat (1)	
Arc to and fro	Change orientation by moving back and forth: 10 (54) hit turtle (1), tap mouth (1), bird wings flap (2), butterfly wings flap (2), strum guitar (5), move shoelaces in and out (1), move guitar up and down (2), beat drum (31), move reins up and down (8), flag wave (1)	
Circular	Move in circular path or rotate around axis: 7 (11) turn bag around (3), turn straw around (1), rotate steering wheel (1), wave balloon string in circle (3), turn crank (1), twist knob (1), wheel rotate (1)	Orientation of object: 1 (4) upturned nose (4)
Open/close	Open or close: 3 (7) umbrella open (1), Santa straighten up (1), scissors cut (5)	

Table 4. *(continued)*

	Action	Description
Bend	Bend: 5 (5) fish swim (1), bird wing flap (1), toes curl (1), press gun hammer (1), press button (1)	
Wiggle	Wiggle: 2 (3) snow flutter (1), play piano (2)	
No motion	Hold object: 7 (24) hold umbrella (1), handle- bars (2), reins (2), banana (2), straw (11), cup (2), stomach (4)	Object exists: 5 (11) hat (2), nose (1), straw (3), scissors (2), coin (3)

tions are not included in Table 4). In addition, 16 (84%) of the 19 motions in David's two-motion signs (not shown in Table 4) were found to conform to the form/meaning criteria established on the basis of the one-motion signs.

Handshape and Motion Combinations

We have shown that David's signs can be described in terms of handshape form/meaning categories and motion form/meaning categories. However, we have not yet shown that a sign in David's system was a composite of hand and motion morphemes rather than one unanalyzed whole, i.e., that handshape and motion are separable units. Since signs are composed of hands moving in space, it is not possible to find handshapes which are actually separated from their motions. Nevertheless, if we find that a handshape is not uniquely associated with one sign but is combined with several different motions in different signs, then we have evidence that the handshape can function as an independent unit in David's system. Similarly, if a motion is combined with different handshapes in different signs, there is evidence for the separability of that motion.

Table 5 presents the number of types (and tokens) of signs produced by David, classified according to handshape and motion. Note that six of the handshapes (Fist, O, C, Point, Palm, and Spread Palm) were found in combination with at least four and as many as eight different motions. Moreover, all of the motions except Wiggle were found in combination with at least two and as many as five of these handshapes. These six handshapes and all of the motions except Wiggle thus satisfy our criterion as independent units in David's signs. In contrast, of the remaining four handshapes, Thumb, L, and F were each found combined with only one motion and V occurred with two motions, one of which was "no motion." Recall that in Table 2 each of these four handshapes was used to

Table 5. Handshape and motion combinations in David's one-motion signs

	Linear	Long arc	Short arc	Arc to and fro	Circular	Open close	Bend	Wiggle	No motion
Fist		2 (4)	2 (2)	2 (20)	2 (4)				3 (5)
O	6 (12)	1 (1)	1 (1)	2 (18)	2 (5)				4 (16)
C	1 (4)			1 (2)	2 (2)	2 (2)			1 (2)
Point	1 (1)	2 (4)	2 (2)		1 (1)				1 (3)
Palm	3 (3)	2 (2)	2 (2)	6 (11)	1 (1)	1 (1)	2 (3)		1 (4)
Palm Spread	1 (1)			2 (3)		1 (1)	1 (1)	2 (3)	
Thumb						1 (1)			
V						1 (5)			1 (2)
L							1 (1)		
F									1 (3)

The first number represents the total number of different types of signs David produced in that category; the number in parenthesis represents the total number of tokens.

represent only one object rather than a class of objects. Thus, the signs in David's system which contain these four handshapes may in fact be unanalyzed wholes in which handshape and motion are *not* isolable units.

Discussion

We have found that the corpus of signs David produced can be characterized as a system of hand and motion morphemes; in particular, David's signs were composed of a limited and discrete set of ten hand and nine motion forms each of which was consistently associated with a distinct meaning and recurred across different lexical items. Thus, David's signs appeared to be decomposable into smaller morpheme-like components, suggesting that his gesture system was indeed structured at the sign level.

Two important points are worth noting about the signs in David's gesture system. First, David used discrete forms to represent the objects, actions, and traits in his world despite the fact that in the manual modality one can represent movements and shapes in a continuous fashion. Although mimetic signs in conventional sign languages such as ASL were originally thought to be built on just such an analog use of movement and space (DeMatteo, 1977), current research has shown the signs of ASL to be composed of combinations of a limited set of discrete morphemes in the sign systems of deaf adults (McDonald, 1982; Newport, 1981; Supalla, 1982). Moreover, during the acquisition process, young deaf children acquiring ASL from their deaf parents do not learn the signs of ASL that can be seen as analog representations of movement and space any more easily than they learn the signs that cannot be seen as analog representations (Meier, 1981). Thus, sign systems, be they conventional or individualistic, appear to be characterized by a system of categorical rather than analogic representation.

Secondly, David's signs appear to be organized in relation to one another, as opposed to being organized only in relation to the objects they represent. One indication of organization across lexical items is the fact that David's signs, at times, adhered to sign-sign constraints (i.e., the fit between a sign and the rest of the signs in the lexicon) at the expense of sign-object constraints (i.e., the fit between a sign and the object it represents). The two-hand exceptions in David's two-motion signs illustrate this point. Recall that only two handshapes seemed to be allowable in David's two-motion signs and that this set included only one HANDLE handshape — the Fist. In exception one, the Fist hand was inappropriately used to represent contacting the back of a turtle, a referent that fits David's meaning category "contact large surface" and (on the basis of the properties of the object) should have been represented by a HANDLE Palm. David appeared to use the formally appropriate Fist rather than the semantically appropriate Palm, suggesting that formal considerations may override semantic considerations in David's system. Similarly, in exception two, the Fist hand was inappropriately used to represent grasping a small short knob, a referent that fits David's meaning category "grasp small object of any length" and (based on the properties of the object) should have been represented by a HANDLE O. Again David substituted a Fist (the handshape for small *long* objects), adhering to the formal constraints on handshapes in two-motion signs at the expense of sign-object constraints.

We have described the gestures developed by a deaf child with hearing losses so severe he cannot naturally acquire oral language, and born to hearing parents who have not yet exposed him to a conventional manual language. Despite his impoverished language-learning conditions, this child developed a gestural communication system with structure at the sign level, i.e., a gestural system whose lexical items were organized with respect to one another, with component pieces of form and component pieces of meaning inter-relating the items. These results suggest that a child can develop the rudiments of a structured communication system — including structure at a morphological level — even without a conventional language model to guide his development.

CHAPTER 14

Gesture in Hearing Mother-Deaf Child Interaction

M. C. DA CUNHA PEREIRA and C. DE LEMOS

Introduction

Among the problems faced by students of language acquisition by deaf children with hearing parents is to explain how they develop gestural systems without sign language input (Lenneberg, 1964; Moores, 1974; Tervoort, 1961). As might be expected, attempts to solve such a problem began by explaining gestural development in those children in terms of innate mechanisms (Feldman, Goldin-Meadow, & Gleitman, 1978; Goldin-Meadow, 1979). In addition, lack of sign language input was considered equivalent to no input at all. The studies mentioned above seem to emphasize that their deaf subjects were submitted to an oral method of teaching in order to make more salient the absence of gestural input. They also point out that the children fail to acquire oral language when exposed to it.

This type of approach neglects the possibility that deaf children in some way or another interact with their parents as well as the empirically relevant questions arising from such a possibility. What happens between the hearing adult and the deaf child? What is the role of the adult's gesture and of the child's gesture in this kind of interaction? Is the different symbolic status of gestural communication and sign language such that hypotheses about their developmental relationship should not be entertained?

Such questions are crucial because they force us to reexamine the concept of input. Preconceptions about the nature of the input such as those mentioned above have prevented researchers from giving greater attention to the interactional processes between hearing and deaf individuals, especially between the hearing adult and the deaf child. A first step in this direction would be to consider a proposal by McNeill (1985) that gesture and speech are integrated in the same matrix of meaning production. For McNeill, gestures are semantically and pragmatically related to the linguistic units instantiated in speech. Furthermore, he states that "the occurrence of gestures, along with speech, implies that during the act of speaking two kinds of thinking, imagistic and syntactic, are being coordinated" (p. 367). According to this proposal, then, the hearing adult does not participate in interaction only through what he or she says or hears, but also through gestures performed and interpreted.

Here it is important to mention Caselli's studies of gesture in the language development of hearing children. Caselli (1983a and this volume) and Caselli, Ossella, and Volterra (1983) show that hearing children develop gestures while interacting with their mothers. The gestures are of the same type as the ones used by young deaf children and they appear in single-element utterances or combined, with both indicative and referential gestures conjoined in two-gesture utterances. These authors assign gesture and speech to a sole and general symbolic capacity but they do not discuss what happens to gestural expressions with the growth of oral and linguistic ability. In other words, how is the matrix of meaning production referred to by McNeill affected by the child's increasing use of spoken language during interaction?

Lock's (1980) work also has as its aim to relate gestural and vocal communication in the linguistic development of hearing children. Its importance lies in the role Lock assigns to adult-child interaction in the qualitative transformation of the child's motor activities into communicative gestures. According to Lock, the mother interprets her child's movements early on as communicative acts. By attributing meaning to the child's movements, she gives them social value; it is through her response to those movements that they become gestures which will later be used intentionally. In this way, the mother mirrors the child's behavior back to him or her, and as a result the child begins, as Lock points out, to express his or her communicative intentions by means of gestures. Lock also states that utterances of more than one gesture are the empirical evidence for an initial combining ability preceding and determining the emergence of multiword combinations or a primitive oral syntax.

Both Lock and Caselli, in their pioneering research, view gestural and oral language as temporally ordered with no attention given to the gestures produced simultaneously with speech in later stages. This approach is understandable given the intellectual context for studies of spoken language. Oral language has only recently become the object of linguistic analysis. As has been pointed out by Kato (1986), writing systems seem to have biased our views on oral language, reducing it to its segmental aspects. Thus, there has been a general neglect of prosodic and gestural components in linguistic research, even though both are an integral part of spoken language activity. The same has not been true for the study of language in some branches of psychology.

Mead (1934) assigned a crucial role to gesture in the origin of mental processes. For him, gestures included manual as well as vocal postures, and meaning was a product of social interaction. Mead pointed out the discrete nature of gestures or postures when defining them as a phase of the broader social act in which they were produced and acquired their meaning. Thus, following this view, in order to become language or symbolic activity, gestures must be shared and their meanings recognized as each conversational partner functions as a mirror for the other.

Mead's statement that gesture is a phase in the social act it represents seems to refer to the fact that a segment of the behavioral or motor chain is framed and raised up to represent the situation to which it first belonged. In this way, the gesture becomes a discrete symbolic or meaningful element. Thus, the gesture or raising a spoon up to the mouth represents the whole act of eating.

How do such processes — framing, raising up, and meaning attribution — come about? Mead suggests that reciprocal imitation plays an important part in such processes. According to him, imitation is not simply doing what you see another person do; it accomplishes agreement with the other person about which aspect of the act is to be raised up as a representation of that act. In this way, it is possible to evoke in oneself the response evoked in the other.

De Lemos (1981), in her discussion of specularity, highlights the role that reciprocal imitation plays in the child's language development. Specularity is closely related to the concepts of reflex and mirroring, attributing to the phenomenon of reciprocal imitation the status of a constitutive process in which dialogue and signs are shared objects. For De Lemos, the specularity process accounts not only for the child's utterances, but also for the mother's, with the framing and construction of linguistic objects resulting from mutual incorporation. When the child incorporates the adult's role and the roles assigned to him or her by the adult in specific situations, he or she gradually becomes able to represent him- or herself and the partner as interlocutors.

The process of specularity, or the incorporation of part or all of the partner's utterance, is the basis for two other processes which, according to De Lemos (1982), seem to govern the building up of adult-child dialogue, namely the complementary process and the reciprocity process. The former comprises both (a) inter-turn complementarity in which the child fills in a semantic, syntactic, and pragmatic locus set up by the immediately preceding utterance; and (b) intra-turn complementarity wherein the child's utterance results from the incorporation of part of the utterance immediately preceding combined with a complementary word. By means of the reciprocity process, the child takes up roles assumed earlier only by the adult.

The notions of meaning-production matrix and of interactive processes enable us to reformulate the questions raised at the beginning of this paper in the following way: are the interactive processes presented above as constitutive of language acquisition in hearing children also responsible for gestural development in deaf children? How can those processes be effective in the interaction of individuals having different access to each other's behavioral chain?

The last question points to issues raised by McNeill's view of the coordination of gestures with speech, specifically the need to define the term "coordination" and to explicate the statement that gesture and speech are products of the same computational stage. Although such a view is based on both temporal and semantic-pragmatic relations between gesture and speech, the reference point implied by McNeill's description of those relations is clearly the speaker's speech production.

Concerning the interaction of hearing adults with deaf children, it would be misleading either to take the speech production of the adult as a reference point or to assume the possibility of the child's doing so. On the other hand, if McNeill's proposal is to be extended to sign language, thus achieving further theoretical relevance, it would be necessary to look at the functioning of the matrix in the cases in which access to speech is partial. A prerequisite for such analysis would be to clarify the relationships between gesture and speech by examining the pragmatic constraints operating on their coordination, in other words, by taking into account the interactive processes which may determine the symbolic status and function of each one of the activities.

At this point, it is worth emphasizing that, throughout this chapter, the term "interaction" is not being used synonymously with "communication." Indeed, the claim that interactive processes are constitutive of language acquisition — and also of language as a symbolic activity — is incompatible with the view of communication as a function of language and, therefore, external to its construction and/or organization processes. Thus, in rephrasing our initial questions, we also had in mind the theoretical consequences of relating McNeill's proposal to De Lemos' hypotheses on language acquisition. Namely, the need for imposing an intersubjective and, thus, dialectical perspective onto the notion of meaning-production matrix. Accordingly, gesture and speech integrated in different ways in different utterance acts should be seen as corresponding to different interlocutionary effects.

The Study

The theoretical points presented above motivated the first author to undertake the analysis of longitudinal data on three deaf children's interactions with their hearing mothers. The study is part of a wider research endeavor aimed at the description of symbolic development in four hearing-impaired children of hearing parents. The subjects were chosen from children entering a specialized school for the deaf in São Paulo, Brazil, who had never been submitted to any special language training. Before being admitted they had been seen by a diagnostic team which confirmed that they all had a severe sensori-neural congenital hearing loss and showed no other impairments. The school uses an oral approach in language teaching, but gestures are accepted if the children do not have any other way to express themselves.

Dyadic interactions between children were videotaped for 30 min per month and interactions of children and their mothers were recorded every 2 months. The recording sessions took place in the school in a room where four or five kinds of toys were available at each session. No instructions were given to any dyad, and the mothers were told that the investigator's aim was to observe the child's general development.

The children were between 2;7 and 3;4 when the first author started the data collection, continuing for 1½ years for two of the children and 3 years for the other two. Videotaped data available for analysis consist of 68 30-min recordings.

Data were transcribed so that gestures, facial expressions, and body motion as well as vocalizations and verbal activities were detailed enough to allow investigators to follow, throughout the transcripts, the qualitative changes taking place over time.

The first point to be made concerning the data is that all the mothers used gestures simultaneously with oral language, interpreted equivalents, or oral translations. Examples 1–3 below, illustrate how, by repeating, translating, or mirroring the child's gesture, the mother shows her acceptance of its form and meaning. It should also be noticed that in example 3 she even requests the child's agreement of her interpretation, which is obtained through the child's nodding:

1.   Marcio and his mother look at pictures in books (M — 6;4.19).
     M: Open hand, palm down, movement with the hand back and forth.
     Mother: "Balanço." (Swing).

2.   Vanessa and her mother look at pictures in books (V — 3;9.14).
     V: Thumb and forefinger near each other, in front of the eye + points to a picture.
     Mother: Makes same gesture as Vanessa, *"Pequenininho"* (Very small).

3.   Vanessa and her mother play with building blocks (V — 3;9.14).
     V: While building a church: points to the church + makes sign of the cross + points to the church.
     Mother: "Ah, a igreja? É assim: Pai, Filho, Espirito Santo" (Ah, the church? It's like this: Father, Son, Holy Ghost).
     V: Nods affirmatively.

Another example demonstrates the role of the specularity process in the negotiation of signs or linguistic objects:

4.   Vanessa and her mother look at pictures in books (V — 3;9.14).
     V: Points at a picture.
     Mother: Points at the same picture + closed hand near side of head, movement of shaking back and forth, *"Ó aí as bandeirinhas, né?"* (Look at the little flags, huh?).
     V: Papi.
     Mother: Points at the same picture, *"Né? É esta aqui"* (Isn't it? It's this one here).
     V: Looks,
     "Não. Não. Papi não" (No. No. Not papi). Still, closed hand in front of body, *"Roda. Roda"* (Turn round. Turn round).
     Mother: Points at the same picture, *"Bandeira"* (Flag).
     V: Still, closed hand in front of body, *"Roda"* (Turn round).
     Mother: Closed hand in front of body, movement of shaking hand back and forth, *"Bandeirinha. Não é pipa, não"* (Flag. It's not a kite, no).
     V: "Papila?"
     Mother: Shakes her head no, *"Não"* (No).
     V: Still, closed hand in front of body, *"Roda"* (Turn round). Repeats gesture, *"Roda"* (Turn round).
     Mother: Nods yes, *"E"* (Yes).

In example 4, mother and child seem to negotiate the form of the gesture, namely hand movement and position, in order to distinguish between a flag and a kite. It is worth noticing that, like her mother, Vanessa presents oral productions simultaneously with her gestures. These productions approximate words in adult Portuguese.

The first occurrences of intra-turn complementarity, that is, of gestural combinations, are also based on specularity or incorporation of the partner's turn:

5. Viviane and her mother look at pictures in books (Vi − 3;4.8).

    Vi: Points at a picture and looks at her mother.

    Mother: Palm of hand up + closed hand, still and near the head, "*O que é? O guarda-chuva?*" (What is it? The umbrella?)

    Vi: Looks at the picture and makes the same gestures as her mother.

    Mother: Points out of the window, "*Tá chovendo, né?*" (It's raining, isn't it?)
    Viviane's sister asks to see the picture.

    Vi: Looks at her sister and points out of the window and repeats mother's gesture: still, closed hand and near the head.

    Mother: "*Tá chovendo. Tá segurando o guarda-chuva.*" (It's raining. He's holding the umbrella).

6. Márcio and his mother look at pictures in books (M − 4;8.5).

    Mother: Points to a picture, "*Andando*" (Walking).

    M: Points to the same picture as his mother + hands beside body, palms backwards, movement of swimming.

    Mother: Nodding affirmatively, "*Tá nadando*" (He's swimming).

In example 5, Viviane produces a two-gesture utterance by combining gestures used separately by her mother. In example 6, Márcio combines the indicative gesture, used by his mother, with a referential gesture and produces a two-gesture utterance based on partial specularity.

The reciprocity process was also observed throughout the recordings: in the first recording sessions it is the mother who points out and names the figures in the pictures; later the child points, and the mother names until the child begins to both point and name the figures in the pictures.

Having made it clear that the same processes observed in the interaction of hearing mothers and their hearing children are also found in hearing mother-deaf child interaction, the importance of those processes in the assignment of meaning to gestures and in the construction of gestural subsystems remains to be demonstrated.

In the following examples it will be possible to see that the mother is able to interpret the gestures produced by the child and to offer the same gesture back to her, mirroring it as a form of agreement and recognition of its symbolic status. Such is the process by which the child's motor activities in specific situations are raised up as gestural indices of a whole interactional episode.

7. Viviane and her mother play with puppets (Vi − 3;0.19).

    Mother: Picking up a puppet: "*Que nenê lindo! Que bonitinho!* (What a beautiful baby! How pretty!). Holds the puppet close to her body and turns from side to side, rocking it.

    Vi: Repeats mother's gesture.

8. Viviane and her mother look at pictures in books (Vi − 3;4.8).
    Vi: Points to a picture + arm crooked, palm up, movement with the arm from side to side.
    Mother: Shakes head no + hand opened, palm up *"Onde tem nenê."* (Where is the baby?). Points to the same picture, *"Não tem nenê. É o menino"* (There is no baby. It's a boy). Open hand, palm down at the waist, *"Já é grande, né."* (He's big already, isn't he?).

The mimicry of rocking the baby is now reduced to one movement, namely the crooked arm, but the resulting gesture, though abbreviated, remained identifiable by someone outside the interaction. The same does not occur in the interaction below in which the gesture is not identifiable by a person unfamiliar with it:

9. Márcio's mother goes to her bag to get a handkerchief (M − 4;5.8).
    M: Nudges his mother + thumbs and forefingers forming a pincer in front of the mouth.
    Mother: *"Bala não tem"* (There's no candy).
    M: Open hands, palm up.
    Mother: *"Acabou"* (All gone).
    M: Hands on waist, displeased facial expression.
    Mother: Closed fingers in except forefinger which extended to left and in front of the body; semicircular movement away from the body, *"Depois"* (Afterwards). Points to herself, then to the door of the room, *"Eu vou lá"* (I am going there). Open hand, palm up; closing hand movement, *Pegar, tá?"* (To get it, OK?).
    M: Moves away.

In example 9, the gesture which stands for "candy" is hardly relatable to the source situation, namely that of unwrapping candy. So one can plausibly say that it is a gesture on its way to becoming a sign. However, further data analysis is needed for understanding how paradigmatic (the example of the flag) and syntagmatic (the example of the umbrella) relations holding among gestures determine abbreviation and ritualization processes; in other words, how formal subsystems are built up and/or become operative. There is no doubt that those subsystems would show a much lower degree of organization than those which seem to result from highly semantically and pragmatically differentiated interactions as is the case among deaf adults.

The fact that the subjects of this research attended a school where there were older deaf children cannot be disregarded — we cannot say that they are acquiring a sign language within a hearing family group. However, it is in their interactions with members of such a group that they seem to develop abilities which make the learning of a sign language possible, namely the ability to assume roles in social interactions and the capacity for symbolic activity.

It should be mentioned, finally, that our data on child-child interaction show that, in spite of the fact that they were attending the same school and belonged to the same age range and socioeconomic class, communication within each pair was definitely impaired at the beginning. Negotiation of the form and meaning of gestures was absent, and one could hardly find processes of mutual interpretation. The following example will serve to illustrate this point:

10. Vanessa and Márcio are looking at pictures in a book (V − 4; 1.18 and M − 5; 0.9).
    Vanessa nudges Márcio who turns his book for her to see. Vanessa continues nudging Márcio. Márcio looks at Vanessa, and she points at a picture in Márcio's book.
    V: Points at the picture of a dog.
    M: Does not look.
    V: Nudges Márcio and points again at the picture + open mouth, makes brusque movement to close it.
    M: Points at the picture of the dog, "*Ah!*" stretches body and sticks out the tongue.
    V: Looks at the picture in Márcio's book + open mouth, makes brusque movement to close it.
    M: Looks at Vanessa with open mouth and tongue out.
    Each child returns to own book.

As illustrated above, each child has his or her own particular gesture to refer to the picture of a dog. It is plausible to look at such a difference as corresponding to different ways of framing their experience with dogs, probably resulting from different interactional experiences. Such observation points again to the need to consider symbols, whether they are vocal or gestural, as originating from shared experiences where intersubjective agreement on pragmatic, semantic, or formal features is gradually obtained.

In brief, what we have been attempting to show is that there is interaction between the hearing mother and the deaf child in spite of the different symbolic modes they have at their disposal. Moreover, the processes which govern such interaction are, in most respects, the same as those described for the hearing mother and her child. It is, indeed, through these processes that speech and gesture are negotiated and thus acquire symbolic status.

It is also worth noting that there was no exclusion of one or the other modality in the dyads we studied. All mothers used both gestures and speech to interact with their children from the first recording session onwards.

Although it is not within the scope of the present work to discuss the vocal production of the children, mention should be made of their attempts to use behavioral modes. Since neither of the two modalities is excluded, it seems appropriate to describe how gestural and vocal/oral production relate to each other, namely, which channel or modality is in the foreground, leaving to the other modality the function of expressive background (C. De Lemos, in preparation). Distance and other factors, mainly those culturally determined, seem to govern the possibilities of gesture being in the foreground or background in hearing adult's communication. Such an observation is a sort of preliminary answer to the questions raised above about the status and function of gesture and speech in McNeill's matrix of meaning-production.

The mother, as the hearing partner, can use both modalities integrated in the matrix. It is her set of expectations regarding her child's capacity and auditory impairment which seems to determine the degree of either gesture or speech foregrounding in her communicative activity. Of course, the child's auditory impairment strongly influences gesture foregrounding at the beginning. However, as far as her vocal behavior is assigned an interactional role, the way the child represents his or her partner also becomes a factor governing, to some extent, the foregrounding of either gestural or vocal production.

There is no doubt how dependent the deaf child's symbolic activity is on his or her auditory and vocal abilities. However, Vanessa's longitudinal data demonstrate clearly that the foregrounding of either gestural or vocal expressions was governed by the image she built up regarding her partner's communicative abilities. Indeed, speech became more and more foregrounded in her interaction with her mother, while gesture was usually foregrounded in her interaction with Márcio and other deaf children at school.

We began this chapter by calling attention to the notion of a meaning-production matrix and arguing for its importance in the description of the linguistic development of both hearing and deaf children. It is also important from an educational point of view. In fact, having in mind that, instead of a gestural system, the deaf child is acquiring a meaning-production matrix, it is possible to look at him or her not from the point of view of the hearing and/or speech deficit, but as someone who functions differently from a linguistic point of view (cf., Cole & Bruner, 1972).

As far as sign language is concerned, it seems clear that acquisition does not occur through the interaction of the deaf child with his or her hearing and nonsigning family. However, as shown in the study reported above, such interaction can be the social "locus" wherein the deaf child acquires symbolic and interactional abilities which are the constitutive basis for the later mastery of a fully developed system.

It also does not seem to be the case that the deaf child's contact with deaf peers is enough for such a process to take place. This view is supported by the evidence presented in example 10 above. What we would suggest is that the acquisition of sign language is likely to develop out of a primitive gestural system, in the deaf child's contact with older deaf children and/or signers, in other words, through contact with individuals whose mastery of a fully developed sign system enables them to assign intention and meaning to the child's gestures and general behavior. Such interaction would establish a second "locus" for the construction of more complex linguistic objects.

CHAPTER 15

The Interaction of Gesture and Speech in the Language Development of Two Profoundly Deaf Children

H. MOHAY

> Man, full of wisdom and divinity, could have appeared nothing superior to a naked trunk or block, had he not been adorned with the hand as the interpreter and messenger of his thoughts. . . . Since Nature has furnished us with two instruments for the purpose of bringing into light and expressing the silent affections of the mind, language and the hand, it has been the opinion of learned and intelligent man that the former would be maimed and nearly useless without the latter; whereas the hand, without the aid of language, has produced many and wonderful effects.
>
> Cresollius, 1620, (Quoted in Critchley, 1975)

Introduction

Most deaf children are born into families in which there is no history of hearing impairment. Hence they have no exposure to the manual communication used in the deaf community, and the spoken language used by the hearing community in which they live is inaccessible to them. Even with amplification, the auditory signal is distorted and incomplete and the lipreading pattern is ambiguous and often impossible to interpret. Under these conditions, deaf children do not acquire spoken language effortlessly as hearing children do. Each word has to be laboriously taught and learned. Language acquisition becomes an arduous and frustrating task and one in which they are frequently unsuccessful. It has long been recognized that because of this hearing-impaired children resort to the use of gestural communication. Heider and Heider (1941), for example, reported that 4- to 6-year-old deaf children used few spoken words, but communicated with each other quite effectively by means of gestures, pantomime, and facial expression. Although the use of nonverbal communication was acknowledged, the prevailing oral education philosophy decreed that all means of communication other than speech be regarded as inferior and not worthy of further investigation. Interest was therefore directed exclusively to the child's acquisition of spoken language. However, as this was frequently very limited and difficult to transcribe accurately because of the distorted speech of deaf children, most research rested heavily on the production of written language and was consequently restricted to school age children.

As a result, little information is available on the spoken language development of young hearing-impaired children. Lenneberg, Rebelsky, and Nichols (1965) and Lenneberg (1967) reported that as early as 6 months of age the vocalizations of deaf infants differ from those of hearing infants in both frequency of production and variety. These results were largely confirmed by Maskarinec, Cairns, Butterfield, and Weamer (1981), and Lack, Ling, Ling and Ship (1970) similarly noted that all seven of the hearing-impaired children in their study had abnormal voice quality when they commenced a preschool training program at ages ranging from 11 to 32 months. Thus it would seem that from an early age the vocal behavior of hearing-impaired children is different from that of hearing children and continues to be so as they struggle to acquire a spoken vocabulary. Both Pugh (1946) and Morkovin (1960) reported that the average spoken vocabulary of 4-year-old deaf children was less than 30 words, and advances in technology seem to have improved this only marginally. Gregory and Bishop (1982), for example, found that 16 of the 24 hearing-impaired children they studied entered school with a spoken vocabulary of fewer than 150 words, and Gregory and Mogford (1981) reported that the two profoundly deaf children whose language development they monitored from the time of diagnosis until 4 years of age failed to acquire even ten words during this period. The moderately and severely hearing-impaired children in their sample did somewhat better with all of them attaining a spoken vocabulary in excess of 100 words before their 4th birthday. However, their first words were produced later than hearing children's and their rate of word acquisition was slower. This was particularly evident after the acquisition of the first 50 words when the hearing-impaired children failed to show the burgeoning of vocabulary usually observed in hearing children at this stage of language acquisition.

In spite of the emphasis on spoken (and written) language, sporadic reports on the gestural communication of deaf children did appear in the literature. Tervoort (1961) and Tervoort and Verbeck (1967), for example, presented a detailed analysis of the development and use of esoteric sign systems by hearing-impaired school children who were denied access to a formal sign language. A little later, Kuschel (1973) described the lexicon of gestures invented by the only deaf man on a Polynesian island, and Scroggs (1981) documented the gestural narrative produced by a similarly isolated 9-year-old deaf boy.

Study of the gestural communication of hearing-impaired children gained increased acceptance as educators modified their attitudes to the use of alternative methods of communication. These changes in educational ideology coincided with changes in emphasis in the study of language acquisition. Developmental psycholinguists turned their attention away from the purely structural aspects of children's language and began to examine its semantic and pragmatic functions, thus opening up avenues for the exploration of the nonverbal precursors of spoken language (Bates, 1976a, 1976b; Bates, Bretherton, Snyder, Shore, & Volterra, 1980; Bruner, 1978; Bullowa, 1977). Techniques and theories developed in the investigation of the early language acquisition of hearing children were then adapted and applied to the communication used by hearing-impaired children.

The first and most detailed developmental studies of the "home signs" used by young hearing-impaired children of hearing parents were presented by Feldman (1975) and Goldin-Meadow (1975). These were subsequently published in Feldman, Goldin-Meadow, and Gleitman (1978), Goldin-Meadow

(1979), Goldin-Meadow and Feldman (1975), and Goldin-Meadow and Feldman (1977). Their results were based on a longitudinal study of six children with varying degrees of hearing impairment (31–100 dB) whose ages at the beginning of the study ranged from 1 year 5 months to 4 years 1 month.

Both Feldman and Goldin-Meadow focused their attention on the communicative gestures produced by the children, Feldman describing the structure and content of the gestural lexicons they developed, and Goldin-Meadow applying a case grammar analysis to the gestural utterances. They concluded that, in the absence of a mature language model, hearing-impaired children were able to invent a language-like gestural communication system. Although Goldin-Meadow (1985) has replicated this study, other people have been unable to find evidence of rich gestural lexicons or grammatical rules governing the gestural utterances produced by the hearing-impaired children they have studied (Gregory & Mogford, 1981; Mohay, 1984, 1986).

Skarakis and Prutting (1977) and Curtiss, Prutting, and Lowell (1979) examined both the verbal and nonverbal communication produced by hearing-impaired children. Unfortunately, no distinction was made between symbolic communication and direct actions on objects and people and, although verbal and nonverbal behavior were coded separately, insufficient information was provided to assess either changes in mode of communication over time or interaction between different modes of communication. Despite these shortcomings, both studies, together with those of Mohay (1982, 1984) and Kricos and Aungst (1984), demonstrated that, although hearing-impaired children use very little speech, they are able to convey, by a variety of means, a range of semantic functions and pragmatic intents which are comparable with those expressed by hearing children at a similar stage of language development.

To date most studies of the language development of young hearing-impaired children have either focused exclusively on spoken or gestural communication or have combined the two in a global assessment of communication. Very few studies have attempted to investigate the relationship between spoken and gestural communication in language development. However, it is clearly essential to understand the interaction of these two modes of communication if they are to be utilized effectively to foster spoken language development. For example, it is important to know whether nonverbal expression predates verbal expression and whether acceptance of gestural communication will facilitate or impede the production of spoken language.

In the present paper I have attempted to describe the interaction between gestural and spoken communication in the language development of two profoundly deaf children and to compare it with the early language development observed in hearing children. The implications of this information for educational practice have also been considered.

Subjects

The subjects, Steven and Annette, were selected for the study as they were the youngest profoundly deaf children attending the oral preschool; they had no other identifiable handicaps, no access to manual communication, and came from English-speaking homes. A summary of relevant background information about each child is presented in Table 1. When Steven was 30 months old, his parents elected to transfer him to a newly opened cued speech program. Annette's parents made the same decision a few months later when she was 38 months old. The present study concluded at this point as the children were then being presented with manual supplements to oral communication which, it was anticipated, would affect the ways in which they used words and gestures (Mohay, 1983).

Table 1. Background information about subjects

	Steven	Annette
Age deafness diagnosed (months)	15	18
Degree of hearing loss	Profound	Profound
IQ at 3 years of age	100	128
Socioeconomic class	3	3
Mother's occupation	Homemaker	Homemaker
Siblings	None	None
Period in study (months)	18–30	21–38

Method

The parents were told that the purpose of the study was to investigate the development of communication in deaf children. Each child's home was visited at monthly intervals, except when illness or vacations intervened. On each visit 30 continuous minutes of the child's activities were videotaped by the experimenter. Recording was interrupted only when the child was out of camera range or was positioned so that his/her hands were not visible. Table 2 shows the number of videotapes for each child. The parents were asked to follow their normal routine as far as possible during the videotaping sessions. The content of the videotapes varied but mainly involved the mother and child engaging in informal play activities. Occasionally other members of the family were also present. The experimenter tried to avoid being involved in interactions during this time. No special techniques were used to elicit communication from the children. However, it was noticed that the mothers attempted to devise situations which would encourage the production of any new vocabulary acquired by the child.

Table 2. Videotapes made of each child

	Period (months)	Tapes (n)
Steven	18–30	10
Annette (a)	21–30	10
Annette (b)	31–38	8

Each videotape was analyzed as soon as possible after it was recorded. A written transcript was made of both the gestural and spoken utterances produced by the child together with notes on the contexts in which they occurred.

As the study was concerned with communication, it was necessary to exclude vocalizations and nonverbal behaviors (e.g., wriggles and ear scratching) which were produced without intent to communicate (Ekman & Friesen, 1972; Wiener, Devoe, Rubinow, & Geller, 1972). Only communicative utterances (words and/or gestures) were included in the transcripts. Intent to communicate was gauged by the child's attempts to engage the mother's attention and the anticipation of a response. Responses made to the mother's words or action were also accepted. In addition, gestures had to be symbolic, i.e., distanced from the object or person to whom they referred (Werner & Kaplan, 1963). Thus, direct actions on objects or people were excluded. Extensive pantomime was also excluded by restricting the definition of gestures to actions of the head, hands, and arms. Gestures were described in terms of the notational system proposed by Stokoe (1960) and were glossed on the basis of their iconic form and the context in which they were used. Glosses were recorded in capital letters. Pointing gestures were recorded as POINTING-object, POINTING-person, or POINTING-location, with the specific referent identified in the context notes.

Spoken words had to approximate English words or be consistently used to express the same meaning. They were transcribed as accurately as possible in standard English orthography and were recorded in lower case letters within inverted commas, e.g., "no." A "rich interpretation" (Brown, 1973) was ascribed to each utterance on the bases of the form of the utterance, the context in which it occurred, and the child's satisfaction with the mother's response.

In addition to defining the gestures and words to be included in the transcripts, it was necessary to establish criteria for the determination of utterance boundaries. Voice onset and pauses of greater than 2 s were used as criteria for the beginning and end of spoken utterances, respectively (Dore, 1974). The beginning of gestural utterances was usually marked by various attention-getting devices, e.g., touching the mother, glancing at her, or vocalizing, followed by moving the hands from the resting position and starting to gesture. Terminal juncture was defined as pausing for more than 2 s, returning the hands to a resting position, and holding a gesture for more than 2 s.

Extensive reliability studies demonstrated that acceptable degrees of inter-rater reliability could be obtained for the transcription of both gestures and words. The reliability with which gestures were identified (0.81) was somewhat higher than that for words (0.74). In view of this it was decided that in doubtful cases words would be accepted if they were either accepted by the mother during the taping session or if the mother reported that they were part of the child's spoken vocabulary. Few disagreements occurred with regard to utterance boundaries (inter-rater reliability 0.98). Similarly, as long as the observers had adequate contextual information, there was little disagreement between them over the meaning of utterances.

All utterances were subsequently analyzed in terms of their semantic functions and pragmatic intents using slightly modified versions of the classification systems proposed by Greenfield and Smith (1976) and Dore (1974). Reliability studies showed over 80% agreement between independent coders for the classification of utterances in both analyses.

Results and Discussion

Structure of the Communication System

Frequency of Gesture and Word Production. In keeping with previous studies of the language development of young hearing-impaired children (e.g., Curtiss et al., 1979; Feldman et al., 1978; Goldin-Meadow, 1985; Kricos & Aungst, 1984), it was found that both Steven and Annette communicated primarily by means of gesture (Figs. 1 and 2). Up to 29 months of age the two children produced similar

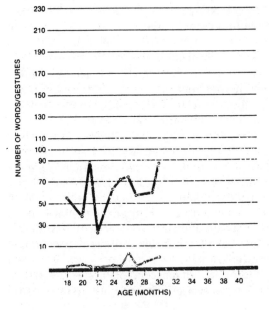

Fig. 1. Comparison of the total number of gestures (*solid line*) and words (*dotted line*) used by Steven on each videotape

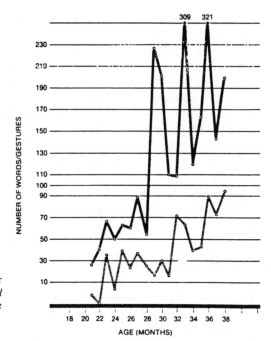

Fig. 2. Comparison of the total number of gestures (*solid line*) and words (*dotted line*) used by Annette on each videotape

numbers of gestures in each videotape. However, at this point Annette showed a dramatic increase in her gesture production which was maintained for the remainder of the study period. This increase in production was matched by a corresponding increase in the diversity of gestures which she used. Interestingly, these changes occurred at a time when she had acquired a gestural lexicon of approximately 50 items (Table 3) and appeared to be analogous to the changes in spoken language observed in hearing children following their acquisition of about 50 words (Braine, 1963; Nelson, 1973). This milestone seems, therefore, to be important, irrespective of the mode of communication. Goldin-Meadow (1985) also reported quantum changes in the gestural output of her hearing-impaired subjects, but it is unclear from her data whether these were related to lexical size.

The data from Annette clearly show the relationship between gesture production and speech production for, on tapes containing a large number of gestures, there are also a large number of words and on those with few gestures there are few words. Furthermore, shortly after the dramatic increase in her gesture production was recorded, a corresponding increase in speech production was observed. A close alliance between gestural and spoken communication has also been noted in the emergent language of hearing children (Bullowa, 1977; R.A. Clark, 1978; MacNamara, 1977; Volterra, Bates, Benigni, Bretherton, & Camaioni, 1979), and their interaction in adult communication has been well documented (Ekman & Friesen, 1969; Freedman & Grand, 1977; Kendon, 1980a). Thus, contrary to the beliefs once expressed by many teachers of the deaf

Table 3. Cumulative number of different words and gestures recorded for each child, including those recorded on only one occasion

Age (months)	Steven		Annette	
	Words	Gestures	Words	Gestures
18	0	8		
19				
20	2	20		
21	3	23	2	9
22	3	25	2	19
23			10	28
24	5	28	11	33
25	6	29	16	34
26	7	31	17	36
27	8	33	19	40
28	9	35	19	41
29			19	56
30	10	35	19	65
31			19	73
32			19	77
33			25	84
34			27	86
35			30	87
36			33	100
37			40	102
38			46	106

(e.g., Ewing & Ewing, 1964), the use of gestures does not appear to impede speech production and may even facilitate it.

Not only did Steven and Annette use more gestures than words, they also used a greater variety of gestures than words, their gestural lexicon grew far more rapidly than their spoken lexicon, and, unlike hearing children, no decline in their use of gestures was observed as speech became established. It is noteworthy that Steven and Annette produced strikingly different amounts of speech thus highlighting the fact that, despite similarities in degree of hearing loss, age of diagnosis, intelligence and social and educational background, large individual differences still exist in deaf children's ability to acquire spoken language.

Spoken and Gestural Lexicons. The items in the children's gestural lexicons can be divided into two groups:

— *Deictic gestures,* i.e., pointing and reaching, which change their reference according to the context in which they are used.
— *Referential gestures,* which have stable semantic content.

Deictic gestures dominated the children's communication on all tapes, with referential gestures occurring infrequently (Table 4). These findings are consistent with those reported in previous studies (Feldman, 1975; Heider & Heider, 1941; Volterra, 1981a). Interestingly, both Hoffmeister (1978a) and Kantor

Table 4. Total number of gestures, number of deictic gestures, and number of different referential gestures occurring on each videotape

	Steven			Annette		
Age (months)	Total gestures (n)	Deictic gestures (n)	Different referential gestures (n)	Total gestures (n)	Deictic gestures (n)	Different referential gestures (n)
18	54	49	5			
19						
20	37	15	12			
21	88	64	9	26	13	8
22	21	19	2	40	23	9
23				68	30	17
24	62	53	8	48	7	15
25	72	61	7	64	29	13
26	73	53	6	60	22	14
27	57	34	9	89	17	15
28	58	51	7	55	15	15
29				225	95	32
30	86	44	14	200	57	32
31				109	49	17
32				108	32	26
33				309	158	31
34				118	38	20
35				163	63	20
36				321	129	36
37				143	52	26
38				198	70	29

(1982b) made the same observations about the communication of young deaf children acquiring American Sign Language (ASL), and a number of studies have reported the use of deictic gestures by hearing children in the early stages of language development (Bruner, 1978; E.V. Clark, 1978; Zinober & Martlew, 1985a). Although deictic gestures are structurally simple, nonspecific and context bound, children use them to fulfill many communicative functions (see Mohay, 1984). Thus, at a semantic and pragmatic level, the deictic system has to be regarded as quite complex, and it seems likely that it provides an important communication base for later language development, irrespective of the form that language takes.

Most of the referential gestures used by Steven and Annette were not substantives (nominals) but were related to the interaction between the child and the mother. The reason for this becomes apparent when it is realized that many of these gestures are ones which are commonly used by the hearing population in the middle-class Australian community in which the children lived. As adults tend to use gestures to regulate children's behavior rather than to name objects, it is hardly surprising to find such gestures as BYE-BYE, BEHAVE-YOURSELF, ALLGONE, and HERE being incorporated into the children's lexicons. Barten

(1977) observed similar gestures being used by young hearing children and referred to them as "instrumental gestures."

Some referential gestures appeared to be derived from activities which the children engaged in at school, e.g., MUSIC-GAME and SIT-DOWN, and some were probably remnants of earlier gestures which expressed the child's emotional state, e.g., DON'T-ANNOY-ME and I'M-FRUSTRATED. Again, similar gestures have been observed in the communicative repertoires of young hearing children (Barten, 1977; Zinober & Martlew, 1985a). A few gestures were abbreviated pantomimes of actions, e.g., THROW, PUSH, and SWIM, and others, especially in Annette's gestural lexicon, were derived from sources such as finger-play books. The origin of most of the children's gestures can therefore be explained. Volterra, Beronesi, and Massoni (this volume) identified similar derivations for the getures used by their hearing-impaired subjects.

In marked contrast to the findings reported by Feldman et al. (1978) and Goldin-Meadow (1985), the children in the present study appeared to invent very few gestures and those which were generated were rarely produced on more than one occasion. This is consistent with Gregory and Mogford's (1981) observation that the hearing-impaired children in their study were not creative in devising new gestures.

At all ages, both Steven and Annette had smaller spoken than gestural lexicons. Like hearing children, there were a few words which they used frequently and a larger group which only occurred now and again. It was anticipated that the words which they acquired would be mainly substantives as these are generally regarded as the easiest words to teach deaf children and also frequently constitute the major portion of the lexicon acquired by young hearing children (Nelson, 1973). In fact, the opposite was found. The children's vocabularies contained proportionally more personal-social and action words and fewer general nominals than the vocabularies of hearing children at a similar stage of language acquisition. These results are very similar to those reported by Gregory and Mogford (1981) to the extent that there is even considerable overlap in the vocabulary items of the children in the two studies.

The reasons for the difference in the vocabularies acquired by hearing and hearing-impaired children are not clear, but a number of possible explanations can be advanced. These include the possibility that they may reflect differences in the features in the environment which attract and hold the children's attention, differences in age at the time of language acquisition, and consequent differences in cognitive and social maturity, differences in maternal language (Nienhuys, Horsborough, & Cross, 1985) or dfficulty experienced by hearing-impaired children in the establishment of joint attention-creating problems in the learning of reference (Bruner, 1983a). Whatever the cause, the outcome is that the hearing-impaired child's acquisition of spoken language is not only slower than that of the hearing child, but also follows a somewhat different pattern.

Combinations of Gestures and Words. Single-gesture utterances dominated Steven's and Annette's communication at all ages. Gestures were combined to form longer utterances and the frequency of production and length of these combinations increased as the children got older (Table 5). Spoken words were rarely combined with each other but they were combined with deictic gestures, referential gestures, and nods and shakes of the head (Table 6). In these utterances the gesture and word were usually produced simultaneously rather than consecutively and the two often carried the same meaning, thus increasing the likelihood of the utterance being correctly interpreted. [Pereira (1985) made the same observations about the communication of deaf children in the process of acquiring Portuguese.] Words and gestures which carried the same meaning (e.g., BYE-BYE, COME-ON, ALLGONE, YES, NO) often appeared for the first time on the same tape. In a few cases the gesture was recorded 1 or 2 months before the first recorded occurrence of the spoken word. Similar findings have also been reported in the early language development of hearing children (Volterra et al., 1979). No instances were found of a word predating its gestural equivalent, although some words had no gestural representation and many gestures had no

Table 5. Number of utterances according to length and mode of production

	Steven	Annette (a)	Annette (b)
Tapes (*n*)	10	10	8
Age (months)	18–30	21–30	31–38
Length of utterance:			
One gesture	426	429	484
Two gestures	37	70	129
Three gestures	5	11	28
Four or more gestures	5	11	24
One word	7	66	111
Two words	0	1	2
Three words	0	0	0
Word + gesture	9	62	129
Complex[a]	0	21	69

[a] Complex utterances were more than two elements long and contained word(s) and gesture(s).

Table 6. Frequency of occurrence of different types of gesture/word combinations

	Steven	Annette (a)	Annette (b)
Tapes (*n*)	10	10	8
Age (months)	18–30	21–30	31–38
Gesture/word combinations:			
Deictic gesture + word	6	22	26
Referential gesture + word	2	31	30
Nod/headshake + word	1	9	73

spoken equivalents. Initially all gestures and words which carried the same gloss were invariably produced together. However, as the children became more confident about their use of the word, they began to use it without the accompanying gesture. Gardner and Zorfass (1983), in a case study of the language development of a child exposed to Manually Coded English (MCE), reported that he too acquired signs before words, then combined signs and words with the same meaning and eventually ceased to use the signs as the spoken equivalents became intelligible.

The children in the present study not only combined gestures and words which had the same gloss, but also gestures and words which had the same functions. For example, in the utterance GO-AWAY "no," both elements appeared to express negative volition and to protest against the action of the mother.

Words also accompanied deictic gestures and usually named the object or person pointed to. These utterances bore a marked resemblance to those produced by young hearing children in the early stages of spoken language acquisition.

Curtiss et al. (1979) made similar observations about the communication used by the hearing-impaired children in their study. They suggested that gestures and words could be combined within a single communicative act in one of four ways. In the first the gesture and word carried the same meaning, for example, "no" accompanied by a head shake, or pointing to an object and naming it. This was the most frequent type of gesture/word combination observed in their group of 2-year-olds and it decreased slightly in frequency of production in the older age groups (3-year-olds and 4-year-olds). This form of gesture/word combination was observed the most often at all ages in the present study. The second type was the production of a gesture and word which were not related. These combinations were rarely produced by the subjects of Curtiss et al. and were not observed at all in the present study. The third type involved the use of a word to supplement a gesture, such as saying "I've got it" while holding up a cookie. This type of utterance was not recorded in the present study as the gesture would have been regarded as a direct action and hence nonsymbolic. However, gesture/word combinations, such as GO-AWAY "no," seem to fit this category as the two elements obviously have the same illocutionary force, even though they do not carry exactly the same meaning. Curtiss et al. reported that this type of utterance occurred more frequently in the older age groups, but no such developmental changes were observed in the present study. These three types of utterance appear to be very similar to the performative utterances in the early language acquisition of hearing children described by Bullowa (1977) and Gruber (1973).

The final type of gesture/word combination described by Curtiss et al. involved the gesture fulfilling a semantic function which was not expressed by the verbal utterance; for example, the child pointed to other children and said "have juice." This type of utterance in which the whole was different from the parts was only produced by the 4-year-olds. The data from the present study indicate that the children were also beginning to produce this type of combination. Very occasionally these were observed in one-gesture/one-word combinations; for instance, Annette at 29 months pointed to a blanket and at the same time said "baby," meaning "I want the blanket for my baby." More often, however, they were observed in complex utterances. These usually consisted of two gestures and a word which carried the same meaning as one of the gestures, as when Annette said "baby" while pointing to a picture of a sleeping baby and then produced a gesture for BE-QUIET. Sometimes, however, the gestures and words carried different meanings. For example, on one occasion Annette was looking at some family photographs when she pointed to the open door then to a picture of her father then to the door again and, while holding this gesture, nodded and said "work." This seemed to mean, "Daddy is out there at work." Few of these complex utterances were recorded but they were increasing in frequency in the later tapes. Gruber (1973) referred to utterances of this type as "constative" and recorded the hearing child he observed using them for the first time at 17 months of age. The ability of hearing-impaired children to produce this type of utterance appears, therefore, to be significantly delayed.

In summary, both hearing and hearing-impaired children initially appear to combine gestures and words to produce utterances with a high degree of redundancy, thus increasing the likelihood of being understood and responded to appropriately. As they become more confident in their use of words, the need for a gestural accompaniment becomes less and accompanying gestures may no longer be used. Annette and Steven rarely combined words but incorporated words into longer gestural utterances. This may represent a precursor of the two-word utterance. Alternatively, it may be a way of optimizing the use of an impoverished gestural and spoken lexicon to permit the expression of complex ideas and maximize the probability of being understood.

Spoken and Gestural Expression of Semantic Functions and Pragmatic Intents

All single-word and single-gesture utterances produced by Steven and Annette were analyzed in terms of the classification of semantic functions of one-word utterances proposed by Greenfield and Smith (1976). This revealed that Annette was able to express verbally all but four of the semantic functions while Steven, with his extremely restricted spoken language, was only able to express a total of four.

Some modifications had to be made to Greenfield and Smith's categories in order to apply them to gestural communication. The categories of Indicative and Indicative Object had to be amalgamated as they could not be distinguished in gestural communication and the categories of Location Associated with an Object or Animate and Locative Question had to be created. The former catered for the children's strategy of pointing to the habitual location of an object or person as a means of referring to them when they were not present. Indeed, as they had few referential gestures, this was one of the few methods available to them for referring to objects and people not in their immediate environment. The category of Locative Question accommodated the WHERE gesture used by the children, although it is debatable whether this was a true question form as it was used primarily either to elicit or indicate search activities.

The children's use of space in the production of gestures sometimes permitted more than one semantic function to be expressed by a single gesture. For example, Steven was observed to hold a flat hand (GIVE-ME) just above a space in a jigsaw puzzle which he and his mother were doing. His fingers were directed towards his mother and his message was clearly, "I want you to GIVE-ME the piece of puzzle to go into this space." In these instances the objective of the utterance was considered in allocating it to a category, and, as Steven was clearly requesting an object, the utterance was placed in the category Volitional Object.

Despite these problems, high levels of inter-rater reliability were achieved in the classification of utterances. Examples of all semantic functions could be found in the single-gesture utterances produced by both children. With the exception of Datives and Objects, which are usually well represented in the one-word utterances of hearing children, the semantic functions which were expressed infrequently by Steven and Annette were also rarely produced by Greenfield and Smith's hearing subjects. By definition the Object category requires the naming of an object which has undergone or is undergoing a change of stage or having an action performed on it. There are, therefore, obvious problems in expressing this semantic relationship gesturally quite apart from the fact that the children had few referential gestures in their lexicons to enable them to specify objects. In addition, it is likely that the children used other nonverbal means such as gaze to indicate recipients (Datives) and Objects.

Curtiss et al. (1979) and Kricos and Aungst (1984) found that the young hearing-impaired children in their studies expressed few semantic functions verbally and also failed to express some nonverbally. The semantic functions which were not observed were the ones which Annette and Steven produced infrequently. It is possible, therefore, that examples of these infrequently occurring utterances were simply not captured in the relatively small language samples on which the results were based.

Not only were the hearing-impaired children in the present sample able to express more semantic functions gesturally than verbally but, in most cases, gestural expression also predated verbal expression (Table 7). Thus, although the children were significantly delayed and limited in their verbal expression of semantic functions, they were able to express gesturally the same notions expressed verbally by hearing children. Several of these semantic functions were recorded on the first videotape and therefore may have existed in the children's gestural communication for some time. All the others were recorded over the ensuing months. Hence, when the use of gestural communication was acknowledged, the children's abilities to express semantic relationships did not appear to be significantly delayed. These findings tend to support the notion of a cognitive basis underlying language development, but more research is required to elucidate this relationship.

The children's spoken and gestural utterances were also analyzed in terms of their communicative functions or illocutionary force. Dore's (1974) classification of primitive speech acts (PSAs) was used for this purpose. Some minor modifications were necessary to allow for the different styles of mother/child

Table 7. Age at which each semantic function was first observed in the spoken and gestural utterances produced by the children

Semantic Function	Steven		Annette	
	Words (months)	Gestures (months)	Words (months)	Gestures (months)
Performative	21	18	23	21
Positive Volition	–	20	29	24
Negative Volition	24	21	21	22
Volitional Object	–	18	30	21
Indicative Object	–	18	21	21
Agent	29	18	–	22
Act or Stage of Agent	–	20	23	22
Object	20	18	27	24
Act or State of Object	–	20	23	22
Dative	–	20	25	23
Object Associated with Object or Location	–	18	–	24
Animate Associated with Object or Location	–	24	–	22
Location	–	22	–	22
Modification of Event	–	21	27	25
Location Associated with Object or Animate	–	21	–	22
Locative Question	–	20	–	21

interaction which occurred with the hearing-impaired children and to accommodate changes in language usage which were probably a reflection of the fact that the hearing-impaired subjects were older than Dore's subjects. The changes were in line with Dore's later expansion and refinement of the PSA categories to cater for the conversational acts of preschool children (Dore, Gearhart, & Newman, 1978).

The results indicated that, like hearing children, the hearing-impaired children frequently imitated maternal speech. In many instances this was a deliberate strategy adopted by the mother, presumably as a teaching device. The hearing-impaired children were also inclined to repeat their own words, either to ensure that they were understood or as a form of rehearsal. As with the expression of semantic functions, Annette was able to express most PSAs verbally while Steven's meagre speech severely curtailed the range of PSAs he could express. Both children expressed all PSAs gesturally, and again gestural expression was found to predate verbal expression in almost every instance (Table 8). These results emphasize once again the importance of gestural communication and its close alliance with the development of spoken language.

Table 8. Age at which each primitive speech act was first observed in the spoken and gestural utterances produced by the children

	Steven		Annette	
Primitive speech acts	Words (months)	Gestures (months)	Words (months)	Gestures (months)
Labelling	20	18	21	21
Description	–	18	23	21
Repeating (self)	29	18	23	26
Imitation of mother	26	21	25	22
Answering	–	24	26	24
Requesting (action)	20	18	23	22
Requesting (answer)	–	18	23	21
Requesting object	–	18	28	21
Calling (attention getting)	–	26	30	22
Greeting (rituals)	21	27	23	23
Protesting	24	21	21	21
Claims	–	20	–	23
Accompaniments	–	20	23	21

Conclusion

The data from the present study show that, even at 2½ and 3 years of age, respectively, Steven and Annette communicated primarily by means of gestures which were usually produced in the form of single-gesture utterances. Spoken utterances were produced less frequently and they too were usually composed of only a single unit (i.e., one word). Clearly, therefore, the communication produced by these children, both in terms of mode of communication and complexity of utterances, was very different from that produced by hearing children of comparable age.

However, when comparisons are made with the communication produced by hearing children at the same stage of language development, some interesting similarities are revealed. The legitimacy of such comparisons is questionable, of course, as in every other respect the hearing-impaired children are substantially more mature than their linguistically matched hearing counterparts. Notwithstanding these limitations, it is important to note that both hearing and hearing-impaired children frequently use gestures to communicate at this stage of language development and often combine gestures (especially deictic gestures) with words (Caselli, 1983a; E.V. Clark, 1978; Volterra, 1981a). In addition, the gesture/word combinations produced by both hearing and hearing-impaired children often have a high degree of redundancy and are tied to the context in which they are produced, i.e., they are unable to represent objects or events which are removed in time or space (Greenfield & Smith, 1976; Gruber, 1973).

E.V. Clark (1978) suggested that gestural communication is an essential intermediary step in the hearing child's acquisition of spoken language, but very little has been reported about the range of different gestures used by hearing children. It is known that, like hearing-impaired children, they use pointing and reaching gestures and nods and shakes of the head. R.A. Clark (1978) reported large individual differences between children, with those who talked later using a wider variety of gestures than those who talked early. However, as she did not document the gestures used, comparison of the gestural repertoires of hearing and hearing-impaired children cannot be made due to lack of information about the range of gestures used by hearing children.

Although the hearing-impaired children in the present study were restricted in their verbal communication, they could express nonverbally the same range of semantic functions and pragmatic intents as those expressed verbally by hearing children at the one-word stage of language development. This suggests that they were isolating similar relationships in their environment to comment on, possibly due to a common cognitive substrate underlying language development.

Spoken language development in the hearing-impaired children was very slow, and in this mode of communication, more differences than similarities existed between the hearing and hearing-impaired children. Not only was acquisition of spoken words slower for hearing-impaired children, but no acceleration in rate of acquisition was observed as their vocabularies expanded. In addition, the content of their vocabularies differed from that of hearing children at the same stage of language development. Thus, although the communication used by the hearing-impaired children appeared to be very similar in some respects to that of hearing children at the same stage of language development, in others it was quite different.

The results of the research presented in this paper suggest that gestural communication should not be regarded as merely an adjunct to, or a substitute for, spoken language and hence to be discouraged. Rather, it should be regarded as intimately related to speech production, being a precursor and possibly even a facilitator of the spoken language development of both hearing and hearing-impaired children. Viewed in this light, it becomes supremely important for teachers and parents to be sensitive to children's gestural communication and to respond appropriately to the messages which they are attempting to convey. In this way gestures and words can become associated and the development of spoken language promoted.

Furthermore, in considering the recent increase in interest in the use of manual supplements such as cued speech or MCE, with young hearing-impaired children, educators should be cognizant of the effect which this may have on the adult's production of natural gesture, for it is undoubtedly true that hearing-impaired children acquire a large proportion of their gestural repertoire from the adults around them.

Kantor (1982b) reported that deaf parents who used ASL modified their language production when interacting with their infants and incorporated the use of a large number of deictic gestures. The various forms of MCE and cued speech may not lend themselves so readily to such modification. Thus, if gestural communication is perceived as a necessary preverbal stage in language acquisition, denying a child access to a range of natural gestures which can be used to direct attention and behavior may have an adverse effect on language development. These factors, therefore, need to be taken into consideration in both day-to-day classroom management and in the more long-term planning of education programs for hearing-impaired children.

CHAPTER 16
How Does Gestural Communication Become Language?

V. VOLTERRA, S. BERONESI, and P. MASSONI

Introduction

The title of this chapter reflects one of the basic questions in language acquisition theory. The study we describe contributes to our understanding of the process through which gestural communication becomes language. Deaf children of hearing parents not exposed to sign language input appear to develop spontaneously efficient visual-gestural communication at the same time they increase their spoken communication (see Goldin-Meadow, 1979; Goldin-Meadow & Feldman, 1975; Mohay, 1982, 1984; Pereira, 1985); but it is not clear how this development takes place. Do they "create" a gestural language or more simply do they transform and develop the limited gestural input they are exposed to? Exploring this process through a single case study can help us to understand better, on the one hand, some similarities between gestural communication of hearing children acquiring spoken language spontaneously and gestural communication of deaf children struggling in order to acquire spoken language. On the other hand, it helps us to clarify some relevant differences between gestural communication and sign language.

The case study we present here is particularly interesting for us because it shows how hearing people living with, teaching, or even studying a deaf child do not often realize how much gestural communication is used when interacting with him or her. The subject of our study was followed in order to observe the development of his spoken communication; only after several months of analysis did we realize the important role that gesturing played in his communicative interaction and consequently in his linguistic development. This paper reports on this discovery.

Methods and Procedures

M is congenitally and profoundly deaf with no other known cognitive or physical disabilities. The cause of deafness is unknown. He comes from a middle-class

A slightly different version of this paper was originally published in Italian as "*Quando la comunicazione gestuale diventa linguaggio*" in G. Attili and P. Ricci-Bitti (Eds.), 1983, *I Gesti e i Segni*. Roma: Bulzoni, pp. 201–212.

family living in Rome, Italy, and both parents are hearing. He has no siblings. The mother is the primary caregiver. Since the age of 2 years the child has been wearing hearing aids, and between the ages of 3 and 10 he received regular vocal/auditory training 3–4 days a week by a speech therapist. From the age of 3 years he was mainstreamed in a regular school, the only deaf child in the classroom. M participated in a research project on spoken language acquisition of deaf children educated through an oral method. This method was designed to follow the developmental linguistic stages hearing children go through (for further details see Facchini, Guidicini, Volterra, Massoni, & Beronesi, 1981; Volterra & Massoni, 1978).

As one of the subjects of the project, M was followed from the age of 3 years 8 months through systematic written observations and audiorecorded sessions while interacting with his mother and the speech therapist; beginning at the age of 6 years, further data were collected through videotaped sessions in a playroom at the laboratory of the Institute of Psychology, at the National Research Council. The room has a one-way mirror, allowing us to videotape him unnoticed.

In the present chapter we will refer only to a limited period of his development, discussing data collected during four videotaped sessions at the following ages:

Session 1:   6 years 2 months
Session 2:   6 years 9 months
Session 3:   6 years 10 months
Session 4:   7 years

Each session lasted about 1 h. In all four of them the child interacted spontaneously with the speech therapist, and in two instances another deaf child and one hearing adult were present. Our focus during the period of data collection was the child's spoken production and not his gestural communication; for this reason the sessions were coded initially for vocal productions only. One year later, looking back on the original videotapes in order to further analyze the child's spoken production, we were struck by his use of the gestural modality progressing in conjunction with his spoken communication. We must remember that from birth until that time the child had never had any contact with adults or children using sign language. At this point the four videotaped sessions were coded again for gestures.

One of the problems to be solved was the transcription of the gestures into written glosses (Italian first and then English). All the gestures of the child and therapist are transcribed in capital letters, the gestures corresponding to actions are not transcribed in infinitive form as we usually do with sign languages; instead they are based on the spoken form, which is produced simultaneously with the gestures.

Data and Results

Of the various perspectives from which these data could be analyzed, we will focus on four:

1. The types of gestures produced by M.
2. The relationship between his gestural and spoken production.
3. The unique way in which M adapts common gestures, discovering by himself some peculiar properties of the gestural modality.
4. Similarities and differences between the gestures of the child and of the speech therapist.

Types of Gestures

Where do the child's gestures come from? Many of M's gestures are commonly used in the nonverbal communication of hearing people. It would be interesting to note that some of these gestures may be unfamiliar to non-Italian readers; however, they are widely used in Italy:

COME-HERE: extended arm, palm down, repeated flexion and extension of hand toward body.
BROKEN: closed fists, palm down, moving out and rotating.
IT-DOESN'T-WORK: both hands with thumb and index fingers extended with wrist rotation.
BE-QUIET: index finger placed against mouth.

Certain gestures produced by M are used less frequently in communication between hearing people:

TO-LOOK: index finger moving from the eye outward.
TO-HEAR: index finger touching the ear.
SMOKE: both hands moving in an upwards spiral.

Certain gestures evidently originate from pantomime:

MONOCLE: hand in a circle against the eye; it was used for the king in "Sleeping Beauty" who wears a monocle.
TO-INFLATE: both hands with spread fingers as if surrounding a sphere moving diagonally upwards.
DEAD: arms drop to ground followed by body.
ELEPHANT: arm used as extension of the nose, moving back and forth.

For certain gestures, M outlines the contours of the object in space:

CHRISTMAS TREE
DOOR
HOUSE.

A few gestures are the result of a conventionalization process between the therapist and the child:

THE-WICKED-FAIRY: two hands, palms forward at the sides of the head.

The meaning of these gestures was inferred on the basis of the words that M himself used together with the gesture, or by the immediate interpretation of the therapist. The gestures were executed with the hands, accompanied by the appropriate facial expression, with the exception of YES which was executed only by nodding the head. Although we have not conducted a detailed analysis of the parameters, gestures are produced with various hand configurations in different locations and with a variety of movements. Some gestures are one-handed, some are two-handed; a few gestures are produced sometimes with one hand and at other times with two. In the first session, two-handed gestures are more numerous than one-handed gestures; in the second session, the opposite occurs. When both hands are used, they follow the constraints described by Battison (1974) for American Sign Language (ASL): the two hands are symmetrical, assuming the same hand configuration and the same movement; in the rare cases where there is no symmetry, the nondominant hand assumes an unmarked configuration, as in the case of SMAMMA (GO-AWAY) where the right hand, palm turned inward, repeatedly hits the palm of the left hand.

Relationship Between Gestural and Spoken Production

The relationship between gestural and spoken production varies during the period considered. A complete list of words and gestures produced in the first and second sessions is reported in the Appendix. In the first session gestural production is less than spoken production: 30 gestures versus 50 spoken words. M produces single gestures and single words as well as combinations of gestures and combinations of words. He uses simultaneously spoken and gestural productions most frequently. For example:

"Questo basta" (That enough).

THAT'S ENOUGH
"Noo e' rotto" (No, it's broken).

NO BROKEN

But not all words are accompanied by the corresponding gestures. For example:

"Donna a balla no" (Women go dance no).

DANCE NO
"Brutta, brutta va via" (Ugly, ugly go away).

UGLY AWAY

We found very few examples of spoken sentences without accompanying gestures:

"Piera, Simone piange" (Piera, Simone cries).
"Questo rotto, ha paura" (This broken, is afraid).
"Io aspetta forte" (I wait strong).
"Piera, metto dov'e'" (Piera, I put where it is).

And we found a few examples of sequences of gestures such as:

WICKED-FAIRY NICE BIRD CRY (meaning "the wicked fairy's nice bird is crying").

Six months later, in the second session, significant changes are observed. There is a noticeable increase in both gestures and words: 82 gestures versus 120 words; M now uses sentences which are significantly longer and richer in meaning. But the most striking observation about this session is that M very consistently uses gestures to accompany his speech. In the following example he was explaining a picture he had drawn about a story he created:

"La mamma porta guarda mannaggia" (The mother door watches, darn it).

THIS　　DOOR WATCH　　DARN-IT!

"Perche' piano piano L'aereo camminato" (Why slow slow airplane walked).

　　　WHY　　SLOW SLOW AIRPLANE WALK.

Many words that did not have a corresponding gesture in the first session now have one: FALL, CHILD, COME. Only rarely do we observe speech without gestures; this occurs only when the therapist asks M to repeat a word or phrase that she proposes.

As far as the third session is concerned, the relationship between gestures and speech is similar to the second session. At the fourth session, however, we observe a new development: M now produces long spoken utterances, without depending on corresponding gestures. Due to the development of M's spoken language, (it is now more complex and comprehensible, his use of gestures is greatly reduced. M makes use of gestures only to clarify or specify certain points of his talk. In these instances, gestural usage is similar to that of the second session. For the most part, however, gestures are no longer expressing the same meaning as the words he produces but instead they accompany his speech in order to underline it. He uses the "illustrative gestures" (IG), also used by hearing people while speaking, to illustrate what is being said verbally (Ekman & Friesen, 1969; Poggi, 1983). Here is an example of his production during the fourth session:

"Una donna è morta perchè uomo cattivo allora ha spara(to)" (One women died why bad man then he shoot).

IG　　　　　SHOOT

"La donna buona uomo cattivo fatto uomo buono" (The good women bad man did good man).

IG　　POINT TO PHONE

"Uomo cattivo aspetta, ha preso la pistola" (Bad man wait, he took the gun).

POINT OUTSIDE WAIT　　　TOOK

"E due Piera e io va bene" (And two Piera and myself, well?).

TWO POINT TO P　　　ME

"Uomo cattivo e uomo buono insieme" (Bad man and good man together . . .).
POINT OUTSIDE   IG   TOGETHER.

From this example it is clear that only some spoken words are accompanied by the corresponding gestures (shoot, wait, together). Many words are instead accompanied by pointing or illustrative gestures.

We can conclude from our data that M resorts to the use of gestures to accompany his speech in a particular phase of his linguistic development, i.e., when he starts to produce more complex syntactic structures (coordinated and subordinated), but his spoken production is still limited with respect to phono-articulatory and morphological aspects (second and third sessions). The use of gestures seems to become less necessary immediately following this phase when he has become more skilled in spoken language production (fourth session).

M's Discovery of Particular Properties of Gestural Modality

The data on the development of gestures bring us to the third point of our analysis. It is important to emphasize that progressively, from the second session on, M discovers, through the use of space and movement, characteristics of the gestural modality which have the potential to be used for morphological and syntactical purposes in sign languages. For example, in the first session the use of space is only observed in two instances: asking the speech therapist to sit near him, he shows with his hand how he wants her to move; a little bit later, remembering the movie *"Cinderella,"* (specifically the scene in which the king and the chamberlain jump from the bed to the chandelier) he attempts to mimic the characters in space, moving the two hands alternately up and down.

These potentialities discovered in the first session are increasingly used in the next sessions. M places the characters of the story in precise locations and then he returns, with a series of gestures, to those points in space, thus producing a kind of pronominal reference.

In the second, third, and fourth sessions M discovers new possibilities in terms of directionality of gestures that express transitive actions. The direction of these gestures changes depending on the location in space where he has placed the agent (performing the action) and the patient (receiving the action):

TO SHOOT: index and thumb in position of a gun with movement of the whole arm forward. The gesture is executed once toward the listener and once toward the speaker.
TO-SLAP-IN-THE-FACE: first executed from right to left, and then from left to right, depending on where the agent was previously located.

Moreover, from the second session on, M discovers the possibility of tracing in space the outline of objects for which he does not yet have specific gestures: the Christmas tree, the door, the house. He also discovers the possibility of representing spatial relations in space: an object on top of the house, the car passing under the bridge, and so on. The same happens with regard to the discovery of the modulation of movement. In the first session, we noticed only a variation in the movement of a few gestures. M changes the rhythm and amplitude of the movement of two gestures (NO and WAIT) as the meaning varies, specifically as the illocutionary force with which the corresponding word is pronounced varies. Also in the first session the amplitude of the gesture SMALL varies in relation to the size of the object to which it refers. From the second session on, we find modulations in a variety of gestures:

— TO BITE becomes TO ATTACK.
— The airplane can FLY at different speeds, TAKE OFF or GLIDE.
— The gesture INFLATE is performed with progressive expansions.
— M repeats several times with different intensity a heart beat, which then stops; death follows with a progressive relaxation of the entire body.

Gestures are also more connected and influenced by each other: the movement of one gesture is often incorporated into the movement of the following gesture. We found also an example of the simultaneous use of the two hands: right hand gestures PLANE-FLY, while the left gestures SLOW.

A Comparison Between the Therapist's and M's Use of Gestures

Through the four videotaped sessions P uses two types of gestures. One is used to accompany speech — gestures follow and punctuate the spoken sentences (Ekman & Friesen, 1969). The second type, far more meaningful, is used by P to express the same content she expresses in her spoken sentences. It is important to note that the first type of gesture is used significantly more often by P than by M throughout the four sessions, and it is rarely used by the child in the first and second.

As far as the second type of gesturing is concerned, if we compare a series of situations in which P, during dialogue, performs some gestures to exemplify parts of her story and M repeats them shortly thereafter, we note that the child uses space, modulation of movement, and facial expression in a more pronounced way than the therapist. The opposite is true in those situations in which P reproduces gestures or sequences of gestures executed a little earlier by M. For example, as far as the location of characters in space is concerned, P limits herself to placing the characters in space and does not point to those locations again for further reference as the child does. As far as the modulation of movement is concerned, in the sequence of gestures referring to the heart which beats and then stops, (showing that the person is dying) M modulates his movements in a much richer and more precise way than P. The same appears to be true for facial expression which is clearly more varied in the child as compared to P. Remember again that at the time of these sessions the child was in a oral program and that the speech therapist was using gesturing unconsciously. She was very surprised, looking back to the original tapes, to notice how much she herself used gestural communication in interacting with the child.

Conclusion

Let us now draw some conclusions from the data presented. M adopts gestures, in a certain period of his linguistic development, as a necessary support to his spoken communication: he realizes a parallel development in his vocal and gestural productions similar to that observed in hearing children at an earlier age and stage of development. Around the age of 1 year, hearing children show a kind of equipotentiality between gestural and vocal modalities in their communicative development, despite the fact they are exposed to spoken input (Volterra, 1981a; Caselli, this volume). M seems to progress further on in the process, which normally stops around the age of 2 years in the case of hearing children. For example, he is able to combine two or more referential gestures in a sentence, a combination which does not appear to be used by hearing children. There is no doubt that this happens because the spoken input he has access to is much reduced compared to the input received by hearing children. In addition, M discovers the potentialities of the gestural input to which he is exposed, unknown even to the hearing adults who are presenting it. He exploits this input to the fullest even if he does not reach a complete and systematic use of it. Location in space, directionality, and modulation of movement and facial expression, although clearly present, do not appear to be used by M systematically to express morphological and syntactical characteristics as seen in sign languages.

These observations of M's gestural communication remind us of an important paper by Newport and Supalla (1980) in which they claim that only ASL used by the second generation signers (i.e., those who have ASL as a native language) displays some of the more complex aspects of internal sign morphology when compared with the ASL used by the first generation signers (i.e., those who, not having deaf parents, have learned ASL as adults or at least after early childhood). In their opinion "complex internal morphological analysis is performed by second generation deaf on an input which does not itself contain this morphology" (p. 205). "Learning may go well beyond what is justified by the input, . . . the output of such a process may be more highly structured than the input" (p. 206). Also, in the case of M, his gestural production (the output) seems to go beyond what the gestural production of the hearing adults (the input) would justify. In the case of M we cannot speak of morphological rules applied systematically to his gestures, but there is an attempt in this direction. It is clear that M tries to express gesturally the same content he tries to express vocally. During the period in which he learns to use a series of morphological rules in the spoken language (from the second session he starts to use verb conjugations and noun gender/number agreement sporadically), he attempts to discover also in the gestural modality, through a reanalysis of input, analogous mechanisms that allow him to express the same grammatical and syntactic phenomena. We have to remember that the gestural modality is natural for him and, above all, permits him, as deaf, to have feedback of his own production. His use of location, directionality, and modulation of movement can be interpreted according to this view.

In the future we propose to study more systematically how and how much M and other deaf children with the same background manage to express themselves through the gestural modality. The paths they choose will help us to understand better which characteristics of sign language are "natural" solutions that is, solutions which are easier to discover given the fact that the gestural modality is used to express the "human language faculty," and which characteristics can appear only after a gestural linguistic system (a sign language) is used within a community for generations.

We would like to add a biographical note on M's story. As a consequence of this study a bimodal approach was used with M beginning when he was 7½ years old. At the present time, at 12 years of age, he has developed competence in written and spoken Italian which is equivalent to his hearing peers and he is attending a special Italian Sign Language class with deaf teachers once a week.

Appendix

List of Words and Gestures Produced by M in the First and Second Sessions

Words	Gestures
Adesso (now)	
Aereo (airplane)	AIRPLANE
	TAKE OFF
	DRIVE (pilot)
Albero (tree)	CHRISTMAS TREE
Alle 5 (at five o'clock)	FIVE
Am	AM
A me (to me)	TO ME
Aperto (open)	OPEN
A posto (things straight)	
Aspetta (wait)	*WAIT
	*I'M WAITING FOR
Attento	BE CAREFUL
Aurora (name)	
Balla (she is dancing)	*DANCE
Bambola (doll)	
Basta (stop it)	*STOP-IT
Batte (beats)	*BEAT
	*TO HIT THE HEAD
Bianche (white)	
Botte (beats)	
Bravo (clever)	
	*FINE (face expression)
Bum	BUM (with various meanings)

Buttare (to throw)
Cade/caduto (it falls down/
   fallen down)   AIRPLANE-FALL-DOWN
Cammina/camminato (he is
   walking-walked   WALK
Carne (meat)
Casa (house)   HOUSE
                              *UGLY
C'e' (there is) (the noise)   TO HEAR
Che e'? (What is?)
Che fa? (What is he doing?)
Che fai? (What are you doing?)   *WHAT?
Che hai fatto? (what did you do)
Cuore (heart)   HEART
                              HEART BEAT

Donna (woman)
Dopo (after)   *AFTER
Dorme (he is sleeping)   TO SLEEP
Dov'e'? (where is?)   *WHERE?
Dove (where)
Due (two)   TWO
E' (is)
E'buono (it is good)   BUONO
Eccola/ecco   *POINTING
E' matto (he is mad)   MAD
E' piccolo (it is small)   SMALL
E' rotto (it is broken)   *BROKEN
E' tuo/e' tua (it is yours)   POINTING TO ADDRESSEE
Fa male (it's hurt)

                              STAB
Fata cattiva (wicked fairy)   *WICKED-FAIRY
Fatto (made)
Finito (finished)   FINISHED
Forte (strong)
Fumo (smoke)   *SMOKE
                              *TO SMOKE
Gesu' (Jesus)   CROSS
Giallo (yellow)
Grr   ATTACK
Grande (big)   *BIG
Guarda (look)   *LOOK
Ha fame (he is hungry)
Ha morso (he has bitten)
Ha paura (he is afraid)   *FEAR
Ho avuto paura (I was afraid)

Il bambino (the child)	CHILD
	BABY
Il cane (the dog)	
Io (I)	*POINTING TO HIMSELF
La' (there)	*POINTING
La bambina (the girl)	
La donna (the woman)	
La luce (the light)	
Latte (milk)	
L'auto (the car)	
L'elefante (the elephant)	ELEPHANT
Levati (get out of)	
Libro (book)	
Lontano (far away)	FAR AWAY
L'orologio (the clock)	
Male (hurt)	
Mamma	
Mangia/mangiato/mangiare (he eats/eaten/to eat)	TO EAT
Mannaggia (darn it)	DARN IT
Matta (mad)	
Mela (apple)	APPLE
Metto (I put)	
Mio (my)	*POINTING TO HIMSELF
Morto (dead)	DEAD
No	*NO
Non (not)	
Non c'e' (there isn't)	*THERE ISN'T
Non importa (doesn't matter)	
Non lo so (I don't know)	
Non parla (he doesn't speak)	DON'T SPEAK
Non va (it doesn't work)	DOESN'T WORK
Orso (bear)	
Otto (eight)	
Papa' (daddy)	
Penso (I think)	
Perche'? (why?)	WHY?
Per il collo (by the neck)	NECK
Piange/piango (she cries/I cry)	TO CRY
Piano (slow)	*SLOW
Piccolo (small)	*SMALL
Piera (name of the speech therapist)	
Pizzica (it pinchs)	
Poi (after)	AFTER
Porta (door)	DOOR

Prima (before)	BEFORE
Pure (also)	
Qua (here)	*POINTING
Quattro (four)	FOUR
Questo (this)	*POINTING
Rosso (red)	
Sangue (blood)	*BLOOD
Scarpa (shoe)	
Scoppiato (burst)	BURST
Scritto (written)	WRITTEN
Sei (six)	
Sente (he hears)	TO HEAR
Sette (seven)	
Si (yes)	*YES (with the head)
Si gonfia (he's inflates)	TO INFLATE
Simone (name of one of his friends)	
Sole (sun)	
Sopra (on)	ON
Spara (he shoots)	TO SHOOT
Tanto (a lot)	A LOT
Tavolo (table)	
Tigre (tiger)	
Tra poco (in a short time)	IN A SHORT TIME
Tre (three)	THREE
Tuo/a (yours)	
Tutto (everything)	EVERYTHING
	EVERYTHING QUIET
Uffa (tired)	
Uno (one)	ONE
Uomo (man)	
Verde (green)	
Via (away)	*AWAY
	*GO AWAY
Viene (he is coming)	
Vieni (come here)	*COME-HERE
Viola (violet)	
Zitto	*BE QUIET
	*MONOCLE
	*BIRD
	SCATTERED
	WIND

*Indicates words and gestures produced in the first session.

PART IV

Hearing Children with Spoken and Sign Language Input

Overview

In this part, we include two chapters which examine the early gestural communication of hearing children who have deaf parents. Bonvillian, Orlansky, and Folven report on a longitudinal investigation of 13 children (all hearing except one) who have been exposed to signing within their families. The authors' main interest is in the precursors of language; they look, in particular, at the interrelationship between gestural and cognitive development of the children in addition to their sign language acquisition. From the results of this study and other studies of signing children, they conclude that the first steps in sign language usage are more rapidly achieved than are comparable milestones in speech. They also conclude that some interrelationships between sign language acquisition and cognitive and gestural development differ from those that have been based on studies of spoken language.

The chapter by Griffith is a case study of one hearing child with deaf parents followed longitudinally from 17 to 23 months of age. The focus of the research is the bilingual acquisition of spoken English and American Sign Language with particular attention devoted to code-switching. From the data, Griffith concludes that hearing children of deaf parents acquire the two languages in a fashion similar to that of children acquiring two spoken languages. There is no advantage for the gestural modality.

These two chapters both examine the early communication of hearing children with sign language input, but they differ with respect to the number of subjects involved, the ages of the children, the research questions asked, and the conclusions reached. Bonvillian et al. discuss data from eight infants between the ages of 9 and 13 months while Griffith describes the communicative behavior of one child at a later stage of development, between 17 and 23 months. The first study is designed to explore cognitive and gestural precursors of language; the second sets out to document bilingual, bimodal language acquisition, including code-switching. These differences may explain the fact that the two chapters present quite different conclusions about the time-tables for spoken and sign language acquisition. Furthermore, the authors use dissimilar criteria in arriving at the definition of gesture and sign. Consequently, there is disagreement about the timing of the onset of language. Bonvillian and his colleagues themselves point out that there are many obstacles to an accurate interpretation of the early gestural communication of young children exposed to sign language.

CHAPTER 17

Early Sign Language Acquisition: Implications for Theories of Language Acquisition

J.D. Bonvillian, M.D. Orlansky, and R.J. Folven

Introduction

During the past 25 years, our understanding of how children acquire language has been considerably expanded by the results of a large number of empirical investigations. Although our knowledge of the language acquisition process has improved, there is as yet no widespread agreement regarding the important questions of when language is first used by children, and what abilities or characteristics should rightly be considered prerequisites or precursors to language.

Inasmuch as symbolic and communicative components have been widely viewed as fundamental to language, many investigators have presumed that their presence is a prerequisite to language. Consequently, it was often assumed, until recently, that language emerged only after certain symbolic and communicative prerequisites have been "mastered." This focus on prerequisites has tended to obscure the concept of language as a skill intimately intertwined with the child's general cognitive, perceptual, gestural, and social development. Moreover, questions regarding the nature of language acquisition have not been restricted to theoretical debates; they have influenced the education and treatment of children as well.

Language Precursors

Theorists typically have taken one of several positions in seeking to explain the development of language. One perspective (Piaget, 1962; Sinclair, 1971) has held that the child's acquisition of cognitive or sensorimotor abilities is a necessary precursor to language. Language, in this model, is viewed essentially as an outgrowth of the child's acquisition of this symbolic function, with the ability to use symbols a consequence of the completion of the sensorimotor period. In the

This research was supported in part by National Science Foundation Grant BNS-8023114. Portions of this research were presented at the Third International Symposium on Sign Language Research, Rome, June, 1983, and at the biennial meeting of the Society for Research in Child Development, Toronto, April, 1985. The authors wish to express their deep gratitude to the families who so generously participated in the study.

development of the symbolic function, Piaget placed special importance on the child's capacity for mental representation, an ability clearly demonstrated by the understanding of the permanence of objects. Many studies conducted within this theoretical framework have compared a child's spoken language development with his or her performance on sensorimotor tasks. In addition, a strong correspondence between young children's symbolic play and their spoken language development has been reported (Casby & Ruder, 1983; Nicolich, 1975, 1977).

Another approach which emphasized the importance of cognitive precursors to language was formulated by Werner and Kaplan (1963). They pointed out that the child's transition from an egocentric conceptualization of self and environment to the realization that objects are entities distinct from the self is a critical development during the sensorimotor period. This process of differentiating or distancing of the self from the referent is considered an early precursor of referential behavior and subsequent language development.

A second major series of models of language acquisition has focused on the interaction between the child and his or her mother (or other principal caregiver). From this perspective, language is primarily constructed socially: over the course of a great many daily interactions, mother and child gradually establish a number of conventionalized routines that enable them to control and understand each other's behavior in an increasingly complex environment. Beginning in early infancy, a mother often reacts to her child's grasping and reaching movements by attributing intentions to them and otherwise interpreting them from her perspective. In many cases, interpretation is supplemented with action, as the mother assists her child in achieving the apparent goal of these movements or actions. As Bruner (1975a) has noted, the child's participation in these early prelinguistic exchanges and turn-taking routines provides a foundation of experience in nonverbal signaling. The visual cross-checking that occurs between mother and infant is also considered important; language is thus viewed as having precursors in the pragmatic aspects of social interaction.

The third major approach to studying the roots of language has centered on the child's early gestural communication. Researchers have focused either on the structural and communicative aspects of the child's nonverbal gestures, or on the co-occurrence of gestures with vocalic utterances in order to determine the meaning of early vocalizations. The various gestures produced by the normal child and their communicative impact have been examined in particular depth by Bates and her associates (Bates, Benigni, Bretherton, Camaioni, & Volterra, 1977, 1979). Bates has contended that minimal gestural communication precedes language and placed the onset of such gestural facility late in the child's 1st year. In this model, during the period between 9 and 13 months, the parent comes to recognize the different gestures and sounds produced by the child. To the extent that the parent and child agree on the specific form and function of the various gestures, it can be argued that these gestures have become a form of conventionalized communication (Bates et al., 1979), although they are highly context bound. Not until about 13 months of age do most children discover that objects and events have names, and that such names can be used to identify referents. It also has been observed (A.L. Carter, 1975b) that early gestures transmit the requests or intentions of very young children with greater accuracy and specificity than speech.

In spite of an extensive body of research and theoretical literature, the empirical support for these models of language precursors and prerequisites has not been decisive. The models, moreover, have all been developed from studies of children's *spoken* language; seldom or never have these models been examined from the perspective of the acquisition of a recognized gestural language, such as one of the manual languages of deaf persons. When data from the present longitudinal study of the acquisition of American Sign Language (ASL) are brought to bear on the previously proposed theoretical relationships among cognition, symbolic play, gestural development, and language, it will become apparent that certain widely held notions need to be re-examined and considerably modified. The perspective that emerges from this investigation is that many aspects of productive language can take place earlier than has been believed, and that language modality is an important factor in the acquisition process.

Early Sign Language Acquisition

Evidence has existed for some time that the interrelationships between sign language acquisition and a child's cognitive, gestural, and social development may differ from those interrelationships that have been predicated on studies of spoken language. Well over 100 years ago, it was observed that the young, normally hearing children of instructors in schools for the deaf, when exposed to both sign language and spoken English, usually acquired the former first (Whitney, 1867). More recent and systematic investigations have substantiated this observation of accelerated sign language development in populations of both deaf and hearing children. Schlesinger and Meadow (1972), for example, studied language development in three children (two hearing, one deaf) who were exposed to sign language. All three of these children reportedly learned to sign before learning to speak, although there was considerable variation in the ages at which signs were initiated: the subjects produced their first signs at 5.5, 10.5, and 12 months. Early emergence of individual signs was also reported in a case study of a hearing child (first sign at 7 months of age) of a deaf mother and hearing father (Prinz & Prinz, 1979), and in two studies of deaf children of deaf parents, in which the three subjects produced their first signs at 8 and 9 months of age (Bergmann 1983; Williams, 1976).

Children who initially learn language in a manual-gestural mode tend to show an accelerated rate of total vocabulary acquisition in addition to an earlier onset of expressive communication. For example, a deaf child studied by McIntire (1977) attained a vocabulary of more than 85 signs by 13 months of age, a point at which most children would probably be mastering only their first few spoken words. Similarly, a young hearing child who was exposed to signs was reported to have developed a vocabulary of 10 signs at 13 months, and of 50 signs at 15.3 months (Holmes & Holmes, 1980). In addition, several of the subjects in these studies displayed the ability to combine signs at an unusually early age — as early as 10 months in the McIntire study. It should be noted, however, that these findings of early acquisition of linguistic skills in the manual mode were restricted to examinations of the first steps of language production. When the acquisition of more complex linguistic functions was studied in manual and auditory-vocal languages, the ages and patterns of acquisition across modalities typically did not differ.

Several potentially important aspects of the subjects' performance were not investigated in the previously reviewed studies of sign language acquisition, including the children's corresponding cognitive and motor development, use of gestures other than those of ASL, and interactions with signing caregivers. In the absence of such information, it was not possible to evaluate the signing children's communicative development in relation to their progress on these other significant dimensions. Also, these studies were based on a very small number of subjects; most investigations, in fact, involved only a single signing child. Especially in light of recent studies that have revealed substantial individual differences in patterns of early language development (see Nelson, 1981), any definitive conclusions had to await larger-scale and more systematic investigations.

With the foregoing concerns in mind, we conducted a longitudinal investigation of children's early sign language acquisition in relationship to their cognitive and gestural development (Bonvillian, Orlansky, & Novack, 1983; Bonvillian, Orlansky, Novack, & Folven, 1983; Folven, Bonvillian, & Orlansky, 1984/85). Over an 18-month period, we made regular monthly research visits to the homes of 13 very young children of deaf parents. With a single exception, all the children appeared to have normal hearing. Both parents were deaf in all but three of the families; two families had a deaf mother and a hearing father, and one family had a deaf father and a hearing mother. The parents reported that their usual means of communication within the home was ASL. In addition, most parents at times used speech to communicate with their children, although the quantity and intelligibility of their vocalizations showed considerable variation.

In the course of each home visit (which lasted a minimum of 1 h), detailed information was obtained about each child's communicative performance and overall development. During these visits, both written reports and videotape recordings were collected of each child's sign language usage and interaction with his or her mother. In addition, the children's parents maintained written journals in which they recorded the date a sign or sign combination was initially produced, its English equivalent, and a description of how the sign was physically formed. Also during each of the visits, the children's cognitive development was assessed using the scales of sensorimotor functioning from the Uzgiris and Hunt (1975) ordinal scales of psychological development. The subject's performance on one of the scales, the Development of Vocal Imitation, was not included in any analyses.

Videotape recordings of the young children's interaction with their mothers, symbolic play, and nonsign gestural development were also made at each home visit. Each mother-child pair was asked to sit on a blanket on the floor and to "play as you normally do," with a box of toys provided. This procedure was followed to ensure some uniformity in setting across the different households, as well as to encourage signing and to foster symbolic play with such items as dolls, bottles, spoons, and cups. The children's symbolic play and production of signs and nonsign gestures were then compared with the findings reported by Bates et al. (1979) and Nicolich (1977; McCune-Nicolich, 1981) for gestural and symbolic play development for children in hearing households learning to speak.

In comparison with the norms for spoken language development (Cattell, 1940; Lenneberg, 1967; Nelson, 1973), the young children learning to sign were accelerated in their acquisition of the first steps of language usage. The subjects typically attained language milestones, in signs, a couple of months in advance of what would have been expected for children learning to speak. Whereas most infants do not utter their first recognizable word until the end of their 1st year, the mean age at which the young signing children produced their first recognizable sign was 8.6 months (Bonvillian, Orlansky, Novack, and Folven, 1983). Because there are substantial difficulties involved in determining when a child first "uses" a word, investigators have frequently utilized the age at which a child achieves a ten-item vocabulary as an important measure of early vocabulary development. On this measure as well, the young signing children were significantly advanced in comparison with children learning to speak (Nelson, 1973), attaining a ten-item sign vocabulary at a mean age of 13.2 months.

Accelerated sign language development was also evident in the subjects' mean vocabulary size of 48.2 signs at 18 months; Lenneberg (1967) describes a range of 3-50 spoken words as normal for this age. Similarly, the subjects first began to combine two or more signs at an average age of 17.1 months, whereas most children learning to speak begin to combine words between 18 and 21 months of age (Gesell & Thompson, 1934; Slobin, 1971). Although the signing children's performance, in comparison with the norms for spoken language development, was quite impressive, it should be noted that there were substantial interindividual differences. While some of the children had well-established vocabularies and were combining signs at the time of their 1st birthday, other children made slower progress.

Gestural Development

The examination of the interrelationships between the children's production of gestures (often referred to as performative or deictic gestures) and their acquisition of a manual language was based primarily on videotape recordings of the young children at age 6-16 months. This period extends down to include the age at which a recognizable sign was first produced, and circumscribes the 9-13-month age range investigated by Bates et al. (1979). Unfortunately, there were adequate videotape recordings on only eight of the 13 children in the present study in this latter age range. Thus, any failure to replicate in sign language the correlational findings of Bates et al. (1979) may be attributable, in part, to the smaller sample size in our study.

In their analysis of the nature of the ties between early gestures and language acquisition, Bates et al. (1979) identified a sequence of communicative gestures that preceded and predicted the onset of spoken language. This sequence consisted of *ritualized requests* (a conventionalized sound or gesture, such as touching an adult's hand and waiting), *showing* (holding out an object to gain an adult's attention), *giving* (offering and surrendering an object), and *communicative pointing* (pointing to an object, usually with arm outstretched and checking for adult confirmation). These four communicative gestures, along with *noncommunicative pointing* (examining objects with the index finger), were found to be significant predictors of language acquisition; that is, those infants who, between 9 and 13 months, produced more of these gestures were also likely to be among those infants with more extensive production and comprehension vocabularies. The reason that these "prelinguistic" gestures were correlated with spoken language development, according to Bates et al. (1979), was that they share three critical characteristics with language: communicative intent, joint reference, and conventionalization of form.

In the present study, seven of the eight children for whom detailed videotape recordings were available during this 9–13-month period exhibited a pattern of co-occurrence of sign and nonsign gestural production. That is, for these children, there was no recorded period during which they produced any of the performative or deictic gestures identified by Bates et al. (1979) that they had not also produced a recognizable sign. The pattern of sign and nonsign gesture acquisition was clearly associated: the onset of signing was closely aligned temporally with the appearance of the deictic gestures, and expansion of the children's sign language vocabularies coincided with an increased frequency of nonsign gestural production. The single exception to this pattern of co-occurrence was a child for whom speech appeared to play a more dominant role, as the child received considerable spoken language input from an older hearing sibling.

Although the pattern of a distinct period of performative or deictic gestures antedating the onset of early sign production use was not found to exist in the manual mode, the analysis of ASL acquisition and the emergence of nonsign communicative gestures did yield results which in some respects were similar to those obtained by Bates et al. (1979) for such gestures and speech. The ages at which the children learning to sign acquired the various nonsign or deictic gestures were close to the ages reported by Bates et al. (1979) for the emergence of these gestures in children learning to speak. Additionally, those gestures which significantly predicted the expansion of the children's sign language lexicons between 9 and 12 1/2 months, communicative pointing and giving, were also the two strongest predictors of the pace of spoken language development in the Bates et al. (1979) study.

That the same gestures were found to be the strongest predictors of both spoken and sign language acquisition probably indicates a substantial underlying similarity in language development in both modes. It should be recognized, however, that although the children exposed to manual language produced signs before most children utter their first words, their early signs were typically directed to objects or events in the immediate context. Moreover, it is difficult to make inferences regarding the signing children's command or understanding of their initial lexical items.

Symbolic Play

Our study also investigated the relationship between the children's acquisition of ASL and their levels of maturity in symbolic play. For children learning to speak, McCune-Nicolich (1981) has reported data that support a structural correspondence between the domains of symbolic play and language. Of particular interest were her contentions that: (a) first words occur during levels 2 and 3 of symbolic play; (b) linear combinations of words (e.g., such unanalyzed phrases as "orange juice" or "Uncle John") appear during level 4 when play schemes are combined sequentially; and (c) syntactic combinations of words emerge contemporaneously with the child's demonstration of level 5 symbolic play (the performance of mentally planned symbolic games). Using the scale devised by Nicolich (1977), a level of symbolic maturity was assigned to each of the signing subjects, reflecting the highest level of spontaneously demonstrated symbolic play that was observed to occur during each videotape segment. Briefly, the milestones in ASL acquisition were attained during earlier stages of symbolic maturity than Nicolich found for similar stages in speech development. More specifically, for the six videotaped visits in which level 3 was the highest demonstrated level of symbolic play (which Nicolich found to be associated with first words), all six subjects were producing at least single sign utterances, and three of the children also were combining signs. For the seven tapes which showed level 4 functioning (associated with sequential word combinations in children learning to speak), all seven subjects were already producing syntactic sign combinations. And by the time some of the subjects demonstrated level 5 symbolic play, these subjects had long been producing syntactic sign combinations. Thus, the structural correspondence between symbolic play and language outlined by McCune-Nicolich (1981) does not appear to apply consistently to infants learning language in a manual or gestural mode, as various linguistic capacities were evident at earlier levels of symbolic play than she and others (e.g., Casby & Ruder, 1983; Lombardino & Sproul, 1984) have reported.

A degree of caution probably should be exercised in interpreting the current findings, given the small number of subjects and the relative brevity of the videotape sessions. Nevertheless, the ages at which our subjects acquired the different levels of symbolic play were largely compatible with those reported by Nicolich (1977).

Cognitive Development

Because of the lack of widespread agreement among investigators as to what criteria should be employed for determining when children first use language, the present subject's performance on the Uzgiris-Hunt scales was computed for the ages at which the children attained several significant sign language milestones. Comparative measures of language and sensorimotor development were taken at the ages when the children produced their (a) first recognizable sign; (b) tenth different sign; (c) first sign for an object, individual, or event not in the immediate context; and (d) first two-sign combination. Overall, the children showed accelerated acquisition in sign of these four language milestones, and, because they were at a younger age when they attained these milestones, their performance on the scales of cognitive development was often considerably below those cognitive levels previously postulated as necessary for language (Bonvillian et al., 1983).

At the time the children of deaf parents produced their first recognizable sign, they scored primarily in stages 3 (30.8%) and 4 (46.2%) across the different scales of sensorimotor development. And for the two scales whose completion has been most frequently viewed as necessary for language (object permanence and means-ends abilities), more than half of the scores were below stage 5. Thus, young children, as a whole, appear to have the ability to produce a sign or an arbitrary gesture for an item in the immediate context long before they complete the sensorimotor period.

By the time the subjects produced their tenth different sign, they were typically able to name reliably a variety of objects or events in their immediate environment. At this stage, the children were usually able to recognize and name objects from different perspectives, as well as a range of exemplars of the same object. Developmentally, the children's overall performance on the Uzgiris-Hunt scales at the time of this language milestone was primarily – about half – in stage 5, with most of the remaining scores spread evenly between stages 4 and 6. On the object permanence scale, the children's performance was almost evenly divided between stages 5 and 6, whereas on the means-ends scale nearly one-third of the children were still performing on a stage 4 level. This finding of a small but well-established vocabulary prior to the completion of the sensorimotor period further accentuates the limitations of the sensorimotor prerequisite to language model.

Determining the point at which the young children first used signs in a truly symbolic fashion proved to be problematic, largely because the children mainly signed about objects, individuals, or events in their immediate environment. The children appeared to shift only gradually from signing about "here-and-now" items to signing about people or things that were upstairs or down the hall, or about past events. In determining when signs were first used in a symbolic manner, it proved helpful to meet with parents, to discuss their interpretations of their children's signing, and to review the diaries that were kept. Inevitably such evaluation has an interpretive component; the dates used in the calculations of symbolic sign usage should be viewed with some caution as they rely on subjective judgments to a higher degree than do the other measures of sign language development. As a group, the children did not appear to use signs in a symbolic fashion until they had established at least a basic vocabulary, usually over ten signs, and in some cases not until they had begun to combine signs. The sensorimotor scales placed the children primarily in stages 5 (47.4%) and 6 (34.2%) by that time, with the majority of the children scoring in stage 6 on the object permanence scale.

By the time the children began to combine signs, their most frequent scores on the Uzgiris-Hunt scales (44.0%) were stage 6 responses, with many of the remaining responses (38.0%) in stage 5. The children were notably advanced, relative to the other scales, on the scale of object permanence, with all but one subject scoring in or completing stage 6. It should be noted, however, that the procedures employed in the Uzgiris-Hunt assessment of object permanence have been criticized (Bertenthal & Fischer, 1983) for sometimes resulting in the premature crediting of the child with object permanence and mental representational skills. The children's performance on the means-ends abilities scales also was advanced, with only two subjects scoring below stage 6. In spite of the elevated performance on these two scales, it should be remembered that over half (56.0%) of the children's total scores across the different scales were below the stage 6 level. Thus, even at the point when the children were beginning to demonstrate more advanced linguistic abilities (i.e., sign combinations), there were substantial sections of the sensorimotor scales that had yet to be traversed.

Modality Factors in Early Signing

The course of acquisition of the first steps of a visuomotor language such as ASL differs notably from that of an auditory-vocal language. Many of the hand movements involved in the adult gestures of pointing, waving, and grasping appear as early as the first few months of life (Trevarthen, 1979), and the hand configurations that occur most frequently in young children's initial sign vocabularies are typically produced by all children during their first 6 months (Fogel, 1981). It is thus quite plausible that these hand configurations and movements could be shaped into and interpreted as recognizable signs by deaf parents of very young children.

Schaeffer (1978, 1980) has suggested that many of the basic cognitive and interactional skills posited as prerequisites for language may actually develop as a result of direct manual language training. For example, early sign training and use encompasses aspects of causality (e.g., seeking eye contact, touching an adult to gain the adult's attention), and gestural imitation, thus tending to entrain stage 4 sensorimotor schemes in the child. Another inherent difference between sign and speech concerns the degree of external control possible in each mode: parents can easily mold and guide their children's hands into the correct formation and movement of a sign, but comparable external manipulation of the speech mechanism is impossible. Overall, then, such a high degree of correspondence among the learning and building blocks of the language, the child's intentions and cognitive development, and parent-child interaction would not exist in an auditory-vocal language.

Piaget's detailed descriptions of the development of motor imitation skills in his own children further attest to the onset of elements of a gestural communication system early in the child's 1st year. Piaget observed that during the third sensorimotor period (about 4–8 months), infants are often successful at imitating other people's movements as long as the infants already have these movements in their gestural repertoire and can see their own production. With the fourth sensorimotor stage (about 8–12 months), Piaget observed that more complex gestures are typically imitated and acquired. First, infants develop the ability to imitate gestures they have never made before, and secondly, they are able to imitate movements that they are unable to see. Not surprisingly, this is the time frame in which many of the present subjects made considerable progress in their ability to imitate their parents' signs and to produce recognizable signs on their own.

Even for young children not exposed to a manual language, gestures continue to play a prominent role in communication over the first 2 years. The use of the two modalities, though, does not remain constant over time. With maturation, the normal child's preferred production modality changes from a predominantly gestural one at about 13 months to a primarily vocal one at about 20 months of age (Bretherton, Bates, McNew, Shore, Williamson, & Beeghly-Smith, 1981). Similarly, Goldin-Meadow and Morford (1985; & this volume) reported that their young hearing subjects initially relied on gesture as their principal means of communication; for example, producing two-gesture combinations 5–9 months before speaking two-word sentences. Even after the subjects began to utter recognizable words, they frequently produced gestures together with speech. The pattern of gesture and word combination, however, changed over time. Initially, the young children used the two modalities in a complementary fashion, typically producing a word and a gesture to indicate the same thing. Later, they would sometimes use words and gestures in what Goldin-Meadow and Morford termed a "supplementary manner" to designate two different semantic elements. With the children's rapid advances in spoken language late in the 2nd year, the complexity of their gestural production declined.

Interestingly, some of the factors that appear to assist children in the early learning of signs also prove to be obstacles to their accurate interpretation by investigators. One difficulty is that some of the first signs reported in various studies closely resemble gestures that all children generate, regardless of linguistic input. Therefore, even though these early gestures may lack any true linguistic component, they may be interpreted as signs by the children's caregivers. The children's "signs" then acquire a degree of linguistic significance for the caregivers and may well become a focus of caregiver-child interactions, with their production differentially reinforced by the caregivers. A second hurdle in interpretation of early signing stems from children's enhanced motor imitation skills at the end of their 1st year, when they become more adept at imitating the arbitrary or conventionalized gestures that constitute their caregivers' sign lexicons. Concomitantly, the young children gradually increase in their ability to delay imitation. Thus a fine line often exists between children's imitation of their parents' signs and truly "new" entries in their sign lexicons. A third obstacle in assessing the children's sign/gesture production is in determining the dependence of the sign on the immediate environmental context. As noted before, many of the early signs produced by the present subjects were made to objects, people, or events in the immediate environment. Even when an arbitrary or conventionalized gesture is reliably produced for a range of appropriate exemplars, such a sign is still far from obtaining its full linguistic potential. As children become more accomplished signers, they learn how and why to modify the formational characteristics of this sign, how to combine this sign in grammatical utterances, and in what situations this sign should be used. The path from an initial recognizable sign to a sign with its full array of linguistic properties, then, is often very lengthy. Where to draw the line between gesture and sign is thus an area of current controversy (Volterra & Caselli, 1985). To some extent, the same difficulties hinder studies of spoken language acquisition, where investigators frequently credit full word knowledge to their young subjects' first word-like utterances. However, because the transition from first sign-like gestural productions to an established sign lexicon often covers many months in children learning to sign, the linguistic interpretive problem appears more difficult in this domain. Also, as Locke (1983) has argued, the comparatively late initiation of words in hearing children is likely more attributable to vocal tract constraints than to cognitive limitations. Thus, when children utter their first recognizable words, they may be more developmentally advanced than their counterparts who are producing their first recognizable signs.

The concept that signs are initially acquired more easily than words is further supported by the results of two recent studies of early language development involving Down syndrome children (Abrahamsen, Brown-Williams, & McCarty, 1986; Abrahamsen, Cavallo, & McCluer, 1985), a population in whom developmental events are slowed down and temporal sequences apparently easier to discern. The investigators reported that the Down syndrome children typically learned first how to imitate several signs. Then some of these signs were produced for a referent without a model, and at this time or later the first spoken words began to appear with those signs. In general, for Down syndrome children, as well as for the normal children examined, there appeared to be an advantage for signs up to at least the developmental age of 20 months, after which this imbalance in modality preference tended to dissipate.

When the overall performance of our 13 subjects is examined along with that of signing children in other studies, a compelling case can be made that the first steps in sign language usage are often more rapidly and readily achieved than are comparable milestones in speech. This result appears to run counter to a widely held axiom in linguistics, namely that no language is more easily learned than any other, as a first language. These findings on sign language, we should note, relate only to the very first steps of language acquisition. The course of sign language acquisition appears to more closely parallel that of spoken language development after the age of 2 years, as cognitive and linguistic components gradually assume a more dominant role over modality factors.

Theoretical Implications

In light of the finding that young children of deaf parents often begin to produce signs several months before the end of their 1st year, some reconsideration of the position that completion, or near-completion, of the sensorimotor period is a necessary cognitive prerequisite to language appears to be in order. Similarly, the finding that signs co-occur with the onset and use of performative or deictic gestures casts doubt on the view that such nonsign gestures are necessarily a step that precedes the production of language.

Earlier models of gestural and language development (Bates et al., 1975; Volterra, 1981a), have depicted children as producing deictic or performative gestures towards the end of their 1st year. These gestures were described as having clear communicative intent and included such gestures as pointing, giving, and showing. The referential meaning in such early communications was provided solely by the context in which the deictic gestures were produced. Referential gestures — gestures that stood for stable referents in the environment, such as pantomiming a drinking motion to indicate DRINK — were considered to be acquired only later by children. However, children who are learning to sign can reliably produce arbitrary or conventionalized gestures (signs) to refer to objects or events in their environment as early as most children acquire context-tied gestures; thus the above model of gestural and language development needs to be revised. Children apparently have the capacity to acquire and use signs earlier than previously believed — provided, of course, that they receive manual input.

The observed pattern of gesture and sign development in the present study also has implications for models of symbol development and early language usage. If the subject's first recognizable signs had emerged after (or even contemporaneous with) giving and communicative pointing, then it would have been reasonable to propose that distancing theory (Werner & Kaplan, 1963) adequately described the transition from communicative gestures to signs. Many of the subjects, however, were able to produce signs, at least for objects or events in the immediate environment, before they used giving and communicative pointing gestures. Apparently, these young children had acquired a sufficient capacity to distance self from referent and the referent from its symbol by the time they produced their first signs. Relatedly, it was not evident that the subjects typically used their first signs within communicative routines. Although many early signs were incorporated into communicative routines, a number appeared to be imitations of parental signs or responses to requests for a label for items in the immediate environment. Thus, it may be that the very first uses of signs are not primarily communicative in nature (see Petitto, 1986).

Of course, one of the problems associated with constructing a model of the transition from nonlinguistic gestures to language has been the lack of agreement among various investigators as to when language begins. Piaget (1962) has argued that children do not demonstrate true language until they use words to recount past events. Such an approach downplays the child's learning of arbitrary or conventionalized symbols to represent persons, objects, and events, and thus may be too strict a criterion for language onset. Another criterion for language onset has been the use of words or signs to *name*. In their model of language development, Bates et al. (1977) have attached considerable significance to the acquisition of this ability to use what they call *referential language*. [Because of the apparent difficulties in determining the course of transition from gesture to language, we have undertaken a second study of early language development in nine children of deaf parents (Folven & Bonvillian, 1987). In this ongoing investigation, the children are being followed from 7 to 15 months of age, and special emphasis has been placed on determining when the children first demonstrate referential signing. These children first produced recognizable expressive signs at a mean age of 9 months. This finding of the onset of recognizable sign production several months before the end of the 1st year essentially replicates the result of the previous investigation that the onset of signing typically precedes the onset of recognizable spoken words. These early sign productions, however, were used as imitations of adult models, as parts of familiar routines, or as requests for activities, persons, or objects. Referential signing did not begin until about 1 year of age. Furthermore, this use of signs to name followed the onset of *communicative pointing* as in the Bates et al. (1975) model of language development. This transition from nonreferential to referential signing was found to co-occur with the same advances in symbolic play previously reported as associated with the onset of referential spoken word usage (McCune-Nicolich, 1981). Shortly after the children started using signs referentially, they often began to combine signs with a gesture (mean age = 12.6 months), typically a point. Within several months after first combining signs with gestures, most of the children had begun to combine two distinct signs. Thus, as in the earlier study (Bonvillian, Orlansky, Novack, & Folven, 1983), young signing children showed accelerated onset of lexical combinations.]

The ability manually to name objects present in the immediate context or to label events that just occurred appears to utilize cognitive skills that children normally acquire by the end of the 1st year. The ability to recognize or identify an object or an event over time would seem to be a necessary skill; Brown (1973) has placed the onset of this ability in stage 4 of the sensorimotor period, which often commences around 8 months of age (cf. Cohen & Strauss, 1979; Fagan, 1976). Moore and Meltzoff (1978) suggested that the concept of object identity — the notion that an object remains the same with itself despite some transformations — must be mastered before the child can learn to use names. Moore and Meltzoff place the concept of object identity at about 11 months of age in normal children; this would still be several months after some of the children of deaf parents had begun to use individual signs. (Cossette-Ricard & Decarie, 1983, place the infant's full acquisition of the concept of object identity at a still later date, about 15 months of age, although they emphasize that the notion of object identity develops throughout infancy). Some degree of object recognition or classification is clearly necessary in order for the child to apply names accurately; this ability evidently was achieved by some of our subjects well before they attained stage 5 of the sensorimotor period. Moreover, the present findings cast doubt on the view that the rather elaborate concept of mental representation at stage 6 is necessary for combining two signs. Similarly, recent accounts of children learning to speak (Ingram, 1981; Smolak, 1982) have also challenged statements about cognitive prerequisites to receptive and expressive language. Ingram, for example, observed that one of his subjects acquired a substantial spoken language vocabulary and the ability to combine words several months before achieving the sensorimotor stage purportedly necessary for language.

A perspective widely shared among developmental psycholinguists is that a child's early language usage reflects his or her mapping of language skills onto pre-existing non-linguistic structures or concepts. If that were the case, then the evidence from the present study of early sign language acquisition would indicate that such mapping could occur several months earlier than previously believed. Indeed, Halliday (1975) observed a systematic relationship between intentions and the production of sounds and gestures in his son at 9 months of age (about when many signing children first produced recognizable signs); the son's productions, however, tended to be intimately tied to the object or action itself rather than arbitrary in nature. If children learning to sign did not understand to some extent the relationship between a sign and its referent, then they would probably misname objects frequently, at least within the context of their available lexicons. Records of early sign usage indicate occasional overgeneralization (e.g., use of the sign MILK to refer to all liquids) and undergeneralization (e.g., use of the sign DOG to refer exclusively to the family dog), but there was no evidence of rampant misnaming within the children's available lexicons. This should not be taken to mean that each child thoroughly understood the concepts underlying each sign that he or she produced for various objects, individuals, events, or properties. Further research is needed to probe the underlying concept boundaries of the children's early signs. Yet the regularity and systematicity in the children's early signs suggests a clear and definite tie between sign, referent, and concept. It may well be that the parent's frequent use of signs to label objects and events in the children's environment, in conjunction with the children's own sign productions, gradually builds an interdependence between language and conceptual development, and thus helps anchor the children's linguistic productions to appropriate referents.

Finally, our observations of the children's acquisition of signing skills make us wary of considering any single point as the definitive point at which language begins. Just as children's mental representational skills appear to unfold gradually over time, the children learning to sign typically demonstrated early aspects of naming and communicative intent during their 1st year and slowly built up their sign language skills over the ensuing months. Seldom did the children exhibit sudden or dramatic changes in sign usage; rather, they gradually extended their signs to objects and events progressively more removed from the immediate context. Thus the onset of language may best be viewed as occurring over an extended period, in conjunction with the attainment of many interrelated skills, instead of emanating directly from the attainment of certain fixed prerequisite skills and concepts. We would urge caution in making *any* claims for specific phenomena being precursors to language, especially when the connections between these occurrences and the onset of language are largely speculative. Moreover, before investigators make strong claims about specific prerequisites to language or for distinct developmental language pathways, they would be well advised to confirm their findings by examining language development in modes other than speech.

CHAPTER 18

Emergence of Mode-Finding and Mode-Switching in a Hearing Child of Deaf Parents

P.L. GRIFFITH

Introduction

Since Piaget distinguished between egocentric and social speech in children from 2 to 6 years of age (Bloom & Lahey, 1978), there have been many reports not only that preschool children are able to use the point of view of the listener (Ervin-Tripp, 1972; Maratsos, 1973; McClure, 1977; Menig-Peterson, 1975; Sachs & Devin, 1976; Shatz & Gelman, 1973; Weeks, 1971), but also that listener-adapted variations in communication may occur at the very earliest stages of language acquisition (Berko-Gleason, 1973; Weeks, 1971). In monolingual English-speaking children, early forms of language alternation have been reported mainly as shifts from talking to not talking, whining to not whining (Berko-Gleason, 1973), and in pitch and speech register (Weeks, 1971). By 3 years of age, however, children have been found able to alternate the content (Maratsos, 1973) as well as the form (Shatz & Gelman, 1973) of their messages, according to their perceptions of the knowledge of their listener.

In bilingual learning environments, alternation across languages has been called code-switching, the occurrence of which is determined by the function, the situation, and the participants present (Kachru, 1978). Although code-switching (alternating across constituents) and code-mixing (alternating within constituents) are commonly described phenomena in fluent bilingual speakers (Kachru, 1978), only a few investigators have described code-switching in very young children (Leopold, 1939–1949; McClure, 1977). Leopold called the ability to adapt language according to the needs of the listener the "person-language principle" (Hatch, 1978) and noted in the study of his daughter that she began to employ this principle shortly after her 2nd birthday. Prior to that time he had not considered her as being truly bilingual, but described her language as a melding of English and German into one system. McClure (1977) noted that code-mixing occurred in her Mexican-American subjects by 3 years of age, but that code-switching did not occur until much later in the process of becoming bilingual.

The study of language acquisition in hearing children with one or two deaf parents provides investigators the opportunity to study not only bilingualism but language learning in two modalities as well. Although there has been an increased interest in the study of sign and speech development in this population over the last decade, there are still few descriptions of bilingual, bimodal language development. The majority of studies have focused on delay in acquisition of spoken language by hearing children of deaf parents (Sachs, Bard, & Johnson,

1981; Sachs & Johnson, 1976; Schiff & Ventry, 1976; Todd, 1975). Others have noted the precociousness of these children's learning sign language at very early ages (Prinz & Prinz, 1981; Wilbur & Jones, 1974). In at least three instances, hearing children of deaf parents were reported to be acquiring spoken language at the same rate as hearing children with hearing parents (Brelje, 1971; Jones & Quigley, 1979; Schiff, 1979). Mayberry (1976) reported that her subjects attended more to speech than to sign if their parents spoke to them. Speech intelligibility of deaf parents did not appear to be a factor in spoken language acquisition by their hearing children (Jones & Quigley, 1979; Schiff, 1979; Schiff & Ventry, 1976; Schiff-Myers, 1982); however, whether deaf parents talked to their children was a factor (Cicourel & Boese, 1972; Sachs & Johnson, 1976).

The development of code-switching has not been a major focus of any previously reported study of hearing children of deaf parents, although several anecdotal accounts have appeared in the literature. Lenneberg (1967) noted vocal alternation by children who "use normal voice and speech for hearing adults and abnormal voice and deafisms for the parents" (p. 137). Meadow (1972) also mentioned code-switching in a 2½-year-old hearing son of a deaf father and hearing mother. He used standard sign language[1] with his father, spoken English with his mother, and nonstandard sign language with his 15-year-old foster sister. Schiff and Ventry (1976) stated that the 52 children they studied seemed to be using two systems to communicate: one with hearing people and one with the deaf. Schiff (1979) also described differences in five 2-year-old hearing children of deaf parents when communicating with their deaf mothers and with the hearing investigator; they used more speech, more simultaneous communication, and longer spoken utterances with the latter but more communication attempts and more signs without speech with their mothers. Schiff pointed out the limitations of studying the children with only the mother and the investigator as interactants; the hearing status of other family members varied across subjects and may have influenced the children's communication behavior.

Prinz and Prinz (1981) (a profoundly deaf mother and hearing father) studied their hearing daughter Anya's language from her 7th to 21st month and found her bilingual-bimodal development very similar to that reported for bilingual children learning two spoken languages (Volterra & Taeschner, 1978). They report the first code-switching in Anya's output at about 19 months of age, and "a more conscious and deliberate attempt was made to code-switch from one linguistic system to the other according to the communicative needs of her addressee" (Prinz & Prinz, 1981, p. 82). At 21 months Anya was still in the transitional stage of becoming bilingual; her code-switching was developing along with the other components of her language system. this account appears to represent the earliest age at which code-switching has been reported in the literature. (Although it is probable that Anya's alternation was within constituents and not across consti-

---

[1]"Standard sign language" is Meadow's term for the more regular form used by educated deaf persons.

tuents, no differentiation is made by the authors between code-switching and code-mixing, nor has any such differentiation been made in any of the studies of hearing children with deaf parents.)

The present investigation followed the language development of a hearing son of deaf parents from his 17th to 23rd month. Various aspects of the child's language acquisition in sign and speech are described and related to data available on other hearing children of deaf parents. The child's early ability to alternate language according to addressee is also described. In order to avoid confusion about his or her adaptations of sign and speech, the term "mode-switching" is used here to mean the child's use of sign or speech depending upon the other participant in the conversation.

Method

Subjects

Dave, the subject, is the second of two children and the only hearing member of his family. His 4-year-old sister and his parents are congenitally deaf. His parents attended Gallaudet College, his father receiving the bachelor's degree and his mother completing 3 years of college. At the time of this study Dave's father worked at night and was home during the day; his mother did not work outside the home. His sister attended an oral preschool program for hearing-impaired children (total communication programs were not available locally at the time) and was present for only two of the investigator's visits.

Both parents stated that signing was their main mode of communicating with their family and friends. In discussing communication preferences with the parents, I found that both parents were concerned about their children's speech development and considered speech to be important for the success of their children. The parent's description of their own communication styles, which were later borne out by observation, were both accurate and insightful. Dave's mother generally spoke and signed to him but did not always speak to his sister when communicating with her. Observations indicated that Dave's mother generally spoke to her daughter only when scolding, directing her toward a task, or calling for her attention. She stated that her use of speech with other people depended upon their signing ability and whether they were deaf. With the investigator she used both signs and speech most of the time. On the other hand, Dave's father never spoke but communicated either through signing or note writing. He stated that he had not used speech to communicate since leaving school and felt that the quality of his voice was unpleasant to hearing listeners.

Dave's mother reported that his sign development seemed slower than that of his sister. She could not tell if at 17 months of age Dave said any words but reported that he knew about three signs (NO, MILK, BATHROOM). Because of her concern over Dave's language development, his parents had recently enrolled him in a nursery school language group with other hearing children. Up until 17 months of age Dave's only exposure to speech had been through his sister, his mother, occasional hearing visitors, the television, and hearing persons at a nursery where his mother bowled for 4 h each week.

Procedure

Observations of Dave were made in his home over a 5½-month period. The sessions lasted for about 2 h each and occurred approximately every 2 weeks for a total of 12 visits. On one occasion a deaf adult relative was visiting and on another a student language clinician from the preschool program came for a home visit. Dave's sister was present on two occasions, his father on five occasions, and his mother on all 12.

Data were collected by recording in a diary. Two means of description were used. First, all vocalizations, signs, and gestures and the context in which they occurred were written and tape recorded. Speech was transcribed in the International Phonetic Alphabet symbols and for signs a system based on Stokoe, Casterline, and Croneberg (1965) notation and Boyes Braem (1973) notation was used. Dave's mother served as informant and interpreter when confusions arose concerning Dave's signs. A sample of diary transcription is shown in Table 1. Secondly, immediately following each observation a log of the observer's impressions was written. This included new signs reported by Dave's mother but not observed during the session, a list of persons present, apparent strategies used by Dave to interact, and any changes noticed in communication since the previous visit. A sample of the log is shown in the Appendix.

Results

Transitional Stage

During initial observations it became obvious that Dave was in transition from a prelexical to a lexical form of representing meaning in both speech and sign modes. No signs were produced during the first observation. Instead Dave clapped, laughed, and rubbed his hands in a circular motion (sign babbling) while the investigator and his mother conversed in sign and speech and watched him. Speech produced during play was in the form of consonant/vowel (CV) strings that accompanied the play but dit not appear to be tied to objects of his interest or to his actions. Interactions with others were accomplished through establishment of joint reference by giving, banging, throwing, and rolling objects. Dave observed but did not approach the investigator during this first visit.

By the fourth observation, at 17½ months, Dave clearly exhibited communicative intent in his interactions. Although interactions with the investigator were carried out via object giving and throwing, more advanced communication was observed with his parents. Both proximal (specific referent) and distal

Table 1. Sample page of log of Dave's interaction

	Speech	Sign gloss	Context
1.	Dada?	POINT + COOKIE (right baby O in left palm with arms extended toward cookies)	Sitting on (M's) lap. Pointed then signed toward box of cookies on the table. Eyebrows raised, eyes widened, smiling and kicking legs.
2.	Dada!	COOKIE (hands more rigid)	(M) said, "No, more, Dave." Eyes narrowed, frowning, kicking legs. Voice more demanding and arms and hands rigid.
3.	Bye bye/ Bye bye/ Bye bye bye bye/		Sitting alone on the floor playing with trucks.
4.	Screaming	Hit (M) on leg several times; raised arms up.	(M) sitting in a chair. Dave ran to her, hit her leg until she looked at him, then put his arms up.
5.	O/o/o/	Shaking head NO. Hit book with fist	(M) gave Dave a book. He hit the book several times while saying "no" and shaking head, then threw the book down.
6.	Crying	PLAY (right hand Y, lax, moving wrist vertically)	(S) signed and told Dave to play with the toys, imitated (S's) sign then ran to kitchen.
7.		MINE (right hand toward chest, tapping chest twice)	Dave held up his toy dog and looked at me while signing.
8.		POINT+COAT (sign for coat made the same as the one for COOKIE)	(M) said, TIME TO GO. WHERE COAT? Dave looked at his coat then signed with arms extended toward the coat.

Pause (L. Bloom, 1974); (M), Mother; (S), Sherry.

(locative) pointing (Hoffmeister & Moores, 1973) were used extensively to express a variety of meanings. Pointing, screaming, physical tapping, tapping objects, and eye gaze, as well as gestures such as shrugging shoulders and opening hands (for "all gone, where?, don't know") were all used to indicate semantic intent. Some examples of Dave's repertoire were:

/Da/ + point;	request for cookie
Scream + point;	directive for candy
Shake head + pushing dog;	directive for get away
Point + eye gaze;	locative, Mom in kitchen
eye gaze + tapping Dad on chest + point;	attentional + directive.

These, among other instances, indicated that Dave's semantic development approximated that reported for other hearing children of deaf parents (Prinz &

Prinz, 1979; Wilbur & Jones, 1974), as well as that reported for subjects in language acquisition studies (L. Bloom, 1974; Brown, 1973) of hearing children the same age.

Differential means of gaining attention according to the person addressed were noted on the fifth visit (Dave at 18 months). He gained access to his father by physical tapping or slapping, while he screamed, banged objects, and tapped his mother to gain her attention. Interactions with the investigator remained mediated by objects, although Dave now maintained eye contact and laughed while the investigator talked and signed about his toys or his actions.

Dave's performance from 17 to 19 months of age suggested that observations had begun just as he was in transition from the use of deictic gestures (showing and giving tied to objects) to early referential gesture use (conventional sign emergence) as defined by Volterra (1981a). Within a 6-week period his communication forms had changed from primarily vocal babbling and whispers as well as pointing and banging to the production of recognizable lexical forms in both sign and speech.

Two instances exemplify this development. Dave's usual means of requesting a cookie was to scream and point toward the cookie jar. This happened on several occasions when the investigator was present. During the sixth observation (at 18½ months) Dave's form of request changed to the production of a point followed by a baby sign for "cookie" (right index finger in open palm of left hand, instead of bent five fingertips in palm). Two weeks later the request was again modified by the incorporation of a locative notion in the sign — the sign made with both hands and arms extended toward the cookie jar and omitting the point. The transition that had occurred in about 6 weeks can be diagrammed thus:

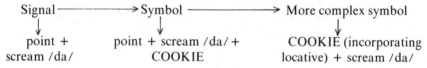

The first spoken word that the investigator could identify as tied to a context was a CV syllable at 18 months, but his first word might have been earlier; his mother could not tell whether he made a word or only sounds. In the initial five observations, all speech sounds appeared to be in the form of CV strings of mostly plosive sounds not tied to any event or object, with the exception of the sound /da/, which was consistently used with a point to request a cookie. In the sixth observation, however, Dave used another CV syllable. His mother and sister were putting together a puzzle of the three little pigs. His sister was signing to their mother about the pig's clothing, when Dave ran over to them, pointed to the puzzle and said, /pI, pI/. His mother responded in sign and speech, "The three pigs." Looking at his mother, he continued with /pI, pI/. His mother was very pleased when the investigator confirmed that Dave's syllable sounded like the word pig — /pIg/.

By the final observation at 18 months Dave had added the word "daddy" to his speech repertoire and a few signs to his sign repertoire, indications that lexical representations were developing in both modes.

Lexical System

Dave's onset of sign and speech acquisition occurred at around 18 months of age — later than reported for several other subjects studied by other investigators. Wilbur and Jones (1974) reported that one of their subjects began to speak and sign at 11 months. First signs and words emerged at 11 months and 9 months in two children studied by Jones and Quigley (1979). What was similar about Dave and these other children was the proximity in time of the first signs to the first words; in all four children production of signs and speech occurred at about the same time. In at least one reported instance (Prinz & Prinz, 1979), the child's first sign appeared several months before her first word; 7 months and 12 months, respectively. Of course for many subjects reported to have delayed speech development, signing had developed within the normally expected time, speech occurring much later (Schiff & Ventry, 1976; Todd, 1975).

The rate of Dave's acquisition of vocabulary in each mode progressed at a rapid pace from 18 to 23 months of age. And although his mother considered his language onset later compared to his sister's, by 23 months of age Dave exhibited no signs of language delay. By 21 months of age his sign and speech development were on a par with that reported for Anya (Prinz & Prinz, 1979) and well within the limits of normal language acquisition (see Table 2).

Table 2. A comparison of the bilingual lexicons of Dave and Anya (Prinz & Prinz, 1979)

Dave			Anya		
Age months	Words	Signs	Age months	Words	Signs
18	3	5	18	8	15
21	20	27	21	14	24

Very little redundancy of vocabulary was found in Dave's two modes, suggesting a sort of economy of effort. The same was found in studies of children acquiring two spoken languages (Leopold, 1939–1949) and acquiring signing and speaking (Mayberry, 1976; Prinz & Prinz, 1979; Wilbur & Jones, 1974). This single lexicon during the early stages of language development supports the hypothesis that the child acquiring American Sign Language (ASL) and English constructs a basic concept of an object or event and encodes it either in one modality or the other but seldom in both (Stokes & Menyuk, 1975). Wilbur and Jones (1974) suggested that sign and speech are acquired as two separate systems that do not overlap nor interfere with one another at least at the early lexical stage. Whether Dave's vocabulary development represents two separate systems developing in parallel or one lexical system with nonoverlapping entries from each mode could not be determined. Determination may depend upon theoretical information not yet available on this population.

Combinatorial Stage

A developmental progression of referential sign and sign-word combinations began almost simultaneously with single representations in sign and speech for Dave. His combinatorial messages from 17 months to 23 months paralleled the progression for referential symbol acquisition described by Volterra for three hearing children learning spoken language and one deaf child learning sign language (Volterra, 1981a), but it differed in possibly significant ways. Volterra distinguished between two main types of gestures, deictic (DG) and referential (RG). The former are context specific and are the actions themselves, such as show, give, point, etc. Referential gestures or "signs" (S), stand for stable referents; i.e., their meaning does not change with context but is conventionalized by the child and adult who use them. Volterra found that her subjects used four main types of combinatorial forms prior to producing referential combinations of two items: DG + DG, DG + S, DG + word (W), and S + W. Her subjects differed from one another in that the patterns DG + W and S + W became progressively more frequent in the productions of hearing children and less frequent in the productions of the deaf child. Her hearing subjects did not produce S + S as did the deaf child, and the deaf child did not produce W + W combinations. Volterra concluded that the use of two fully referential symbols (W or S) seemed to depend directly upon the linguistic environment, and that children not exposed to a stable linguistic input (a signed language or a spoken language) will not progress to the stage of communication in which two referential symbols of the same kind are combined.

Dave's production, and evidence from other studies of hearing children exposed to bimodal language input, suggest an additional alternative in the progression of gestural combinations acquired, one that does not occur in hearing children learning spoken languages or deaf children learning sign languages. This alternative is illustrated by the sequence of Dave's combinatorial productions shown in Table 3.

Table 3. Dave's progression in combining gestures, signs, and words

Sequence	Age (months)	Example
DG + DG	17	Giving ball; hitting ball
DG + S	18	NO + hitting dog
DG + W	18	Showing book + "daddy"
S + W	19	Point (DOWN) + "basement"
S + S	20	MY + BOOK
S + S + W + DG	20	ME + NO + "I" + point to toy
W + W	21	"No"; "book"

At the age when hearing speaking children exposed to speech alone produce W + W combinations and deaf children learning sign language produce S + S, Dave, exposed to both modes and both languages, produced increasingly complex combinations in the following sequence: S + W, S + S, S + S + W, W + W, S + W + W, S + S + S, S + S + W + W. Moreover, he returned to the visual-manual code for his first combinations at each new level of complexity. The fact that he used his visual-manual mode as a basis for symbolizing increasingly complex information supports the suggestion of Wilbur and Jones (1974) that young children may be capable cognitively of producing more complex language in gesture than they are motorically capable of producing in speech. At the point where hearing children exposed to speech begin to combine words, gestures drop out or become backgrounded (Volterra, 1981a); however, children with a sophisticated manual system (i.e., ASL) available to them are able to use that system to communicate more complex information than they are able to do by talking alone. At least this was the case for Dave.

Mode-Switching

Listener-adapted communications, first observed as different devices Dave used with each parent to get attention, became progressively more evident in other aspects of his language repertoire. Examples of mode-switching at 19, 20, and 21 months included accommodations to individual familiar partners, one unfamiliar partner, and to small groups of familiar partners.

Analysis of production in three conversational dyads, Dave-father, Dave-mother, and Dave-investigator, showed that Dave's mode selection with each partner changed over time to match the mode most frequently used by that partner. This accommodation behavior is illustrated in Table 4. Frequency counts of modes used by Dave in each of the three dyads are shown for two sessions about 1 month apart.

With his father Dave increased his use of sign and decreased the use of speech and combined modes. With his mother his preference was less clearly delineated but continued to include speech in most utterances. With the investigator Dave came to use the combined mode most frequently.

Analysis of conversational turns in the Dave-parent dyads showed that information about the partner was abstracted from various sources. Both response and lack of response were important sources of information for Dave; e.g., his

Table 4. Modes Dave used with communication partners

Mode/session:	With Dad 4th	8th	With Mom 5th	9th	With investigator 7th	11th
Sign	4	9	1	3	3	3
Speech	1	2	1	5	1	0
Combined mode	3	1	4	4	2	8

speech utterances were rarely acknowledged by his father unless they occurred at the same time as eye contact, in which case his father smiled or nodded to him. Dave's bimodal utterances received signed responses from his father; these were either repetitions of the signed portion of Dave's utterances or expansions of the signed portion. Information from father to Dave about mode can be summarized as follows:

D: Speaking (looking)   F: No response (not looking)
   Speaking (looking)   Smiles or nods (looking)
   Speaking and signing   Repeats or expands sign part
   Signing   Responds or takes turn

Dave's father not only conversed in sign but played sign teaching games with Dave, often making signs on Dave's body, shaping Dave's hands into a sign, or making signs on toys or pictures.

Analysis of Dave-mother interactions indicated that Dave used all three means of communicating with his mother: sign, speech, and both combined. Most notable in these interactions was Dave's continued use of speech over time. Examinations of conversational turns revealed that his mother responded to Dave's speech initiations very often, even though she did not always understand him; e.g., the following exchange took place while Dave and his mother were looking at a book:

D: (Pointing to picture of pumpkin) HAVE + tee teet (trick or treat)
M: YES + HAVE + you had pumpkin
D: Tee teet (louder)
I: Halloween? Did you trick or treat with a pumpkin for your candy? (In simultaneous mode)
D: (Shakes head no)
M: Oh! COSTUME PUMPKIN, costume
D: (Nods yes) HAVE + tee teet, PU
M: (To investigator simultaneously) I sewed two. One, pumpkin for Dave, other one, witch, for Sherri.

Dave's mother played both sign and speech games similar to those played with his father. She would say words and Dave would run and point or bring the object to her. She often asked the investigator whether Dave had said words correctly and prompted Dave to talk for the investigator. Prompting, however, was rarely a successful means of getting Dave to talk. In summary, his mother's approach was to sign and speak to Dave most of the time. This is not to say that there was an isomorphic relationship between her signs and her speech; rather, most of her utterances to Dave contained some speech. Information for Dave about communicating with his mother appeared as follows:

D: Speaking   M: (Looking) sign and speech sometimes topic mismatch
                         (Looking) responds in both
   Sign and speech   (Looking) responds in both

Over the 5½-month period, Dave's differentiation between the communicative needs of his two parents became more and more evident in his selection of mode to use with each. He was able to make use of the fact that speech was not appropriate in communicating with his father and the fact that sign alone was not necessary with his mother.

Mode-Finding

Two sources of data illustrate Dave's mode-finding behavior. In the first instance, at 20 months of age, his communication partner was a nonsigning student language clinician who was visiting Dave's home for the first time. For 1 h of this visit the clinician and Dave played alone in the living room, while Dave's mother and the investigator observed from the kitchen. The chronology of Dave's utterances are shown in Fig. 1. His first addresses to the clinician show a searching behavior: first a sign, then a sign with a word, then a word, a sign, and back to a word. Analysis of the interaction shows that when Dave signed, the clinician either changed the topic or did not respond, but when the clinician spoke, Dave responded in speech. On the sixth turn, Dave used sign and speech to respond to questions about his family. Only one more sign alone appeared in the rest of the

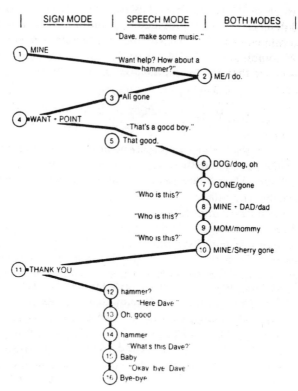

Fig. 1. Dave's search behavior

conversation: Dave signed THANK YOU (to which he received no response) when the clinician handed him a toy. For the remaining utterances Dave used speech alone to communicate with the clinician. Though not conclusive, this instance suggests that by 20 months of age Dave was quite skillful at applying the "person-language principle," even with strangers.

The second evidence of mode-finding is drawn from Dave's utterances to the investigator over the 12 visits to his home. This data showed that he not only adapted his mode to the style of the partner but was also able to adjust his mode selection to the communicative styles of other persons present. During the first four visits his only voluntary interactions with the investigator were nonverbal and consisted of bringing items to the investigator and then running away. His speech utterances to the investigator at this time were few and followed directives from his mother to say words. His first spontaneous expressions directed to the investigator took place on the fifth visit, when Dave was 19 months old. Dave was sitting in his father's lap while his father was reading in sign to him from a book. Occasionally he would look over at the investigator and sign the name of a picture in the book. Analysis of all his communications with the investigator indicated that when his father was present he used more signs and less speech to the investigator, but when his mother and father were both present or his mother and sister, he used both sign and speech modes or combined the two. He rarely used speech alone to communicate with the investigator, even though he did use speech alone with his mother. It is not clear why this occurred. The investigator's continual use of simultaneous communication may have been a factor in his restricted use of speech with the investigator; however, his communication mode appeared to be dictated more by the presence of his family members. His criteria for mode selection with the investigator seemed to be as follows:

1. If Dad is present, sign to investigator.
2. If Mom is present, sign or use both modes.
3. If both parents are present, use sign or both modes with investigator.

Unfortunately, there were no instances of communication to the investigator when family members were not present; therefore it is not possible to know whether Dave might have used speech only with the investigator had they been alone.

Discussion

Evidence presented in this investigation supports the notion that code-switching in bilingual children is a developmental process and that it emerges along with other components of the child's two languages (Leopold, 1939–1949; McClure, 1977). Hearing children of deaf parents appear to acquire their two languages in a similar fashion to that of children acquiring two spoken languages.

Code-switching and alternation of language can, of course, occur within single language learning as well as across languages (Berko-Gleason, 1973; Weeks,

1971). However, studying this aspect as well as other aspects of language de-velopment in a bilingual/bimodal environment provides richer examples of the phenomena and two channels through which to obtain data. The use of two modes by the children also offers a broader base from which we can make inferences about their cognitive and linguistic abilities. Studying infants exposed to a complex visual-gestural language system as well as an auditory-vocal language system will inevitably lead us to a clearer understanding of the early development of intentionality and other language precursors, and it may allow us to trace the development of phenomena such as code-switching from birth.

Appendix

Observation 3. Dave's mother reported that he now uses the sign NO along with the word. During my last observation Dave said the word "no" several times, but did not use the sign. I did not see him use the sign during this observation; however, he said "no" several times.

No actual signs were produced by Dave during my visit. He often clapped his hands or rubbed them together in a circular motion, while smiling and looking at us. While some of his movements may have been approximations of signs, it was difficult to distinguish approximations and intentional movements from un-intentional ones. (I may be reading too much into his use of hands, but he seemed to know when he should be doing something with them; i.e., he always gave eye contact and smiled when he rubbed his hands in the circular motion, and his clapping followed pleasant activity.)

One time his hand movements could have been an approximation of "horse," since this movement was easily distinguished from the frequent circular motion, and was done at an appropriate time. His mother was not sure either and suggested that he "might be trying to sign 'horse'." He would not imitate either the sign or the word, however, and stopped his hand movement when he tried to get him to imitate.

His speech activity (I don't know what else to call it) was very different from that of previous visits.

PART V

Hearing Children and Deaf Children Compared

Overview

In this section, studies comparing deaf and hearing children are reported. Caselli and Volterra analyze the earliest stages of communicative and linguistic development of two deaf children of deaf parents, one American and one Italian, and two Italian hearing children of hearing parents; the children range in age from 10 months to 30 months. Their conclusion is that deaf and hearing children show similar development in the semantic content they express, the contextual and interactional situations in which gestures, sign, and words are produced, and the combinations which occur.

Goldin-Meadow and Morford describe in their chapter the relation between gesture and speech in three hearing children followed longitudinally from 10 to 30 months of age. The gestures produced by each hearing subject were coded according to a system developed previously to analyze the gestures produced by deaf subjects with hearing parents. The authors found, through a detailed comparison, that both hearing and deaf children develop single gestures and two-gesture forms to convey information. The gestures the hearing children produce, however, are not as linguistically complex as the deaf children's gestures.

The study by Bellugi, O'Grady, Lillo-Martin, O'Grady Hynes, van Hoek, and Corina deals with a central issue: the interplay between the development of a spatial language and its spatial cognitive substrate. Comparing deaf signing children's performance on a selected battery of visual-spatial tests to the hearing norms, they found that, especially for certain spatial tasks, deaf subjects' scores differ from those of hearing children. They conclude, then, that the acquisition of the spatial linguistic devices of American Sign Language (ASL) results in greater nonlinguistic spatial abilities.

The first two chapters in this section report similar findings. Caselli and Volterra's chapter provides detailed examples while Goldin-Meadow and Morford include information on frequency data. Both studies agree for example that the hearing children did not develop gesture + gesture combinations as complex as were the deaf children's combinations. None of Caselli's hearing subjects produced a combination of two referential gestures and only one of Goldin-Meadow and Morford's hearing subjects combined, on only one occasion, two characterizing gestures (referential and characterizing gestures seem roughly equivalent). Furthermore, these studies support the idea that the pointing gesture plays a special role in the communication of both hearing and deaf children.

In spite of the congruity in their findings, the authors of these two chapters interpret their results quite differently. Caselli and Volterra emphasize the similarities of timing and sequence of development in the two modalities while Goldin-Meadow and Morford support the position that the manual modality may provide a child with easier access to language than does the oral modality at the earliest stages of language acquisition. Bellugi et al. provide evidence in favor of the first position. The authors show how the transparency of ASL forms at all levels have little or no effect on the acquisition of grammatical processes. Their findings do suggest, however, that linguistic functioning in a visual medium might both require and result in greater visual-spatial processing abilities.

CHAPTER 19
Gesture in Early Child Language

S. GOLDIN-MEADOW and M. MORFORD

Introduction

When communication is blocked from the oral modality, the manual modality frequently assumes the functional burdens of speech (Kendon, 1980c). Elaborate signed systems resembling spoken language in many crucial aspects have been observed to arise in a number of situations where speech has been made impossible, whether by sensory incapacity (Klima & Bellugi, 1979; Newport, 1982; Supalla, 1982; Wilbur, 1979), by environmental circumstances (as in sawmill factories, Meissner & Philpott, 1975), or by speech taboos (as in Australian aborigines, Kendon, 1980b; or Trappist monks, Wundt, 1900/1973). It thus appears that communication in humans is a resilient phenomenon – when prevented from coming out the mouth, it emanates almost irrepressibly from the fingers.

One of the most striking examples of the resilience of communication in humans is found in deaf children who are not able to process the oral language which surrounds them and who have not yet been exposed to a conventional manual language by their hearing parents. These children, unable to learn a spoken language naturally, have been observed to spontaneously exploit the manual modality for communication and to invent their own gestural systems (Fant, 1972; Lenneberg, 1964; Moores, 1974; Tervoort, 1961). Moreover, the gestural systems these deaf children develop have been found to be organized in language-like ways (Feldman, Goldin-Meadow, & Gleitman, 1978; Goldin-Meadow, 1979, 1982, 1985; Goldin-Meadow & Feldman, 1975, 1977; Goldin-Meadow & Mylander, this volume), and have been found to be structurally more complex than the gestures their hearing parents produce (Goldin-Meadow & Mylander, 1983; 1984b). Thus, even a young child appears able, without tutoring, to make effective use of the manual modality when communication is blocked in the oral modality.

This chapter is adapted from an article originally published in the *Merrill-Palmer Quarterly*, 1985, *31*(2), 145–176. We thank our subjects and their families for their continued cooperation throughout the study. This work was supported by National Science Foundation Grant BNS 77–05990, by grants from the Spencer Foundation and the Benton Foundation, by a Biomedical Sciences Support Grant PHS 5 507 PR-07029 to The University of Chicago, and by funds from the Child Psychiatry Section of the Departments of Psychiatry and Pediatrics at The University of Chicago. Portions of this work were presented at the first meeting of the Merrill-Palmer Society in Detroit, 1982, and at the Society for Research in Child Development meeting in Detroit, 1983.

But what is the role of gesture in child language when both manual and oral channels are available to the child? Gestures have often been observed in the spontaneous speech of hearing adults, and several descriptive systems have been proposed to capture the relationship between those gestures and the speech they accompany (Efron 1941/1972; Ekman & Friesen, 1969; Kendon, 1980c; McNeill & Levy, 1982). These gestures have been found to complement the concurrent spoken utterance, for example, by indicating the particular entities referred to in speech (Marslen-Wilson, Levy, & Tyler, 1982), or to supplement the spoken utterance by conveying elements that might otherwise have been spoken; for example, a film director indicates a location to his electrician verbally ("Five balcony") while requesting the action he desires at that location gesturally by moving a light switch in pantomime (Slama-Cazacu, 1976, p. 222).

Hearing children have been reported to use gesture spontaneously several months before they begin to speak (Bates, 1976a). Moreover, observations by Bates, Benigni, Bretherton, Camaioni, and Volterra (1979), A.L. Carter (1975b), and Greenfield and Smith (1976) suggest that, even after a child has begun to speak, he or she continues to use gesture to support the verbal communications. As in adults, hearing children have been observed to use their spontaneous gestures to complement their concurrent spoken utterances, typically to point out the objects referred to in speech (Bates, 1976a; Bates et al. 1979; De Laguna, 1927/1963), or to supplement their concurrent spoken utterances (e.g., a child of 21 months verbally produced the word "touch" while gesturally pointing at a tape recorder, Greenfield & Smith, 1976, p. 115). While previous studies have isolated instances of complementary and supplementary uses of gesture in relation to early speech, few studies have attempted to systematically characterize the young child's gestural corpus. In the present study, we attempt to describe the spontaneous gestures produced by three hearing children, focusing primarily on how those gestures are used alone and in relation to speech. We thus attempt to determine the role spontaneous gesture plays in a young child's communications when the child can make use of *both* the manual and oral channels.

Methods and Procedure

Subjects

Our goal was to observe spontaneous gestures during the earliest stages of language acquisition, in particular, during the child's one- and two-word stages. Thus, we began observing the children between 10 and 17 months of age and stopped observing them at approximately 30 months (one of the children, Carl, moved from Chicago at 22 months, forcing us to conclude our observations on him prematurely). The age range and number of observation sessions for each of the three children is shown in Table 1.

Table 1 also presents descriptive data on the children's speech during this period (see Goldin-Meadow & Morford, 1985, for a detailed analysis of the

Table 1. Summary description of speech samples

Child	Sessions (n)	Age range	Mean length (range)[a]	Upper-bound (range)[b]	Rate per hour (range)[c]
Carl	5	1;5–1;11	1.00–1.23	1–3	25.5–303.0
Ann	12	0;10–2;6	1.00–1.95	1–11	30.0–420.4
Beth	9	1;2–2;5	1.00–2.85	1–10	3.6–260.3

[a] The figures in this column represent the lowest and the highest mean utterance length (the average number of words produced per utterance, calculated by session) achieved by each child throughout our observations.
[b] The figures in this column represent the lowest and the highest upper-bounds (the number of words in the longest utterance produced in a session) achieved by each child throughout our observations.
[c] The figures in this column represent the lowest and the highest production rates (the number of utterances produced per hour, calculated by session) achieved by each child throughout our observations.

linguistic complexity of the three children's spoken utterances). The table displays two measures of sentence length for each of the children: mean length of utterance (MLU, the average number of words in a child's utterances) and upper-bound (the number of words in a child's longest utterance). The lowest and highest MLU and upper-bound (calculated by session) for each of the three children are given in the table. Note that all three children were one-word speakers at the beginning of our observations. In addition, Table 1 also displays the lowest and the highest production rates (the number of utterances produced per hour, calculated by session) for each of the children.

All three children were from white middle-class two-parent families with mother as primary caregiver. None of the three had any apparent hearing difficulties, nor had they any other known cognitive or physical disabilities.

Experimental Procedure

Each child was videotaped periodically (approximately every 2–3 months) at home during informal play sessions. The primary caregiver, the mother in every instance, was asked to interact with her child for at least 30 min of each session. Either the mother then continued to play with the child, or an experimenter played with the child for the remainder of the session. A large bag of toys, books, and puzzles (described in Goldin-Meadow, 1979) served to facilitate interaction. Each session lasted 1–2 h, depending upon the child's attention span.

We coded the gestures produced by each child according to a system developed previously to transcribe and analyze the gestures produced by deaf children generating their own gestural communication systems (see Goldin-Meadow & Mylander, 1984b, for detailed information on this system). We first reviewed each child's videotapes to isolate communicative gestures from the stream of ongoing motor behavior. In order to qualify as a gesture, a motor act must satisfy two criteria: (a) the act must be directed to another individual, i.e., it must be communicative; and (b) the act must not be a direct manipulation of some relevant person or object, i.e., it must not serve any function other than communication; acts used in symbolic play were thus excluded (see Goldin-Meadow & Mylander, 1984b, p. 55, for discussion of how these criteria relate to the criteria used in other investigations of gesture in hearing children).

After extracting motor acts which met the criteria for a gesture, we segmented those acts into units, noting whether a gesture occurred alone (e.g., the child pointed at a bubble jar and then relaxed his or her hand), or in combination with other gestures (e.g., the child pointed at the bubble jar and then, without relaxing his or her hand, pointed to a table).

Gestures were classified into two types: *deictic* gestures were used to single out objects, people, places, and the like in the surroundings, e.g., a point at a toy, or a gesture in which a toy was held up for display. *Characterizing* gestures were stylized pantomimes whose iconic forms varied with the intended meaning of each gesture, e.g., a fist pounded in the air used to represent hammering (characterizing gestures will hereafter be denoted in upper-case type; in this instance, as HAMMER). The children produced a third type of gesture, the marker (e.g., nods, headshakes) which they used to modulate (e.g., affirm, negate) meanings but which were not analyzed in this study.

We assigned semantic meanings to each gesture, using as guides Bloom's (1970) method of rich interpretation and Fillmore's (1968) case descriptions. We assigned gestures to one of three categories: (a) *indicators* were deictics used to indicate the existence of objects, persons, places, e.g., a point at a jar of bubbles used to draw someone's attention to the object; (b) *cases* were deictics used to indicate objects which, in context, appeared to play a role in a semantic relation, e.g., a point at a bubble jar used to request that the jar be opened, the pointing gesture thus indicates the patient of the 'open' relation; (c) *predicates* were characterizing gestures used to represent either action or attribute relations, e.g., a flat hand extended palm-up used to request that a toy be given to the child (GIVE), or an arced motion pulled away from the child's nose used to represent an elephant's long trunk (ARCED). Cases and predicates could be coded for single gestures, as in the above examples, or for gesture + gesture combinations, e.g., if a child pointed at a bubble jar and then produced the characterizing gesture GIVE, the deictic point would be classified as representing a case (in particular, the patient case), and the characterizing GIVE would be classified as representing a predicate (the predicate "give").

Gestures were also distinguished according to whether they occurred with speech or without speech. Gesture + speech combinations were further classified into two types according to the role gesture played vis-à-vis speech in that combination: complementary and supplementary combinations. In *complementary* combinations, gesture denoted the same or a subset of the same semantic elements as were denoted in speech. Gesture could complement speech in one of three ways: (a) a gesture and a word could both function as an *indicator* for the same object, e.g., point at glasses + "glasses" produced to draw attention to the glasses; (b) a gesture and a word could both represent the same *case*, e.g., point at a box + "box" produced to request that a toy be placed in the box; the word and gesture thus both represent the recipient case; (c) a gesture and a word could both represent the same *predicate*, e.g., GIVE + "give" produced to request that a cookie be given to the child. In *supplementary* combinations, gesture denoted different semantic elements from those denoted in speech. Gesture could supplement speech in two ways: (a) gesture could represent one case while speech represented either a different case or a predicate, e.g., point at glasses + "out" used to request that the glasses be taken out of the case; the gesture represents the patient case, the word the act predicate; (b) gesture could represent a predicate while speech represented a case, e.g., GIVE + "puzzle" used to request that the puzzle be given to the child; the gesture represents the act predicate, the word the patient case.

Reliability on coding the hearing children's gestured communications ranged between 88% and 100% agreement between two coders, depending on the coding category.

Results

The Distribution of Gesture and Speech in Hearing Children

The goal of this study was to describe the relation of gestures to speech in three children. Our first task was to determine whether the children would use their hands to gesture at all. The second task was to determine whether their gestures would form a communication system separate from speech or, alternatively, would serve as an adjunct system well-integrated with speech. To address these issues, we began by classifying the children's gestures according to whether they occurred alone or in combination with spoken words.

Table 2 presents the proportions of the children's communications which contained gestures alone, speech alone, or gesture and speech combined. All three children tended to use gesture alone approximately as often as they used gesture in combination with speech. However, Beth used proportionally less gesture overall (30%) than either Ann (56%) or Carl (59%). Similarly, in terms of rate of production, Beth used gesture less often than either Ann or Carl: Beth's highest rate of gesture production (i.e., the number of gestures alone and gesture + speech combinations produced per hour) was 25.5 gestured communications per hour (at age 1 year 4 months, hereafter given, for example, as 1;4), while Ann's was 145.6 (age 1;7) and Carl's was 120.1 (age 1;11). Overall, even though these children used speech as their primary means of communication, they produced gestures alone or in combination with speech relatively often.

Gesture production did, however, begin to decline during the course of our observations for two of the three children. Ann and Beth reached a production peak for gesture alone sometime in the middle of the study after which their production rates for gesture alone declined steadily. Ann's peak production for gesture alone occurred at 1;8 (99.2 gestures alone per hour) and Beth's at 1;4 (23.7

Table 2. The distribution of gesture and speech

Child	Gesture alone[a] (%)	Gesture + speech (%)	Speech alone (%)	Total communications (n)
Carl	34	25	41	746
Ann	24	32	43	1599
Beth	17	13	71	1005

[a] It is should be noted that the children tended to vocalize even when they produced gestures without speech: 82% of Ann's, 35% of Beth's, and 80% of Carl's gestures which were not accompanied by meaningful speech (i.e., gestures alone) were, in fact, accompanied by meaningless vocalizations (e.g., point at bubbles + "uh").

gestures alone per hour). In addition, Beth also reached a production peak for gesture + speech during the study at 1;10 (16.4 gesture + speech combinations per hour). Note that Beth's production peak for gesture alone occurred 6 months earlier than her production peak for gesture + speech combined. At the end of the observations, Ann's production rate for gesture + speech was still increasing at 2;6 (118.3 gesture + speech combinations per hour), and Carl's production rates for both gesture alone and gesture + speech combined were still increasing at 1;11 (21.8 gestures alone per hour; 90.1 gesture + speech combinations per hour). Moreover, all three children were continuing to increase their production rates for speech at the end of the study (124.7 spoken utterances per hour for Beth at 2;5, 148.3 for Ann at 2;6, and 162.9 for Carl at 1;11).

In sum, all three children were found to gesture. In fact, 17%–34% of each child's communications contained gestures alone accompanied by no speech. In addition, the children produced gestures along with speech in another 13%–32% of their communications. Thus, even children learning spoken languages appear to make use of gesture to communicate. We turn next to an analysis of the linguistic complexity of the gestures the children produced.

Types of Gestures

All three children were found to produce deictic gestures, typically pointing acts but also acts which functioned to "point out" an object by holding that object up for display. The children used their deictic gestures to refer to the same range of objects that they referred to with their spoken nouns and pronouns (i.e., toys, vehicles, food, animals, body parts, people, places, and clothing), with a few exceptions: Beth did not use gestures to indicate food, places, or clothing, and Carl did not use gestures to indicate clothing – objects that both children did indicate with words.

The children produced characterizing gestures, but less often than they produced deictics. Characterizing gestures comprised a small proportion of each child's total gestures: 19% of total gestures for Beth, 8% for Ann, and 3% for Carl. Moreover, the range of predicates the children conveyed with their characterizing gestures was quite restricted — far more restricted than the range of predicates they conveyed with their spoken verbs and adjectives. All three children produced the action characterizing gesture GIVE (open palm extended to request an object), and this gesture accounted for almost all of each child's characterizing gestures (100% of Beth's characterizing gestures, 82% of Carl's, and 76% of Ann's). Beth produced no characterizing gestures other than GIVE. Ann produced no other types of action characterizing gestures without accompanying speech but 14 other types with accompanying speech (18 tokens, accounting for 24% of her characterizing signs), e.g., "brush teeth" + BRUSH, fist moving up and down near teeth, to comment on a picture of a toothbrush. Carl produced one attribute characterizing gesture without accompanying speech (two tokens, accounting for 18% of his characterizing signs), i.e., ARCED, index finger moved from nose away from body in an arc to comment on the shape of an elephant's trunk.

Single Gestures

We found that the children began producing single gestures several months before they began producing single words. Both Beth and Ann produced their first deictic gestures at 1;2, but did not produce their first spoken nouns until 1;4 and their first spoken pronouns until 1;7 (Carl was producing deictic gestures and spoken nouns during his initial observation session at 1;5 but, like the other two children, did not begin producing spoken pronouns until several months later at 1;11). Thus, two of the three children used single gestures approximately 2 months before they used single words.

The hearing children tended to use their single gestures in the same way they used their single words. Table 3 presents the proportions of single gestures used as indicators, cases, and predicates. As was the case for their single words (see Goldin-Meadow & Morford, 1985), the children's single gestures were most often used to indicate the existence of objects and were infrequently used to represent cases and predicates.

Table 3. Single Gestures

Child	Indicators (%)	Cases (%)	Predicates (%)	Total single (n)
Carl	78	19	03	183
Ann	83	04	13	362
Beth	75	01	24	169

Gesture + Gesture Combinations

Each of the three children was found to produce a small number of communications which contained two distinct gestures, each denoting a different semantic element, e.g., GIVE + point at toy dog. Overall, the children produced 31 gesture + gesture combinations, accounting for less than 3% of each child's total gestured communications. All but one of these 31 combinations contained only two gestures, typically a deictic point combined with a GIVE characterizing gesture (e.g., point at cookie + GIVE, requesting that a cookie be given to the child) or a deictic point combined with another deictic (e.g., point at puzzle-piece + point at puzzle-board, requesting that the puzzle-piece be put on the puzzle-board). Ann was the only child who combined a deictic point with a characterizing gesture other than GIVE, always to describe some aspect of a picture and always accompanied by speech, e.g., point at a picture of a dog baseball player + SWING (two fists, held end-to-end, swung as though hitting a ball with a bat) + "game." In addition, Ann produced one instance of a combination containing two characterizing gestures, also to describe a picture and also accompanied by speech – TYPE (fingers moved up and down as though typing) + "write" + WRITE (fist jiggled up and down as though writing) + "write" + point at a picture of a turtle typing.

The children produced their few gesture + gesture combinations for only a relatively short period of time. However, the timing of these infrequent two-gesture sentences relative to the onset of two-word speech was of interest: all three children produced their two-gesture sentences *prior* to the onset of their two-word sentences, beginning production 5–9 months and stopping production 2–5 months before two-word speech began (see Fig. 1; the figure displays only those gesture + gesture combinations which were *not* accompanied by speech).

In sum, although the children produced an occasional gesture conveying an action or attribute predicate, most of the gestures the children produced were single points or hold-ups used to indicate objects, people, or locations in the immediate environment. Moreover, the children produced very few gestures in combination with other gestures. In fact, the children were much more likely to combine their gestures with words than with other gestures. We turn now to an analysis of these gesture + speech combinations.

Gesture + Speech Combinations

Table 4 displays the proportions of gesture + speech combinations which were complementary (point at glasses + "glasses") vs. supplementary (point at glasses + "out"). All three children produced many more complementary gesture + speech combinations (71%–89%) than supplementary gesture + speech combinations (11%–29%). Thus, the children tended to use gesture to reinforce rather than to add to the information conveyed in speech.

Complementary Combinations. Table 5 displays the hearing children's complementary gesture + speech combinations categorized according to the par-

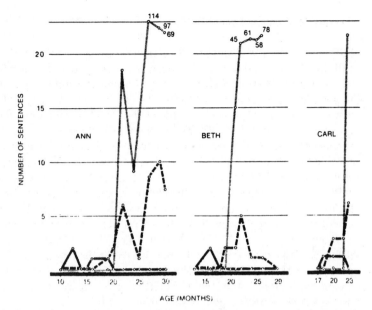

Fig. 1. Number of two-unit sentences conveying two different semantic elements produced by the three children at each observation session. The sentences are classified according to the modality used to convey the two semantic elements: gesture + gesture sentences (*solid line*) (e.g., point at bubbles + point at table), gesture + word sentences (*broken line*) (point at bubbles + "table"), and word + word sentences (*dotted line*) ("bubble table")

Table 4. Gesture + speech combinations

Child	Complementary combinations (%)	Supplementary combinations (%)	Total gesture + speech combinations (n)
Carl	88	12	184
Ann	89	11	516
Beth	71	29	.117

Table 5. The semantic category of the gesture in complementary gesture + speech combinations

Child	Indicators (%)	Cases (%)	Predicates (%)	Total complementary gesture + speech combinations (n)
Carl	88	12	00	162
Ann	72	25	03	461
Beth	55	45	00	83

ticular semantic category assumed by the gesture. Most of the children's complementary gesture + speech combinations were used as indicators (e.g., point at bottle + "bottle," produced to draw attention to the bottle). In addition, all of the children (but Beth in particular) produced complementary gesture + speech combinations in which the gesture assumed a case role, either concatenated with a single spoken word (e.g., point at bubbles + "bubble," used to request the listener to open the bubbles, the patient) or concatenated with a spoken sentence (e.g., point at bubbles + "open bubble"). Finally, one of the children, Ann, produced a small number (13) of complementary gesture + speech combinations in which her gesture assumed a predicate role, e.g., "and cut salami" + CUT (fist moving down abruptly in air).

Interestingly, there was a difference in the type of word (noun vs. pronoun) combined with gesture, as a function of whether the complementary gesture + speech combination was used as an indicator or as a case. In almost all of the complementary gesture + speech combinations used as indicators, the children combined nouns with their points, e.g., point at dog + "dog": 83% (253/333) of Ann's, 98% (45/46) of Beth's, and 87% (123/142) of Carl's gesture + speech indicators were point + noun combinations. In contrast, in the complementary gesture + speech combinations used as cases, the children tended to combine pronouns with their points, e.g., point at dog + "that": 49% (56/115) of Ann's, 64% (23/36) of Beth's, and 40% (8/20) of Carl's complementary gesture + speech cases were point + pronoun combinations.

Supplementary Combinations. An analysis of the semantic category assumed by the gesture in the children's few supplementary gesture + speech combinations revealed that, for two of the children (Ann and Carl), the supplemental gesture was used primarily to represent a case (e.g., "blow" + point at bubbles, where the gesture represents the patient "bubbles"): 92% (67/73) of Ann's and 100% (22/22) of Carl's supplementary gesture + speech combinations were of this type. In contrast, the third child (Beth), tended to use her supplemental gesture as a predicate (e.g., GIVE + "bubbles," where the gesture represents the predicate "give") more frequently (62%, 21/34) than as a case (38%). A supplementary gesture + speech combination could not be classified as an indicator (i.e., as a combination whose only function was to indicate the existence of an object) simply because, by definition, a combination of this type contained at least two different semantic elements, one represented by a word and a second represented by the supplemental gesture.

Developmental Onsets of Gesture + Speech Combinations

The children produced their first *complementary* gesture + speech combinations (point at bubbles + "bubble") at 1;4 for Ann, 1;6 for Beth, and 1;5 for Carl, 1–4 months *before* they produced their first *supplementary* gesture + speech combination (GIVE + "bubble," or point at bubble + "open") at 1;6, 1;7, and 1;8, respectively. Thus, the gesture + speech combination appears to be used first to denote the same semantic element (complementary information) and only later to denote two different semantic elements (supplementary information).

Moreover, the supplementary gesture + speech combination seemed to serve as a transitional form between the children's two-gesture sentences and their two-word sentences. All three children produced supplementary gesture + word sentences 2–4 months *after* they began producing two-gesture sentences but 2–3 months *before* they began producing any two-word sentences (gesture + gesture sentences at 1;1, supplementary gesture + word sentences at 1;6, and word + word sentences at 1;8 for Ann; 1;4, 1;7, and 1;9 for Beth; and 1;6, 1;8, and 1;11 for Carl; see Fig. 1). These data suggest that a gestural transition period may precede the child's entry to the two-word stage, just as a gestural transition period seems to precede his or her entry to the one-word stage. The child appears to have the ability to convey two semantic elements in one combination prior to his or her first two-word sentence, and he or she exhibits this ability initially in the (presumably easier) gesture + gesture and gesture + word forms.

Discussion

The Transitional Nature of Gesture

We found that all three of our subjects used gesture to communicate. In fact, gesture seemed to be a relatively easy way for the children to express themselves. The children produced single deictic gestures to indicate objects months before they produced single words to indicate those same objects. Moreover, all three children conveyed two concatenated semantic elements first in a gesture + gesture sentence form (point at bubbles + point at table, a request to put the bubbles on the table), next in a gesture + word sentence form (point at bubbles + "table"), and only months later in a word + word sentence form ("bubble table"). Gesture thus seemed to serve as a transitional form en route to speech. All three children stopped producing the two-gesture sentence prior to their first two-word productions. Moreover, for Ann and Beth, the production rate for gesture alone, and for Beth, the production rate for gesture combined with speech reached a peak sometime during the middle of the study and declined steadily thereafter. Thus, for all three children, as they grew older speech appeared to assume the communicative functions which were once filled, however briefly, by gesture.

These data suggest that the manual modality may provide a child with easier access to language than does the oral modality at the earliest stages of language acquisition. Another example of the ease with which children can exploit the manual modality at the beginning stages of language acquisition comes from the literature on sign language learning in deaf children of deaf parents. When exposed to a language model in the manual modality, deaf children appear to make more progress initially learning language in the manual modality than do hearing children learning language in the oral modality. For example, Orlansky and Bonvillian (1985) have shown that deaf children learning American Sign Language from their deaf parents acquire their first signs and achieve a ten-sign vocabulary several months in advance of the norms for the acquisition of words in hearing children. Moreover, when hearing children are exposed to usable language models in *both* the oral and manual modalities, those children seem to make more progress initially in the manual language than in the spoken language. For example, Prinz and Prinz (1979) studied a hearing child exposed to American Sign Language by her deaf mother and exposed to English by her hearing father, and found that the child began to acquire signs several months before she began to acquire spoken words. Taken together, these data suggest that the manual modality may provide a child, hearing or deaf, a particularly accessible means of early communication.

The Linguistic Complexity of Gesture

The children in our study not only gestured, but they gestured relatively often. Ann and Carl produced as many as 145.6 and 120.1 gestures per hour, respectively, and even the third child, Beth, produced gestures at a rate of 25.5 per hour. As noted previously, deaf children who are not exposed to a usable conventional language model in either the manual or the oral modality nevertheless develop gestures for the purposes of communication (cf., Goldin-Meadow & Mylander, 1984b). If we compare the gesture production rates for our three hearing children to those of deaf children using gesture as their only means of communication, we find that two of the three children in our study (Ann and Carl) had gesture production rates which were within the range of the deaf children's highest gesture production rates (range 93.0–384.0 per hour, Goldin-Meadow & Morford, 1985).

In addition, the gestures produced by the three hearing children in our study were comparable to those of the deaf children in certain respects. Both the deaf and hearing children produced deictic and characterizing gestures. Moreover, when they used these gestures alone as single gestures, the deaf and hearing children produced the gestures primarily to indicate objects rather than to represent case or predicate relations (cf., Goldin-Meadow & Morford, 1985).

However, the gestures the hearing children produced, when taken as a whole, were not as linguistically complex as the deaf children's gestures. The range of characterizing gestures used by the hearing children was far more restricted than the range of characterizing gestures used by the deaf children. Over 76% of each hearing child's characterizing gestures were GIVE gestures (open palm extended), while the GIVE gesture represented less than 30% of each deaf child's characterizing signs (Goldin-Meadow & Mylander, 1984b, p. 56). Thus, the hearing children did not develop as extensive a gestural lexicon as did the deaf children. Moreover, the hearing children did not develop gesture + gesture combinations which were as complex in either content or form as were the deaf children's gesture combinations. The hearing children produced very few two-gesture combinations (less than 3% of each child's gestured communications), while gesture + gesture combinations ranged between 30% and 51% of the deaf children's gestured communications (Goldin-Meadow & Mylander, 1984b, p. 55). Only one of the three hearing children (Ann) on one occasion combined a characterizing gesture with another characterizing gesture, while all of the deaf children produced characterizing + characterizing combinations; for some, as many as 18% of the deaf child's gesture combinations were of this type (Goldin-Meadow & Mylander, 1984b, p. 55). Indeed, the deaf children's characterizing + characterizing combinations were quite complex, conveying two or more propositions within a single combination, e.g., point at a tower + HIT + FALL, a comment on the fact that the child had hit (act 1) the tower and that the tower had fallen (act 2); or TAKE-OUT + point at a pair of glasses + DON, a request for the partner to take out (act 1) the glasses so that the child could then don (act 2) those glasses.

Other investigations of gesture in hearing children similarly suggest that the children do not produce particularly complex gestures and do not often combine those gestures with other gestures. Greenfield and Smith (1976), in a study of two hearing children learning English, report that their subjects used three different types of gestures (pointing, holding objects out, and reaching) either in isolation or with speech. They did not report that the children combined these gestures with other gestures. Bates et al. (1979), in a study of 25 hearing children, 12 learning Italian and 13 learning English, found that their subjects used gestures such as showing, giving, communicative pointing, and ritual requests, but again they did not report any gesture + gesture combinations. Masur (this volume), in a study of four hearing children learning English, did find that her subjects combined gestures with other gestures but that they did so rarely. One of Masur's subjects produced no gesture + gesture combinations at all, one combined hand reaches with headshakes, one combined points with nods, and the fourth combined points, reaches, and waving. Finally, Volterra (1981a) found that three hearing children learning Italian also combined gestures with other gestures (she does not report how frequently), but she found that none of her subjects combined referential gestures (gestures that seem roughly equivalent to our characterizing gestures) with other referential gestures.

Thus, these results suggest that, even though gesture can be elaborated by a child into a system sufficiently complex to take over the major functions of spoken child language, such elaboration does *not* take place if speech is the child's primary means of communication. The hearing child learning spoken language may make use of gesture early in development but, under normal circumstances, the frequency and complexity of gesture use will reach a plateau and decline as the child begins to talk (although gesture does not disappear and indeed has been found to play an important role in conjunction with speech later in development (cf., Church & Goldin-Meadow, 1986; McNeill, 1985).

The Role of Gesture in Relation to Speech

When the children in our study combined their gestures with speech, the gestures tended to play a complementary role vis-à-vis the spoken utterance; that is, the gesture referred to precisely the same semantic element as did the word.Only rarely did the gesture add supplemental information not conveyed in a word to the spoken utterance. In addition, the children tended to use these complementary gesture + speech combinations as they used their single gestures, primarily to indicate the existence of objects and only occasionally to represent either predicate relations or the case roles of objects. Thus, not surprisingly given that these children were acquiring a spoken language, gesture did not come to take over all, or even many, of the functions of communication in these young children.

Our data suggest that the role of gesture in hearing children's early communications is as an adjunct to speech. The three children in our study used their gestures in combination with speech primarily to indicate the objects labeled by their spoken nouns, a function which gestures serve in adult spoken discourse as well (Marslen-Wilson, Levy, & Tyler, 1982). Note that the deictic pointing gesture directs a communication partner's attention to the existence of a particular person, place, or thing, and (of necessity) to its location as well. Since a noun cannot on its own locate the particular object to which it is referring, the deictic point is serving an important referent-locating function in discourse, a function which even very young hearing children seem to know about.

In conclusion, a young child, deaf or hearing, appears able to exploit the manual modality and develop single gesture and two-gesture forms to convey information to others. If the child is deaf and is not exposed to a conventional manual language model, the child is likely to develop his or her gestures into a fully fledged child language system. In contrast, if the child is hearing and is exposed to a spoken language model, that child will, as speech develops, come to gesture less often and less elaborately, treating gesture as an adjunct to speech.

CHAPTER 20
From Communication to Language in Hearing and Deaf Children

M.C. CASELLI and V. VOLTERRA

Introduction

In this chapter, we present the results of two studies previously reported separately (Caselli, 1983a; Volterra, 1981a). These studies deal with the earliest stages of communicative and linguistic development comparing hearing children exposed to spoken language with deaf children of deaf parents exposed to sign language.

Recent research has shed light on the role of gestures in the preverbal period of communicative development of hearing children. These studies stress how gestures are used with different (vocal) performatives in a rich and effective way (Bruner, 1975b; Camaioni, Volterra, & Bates, 1976; R.A. Clark, 1978); and how gestural communication, cognitive and symbolic development, and the acquisition of language are related to one another (Bates, Benigni, Bretherton, Camaioni, & Volterra, 1979; Nokony, 1978; Caselli, this volume). In particular two types of communicative gestures have been identified in hearing children, specifically, *deictic* and *referential*.

Deictic gestures, such as showing, giving, and pointing, appear when the child is about 10 months of age, and at the very beginning they are produced one at time and often simultaneously with vocal signals. Elsewhere (Bates, Camaioni, & Volterra, 1975), these gestures were called "performative": they express only the child's communicative intention to request or to declare; the referential meaning communicated is given entirely by the context in which the communication takes place. A developmental sequence from showing and giving to pointing was also described. Pointing out an object to others, which is the last of these gestures to appear, represents the final detachment from physical contact with the object. The child gradually acquires the capacity to refer to an object or an event in order to communicate with others about it without physically making contact with it. All these deictic gestures change their semantic content according to the context to which they are referring.

Referential gestures, which some researchers call 'signs' (see Acredolo and Goodwyn, this volume), stand for or represent stable referents. Their meaning is

The two studies reported in this chapter were originally published separately in slightly different versions as "Communication to language: Deaf children's and hearing children's development compared" by M.C. Caselli, *Sign Language Studies*, 1983, *39*, 113–143; and as "Gestures, signs, and words at two years: When does communication become language?" by V. Volterra, *Sign Language Studies*, 1981, *33*, 351–361.

conventionalized by the children and their caregivers. The basic semantic content of these referential gestures does not change with varying contexts. These signs or referential gestures tend to appear a little later than the deictic gestures and often specify what was an earlier stage referred to only through pointing or other deictic gestures. We have noted elsewhere that these gestures pass through the same decontextualization process as words, and they become true symbols only at the end of this process (Caselli, this volume).

According to these findings, we have analyzed the earliest phases of communicative and linguistic development of deaf children with deaf parents who are exposed from birth to sign language in order to compare their gestural communication with that observed in hearing children. For this comparison, we have analyzed the data on the prelinguistic and linguistic communication of both deaf and hearing children using the same criteria.

Our first question was: can we find differences between the gestural communication of a child exposed to a sign language and of a child exposed to a spoken language? If so, at what point do the differences occur? The results of this comparison might provide an opportunity to understand the role of linguistic input in prelinguistic communication and language development. Our purpose here, then, is to show the similarities and differences between the hearing and the deaf child in gestural communication and to illuminate the process children go through when making the transition from an earlier communicative system to a specific spoken or signed language. We also address the question of linguistic advantage, whether held by children acquiring spoken language or children acquiring sign language, a question raised in recent years by several investigators (Boyes Braem, 1973; Maestas y Moores, 1980; McIntire, 1977; Schlesinger & Meadow, 1972; Wilbur & Jones, 1974).

The operating hypothesis is that for language expressed and perceived in different modes it is possible to identify similar stages of acquisition, both in chronology and in sequence of development.

Method

The data reported here refer to four subjects, two deaf children of deaf parents and two hearing children of hearing parents. One deaf child (K) was exposed from birth to American Sign Language (ASL). The data on this subject are part of a larger corpus collected by Bellugi and her colleagues at Salk Institute. For the present study only eight videotapes from 10 to 22 months of age were transcribed and analyzed. No data on spoken production were collected. The second deaf child (M) was exposed from birth to Italian Sign Language (LIS). From the age of 2 years, M went to school with hearing children and received oral training from a speech therapist 3 h a week. The data on M were collected by means of diary accounts kept by the child's mother and videotaped session at 3-month intervals. In the present work we refer to data from 24 to 30 months of age. Vocal productions were also reported and analyzed.

Table 1. Subjects' age and linguistic input

Subjects	Age (months)	Linguistic input
K (deaf)	10–22	ASL
L (hearing)	10–17	Italian
M (deaf)	24–30	LIS
G (hearing)	27–30	Italian

The data on the two hearing children (L and G) were collected using the same methodology reported for M. More information on L is reported in Caselli (this volume). In the present work we refer to data from 10 to 17 months for L and from 27 to 30 months for G. The latter child was chosen because he exhibited gestural communication that was much richer than his verbal production. He is a typical of children whose parents would say: "He doesn't speak but I can understand everything he wants." Table 1 summarizes age and linguistic input for each subject.

In the first study reported here we compare one deaf child (K) and one hearing child (L) with particular attention to the communicative routines from which gestures, signs, and words emerge and the process of decontextualization through which they progress. In the second study we compare the types of combinations produced by the older deaf subject (M) and the older hearing subject (G).

Glosses of the gestures used by children are written in capital letters, while the glosses of the words spoken by children are written in *lower case letters* between quotation marks.

Gestures, Signs and Words: K and L Compared

From 10 to 12 Months

In analyzing K's videotapes at 10 months, numerous instances of the pointing gesture and a small number of signs were found:

LOVE   BIRD   MOTHER
WANT   NO   WHICH

K used the pointing gesture both to ask for something and to draw the attention of the mother to a particular object. For example, there is a long videotaped sequence in which the child points to a pin the mother is wearing and moves forward to touch it; the mother responds by signing BEAUTIFUL and BIRD (the pin is a little bird); the child again points and touches the pin.

K's pointing gestures are interpreted by her mother as forms of naming or as requests for names; indeed, she immediately offers the child the sign name for the object indicated. Later, in similar situations, the roles are reversed: the mother points to something and the child produces the sign name.

Deictic gestures used to request an object are of the following types: the child leans toward an object and then points to it, she produces an opening and closing gesture of the hand, or both. The opening and closing hand is similar to the ASL sign WANT. This manual sign is sometimes produced with one hand while the other points upward. For example, K wants a toy dog that the experimenter has in her hand; she leans toward the dog and then signs WANT while pointing upward.

This sequence was also analyzed by Petitto (1980), who suggested that the pointing gesture accompanying the sign WANT may be interpreted as a linguistic point produced when the child wants to grasp an object. Petitto notes that this child seems only to have this grasping gesture mediated by the following behavioral sequence: (a) nearing the object; (b) pausing again before the object; (c) emitting this 'sign-like' gesture looking at her own hands at times but more often maintaining eye contact with the adult. We propose a different interpretation. First, this pointing gesture is not readily separable from the ASL sign WANT made with the other hand. Secondly, it is unclear what is meant by "linguistic" when referring to this pointing gesture, since it is difficult to determine its exact semantic and syntactic function. Analysis of the situations in which this combination of WANT and pointing appears suggests that it refers to the whole exchange situation. These gestures, then, are not used only when she is requesting an object but also when she already has it in her hand or when a new object is presented and offered to her for the first time; instead of being accompanied by other signals of request, they are accompanied by manifestations of happiness and excitement. Such is the case, for example, when the experimenter presents a wooden doll and moves it toward the child. She leans toward the doll and touches it with one hand while opening and closing the other hand rhythmically; then she opens and closes both hands several times, very excitedly. In this instance, it is not evident that she is producing the sign WANT as a part of a routine.

It could also be maitained that during this phase (at 10 months) the request is more recognizable in signals like "leaning toward" with accompanying facial expression and whimpering sounds and cries or both, than it is in the content or intention of what resembles an ASL sign. Furthermore, the mother does not often interpret this "sign" WANT in just one way; sometimes she responds "WHAT? YOU WANT MILK?". On other occasions she claims that she is unable to interpret the meaning of the "sign."

This behavior is comparable to the behavior of hearing children who are just beginning to talk (also reported in Camaioni et al., 1976). Sounds like the word "dà" (I give, give me, or take), "grazie" (thank you), and "tieni" (take or hold) are not used by the child at first to ask for an object or to thank or to offer something; instead they refer to the whole exchange situation. The child says "dà" while receiving or offering an object, when it had just been received, or even to express possession of the object. These 'words' (analogous to the "sign" WANT in K's performance) are used initially in routines that accompany the entire exchange situation; later they may be applied to a part of the scheme, or they may be used to anticipate or describe the whole or part of the exchange. Such words may be used along with or may be replaced entirely by a rhythmic gesture of opening and closing of one or both hands similar by to the "sign" analyzed here. Bates (1976a) calls such motor activity in hearing children a "ritualized request."

K produces the sign LOVE (made by crossing her arms on her chest with 5-handshapes open and spread) in two different situations. In the first case she looks at the camera, points to it, and signs LOVE. In the second, she has a doll in front of her. Her mother signs DOLL, first on her own body and then on the child's, and the child then touches the doll and signs LOVE. In both situations K appears to be expressing some judgment, and, in fact, the mother too interprets K's gesture to mean "like." Semantically, this sign is comparable to the gesture GOOD (placing the tip of index finger on the lower cheek and slightly rotating the forearm in pronation) used by the hearing child L, to comment on food, as a response to questions like "How is the food?" or as a name for cookie. The form of K's sign LOVE, especially in those situations where the doll was present, is similar to L's gesture TO ROCK (crossing arms on the chest and rocking the body). This gesture is used when recognizing certain objects (dolls, stuffed animals) or for asking the adult to rock the dolls or stuffed animals.

K's sign BIRD, unlike the signs above, is produced the first time in imitation. The child points to the mother's pin and touches it. The mother signs BEAUTIFUL BIRD; the child points and touches the pin again, then signs BIRD in a manner only approximating the adult sign. (She uses the O handshape, opens and closes it slightly, and holds it so that her palm and fingers are directed toward herself instead of away as in the ASL sign.) The mother smiles and repeats the sign as the child has produced it but with a questioning look and then immediately produces the correct form, nodding. The child produces BIRD once again, modifying the orientation of the hand slightly and combining it with a point toward the mother's pin.

Other signs produced by K include NO (headshake), in reply to a command from an adult, and WHICH. The latter is made by imitating the adult's sign when the experimenter, presenting two stuffed animals, asks the child WHICH DOG; K responds by imitating part of the adult phrase. Later when the experimenter offers K two other animals, she immediately makes the sign WHICH demonstrating no understanding of the linguistic significance of the sign but apparently associating it with the "two animals" situation.

From 12 to 15 Months

When K is 12 months old, she produces eight new signs and uses them spontaneously in a less ritualized way than she did 2 months earlier. Her new signs (which are close approximations of the adult forms) are:

COME	MILK	FATHER	DOG
EAT	COW	QUESTION	LIGHT

Careful analysis reveals that both EAT and MILK are produced spontaneously with the communicative intention of requesting and they appear to refer
to the same referent. In other words, K uses these two signs interchangeably to ask
for food in general, as well as for the bottle, even when it is empty. Thus, while her
mother is feeding her, K refuses the food, signs EAT and MILK (she wants neither
to eat nor drink but only to have the bottle to hold in her mouth). Again, while her
mother is eating a sandwich, K leans toward her and points to the sandwich in a
requesting manner. The mother gives her some of the sandwich but K wants more,
signs EAT (performed simultaneously with opening and closing her mouth) and
once again she leans toward the sandwich. Then, while playing with some small
pieces of ham in her dish, she signs MILK.

Similarly, hearing children in the initial phases of linguistic development
may display behaviors of "overextension," "underextension," and "generalization," wherein they use the same word to refer to more than one referent (the
referents often sharing some common property). Conversely, they may use
different words to refer to only one referent. For example, L uses words like
"*ahmme*" (yummy) and "*pappa*" (childrenese for "food") simultaneously bringing the empty hand to the mouth and opening and closing the mouth in a
chewing action to refer to any kind of food, the act of eating, or objects or
situations related to eating. It is not until 17 months that different words begin to
be used by L for different types of food, for example, "*otto*" (cookie) and "*chicca*"
(candy).

The signs K uses to name animals are produced as she turns the pages of a
book with her mother. Sometimes they are imitations of her mother's signs; other
times they are used for naming, produced along with the pointing gesture. The
mother's attempt to elicit the animal name by pointing and using the ASL sign
QUESTION is unsuccessful; as in the previous example with WHICH, K imitates
the sign QUESTION instead of responding with the sign for the name of the
animal.

In the same videotape, K, with her hand spread, repeatedly taps the tip of her
thumb on the counter of her high chair; the mother asks the meaning of that
"sign" by imitating it and signing QUESTION. This time K responds correctly to
her mother's question, and, moving her hand (still with the 5 handshape) to rest
the thumb tip on her temple, she signs FATHER (she is referring to her father who
is filming her with the videocamera). We found a similar interaction between L
and his mother (see example 23 in Caselli, p 64, this volume).

On the videotape of K at 12 months, we observe progress in both the
spontaneous and truly referential use of signs (i.e., apart from ritualized schemes)
and an increase in their number. At 13 and 15 months this progress in both areas
is consolidated, and the child uses signs more precisely and more appropriately.
Nevertheless, the signs are still frequently produced in response to specific
questions asked by the adult; these questions are simple and context specific with
little variation, almost always referring to names of objects or persons present, to
actions the child habitually performs, or to pictures in books that mother and child
"read" together.

From 15 to 17 Months

When K is 15 months old, the first combination of two signs (EAT CEREAL) appears. Then, at 16 months we see a considerable increase in the number of referents that the child expresses, with a repertoire at this time of about 30 signs. Several combinations of signs also appear:

EAT MILK
DOG ME
RABBIT BRUSH-TEETH
WATER BRUSH-TEETH

These findings agree with those reported for hearing children; that is, the first combinations of lexical elements occur when the lexical repertoire of the child is between 20 and 40 words.

L combines his first words at approximately 17 months, but during the preceding months he already produces "mixed" combinations of a referential gesture with a spoken word:

"Papà" BYE-BYE (daddy bye-bye)
"Mamma" BLOW (mommy blow)
"Otto" GOOD (cookie good)

The sum of the gestural and vocal referents signified by L confirms that the overall number of gestures and words in his repertoire is about 20. Table 2 lists the signs, referential gestures, and words produced by K and L, respectively, at the ages considered above. Only signs observed on the videotapes are listed in Table 2 for K, but L's productions include both the referential gestures and words found on the tape and those noted in the diary his mother kept. Note also that between 15 and 16 months, when there is a noticeable acceleration in K's use of signs as well as an increase in their number, L produces very few new referential gestures; his use of the "old" gestures becomes sporadic, but there is an increasing number of new words used spontaneously and in a decontextualized manner. Both children demonstrate their first combinations of two or more elements during this period. Two of K's combinations warrant further examination:

RABBIT BRUSH-TEETH
WATER BRUSH-TEETH

It is useful to analyze this combinatorial pattern using the framework adopted by Scollon (1979) for the acquisition of spoken language (see also Caselli, p 60-61, this volume). He claims that in the structuring of utterances of one or more element, the child goes through easily recognizable phases. The first period is characterized by "vertical constructions." These are constructions in which the elements are related to one another (and to the same argument) but structured only through the adult's intervention with questions, approvals, repetitions, and the like.

The second phase is characterized by "horizontal constructions" in which the child combines two or more elements without "making use of the adult's

Table 2. Signs, referential gestures and words in K's and L's repertoires from 10–17 months

Age (months)	K Signs	Referential gestures	L Words
10–11	LOVE WANT BIRD NO WHICH MOTHER	GOOD BOY BYE DANCE GOOD	brrr brrr (car) Ahmme (food) Bau (dog) Pu (all gone)
12	COME HAT MILK COW FATHER WHAT? DOG LIGHT	NO COMB EAT HIT GO OUT	A pà (food) Amba (water)
13	DRINK ALL GONE BYE	HAT DRINK SLEEP SUCK PHONE	Mamma (mommy) Bobò (hit) Bam (fall down) Miu (cat) Qua qua (duck) Pupù (dirty)
14		DRIVE SHAMPOO BLOW	Appa (shoe) Pio pio (bird) Pa (ball) Nonna (grandmother) Ciuccio (pacifier)
15		CLOCK WAG ITS TAIL	Ghighi (Luigi) Tittà (clock) Papà (father) Pitzy (Pitzy) Tatta (turtle) Bua [ache (boo-boo)]
16	BEAUTIFUL HAT SHOES RABBIT TOOTH-BRUSH NO (with finger-spelling) BABY SLEEP WATER DRESS (verb) EAT MILK DOG WHERE DOG		Bimbi (children) Pappa (food) Mimmi (Mimmi) Pao (Paolo) Cocco (dirty) Otta (burns) Coccò (hen) Din don (bell) Uca (Luca) Cane (dog) Cane (dog) Chia .... brr brr (key car) *Piccolo* piange (*baby* cries) *NO* brr brr (*NO* car)

Table 2. (*continued*)

Age (months)	K		L
	Signs	Referential gestures	Words
	RABBIT BRUSH-TEETH WATER BRUSH-TEETH		Otto *buono* (cookie *good*) Papà *ciao* (daddy bye) Mamma *soffiare* (mommy *blow*)
17			Pigna (pen) Di là (over there) Li (there)
			Mamma più più (mommy no more, no more) più ciuccio (all gone pacifier) Nonno brr brrr (grandfather car)

expressions." Scollon stresses, however, that vertical constructions are retained and used at least into the second phase. In order to correctly interpret the quoted combinations, the entire context must be examined. Then it is clear how K's production of signed language, though more spontaneous and fluent at this age, still acquires its structure through communicative exchanges with the mother. Table 3 shows an example of this. The sequence of signs is representative of both the level of K's sign production during this period and of the dialogues of the mother and child. The combinations of signs in the last part of the sequence are built from the preceding exchanges in which the mother offers a "piece" of language, K repeats the "piece" and offers a new one (first through pointing then with the sign; e.g., WATER), or K produces an element introduced previously by the child herself or by her mother. The RABBIT BRUSH-TEETH sequence is a case in which the "pieces" had been given in the preceding dialogue, the first only by mother and not repeated until now by the child. In WATER BRUSH-TEETH, the first element had not been introduced previously.

L also produces expanded vertical constructions at approximately 16 months of age, as shown in Table 4. At this same age L uses constructions in which one or more words are combined with a referential gesture, always in dialogue. (See examples 27 and 28 in Caselli, p. 65, this volume).

The videotape of K at 16 months also shows a qualitative change in her spontaneous production — a change in form and function. In the earlier videotapes, initiations were almost exclusively executed by pointing, expressing either a request for action or naming, and aimed at eliciting agreement or attracting the mother's attention to particular objects. The mother was required to interpret the gesture produced by the child. At 16 months, however, much of K's spontaneous production is expressed through signs and no longer tends only to name objects.

272   M.C. Caselli and V. Volterra

Table 3. Example of "vertical construction" in K at 16 months

Mother:	Looks in the book, points to a figure, signs SLEEP.
K:	Looks in the book and signs SLEEP.
Mother:	Turns page, points to a figure, signs BRUSH-TEETH; takes K's hand and moves it toward K's mount.
K:	(Guided by mother) signs BRUSH-TEETH.
Mother:	Nods and signs YES RABBIT BRUSH-TEETH.
K:	Looks at book and signs BRUSH-TEETH.
Mother:	Nods and signs RABBIT SLEEP WAKE-UP, BRUSH-TEETH, LIKE YOU.
K:	(Is distracted by other action in room)
Mother:	(Explains about subject introduced by K.) She returns to the book, points to a figure and signs COMB, first on her own head then on K's.
K:	Goes back a few pages in book and signs SLEEP.
Mother:	Nods and signs SLEEP, then turns page, points to a figure and asks, WHAT?
K:	Signs BRUSH-TEETH and points to a figure in book.
Mother:	Nods and signs BABY, RABBIT CRADLE BABY, BABY RABBIT, points in the book and signs MOMMY RABBIT, points to figure and signs DRESS, signs TROUSERS, JACKET.
K:	Repeats DRESS, signs DRESS. Looks in book, looks at mother and signs RABBIT BRUSH-TEETH, points at the page and signs WATER − BRUSH-TEETH.

Table 4. Example of "vertical construction" in L at 16 months

Mother:	"*Vuoi la palla?*" (You want the ball?)
K:	"*A pà*" (Ball)
Mother:	"*Già, non c'è più*" (Right, it's not here any more)
L:	"*Più*" (No more)
Mother:	"*Ah sì, l'ha preso il gatto*" (Oh, yes; the cat took it)
L:	"Miao" (Cat)

Instead her signs refer to states or aspects of objects themselves; thus, we find modifiers like BEAUTIFUL. During the "reading" of the book, K signs the various actions that the characters perform and does not limit herself merely to naming them as she did in previous sessions. In addition, at 16 months, K changes her expression of negation from the headshake *no* to the manual ASL sign made by the two fingers of an H handshape closing to the opposed extended thumb.

Undoubtedly, in response to K's increased lexical repertoire and her greater communicative and linguistic competence at 16 months of age, K's mother now interacts differently with her child; she no longer limits herself to naming or to asking K for labels in rather ritualized form; instead she expands her expressions by signing statements about the characters they have seen and named in the book game. She no longer encourages K to imitate but rather to give new information about the states and actions of the characters. This behavior of the mother so well adapted to the various stages of the child's growing competence seems to be extremely important for the development of communicative and linguistic competence. Bruner (1975a) claims that a mother seems to know just how far she can go. For example, after having asked the question "What is that?" and the child has answered "*tore*" for doctor, she may ask "And what is the doctor doing?", signalling that she wants the child to express something new. Language, according to Bruner, is always marked in terms of *given/new*. The mother speaks at a level only slightly higher than the child's to enable the child to progress to the use of new information in his or her own language production. Once again, progress observed in K at 16 months is similar to the progress of L at the same age. In fact, it is between 16 and 18 months that we find L's structured exchanges with his mother, with several rounds of turn-taking, and combinations of one referential gesture with one or two words. Here also modifiers such as "*piccolo*" (small) and "*grande*" (big) first appear. The lexical repertoire of L at this stage is about 30 referents (vocal and gestural modalities combined). It is important to state once again that, for L, until 13–14 months the number of vocally expressed referents is very close to the number of referents expressed gesturally (see Table 1). From the 16th or 17th month on there is a rapid increase in the number of words (vocally expressed referents) and a freezing of the gesturally produced lexicon; new referential gestures do not appear and those already in the lexicon are used sporadically.

At this stage we find a marked difference between K on the one hand, and L on the other: the deaf child combines two signs, the hearing child does not; he does, however, combine a single referential gesture with one or two words. This point will be examined in more detail in the next section.

The more important conclusion to be drawn from this first comparative study is that it is not only the words of hearing children that must be compared with the signs of deaf children but also the communicative gestures produced by both must be considered. Only in this way can valid assessments of similarities and differences be made. In particular, we should point out that we have been purposely ambiguous in the use of the terms "sign" and "referential gesture". The signs of the deaf child and the referential gestures of the hearing child in fact appear very similar especially when they are used in recurring routines, calling their linguistic status into question.

Furthermore, gestures or signs used by young deaf children often have only a vague resemblance to the signs used by the adult deaf community. It is not the resemblance or lack of resemblance to signs of a codified adult system that differentiates signs from gestures. The child's signals are often the result of a particular, yet conventional agreement between the child and his or her caregivers. Indeed, they may be idiosyncratic forms that have no meaning, or even a different meaning in the adult's system. The important criterion determining symbolic status of both signs and referential gestures is that they are used by the child in a decontextualized way, that is, to refer to the same referents in different contexts and to refer also to absent objects or events.

Combinations of Communicative Signals: M and G Compared

When we began data collection, both M, the deaf child, and G, the hearing child, produced combinations of communicative signals. Considering the similarity of signs and referential gestures, as mentioned above, we can see that certain combinations were in the repertoire of both children:

> Deictic gesture + deictic gesture (DG + DG)
> Deictic gesture + referential gesture/sign (DG + S)
> Deictic gesture + word (DG + W)
> Referential gesture/sign + word (S + W).

The combinations DG + W and S + W became progressively more frequent in the productions of the hearing child, but they were less frequently produced by the deaf child. M more often produced the sign and the corresponding word referring to the same referent; e.g., he said "*brrr*" (car) and performed the sign CAR at the same time. His most frequent combinations containing words were those with "*mama*," the only word M used without making the corresponding sign. Furthermore, the sign + sign combination (S + S) appeared only in the deaf child, while the word + word combination (W + W) was produced primarily by the hearing child.

In Table 5, examples from each type of combination produced by G and M are reported. From the examples reported in this table it is clear that the striking differences the deaf child and the hearing child concerns the last two types of combinations. It is not surprising that M, the deaf child, produced only one W + W combination at the age considered ("*mama apo*"; mommy open), but it is peculiar that the hearing child, who was particularly prone to gestural communication, did not produce combinations of two referential gestures. Subject L, discussed in the first part of this chapter, also never produced combinations of two referential gestures. From this finding we want to propose a more general hypothesis.

Linguistic capacity implies particular abilities, specifically the ability to use symbols and the ability to combine these symbols. Children must learn to separate different aspects or parts of the world (different actions, objects, people, and events). They must learn to make direct reference to these parts in order to communicate this reality. They can reach this goal in two ways: by referring directly to these parts by deictic gestures like pointing, or by using appropriate and unique referential symbols (vocal words or gestural signs) for these different parts, or by both. It is likely that this is not a one-way process; the use of deictic gestures and symbols may help the child distinguish aspects of the world around him or her.

Finally, in order to communicate progressively more complex messages, children must combine these gestures. They can reach this goal by producing two or more deictic gestures and referential gestural or vocal symbols sequentially. But clearly to combine symbols implies a more advanced cognitive ability than the combination of deictic gestures, the child must reconstruct at the representational

Table 5. Examples of each type of combination produced by G and M

Subject	Type of combination	Examples	Translation
G M		QUELLO QUI	That here
G M	DG + DG	TU QUELLO	You that
G M		QUI LUI	Here him
G M		IO QUELLO	Me that
G M		QUELLO *brrrr*	That car
G M		QUI *mamma*	Here mommy
G	DG + W	QUELLO *ape*	That open
G M	or	TU *ahm*	You eat
G M	W + DG	*ahm* QUELLO	Eat that
G		*nanna* QUI	Nap here
G M		QUELLO BERE	That drink
G M		TU TELEFONARE	You phone
G M		A ME PIANOFORTE	To me piano
G M	DG + S	MANGIARE QUELLO	Eat That
G M	or	PRENDERE QUELLO	Take that
G M	S + DG	VENIRE QUI	Come Here
G M		CIAO IO	Bye me
M		MAMMA LI'	Mommy there
G M		QUELLO GRANDE	That big
G		PICCOLO *piange*	Little cry
G M	S + W	NO *brrrr*	No car
G	or	OTTO *buono*	Cookie good
G	W + S	*papà* CIAO	Daddy bye
G M		*mama* SOFFIARE	Mommy blow
G		*papa più*	Food no more
G	W + W	*da brrrr*	Give car
G M		*mamma apo*	Mommy open
M		POMPA PALLONE	Pump balloon
M	S + S	PALLONE SCOPPIARE	Balloon pop
M		SOLDI CAVALLO	Money go-horse

level all the aspects of the reality he or she wants to communicate with only very limited support from present objects.

From our data it appears that hearing children — despite their exposure to a predominantly vocal input — show the capacity to use symbols in both modalities. That is, they produce vocal and gestural signals with referential force. Furthermore, hearing children show the capacity to combine two or more signals in the gestural modality as well; they produce combinations of two or more deictic gestures and combinations of a deictic gesture with a symbol (word or sign). They do not, however, combine signs; they do not put together two referential gestures though they do combine two vocal symbols (spoken words). The final movement toward the vocal modality takes place when they begin to use simultaneously the symbolic and the combinatorial capacity.

This combinatorial capacity, the combining of two symbols in order to communicate, seems to depend directly on the linguistic input to which the child is exposed. At this point, and only at this point, we note a difference between the child exposed to a spoken input and the child exposed to a signed input: the former combines two vocally produced symbols, the latter combines two gesturally produced symbols.

Conclusion

Comparing the acquisition of language by children exposed to a signed language and by children exposed to a spoken language can be particularly fruitful, especially if the analysis of the process is performed using the same criteria for both. In particular, this endeavor helps determine which aspects of the acquisition process are dependent on the modality of production and reception and which are unaffected by modality. The systematic comparison that has been made here brings us to the following conclusions. First, the stages in the process of language acquisition follow one another in a specific order and are fundamentally the same for all children, independent of the modality of expression and reception. Secondly, both deaf children and hearing children use only deictic gestures in the first period. In the subsequent period, the first signs, referential gestures, and words appear. Signs, gestures, and words at first refer not to specific referents but to complex schemes of action and derive from ritualized exchanges with the mother. In the next period the signs, gestures, and words are separated from the action scheme or ritual and serve to represent only a part of the scheme: an object or an action, for example. In this period it seems that the communicative interaction with the mother is of great importance. The mother stimulates the production of signs, gestures and words through requests for naming and through the presentation of a very simple model adapted to the level of the child's language, one that is highly contextualized and refers to the child's own world of experience.

The child produces signs, gestures, and words at first imitating more or less correctly the model offered by the adult and producing them in response to adult elicitations. Later the signs, gestures, and words are used spontaneously to communicate the child's own needs or states, or to name objects and actions.

In the same period the first combinations of elements appear in vertical and horizontal constructions. We want to emphasize again the fact that both hearing and deaf children begin to combine two elements at the same age, that is, at around 17–18 months when the number of items in their vocabularies is between 20–40 referents.

The specifically linguistic abilities of producing symbols and combining them can be expressed in both modalities, gestural and vocal. Because hearing children exposed to spoken language input and deaf children exposed to sign language input (or not exposed to any input at all) use signs and combine signs with gestures or combine gestures, we can argue that both these abilities do not depend directly on exposure to a linguistic input. What does appear to depend crucially on exposure to a linguistic input, however, is the capacity to combine symbols (referential words or signs), i.e., the capacity to use both abilities, symbolic and combinatorial, simultaneously in order to communicate. This demonstrated dual ability seems to be the indication that the child is passing from using a general communicative capability to managing a real linguistic system.

Finally, the comparison made here affords another look at precocity, that is, the appearance and use of first signs in deaf children as compared with first words in hearing children. From the data and the kind of analysis presented here, where the development of gestural communicative capacity in deaf children is compared with the development of the gestural *and* vocal capacity of hearing children, we submit that there is a substantial parallel between the two groups of children. It is not that deaf children begin to communicate earlier, but that both deaf and hearing children use gestural expression in the early stages of their communication with adults. Definitive settlement of the question of chronology can come only from research based on data from a large sampling of both hearing and deaf subjects analyzed, as we have done here, by applying the same criteria to both.

CHAPTER 21

Enhancement of Spatial Cognition in Deaf Children

U. Bellugi, L. O'Grady, D. Lillo-Martin, M. O'Grady Hynes, K. van Hoek, and D. Corina

Notation

We use the following notation in this chapter:

SIGN	=	Words in capital letters represent English labels (glosses) for ASL signs. The gloss represents the meaning of the unmarked, unmodulated, basic forms of a sign out of context.
SIGN[X:]	=	A form that has undergone indexical change. The form or meaning may be specified, as in INFORM[X:1 to 2] or INFORM[X:I to you].
SIGN[N;M]	=	A form that has undergone inflection for number and distributional aspect or for temporal aspect, focus, or degree.
SIGN[D:]	=	A form that has undergone derivational process.
*SIGN	=	An asterisk preceding a sign form indicates that it is ungrammatical within adult ASL.

Introduction to Language in a Spatial Medium

Deaf children who have been deprived of auditory experience and who rely on a sign language as their principal mode of communication provide a privileged testing ground for investigating the interplay between the development of a spatial language and its spatial cognitive underpinnings. The study of the

This work was supported in part by National Institutes of Health Grants NS 15175, NS 19096, NS 22343, HD 13249; National Science Foundation Grant BNS83-09860 to the Salk Institute for Biological Studies; and the John D. and Catherine MacArthur Foundation Research Network on "The Transition from Infancy to Early Childhood." We would like to thank Edward S. Klima, Howard Poizner, Dennis Schemenauer, and Helene Sabo for their discussions and help with the research. We are grateful to the deaf children and parents who have taken part in our longitudinal studies of the acquisition of sign language from the onset of first gestures to the mastery of the spatially organized syntax and its underpinnings. We are very grateful to Dr. Henry Klopping, to the teachers and staff of the California School for the Deaf, and to the children and their families for their spirited participation in these studies which provide a new perspective on the human capacity for language.

acquisition of American Sign Language (ASL) in deaf children brings into focus some fundamental questions about the representation of language and the representation of space.

In research over the past decade, we have been specifying the ways in which the formal properties of languages are shaped by their modalities of expression, sifting properties peculiar to a particular language mode from more general properties common to all languages. ASL exhibits formal structuring at the same levels as spoken languages and similar kinds of organizational principles (constrained systems of features, rules based on underlying forms, recursive grammatical processes). Yet our studies show that at all structural levels, the form of an utterance in a signed language is deeply influenced by the modality in which the language is cast (Bellugi, 1980).

ASL has been forged into an autonomous language with its own internal mechanism for relating visual form with meaning. ASL has evolved linguistic mechanisms that are not derived from those of English (or any spoken language), thus offering a new perspective on the determinants of language form (Bellugi, Klima, & Poizner, 1988; Klima & Bellugi, 1979). ASL shares underlying principles of organization with spoken languages, but the instantiation of those principles occurs in formal devices arising out of the very different possibilities of the visual-gestural mode (Bellugi, 1988; Bellugi and Studdert-Kennedy, 1980). We consider briefly the structure of ASL at different linguistic levels — the layered structure of phonology, three-dimensional morphology, and the spatially organized syntax.

"Phonology" Without Sound

Research on the structure of lexical signs has shown that, like the words of spoken languages, signs are fractionated into sublexical elements. The elements that distinguish signs (handshapes, movements, places of articulation) are in contrasting spatial arrangements and co-occur throughout the sign.

Vertically Arrayed Morphology

The grammatical mechanisms of ASL exploit elaborately the spatial medium and the possibility of simultaneous and multidimensional articulation. Like spoken languages, ASL has developed grammatical markers that serve as inflectional and derivational morphemes; these are regular changes in form across syntactic classes of lexical items associated with systematic changes in meaning. In ASL, families of sign forms are related via an underlying stem: the forms share a handshape, a location, and a local movement shape. Inflectional and derivational processes represent the interaction of the stem with other features of movement in space (dynamics of movement, manner of movement, directions of movement, spatial array, and the like) all *layered* with the sign stem.

Spatially Organized Syntax

Languages have different ways of marking grammatical relations among their lexical items. In English, it is primarily the *order* of the lexical items that marks the basic grammatical relations among verbs and their arguments; in other languages, it is the morphology of case marking or verb agreement that signals these relations. ASL, by contrast, specifies relations among signs primarily through the manipulation of sign forms in *space*. Thus in sign language, space itself bears linguistic meaning. The most striking and distinctive use of space in ASL is in its role in syntax and discourse, especially in nominal assignment, pronominal reference, verb agreement, anaphoric reference and the referential spatial framework for discourse. Nominals introduced into ASL discourse may be associated with specific points in a plane of signing space. In signed discourse, pointing again to a specific locus clearly "refers back" to a previously mentioned nominal, even with many other signs intervening. The ASL system of verb agreement, like its pronominal system, is also in essence spatialized. Verb signs for a large class of verbs move between the abstract loci in signing space, bearing obligatory markers for person (and number) via spatial indices, thereby specifying subject and object of the verb, as shown in Fig. 1a. This spatialized system thus allows explicit reference through pronominals and agreement markers to multiple, distinct, third-person referents. The same signs in the same order, but with a reversal in direction of the verb's movement, indicate a reversal of grammatical relations. Furthermore, sentences with signs in different temporal orders can still have the same meaning, since grammatical relations are signified spatially. Coreferential nominals are indexed to the same locus point, as is evident in complex embedded structures, such as shown in Fig. 1b. Different spaces may be used to contrast events, to indicate reference to time preceding the utterance, or to express hypotheticals and counterfactuals, as schematically diagrammed in Fig. 1c. This use of spatial loci for referential indexing, verb agreement, and grammatical relations is clearly a unique property of visual-gestural systems.

ASL is markedly different in surface form from English, and from spoken languages in general. The inflectional and derivational devices of ASL, for example, make structured use of space and movement, nesting the basic sign stem in spatial patterns and complex dynamic contours of movement. ASL is unique in its use of space at all levels of linguistic organization. Other signed languages examined suggest that these characteristics turn out to be general characteristics of primary signed languages (Volterra, 1981b).

In addition to the structured use of space in syntax, ASL is different from spoken language in the extent and degree of "motivatedness" between meaning and form. Characteristically, ASL lexical items themselves are often globally iconic, their form resembling some aspect of what they denote. At the morphological and syntactic levels also, there is often some congruence (motivatedness) between form and meaning. Spoken languages are not without such direct clues to meaning (reduplication processes and ideophones provide

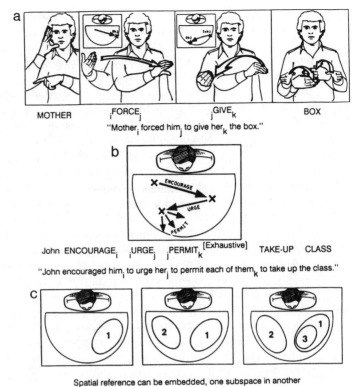

MOTHER   ᵢFORCEⱼ   ⱼGIVEₖ   BOX

"Motherᵢ forced himⱼ to give herₖ the box."

John ENCOURAGEᵢ   ᵢURGEⱼ   ⱼPERMITₖ [Exhaustive]   TAKE-UP   CLASS

"John encouraged himᵢ to urge herⱼ to permit each of themₖ to take up the class."

Spatial reference can be embedded, one subspace in another

Fig. 1a-c. Spatial linguistic contrasts in ASL

direct methods of reflecting meaning through form, for example), but in sign language such transparency is pervasive. ASL thus bears striking traces of its representational origins, but at the same time is fully grammaticized.

The Acquisition of a Visuospatial Language

The relationship between nonlinguistic gesture and language development has been highlighted by recent research, which is well represented in this volume and illuminated in Volterra (1981a) and Volterra and Caselli (1986). The issues involved are brought into particularly clear focus when one examines the sign languages of the deaf. Linguistic signs may be similar to or even identical with the nonlinguistic gestures used by prelingual children and hearing adults. One might therefore expect that the transition from gesture to linguistic symbol would happen smoothly and rapidly, and that the acquisition of those signs which resemble gestures might be facilitated by the transparent similarity between the gesture and the sign. When the form of a sign is identical to that of a gesture, is the linguistic function of the sign learned at the same time as the gesture to which it is transparently related? The nature of the relationship between nonlinguistic development and language can be illuminated by the study of spatial abilities and spatial language in deaf children acquiring ASL.

We have completed a battery of experimental studies and longitudinal studies of deaf children of deaf parents, spanning the age range from 6 months to 10 years. The longitudinal studies involve videotaping spontaneous mother-child interaction in situations designed for eliciting rich information on the grammatical systems which are the focus of our research: transcribing and analyzing the videotapes in notation devised to capture the crucial contrasts. We supplement the naturalistic data with experimental studies of groups of deaf signing children. We have designed a battery of elicitation, imitation, and comprehension tests. These tests tap signing children's knowledge of the equivalent of phonological processes, morphological processes, and syntactic processes in ASL. These allow us to chart the course of acquisition of grammatical structures of ASL. These methods together – naturalistic and experimental – give us the best means for investigating the course of language development in the deaf child.

In this chapter we will focus primarily on how the spatial properties of ASL influence its acquisition in deaf children of deaf parents who are learning sign language as a native language. By examining the acquisition of specifically linguistic space in ASL (as opposed to other types of more general spatial cognitive knowledge), important information about both the representation and the organization of space in development may be uncovered.

The Transition from Gesture to Symbol

The system of personal pronouns in ASL gives rise to a particularly striking issue in the relationship between gesture and sign in the acquisition of language, and also affords a dramatic example of the unexpected similarities between the acquisition of spoken and signed languages (Bellugi & Klima, 1982a, 1982b; Petitto, 1983a, 1983b). Deixis in spoken languages is considered a verbal surrogate for pointing. In ASL, however, deixis *is* pointing. The pronominal signs in ASL are, in fact, the same as pointing gestures that hearing people use to supplement their words nonverbally. This directness of reference should, in principle, lead to ease of acquisition of such forms by young deaf children learning ASL as compared with spoken languages.

The problems children have in learning terms that "shift" with speaker and addressee (such as I and YOU) are well known and well documented for spoken languages. The hearing child's problems with the shifting nature of such arbitrary strings of sounds as YOU and ME are readily understandable. In hearing children, problems with such deictic pronominal terms involving shifting reference are usually resolved by the age of 2;6-3;0. In contrast, we fully expected that because of their transparent nature, the learning of the sign equivalents of pronominal reference in ASL would be early and error-free ("trivial" is the way we expressed it). In ASL, the pronoun signs are exactly the same as the pointing gestures we would use to indicate self and addressee. Given such obvious gestures, directness of reference would seem inescapable. However, to our surprise, our early videotapes revealed that mothers, rather than use pronoun signs with their young deaf children, tended to employ name signs; moreover, their children did the same.

Petitto studied this important aspect of the acquisition of ASL in depth (Petitto, 1983a, 1983b, 1988). Her involvement in the study of pronominal reference surfaced very naturally; one day a deaf mother and child (age 1;11) were visiting, and the child began signing YOU where she clearly meant herself (shown in Fig. 2a). The mother, embarrassed, signed "NO, NO, (YOU) MEAN (YOU)" taking the child's hand and making the pointing sign directly and forcibly on the child herself. In a language where the "speech organs" are directly visible, and moreover, manipulable, the form of mother-to-child correction is remarkably direct; yet the mother's corrections at this period had no effect on the child's productions, and the child continued to walk around the laboratory

Fig. 2a,b. Deaf children's signing errors: pronoun reversal and verb agreement

blithely pointing *incorrectly* for reference to herself. Thus the child was patently ignoring the transparency of the pointing gesture.

Petitto found that deaf children display precisely the same progression — at the same ages — as do hearing children learning pronominal reference systems in spoken languages. Her results provide dramatic evidence of the transition from gesture to sign. It is a transition marked, first, by the emergence of a form used as a pointing gesture, then its absence over a period of several months, and finally the re-emergence of the same form as a pronominal sign that is integrated into a linguistic system but marked by some systematic errors. Importantly, the errors and their resolution occur exactly on target with those observed in children learning spoken languages, at the same ages. It appears to make little difference, then, whether pronominal terms are symbolized by arbitrary streams of sound segments, as in spoken language, or by pointing signs which are indistinguishable in form from pointing gestures, as in sign language. These studies suggest a *discontinuity* in the transition from prelinguistic gesture to linguistic system, even when the form of the two is identical and shares a single channel of expression.

The Spatial Marking for Verb Agreement

We turn now to another subsystem of ASL that involves spatial loci; the level of inflectional morphology by which verb signs are systematically modified to indicate grammatical categories such as agreement for person and number. For a specific subclass of verbs in ASL, "verb agreement" involves articulating the verb sign so that it moves from the position of the subject to the position of the object. Some verbs have obligatory agreement, some optionally undergo agreement, and some can agree with only a single argument. The general mechanism is the same for all verbs that are indexible: movement between the spatial loci established for the noun arguments, either in accordance with actual loci for present referents or with abstract loci established in signing space (Klima and Bellugi, 1979; Lillo-Martin, 1988; Padden, 1983). Thus, for a sign like GIVE, to sign a sentence such as "I give to you," the signer moves a flat grasping hand from in front of his or her own chest to the area in front of the addressee's chest; and to sign "you give to me," the movement of the verb is from addressee to signer. Aside from the structural regularities that make this utterance part of a visual language (such as the form of the handshape, and the position of the utterance within a syntactic context), this sign resembles an iconic mime of giving, between "me," and "you."

A priori, one might think, therefore, that such forms would be acquired relatively early, that the transparency in the form of the sign would facilitate its acquisition, regardless of the fact that in the adult language it is analyzed as a morphologically inflected form. How do children acquire a morphological system which is grammaticized but which nevertheless displays a large amount of iconicity? Meier (1981) analyzed the acquisition of such verb agreement both longitudinally and by experimental elicitation techniques. Working with more than a dozen deaf children of deaf parents, ranging in age from 1;6 to 7;0, Meier mapped out three clear periods in their acquisition of verb agreement.

In the first stage of two to three signs (around the age of 2 years), signing children do not make use of the inflectional apparatus of ASL. Even when these children imitate, their imitations do not copy parental inflected utterances; they use instead the *uninflected* (or citation) form of the sign. Thus the signing child begins by analyzing uninflected forms out of the various patterns he or she is exposed to and uses only these forms. Furthermore, as Newport and Ashbrook (1977) showed, young deaf children at this stage tend to use sequential *order* of their uninflected signs, rather than spatial organization, to mark grammatical relations in their signing.

At the next stage, between the ages of 2 and 3 years, deaf children begin to produce inflected forms of the verb. Then, by 3-3½ years, in required contexts they master and consistently use the appropriate verb agreement system with present referents. In fact, they overgeneralize the system to nonindexible verbs (Meier, 1981, 1982). As shown in Fig. 2b, some of these over-regularizations of object marking to nonindexible verbs by young deaf children result in the production of forms which are ungrammatical in the adult language, for example, *SPELL[X:'to me'], *SAY[X:'to you'], and *LIKE[X:'to it'].

Despite the difference in form of marking, the mastery of the inflections for verb agreement in ASL appears at the same age as mastery of comparable processes in spoken languages, as Meier argues. Moreover, the general pattern of acquisition — from no inflections, through consistent use of the inflectional system but with related over-regularization, to complete mastery — is the same for ASL and spoken languages. Thus, the iconicity of the ASL forms presented to the child again appears to have remarkably little effect on the acquisition process.

The evidence suggests that young children do not acquire these mimetic forms early, despite their iconicity. Nor do they acquire them in analogue or holistic fashion; but rather, as the evidence across our range of acquisition studies also indicates, they do so by acquiring them morpheme by morpheme just as do hearing children acquiring spoken languages.

We have examined some of the first morphological systems to be mastered by the signing child. Because of the transparency of ASL forms, we surmised that these would be systems profoundly influenced by iconicity. What we found, instead, was that their transparency at all levels appears to have little or no effect on acquisition. Indeed Meier (1982) has argued that the young child may not be disposed to make use of the transparency of forms. Rather than focusing on iconicity, the deaf child, in an ordered and orderly fashion, analyzes morphological components of the system presented to him or her. The fact that the articulators in sign language are visible and manipulable could plausibly be thought to provide a special route to learning: mothers do occasionally mold and shape young children's hands in signing. Our evidence suggests, however, that this manipulation is steadfastly and systematically ignored by signing children who firmly hold their ground, continuing the incorrect analysis and resulting errors until they arrive at their own reorganization of the language system. The course of acquisition of grammatical processes in ASL is remarkably like that for spoken languages.

The Interplay Between Spatial Cognition and Spatial Language

In our studies, we focus on the spatial underpinnings of syntax and the ways in which manipulation of points in space figure stucturally at the syntactic level. However, at all levels of the language, spatial locational contrasts convey linguistic information; processing linguistic structure in sign language crucially involves processing spatial relations, and sign discourse requires planning across spatial relationships. Young deaf children learning ASL sometimes have difficulty coping with the referential spatial framework involved in sentence, discourse, and narrative, as Fig. 3 shows. A deaf child of 3 years does not yet explicitly establish identities for loci. Furthermore, he or she tends to use one locus for several referents, stacking them up at one locus point, thus still leaving reference unclear and ambiguous (Bellugi, 1988; Loew, 1983). In a series of studies we ask whether the special requirements of spatial representation that

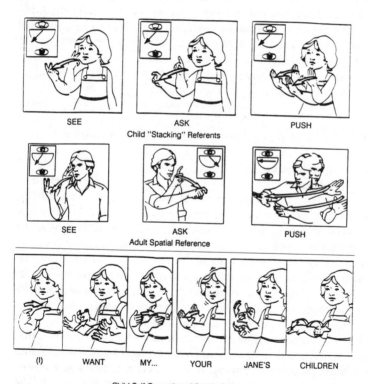

Fig. 3. Acquisition of spatial syntax

underlie sign language structure limit the deaf child's acquisition of language in this domain (van Hoek, O'Grady, & Bellugi, 1987).

The young deaf child is faced with the dual task in sign language of spatial perception, memory, and spatial transformations on the one hand, and processing grammatical structure on the other, all in one and the same visual event. How will these complex requirements for spatial processing affect the development of particular visuospatial capacities? The complex linguistic manipulations of the space in front of the signer's body in ASL place complex spatial-cognitive demands on the child acquiring such a system. Indeed, aspects of the acquisition of this spatial framework appear later than we might expect (Bellugi, 1988; Bellugi & Klima, 1982a; Lillo-Martin, 1985a, 1985b, 1986b; Lillo-Martin, Bellugi, Struxness, & O'Grady, 1985). The young deaf child, unlike his or her hearing counterpart, must acquire nonlanguage spatial capacities that serve as prerequisites to the linguistic use of space. We now investigate whether acquiring linguistic structures that are so intimately intertwined with elaborate spatial manipulation and representation affects the processing of nonlanguage spatial information.

The studies which we have been conducting suggest that, in fact, acquisition of a signed language may indeed have an impact on spatial-cognitive development. We investigate here the interplay between a spatial language and spatial cognition in young children. Is spatial representation conceptually difficult for the child and therefore a cognitively complex medium in which to signal linguistic functions? Or does the acquisition of the spatial linguistic devices of ASL result in greater nonlinguistic spatial abilities? We examine the interplay between development of spatial language and its spatial-cognitive substrate.

Spatial-Cognitive Development in Deaf and Hearing Children

We describe results of a series of studies of nonlanguage visuospatial processing which include spatial-cognitive functions which may underlie spatial syntax in ASL (spatial memory, spatial attention, as well as higher-order spatial transformations and spatial representations). The issues underlying the development of spatial cognition are so important to our studies that we organized a conference around this theme which has resulted in a book (Stiles-Davis, Kritchevsky, & Bellugi, 1988). Spatial cognitive tests were administered to deaf children who were learning ASL as a primary native language. Instructions were given in ASL by a deaf native signer. Responses to all tests were videotaped for later analysis. For tests described below, we used hearing norms, where they were available, to compare with the deaf children in these studies.

Deaf children ranging in age from 2 to 10 years old took part in these studies. All of the children tested had deaf parents and/or older deaf signing siblings and used ASL as a primary mode of communication. The same children took part in our studies of the processing of ASL linguistic structure, and in studies of the development of hand dominance in deaf signing children; thus we can make comparisons across domains (see Bellugi, 1988; Lillo-Martin, 1986b; Lillo-Martin et al., 1985; Petitto and Bellugi, 1988).

We present an analysis of the performance of deaf signing children on the following tasks: drawing; copying geometric shapes; spatial construction; spatial organization; facial discrimination under different spatial orientations; spatial analysis of dynamic displays. No single performance will be taken to indicate definitively whether or not there are differences between deaf signing children and hearing children for nonlanguage visuospatial processing. Rather, converging evidence from the array of tasks will provide the necessary test.

Drawing

We asked deaf signing children of different ages to copy drawings from a model. Each of the deaf children was asked to draw a daisy and a house (front and sides) based on a model from the Boston Diagnostic Aphasia Examination (Goodglass & Kaplan, 1983). Our previous research has shown that this test reliably taps the distinguishing characteristics of the two cerebral hemispheres (Poizner, Klima, & Bellugi, 1987). Figure 4 shows sample drawings of a flower and of a house done by young deaf children of deaf parents and illustrates the development of such visuospatial abilities in young signing children. The youngest children were quite unable to perform the task accurately, but by 4 years of age the children's drawings tended to resemble the target, with recognizable shapes and good

Fig. 4. Sample drawings of house and flower

spatial organization. By the age of 6 years, the children were able to incorporate depth and perspective information, and the overall configurations of the drawings — as well as the internal features — were quite accurately depicted.

Copying Geometric Shapes

In order to compare the performance of deaf and hearing children in a more structured task, we turn next to a widely used drawing task which is normed on young children, the Visual-Motor Integration Test. The Developmental Test of Visual-Motor Integration (VMI) is a test consisting of 24 geometric forms arranged in order from simple to complex (Beery, 1982). We administered a shortened version of the test (15 items). The child is asked to copy each form on paper. Forty-seven deaf, signing children took this task. The left side of Fig. 5 shows sample drawings from a model (three intersecting lines of differing orientations) from hearing and from deaf children. In our sample, the youngest children were unsuccessful at completing this task, as were the age-matched hearing children. The earliest successful performance on this task was at the age of 5;9, which corresponds to the age norm at which 50% of hearing children master this form. Note the strong similarities between typical responses at different ages by hearing and deaf children.

In general, the deaf children appear to be approximately on target in this task, neither early nor late in their ability to copy visuospatial geometric forms. These results are from a small sample of children; it appears that with a larger sample of children, we may find that the young deaf child may be more adept at this task than the hearing child.

Spatial Construction

We next turn to a task where the deaf children show suggestive advantage appears more clearly. The Block Design subtest of the Wechsler Intelligence Scale for Children (WISC-R. Wechsler, 1974) was administered to 20 deaf children of deaf parents. In this test, the child must assemble either four or nine three-dimensional blocks — whose surfaces are colored red, white, or half-red, half-white — to match a two-dimensional model of the top surface. Typical constructions made by the deaf children at different ages are shown immediately below the model. In Fig. 6 age-equivalent scores of deaf children are compared to those of hearing children. We see differences in performance between the deaf signing children and their hearing counterparts of the same age. Several deaf children's scores were, as Fig. 6 shows, greater than the mean of their hearing peers. The deaf children of deaf parents thus performed extremely well on this spatial construction task. On this test of spatial arrangement and spatial manipulation, a number of the deaf children show an advantage when compared with their hearing counterparts.

290

U. Bellugi et al.

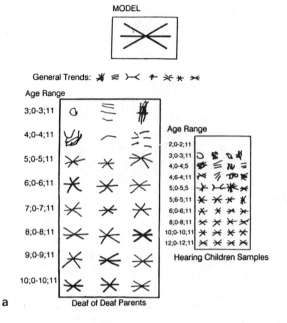

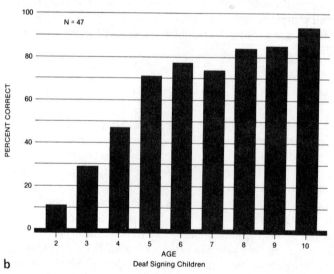

Fig. 5a,b. Sample item from Visual-Motor Integration Drawing test (**a**) and results of the test (**b**)

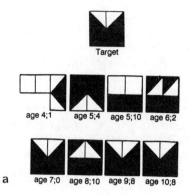

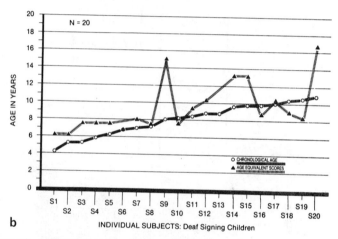

Fig. 6a,b. Spatial construction: WISC-R blocks. **a** Representative deaf signing children's block construction; **b** results; *solid line,* chronological age; *dotted line,* age-equivalent scores

Spatial Organization

The Hooper Visual Organization Test was used to assess perception of form and ability to perceive a whole from disorganized parts. This is a test in which line drawings of objects (which have been cut up into parts and rearranged on the paper) are presented. The child's task is to decide what the object is when the parts are rearranged, so that the correct naming may involve mentally reconstructing the whole out of its spatially separated parts (Hooper, 1980). The Hooper test contains 30 items, arranged in order of difficulty.

We gave the test to 39 deaf, signing children, all of whom had deaf parents or older deaf siblings. The test manual presents averages for junior high school students, not for younger children. These indicate that the junior high school group obtained mean scores of 85% correct. Based on these data, the authors derived a cut-off score of 20 to indicate normal level of functioning. Figure 7 shows the raw scores and percentage correct of deaf children, by ages, from 3 to 10 years. There is a very rapid increase from 32.7% at the 3-year-old level to almost 70% correct by the age of 4 years.

The scores show that the 4-year-olds were already doing rather well on the task. Sample items are given in the figure. One item illustrated involves reconstruction of a cane. A total of 95% of the children got the item correct, and the two incorrect answers were highly plausible ("hammer" and "wood"). Based on a cut-off score of 20, all of our subjects, except for the 3-year-olds, would be

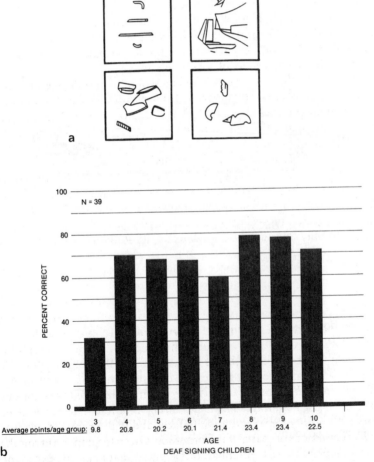

Fig. 7a,b. Spatial organization: Hopper test

considered unimpaired on this task. This test involves mental reorganization of parts to form an object percept, as well as recognition and naming of objects and may be relevant to the spatial underpinnings of sign language syntax.

Facial Discrimination Under Different Spatial Orientations

We now turn to a facial recognition test which we have used with brain-damaged deaf adults (Poizner et al., 1987). The test involves recognition of faces under varying conditions of lighting and changes in position and, thus, measures both facial recognition and spatial transformation. We used the Benton, Van Allen, Hamsher, and Levine (1978) Test of Facial Recognition which consists of three parts. The stimuli for all three parts are single, front-view photographs of a face. In the first section of the test, the child must identify the stimulus in a display of six front-view photographs appearing below it. In the second part, the child matches the front-view photograph to three of six three-quarter view photographs. In the third part, the child matches the stimulus to three of six front-view photographs taken under different lighting conditions. A single photograph must be located three times in a display of six photographs.

Figure 8 presents a sample item from the test and the results of testing with deaf children of deaf parents. There were 42 subjects ranging in age from 3 to 10 years (all were prelingually deaf and had deaf parents or older deaf siblings). As is evident from the figure, the deaf children were markedly in advance of the hearing children at all age levels on this task. Note that the norms for hearing children begin only at the age of 6 years, yet even at the age of 3, the deaf children were performing at the 6-year-old level. On this task, the deaf children consistently achieved higher scores than their hearing counterparts at each age level.

In ASL, a variety of specific facial signals have arisen as a part of the grammaticized apparatus co-occurring with manual signs and the structured use of space, thus adding additional "layers" to the grammatical structure of the language. Facial signals during signing function in two distinct ways: one is nonlinguistic (e.g., signals which convey emotion), and the other is specifically linguistic (e.g., the specialized facial markers in ASL for the functional equivalence of relative clauses, conditionals, topicalizations and the like; see Corina, 1987). We have been analyzing the acquisition of linguistic and non-linguistic facial markers in deaf signing children (Reilly, McIntire, & Bellugi, this volume). We are particularly interested in comparing deaf and hearing children on tasks relevant to the spatial cognitive prerequisites of sign language in order to examine the ways in which language and cognition may be intertwined or separated. In the nonlinguistic task of facial recognition presented here, the deaf children scored higher than age-matched hearing children. This suggests enhancement of the ability to pay attention to faces and to discriminate one from another under conditions of spatial transformation. Given the important role that facial expression plays in ASL grammar, this suggests that linguistic experience may impact on nonlinguistic cognitive development.

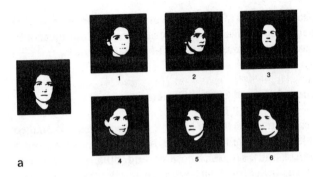

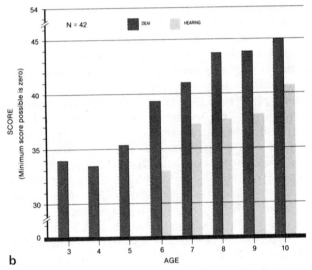

Fig. 8. a Facial discrimination under different spatial orientations, Benton Facial Recognition Test; **b** comparison of deaf signing children (*solid columns*) with hearing children (*screened columns*) on visuoperceptual task

Spatial Analysis of Dynamic Displays

We designed a special test of the ability of deaf children to decode, analyze, and remember movement in space which was carried out with deaf children in Hong Kong who are exposed both to a visuospatial primary language (Chinese Sign Language) and a visuospatial script (Chinese kanji or logographs). In separate studies, we have shown that deaf children just beginning to learn to write Chinese characters actively seek to discover the internal regularities underlying the architectural forms of the characters and make use of such regularities in creating new character forms (Fok and Bellugi, 1986). The forms invented by both hearing and deaf children alike are almost always perfectly acceptable character forms following all the implicit rules of character formation. Furthermore, the deaf children bring their own knowledge of sign language to the process of constructing characters. The evidence suggests that they actively seek to impose principles of sign construction borrowed from sign language and apply them to the written form of Chinese they are learning.

In a new experiment, we investigate the ability of deaf and hearing children who are just beginning to learn to read and write Chinese to analyze Chinese script through movement patterns in space (Fok and Bellugi, 1986). In order to capitalize on movement and to extract movement in a direct way, we use a technique which enables us to highlight movement patterns as dynamic patterns of light. We use a small light-emitting diode attached to the fingertip and record patterns of movement on videotape in a darkened room, so that the resultant display is a trace of a point-light as the finger moves in the process of writing Chinese characters (see Poizner, 1981; Poizner, Bellugi, & Lutes-Driscoll, 1981, for other uses of this technique). In this way, only the dynamic pattern of movement representing the character is shown on the videoscreen. We presented pseudocharacters written in the air as separate strokes, but on the videotape a continuous trace of motion is seen, a dynamic flow of movement as point-light

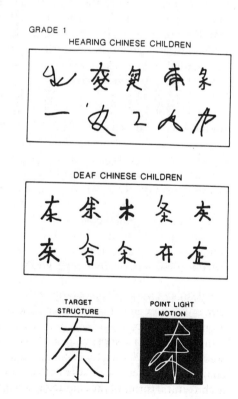

Fig. 9. Spatial analysis of dynamic displays
(Chinese pseudocharacters in lights)

display. The top portion of Fig. 9 presents a Chinese pseudocharacter as written (on the left), and the pattern of continuous moving light traced from the videoscreen (on the right). We asked deaf and hearing children in the first grade in Hong Kong schools — who were just beginning to read and write — to watch 60 such continuous movement patterns, and each time, write down the pseudo-character (involving discrete strokes) that was represented by the continuous flow of motion.

We were interested in whether or not deaf and hearing children might approach the task differently, and thus presented these moving point-light displays to very young children. The results were dramatic indeed. The lower portion of Fig. 9 presents the responses from hearing children and the responses from deaf children in the first grade, on the sample item. Recall that the children see a continuous path of movement in space as a point-light display and are asked to write down the discrete strokes that would represent the pseudocharacter as it was originally written. The experimenter commented that in general the hearing children found the task very difficult, but the deaf children appeared to find it easy, and the results strongly support a difference between the two groups. As the figure shows, the hearing children produced continuous lines, often simplified. The deaf children were significantly better than the hearing children in remembering, analyzing, and decoding the movement in space into its discrete components. They were able to distinguish between the movements representing strokes and the transitional movements, and to remember the sequence and spatial arrangements. It is evident that this task taps special abilities for spatial analysis of movement on the part of deaf children. Deaf children exposed to a visuospatial language appear to bring markedly enhanced spatial abilities to this task (Fok and Bellugi, 1986).

Spatial-Cognitive Enhancement in Deaf Children

We have presented here the results of deaf, signing children's performances on a selected battery of visuospatial tests measuring spatial construction, perception, and organization. The assessment of performance on these tests is theoretically important if we are to understand the effect of linguistic experience on the development of spatial cognition.

Emerging from this battery of spatial tests is a picture of deaf, signing children's spatial abilities which is comparable to that of hearing children and indeed; enhanced for some aspects of spatial cognition. Interesting is the finding that in several tests, young, deaf children below the age of 6 years appear particularly adept as compared to age-matched hearing children's norms. In some instances the deaf children are performing ahead of their age expectancies. This enhanced performance was particularly evident at the younger ages and then levelled off. In the facial recognition task, for example, the means for deaf children are consistently higher than for hearing children. The scores of the youngest children (between 3 and 5 years) are particularly noteworthy; these younger deaf children were scoring as high as hearing 6-year-olds. It thus appears that there may be an enhancement of spatial capacities in deaf signing children, particularly at younger ages.

Some of the tasks appear to tap abilities that are more sensitive to differences between groups than others. On the drawing tasks, the deaf children were neither behind nor ahead of hearing children but exactly on target. However, on processes of spatial construction, spatial orientation, and mental rotation, deaf children's scores appeared to differ from hearing children. In tasks such as facial recognition under different spatial orientations and spatial construction, we find that the deaf children may show a consistent advantage.

The difference between deaf and hearing children appears most strongly in the task of spatial analysis of dynamic displays, where the performances of deaf and hearing children are significantly different. Deaf children, even in the first grade, show a marked advantage in the ability to remember, attend to, and analyze such spatial displays which involve movement patterns. The deaf children's abilities at analyzing spatial displays of movement involved in writing characters is impressive. In order to focus on the effects of deafness and the acquisition of sign language (without considering the influence of knowledge of characters), we asked deaf and hearing Americans who had no experience with Chinese to perform the same task. The deaf subjects were all highly proficient signers who learned ASL as young children from deaf parents or older siblings. We found that there were differences between the hearing and deaf subjects on the task; again the deaf subjects were significantly better than the hearing at the spatial analysis of dynamic point-light displays. This task, then, taps consistent differences between deaf and hearing subjects and suggests that the enhancement of spatial abilities seen in deaf children may have a lasting effect into adulthood as well in certain spatial cognitive tasks.

The Separation Between Spatial Cognition and Spatial Language

In a separate series of studies, we are investigating the effects of unilateral lesions to the left and the right hemisphere in deaf signers. Since ASL displays the complex linguistic structure found in spoken languages but conveys much of its structure by manipulating spatial relations, it exhibits properties for which each of the hemispheres of hearing people show a different predominant function. The study of brain-damaged deaf signers offers a particularly revealing vantage point for understanding the organization of the brain for language and spatial cognitive functions in deaf signers (Poizner et al., 1987).

We found that on spatial tasks, there were clear-cut differences in performance between left hemisphere-damaged signers and right hemisphere-damaged signers across a range of tasks. In nonlanguage spatial tasks, the right hemisphere-damaged signers were severely impaired; they tended to show severe spatial disorganization, were unable to indicate perspective, and neglected the left side of space, reflecting the classic visuospatial impairments seen in hearing patients with right hemisphere-damage. These nonlanguage data suggest that the right hemisphere in deaf signers develops cerebral specialization for nonlanguage visuospatial functions. On linguistic tasks and in analyses of ongoing signing, the two groups of patients were also markedly different. The signers with right hemisphere damage were not aphasic. They exhibited fluent, grammatical, virtually error-free signing, with a good range of grammatical forms, no agrammatism, and no signing deficits. This preserved signing existed in the face of marked deficits in the processing of nonlanguage spatial relations. The signers with left hemisphere damage, in great contrast, were not impaired in nonlanguage visuospatial tasks, but were very impaired in language functions. They showed distinct sign aphasias; one left hemisphere-damaged signer even had impairment of spatially organized syntax. These data show that in deaf adult signers, it is the left hemisphere that is dominant for sign language, even though processing sign language involves processing spatial relations at all linguistic levels.

These results are consistent with the studies of Neville, using correlations between electrophysiological measures and behavior, showing that in a spatial attention task, deaf signing subjects are superior to hearing subjects (Neville, 1988). Perhaps, unexpectedly, the complex requirements for spatial processing in sign language may accelerate the development of particular visuospatial capacities.

Language and spatial representation are attributes for which the two cerebral hemispheres in hearing people show different specializations, and we have extended this finding to deaf signing adults as well. The use of the two hands in sign language may provide clues to hemispheric specialization that one cannot obtain from speech, since in sign language, the hands themselves are the language articulators. The development of hand dominance in very young deaf signers affords a unique opportunity for marking the onset of cerebral specialization. Indeed our preliminary studies suggest that hand dominance for sign language appears very early in some deaf children (perhaps as early as the first signs) and is much stronger than hand preference for nonlanguage activities in the same young children (Bellugi, Klima, Lillo-Martin, O'Grady, & Vaid, 1986; Vaid, Schemenauer, Bellugi, & Poizner, 1984). In these ways, then, the study of the acquisition process in sign language may provide additional clues to the biological foundations of language.

Conclusion

C.J. ERTING and V. VOLTERRA

A comparison of the chapters included in this volume leads us to conclude that there are the following points of agreement among the authors:

1. Both hearing and deaf children use gestures to communicate.
2. This stage of communicative development is an important step in the language acquisition process.
3. There is a progression and change in the use of these gestures over time so that we cannot speak of gestures as a whole.
4. Distinctions which should be made include:
   - Whether the gesture is used within or outside of a communicative situation.
   - The degree to which the gesture is detached from the context.
   - The relationship between the gesture and the input to which the child has been exposed.
   - The relationship between the child's gestural communication and the child's communication through other modalities.
   - The communicative function of the gesture.

There remain, however, numerous differences among the authors, as we have noted in the introductions to each section of this book. One of the most important and confusing of these relates to terminology. For example, some researchers label the earliest gestures the children produce "signs" while others label similar communicative behaviors "gestures" or "referential gestures." This problem is not simply a question of terms; it is essentially a theoretical issue. If a child production is labeled a "sign," the implication is that it is part of a linguistic system and, therefore, a symbolic act. But, if the production is labeled a "gesture," its symbolic status is unclear and must be specified, for example, as referential. In addition, the degree of decontextualization requires clarification. Often an author's choice of terms depends upon whether the child is hearing or deaf or upon the linguistic input to which the child is exposed. It appears to us that many of the apparent contradictions in the results of the studies reported here are a consequence of the lack of uniformity in the use of terms.

While terminological inconsistencies may obscure similarities as well as differences in research reports making it difficult to compare findings, terminology is not the only source of confusion. A lack of uniformity in the criteria applied to communicative productions of children when classifying them as linguistic or nonlinguistic is a major obstacle to comparability of results. In order to advance our understanding of the transition from gesture to language, researchers should adopt uniform criteria for deciding upon the status of a gestural production. These criteria should not be based on the hearing status of the child or on the communicative and linguistic environment to which the child has been exposed. Rather, the criteria should be based on the degree to which the gesture is detached from the context in which it is used.

This problem of determining the linguistic status of a communicative production is not restricted to the gestural modality. It also arises in the study of spoken communication. Vihman and Miller (1988) address this problem in a study designed to explore the relationship between babbling and early words. The criteria for coding a vocalization as a word are phonetic resemblance to an adult word and contextual appropriateness. But, as Snow (1988) points out, recent research demonstrates the relative independence of the child's developing phonological system from the early lexicon as a systematic communicative and symbolic system. There is a tendency to label any of the child's vocalizations that approximate adult forms as "words" without taking into account their symbolic status, the degree of decontextualization, and whether or not they appear within or outside of a communicative situation. If a comparison of the gesture to language transition of children acquiring a spoken language and children acquiring a sign language is to be fruitful, it is necessary to apply the same criteria to the children's vocal and manual productions in order to determine their communicative, symbolic, and linguistic status.

Recently, Volterra and Caselli (1985) proposed a terminological framework for the vocal and gestural modalities in an effort to facilitate comparison of studies of hearing children and studies of deaf children making the transition from gesture to language. Implicit in this labeling scheme, shown in Table 1, is the idea that the same criteria for determining the communicative, symbolic, and linguistic status of children's productions should be applied in both modalities.

Table 1. Terminological framework for vocal and gestural modalities. (From Volterra & Caselli, 1986)

Approximate age (months)	Child production	Terminology
0– 7	Motor/vocal behavior	SOUND MOVEMENT
7–12	Intentional communicative signals	VOCALIZATION GESTURE
12–16	Symbolic reference	WORD SIGN
16–20	Symbol combination	SPOKEN LANGUAGE SIGN LANGUAGE

According to this proposed terminological framework, motor behavior that is not communicative is labeled "movement" while vocal behavior in this category is labeled "sound." These kinds of behaviors are most in evidence from birth to approximately 7 months of age. From approximately 7 to 12 months, children produce a greater number of intentional communicative signals. In the gestural modality these productions are labeled "gestures" and in the vocal modality they are labeled "vocalizations." As these communicative signals become decontextualized, usually between the ages of 12 and 16 months, they are used by the child for symbolic reference. In the gestural modality, Volterra and Caselli use the term "sign" and in the vocal modality, the term "word." Finally, with the combination of two symbols, typically between the ages of 16 and 20 months, the children produce "sign language" or "spoken language."

Since the terms "vocalization," "gesture," "word," and "sign" are all terms that are commonly used in a variety of contexts and carry numerous connotations, perhaps a terminological system that seeks to use these same terms in a more specialized manner will not be readily accepted and may even add to the confusion. The point, however, is that more uniformity and greater specificity of meaning is needed in the literature if researchers are to improve communication with each other and make progress in the analysis and comparison of results. Perhaps a more descriptive terminological scheme, though more cumbersome, would present fewer obstacles for adoption. Table 2 shows such a descriptive terminology. In this scheme, the first productions of the infants are labeled "vocalizations" and "gestures." Intentional communicative signals are labeled "communicative vocalizations" and "communicative gestures." As the children's

Table 2. Descriptive terminological framework for vocal and gestural modalities

Approximate age (months)	Child production	Terminology
0– 7	Motor/vocal behavior	VOCALIZATION GESTURE
7–12	Intentional communicative signals	COMMUNICATIVE VOCALIZATION COMMUNICATIVE GESTURE
12–16	Symbolic reference	SYMBOLIC VOCALIZATION SYMBOLIC GESTURE
16–20	Symbol combination	SPOKEN LANGUAGE (WORD + WORD) SIGN LANGUAGE (SIGN + SIGN)

productions become more decontextualized, they are termed "symbolic vocalizations" and "symbolic gestures." Only during the linguistic stage, when two symbols are combined, are the terms "words" and "signs" applied. They are the individual symbolic components, vocal and gestural, respectively, of spoken language and sign language.

The point to be emphasized here is that criteria for determining the communicative, symbolic, and linguistic status of a child's productions should be made explicit and these criteria should drive the development of a terminological system. Furthermore, the same criteria should apply to the productions of both hearing and deaf children whether they have been exposed to spoken language, sign language, or both. Volterra (1987) proposed a set of criteria which would need to be satisfied for a communicative signal to be classified as symbolic. According to these criteria, it is not the signal's form, that is, whether or not it belongs to a codified system, that differentiates words from vocalizations and signs from gestures. Rather, it is the presymbolic or symbolic stage attained by the child and especially the degree of decontextualization evident in usage.

As for the linguistic status of the child's gestural or vocal communicative productions, two conditions must be satisfied: (a) the signals must be symbolic; and (b) they must be produced in combination with other symbols. Caselli and Volterra (this volume) argue that it is this specifically linguistic capacity in both modalities which seems to relate directly to the linguistic input to which the child is exposed. They argue that, when the vocal and gestural communicative productions of both deaf and hearing children are analyzed according to these criteria, the linguistic advantage for signing children reported by Schlesinger and Meadow (1972), McIntire (1977), Bonvillian, Orlansky, Novack, and Folven (1983), and others disappears. Instead, there is a similar timetable in the developmental stages of the speaking and the signing child. A comparison of the so-called first signs used by deaf children with first gestures of hearing children acquiring a spoken language reveal that their symbolic status is essentially the same: they are produced by infants only as imitative routines or in highly ritualized contexts. Truly symbolic communicative productions, that is first *signs* and first *words*, tend to appear at approximately the same time for hearing and deaf children, after having passed through a similar decontextualization process.

The crucial difference between hearing children exposed to a spoken language and deaf children exposed to a sign language appears during the stage of symbol combination. Prior to this stage, hearing children with a predominantly vocal input show the ability to use communicative symbols in both modalities. They even produce combinations of communicative signals: two or more pointing gestures, pointing gesture with a symbol (word or sign), and a word and a sign. They do not, however, combine two symbolic gestures but rather they move to the linguistic stage with the combination of two symbolic vocalizations, i.e., two words. The child exposed to sign language, on the other hand, demonstrates true linguistic capacity with the combination at this stage, of two symbolic gestures, i.e., two signs.

To summarize, *the fundamental stages of sign language and spoken language acquisition are the same.* In addition, *the timing of the achievement of milestones in sign language acquisition corresponds fairly well to the achievement of their counterparts in spoken language acquisition.* The evidence indicates that *iconicity does not have a facilitating effect on acquisition of sign language as a native language by infants.* As a consequence, many interpretations or explanations concerning acquisition of spoken languages must now be reconsidered. Children seem to pay particular attention to the actions or functions of objects which are products of these children's activities carried out by themselves or in their interaction with adults. They use actions as a kind of recognitory label for the object. For example, the action of bringing the telephone to the ear becomes a gesture that represents the telephone. It does not mean that the child exploits the iconicity of this gesture with respect to the telephone; the child simply uses an action frequently associated with the object to represent it in the same way that the word "hello," a word frequently associated with the telephone, might be used to label it. The first gestures or onomatopoeic words are adopted by children acquiring spoken languages not because of their iconicity but instead because they are the "simplest" labels associated with particular objects or events. "Simple" here means easier to reproduce with respect to the motor or vocal development of the children.

Our belief is that *the sign advantage observed in children exposed to a sign language does not reflect a true advantage in linguistic development.* Rather, a careful comparison of hearing and deaf children's communicative and linguistic development supports the view that there is a basic equipotentiality between the gestural and vocal channels, the final result depending on the modality in which the linguistic input is offered to the child.

We have attempted to put together a representative though not exhaustive collection of papers dealing with the gesture to language transition of deaf and hearing infants. One of our goals was to assess the state of our knowledge about this stage of language acquisition. Another goal was to demonstrate the relevance of the study of the deaf child's acquisition of language for language acquisition theory more generally. Finally, our purpose in bringing together different theoretical and methodological perspectives as well as work in a variety of cultures and languages was to confront ourselves and the reader with difficulties in the literature. We have identified these as a lack of uniformity of criteria for deciding upon the communicative, symbolic, and linguistic status of a child's production and a concomitant disparity in terminology adopted to categorize such behaviors. We suggest that it is time for a dialogue about these problems so that we can move toward consensus and meaningful comparison of data. In the meantime, greater explicitness regarding theoretical assumptions and terminological definitions as well as more detail and clarity in the presentation of data will contribute to progress in our understanding of this theoretically important and most fascinating period of language acquisition — the transition from gesture to language.

References

Abrahamsen, A., Brown-Williams, & McCarty, S. (1986). *The sign modality as a base for speech in Down syndrome toddlers.* Paper presented at the Theoretical Issues in Sign Language Research Conference, Rochester, NY.

Abrahamsen, A.A., Cavallo, M.M., & McCluer, J.A. (1985). Is the sign advantage a robust phenomenon? From gesture to language in two modalities. *Merrill Palmer Quarterly, 31,* 177–209.

Acredolo, L. & Goodwyn, S. (1985a). *Spontaneous signing in normal infants.* Paper presented at the biennial meeting of the Society for Research in Child Development, Toronto, Ontario.

Acredolo, L. & Goodwyn, S. (1985b). Symbolic gesturing in language development. A case study. *Human Development, 28,* 40–49.

Acredolo, L.P. & Goodwyn, S.W. (1988). Symbolic gesturing in normal infants: Cross-sectional and longitudinal evidence. *Child Development, 59* (2), 450–466.

Adamson, L.B. & Bakeman, R. (1982). Affectivity and reference. In T. Field & A. Fogel (Eds.), *Emotion and early interactions.* Hillsdale, NJ: Erlbaum.

Adamson, L.B. & Bakeman, R. (1984). Mothers' communicative acts: Changes during infancy. *Infant Behavior and Development, 7,* 467–478.

Adamson, L.B. & Bakeman, R. (1985). Affect and attention: Infants observed with mothers and peer. *Child Development, 56,* 582–593.

Attili, G. & Ricci-Bitti, P. (Eds.) (1983). *I gesti e i segni.* Roma: Bulzoni.

Bakeman, R. & Adamson, L.B. (1984). Coordinating attention to interaction. *Child Development, 55,* 1278–1289.

Bakeman, R. & Adamson, L.B. (1986). Infant's conventionalized acts: Gestures and words with mothers and peers. *Infant Behavior and Development, 7,* 215–230.

Bakeman, R. & Gottman, J.M. (1986). *Observing interaction: An introduction to sequential analysis.* New York: Cambridge University Press.

Baker, C. & Cokely, D. (1980). *American Sign Language: A teacher's resource text on grammar and culture.* Silver Spring, MD: T.J. Publishers.

Baker, C. & Padden, C. (1978). Focusing on the nonmanual components of American Sign Language. In.P. Siple (Ed.), *Understanding language through Sign Language Research.* New York: Academic.

Baker-Shenk, C. (1983). *A microanalysis of the non-manual components of questions in American Sign Language.* Unpublished doctoral dissertation, University of California, Berkeley.

Barten, S. (1977). Development of gesture. In N.R. Smith & M.B. Franklin (Eds.), *Symbolic functioning in childhood.* Hillsdale, NJ: Erlbaum.

Bates, E. (1976a). *Language and context.* New York: Academic.

Bates, E. (1976b). Pragmatics and sociolinguistics in child language. In D. Morehead & A. Morehead (Eds.), *Normal and deficient child language.* Baltimore, MD: University Park Press.

Bates, E. (1979). *The emergence of symbols: Cognition and communication in infancy.* New York: Academic.

Bates, E., Camaioni, L., & Volterra, V. (1975). The acquisition of performatives prior to speech. *Merrill Palmer Quarterly, 21,* 205–226.

Bates, E., Benigni, L., Bretherton, I., Camaioni, L., & Volterra, V. (1977). From gesture to first word: On cognitive and social prerequisites. In M. Lewis & L.A. Rosenblum (Eds.), *Interaction, conversation and the development of language.* New York: Wiley.

Bates, E., Benigni, L., Bretherton, I., Camaioni, L., & Volterra, V. (1979). *The emergence of symbols: Cognition and communication in infancy.* New York: Academic.

Bates, E., Bretherton, I., Snyder, L., Shore, C., & Volterra, V. (1980). Vocal and gestural symbols at 13 months. *Merrill Palmer Quarterly, 26*, 407–423.

Bates, E., Bretherton, I., Shore, C., & McNew, S. (1983). Names, gestures & objects: symbolization in infancy and aphasia. In K. Nelson (Ed.), *Children's language, Vol. 4.* Hillsdale, NJ: Erlbaum.

Battison, R. (1974). Phonological deletion in American Sign Language. *Sign Language Studies, 5,* 1–19.

Bauer, P. (1985). *Referential and expressive styles in linguistic and nonlinguistic domains: A longitudinal examination.* Unpublished doctoral dissertation. Miami University, Oxford, OH.

Beery, K.W. (1982). *Administration, scoring, and teaching manual for the developmental test of visual-motor integration.* Cleveland: Modern Curriculum.

Bellugi, U. (1980). The structuring of language: Clues from the similarities between signed and spoken language. In U. Bellugi & M. Studdert-Kennedy (Eds.), *Signed and spoken language: Biological constraints on linguistic form.* Weinheim: Verlag Chemie.

Bellugi, U. (1988). The acquisition of a spatial language. In F. Kessell (Ed.), *The development of language and language research: Essays in honor of Roger Brown.* Hillsdale, NJ: Erlbaum.

Bellugi, U. & Studdert-Kennedy, M. (Eds.) (1980). *Signed and spoken language: Biological constraints on linguistic form.* Wienheim: Verlag Chemie.

Bellugi, U. & Klima, E.S. (1982a). The acquisition of three morphological systems in American Sign Language. *Papers and Reports on Child Language Development, 21,* 1–35.

Bellugi, U. & Klima, E.S. (1982b). From gesture to sign: Deixis in a visual-gestural language. In R.J. Jarvella & W. Klein (Eds.), *Speech, place and action: Studies of language in context.* New York: Wiley.

Bellugi, U., Klima, E.S., Lillo-Martin, D., O'Grady, L., & Vaid, J. (1986). *Examining language dominance through hand dominance.* Paper presented at the 11th Annual Boston University Conference on Language Development.

Bellugi, U., Klima, E.S., & Poizner, H. (1988). Sign language and the brain. In F. Plum (Ed.), *Language, communication and the brain.* New York: Raven.

Benelli, B., D'Odorico, L., Levorato, M.C., & Simion, F. (1977). Formation and extension of a concept in a prelinguistic child. *Italian Journal of Psychology, 4,* (3), 429–448.

Benelli, B., D'Odorico, L., Levorato, M.C., & Simion, F. (1980). *Forme di conoscenza prelinguistica e linguistica.* Firenze: Giunti.

Benton, A.L., Van Allen, M.W., Hamsher, K., & Levine, H.S. (1978). *Test of facial recognition, form SL.* Iowa City, IA: University of Iowa, Benton Laboratory of Neuropsychology.

Berges, J. & Lezine, I. (1965). The imitation of gestures. *Clinics in developmental medicine, No. 18.* London: Heineman Medical.

Bergmann, R. (1983, July). *Sign language as mother tongue.* Paper presented at the Ninth Congress of the World Federation of the Deaf, Palermo, Sicily.

Berko-Gleason, J. (1973). Code switching in children's language. In T. Moore (Ed.), *Cognitive development and the acquisition of language.* New York: Academic.

Bertenthal, B.I. & Fischer, K.W. (1983). The development of representation in search. *Child Development, 54,* 846–857.

Birch, H.G. & Lefford, A. (1963). Intersensory development in children. *Monographs of the Society for Research in Child Development, 28.*

Birch, H.G. & Lefford, A. (1967). Visual differentiation, intersensory integration and voluntary motor control. *Monographs of the Society for Research in Child Development, 32* (2), 1–87.

Bloom, K. (1974). Eye contact as a setting event for infant learning. *Journal of Experimental Child Psychology, 17,* 250–263.

Bloom, L. (1970). *Language development: Form and function in emerging grammars.* Cambridge, MA: MIT Press.

Bloom, L. (1974). *One word at a time.* The Hague: Mouton.

Bloom, L. & Lahey, M. (1978). *Language development and language disorders.* New York: Wiley.

Bloom, L., Lightbown, P., & Hood, L. (1975). Structure and variation in child language. *Monographs of the Society for Research in Child Development, 40* (2, Serial No. 160).

Blount, B. (1982). Culture and the language of socialization: parental speech. In D. Wagner & H. Stevenson (Eds.), *Cultural perspectives on child development.* San Francisco: Freeman.

Bonvillian, J.D., Orlansky, M.D., & Novack, L.L. (1983). Developmental milestones: Sign language acquisition and motor development. *Child Development, 54,* 1435–1445.

Bonvillian, J.D., Orlansky, M.D., Novack, L.L., & Folven, R.J. (1983). Early sign language acquisition and cognitive development. In D.R. Rogers & J.A. Sloboda (Eds.), *The acquisition of symbolic skills.* New York: Plenum.

Boyes Braem, P. (1973). *The acquisition of the dez (handshape) in American Sign Language: A preliminary analysis.* Unpublished manuscript, Salk Working Papers, Salk Institute, San Diego, CA.

Boyes Braem, P. (1975). *The acquisition of handshape in ASL.* Salk Institute working paper, The Salk Institute, La Jolla, CA.

Braine, M.D.S. (1963). The ontogeny of English phrase structure in the first phase. *Language, 39,* 1–13.

Brazelton, T.B., Koslowski, B., & Main, M. (1974). The origins of reciprocity: the early mother-infant interaction. In M. Lewis & L. Rosemblum (Eds.), *The effect of the infant on its caregiver.* New York: Academic.

Brazelton, T.B., Tronick, E., Adamson, L., Als, H., & Weise, S. (1975). Early mother-infant reciprocity. In: *The parent-infant relationship.* New York CIBA, Elsevier, pp 137–154.

Brelje, H. (1971). *A study of the relationship between articulation and vocabulary.* Unpublished doctoral dissertation, University of Portland, Oregon.

Bretherton, I. (1988). How to do things with one word: The ontogenesis of intentional message making in infancy. In: M.D. Smith & J.L. Locke (Eds.), *The Emergent lexicon.* New York: Academic.

Bretherton, I. & Bates, E. (1984). The development from 10 to 28 months: Differential stability of language and symbolic play. In R.N. Emde & R.J. Harmon (Eds.), *Continuities and discontinuities in development.* New York: Plenum.

Bretherton, I., Bates, E., McNew, S., Shore, C., Williamson, C., & Beeghly-Smith, M. (1981). Comprehension and production of symbols in infancy: An experimental study. *Developmental Psychology, 17,* 728–736.

Bretherton, I., McNew, S., & Beeghly-Smith, M. (1981). Early person knowledge as expressed in gestural and verbal communication: When do infants acquire a 'theory of mind'? In M.E. Lamb & L.R. Sherrod (Eds.), *Infant social cognition: Empirical and theoretical considerations.* Hillsdale, NJ: Erlbaum.

Bridges, A. (1979). Directing two-year-olds' attention: Some clues to understanding. *Journal of Child Language, 6,* 211–226.

Brown, R. (1973). *A first language: The early stages.* Cambridge, MA: Harvard University Press.

Bruner, J.S. (1975a). From communication to language: A psychological perspective. *Cognition, 3,* 255–287.

Bruner, J.S. (1975b). The ontogenesis of speech acts. *Journal of Child Language, 2,* 1–19.

Bruner, J.S. (1978). Learning how to do things with words. In J.S. Bruner & A. Garton (Eds.), *Human growth and development,* Oxford: Oxford University Press.

Bruner, J.S. (1983a). *Child's talk.* New York: Norton.

Bruner, J.S. (1983b). *Learning to talk.* Oxford: Oxford University Press.

Bullowa, M. (1977). From performative act to performative utterance. An ethological perspective. *Sign Language Studies, 16,* 193–218.

Camaioni, L., Volterra, V., & Bates, E. (1976). *La comunicazione nel primo anno di vita.* Torino: Boringhieri.

Campos, J., Barrett, K.C., Lamb, M.E., Goldsmith, H.H. & Stenberg, C. (1983). Socioemotional development. In M. Haith & J. Campos (Eds.), *Handbook of child psychology: Vol. II. Infancy and development: Psychobiology.* New York: Wiley.

Carter, A.L. (1975a). The transformation of sensorimotor morphemes into words: A case study of the development of 'here' and 'there'. *Papers and Reports on Child Language Development. 11,* 31–48.

Carter, A.L. (1975b). The transformation of sensorimotor morphemes into words: A case study of the development of 'more' and 'mine'. *Journal of Child Language, 2,* 233–250.

Carter, A.L. (1975c). The transformation of sensorimotor morphemes into words. *Papers and Reports on Child Language Development, 10,* 31–47.

Carter, A.L. (1978). The development of systematic vocalizations prior to words: A case study. In N. Waterson & C. Snow (Eds.), *The development of communication.* New York: Wiley.

Carter, M. (1981). *The acquisition of British Sign Language (BSL: A first analysis)*. Unpublished manuscript.

Casby, M.W. & Ruder, K.F. (1983). Symbolic play and early language development in normal and mentally retarded children. *Journal of Speech and Hearing Research, 26*, 404–411.

Case, R. (1985). *Intellectual development: Birth to adulthood*. New York: Academic.

Case, R. & Khanna, F. (1981). The missing links: stages in children's progression from sensorimotor to logical thought. In K. Fischer (Ed.), *New Directions for child development: Vol. 12*. San Francisco: Jossey-Bass.

Caselli, M.C. (1983a). Communication to language: Deaf children's and hearing children's development compared. *Sign Language Studies, 39*, 113–143.

Caselli, M.C. (1983b). Gesti comunicativi e prime parole. *Età Evolutiva, 16*, 36–51.

Caselli, M.C., Ossella, T., & Volterra, V. (1983). Gesti, segni e parole a due anni. In G. Attili & P. Ricci-Bitti (Eds.), *I gesti e i segni*. Roma: Bulzoni.

Cattell, P. (1940). *The measurement of intelligence of infants and young children*. New York: Psychological Corporation

Chappell, P.F. & Sander, L.W. (1979). Mutual regulation of the neonatal-maternal interactive process: context for the origins of communication. In M. Bullowa (Ed.), *Before speech: The beginning of interpersonal communication*. New York: Cambridge University Press.

Charney, R. (1978). *The development of personal pronouns*. Unpublished doctoral dissertation, University of Chicago.

Charney, R. (1980). Speech roles and the development of personal pronouns. *Journal of Child Language, 7*, 509–528.

Chiat, S. (1981). Context-specificity and generalization in the acquisition of pronominal distinctions. *Journal of Child Language, 7*, 509–528.

Chiat, S. (1982). If I were you and you were me: The analysis of pronouns in a pronoun-reversing child. *Journal of Child Language, 9*, 359–379.

Church, R.B. & Goldin-Meadow, S. (1986). The mismatch between gesture and speech as an index of transitional knowledge. *Cognition, 23*, 43–71.

Cicourel, A. & Boese, R. (1972). The acquisition of manual sign language and generative semantics. *Semiotica, 7*, 225–256.

Clark, E.V. (1978). From gesture to word: On the natural history of deixis in language acquisition. In J.S. Bruner & A. Garton (Eds.), *Human growth and development*. Oxford: Oxford University Press.

Clark, R.A. (1978). The transition from action to gesture. In A. Lock (Ed.), *Action, gesture and symbol*. London: Academic.

Cohen, L.B. (1973). A two process model of infant visual attention. *Merrill Palmer Quarterly, 19*, 157–180.

Cohen, L.B. & Strauss, M.S. (1979). Concept acquisition in the human infant. *Child Development, 50*, 419–424.

Cohn, J. & Tronick, E.Z. (1987). Mother-infant face-to-face interaction: The sequence of dyadic states at 3, 6, and 9 months. *Developmental Psychology, 23*(1), 68–77.

Cole, M. & Bruner, J.S. (1972). Cultural differences and inferences about psychological processes. *American Psychologist, 26*, 867–876.

Connolly, K. & Jones, B. (1970). A developmental study of afferent and reafferent integration. *British Journal of Psychology, 61*, 259–266.

Conrad, R. (1979). *The deaf child*. London: Harper and Row.

Corina, D. (1987). *Recognition of affective and noncanonical linguistic facial expressions in hearing and deaf signers. Affective and linguistic expressions*. Unpublished manuscript, The Salk Institute, La Jolla, CA.

Cossette-Ricard, M. & Decarie, T.G. (1983). *Object identity in infants*. Paper presented at the Biennial Meeting of the Society for Research in Child Development, Detroit.

Coulter, G. (1979). *American Sign Language typology*. Unpublished doctoral dissertation, University of California, San Diego.

Coulter, G. (1980). Continuous representation in American Sign Language. In W.C. Stokoe (Ed.), *Proceedings of the First National Symposium on Sign Language Research and Teaching*. Silver Spring, MD: National Association of the Deaf.

308   References

Critchley, M. (1975). *Silent language*. London: Butterworth.
Cromer, R.F. (1974). The development of language and cognition: The cognition hypothesis. In B. Foss (Ed.), *New perspectives in child development*. Hardmondsworth, England: Penguin.
Curtiss, S. (1977). *Genie: a psycholinguistic study of a modern-day "wild child."* New York: Academic.
Curtiss, S., Prutting, C.A., & Lowell, E.L. (1979). Pragmatic-semantic development in young children with impaired hearing. *Journal of Speech and Hearing Research, 22,* 534–552.
DeLaguna, G.A. (1927). *Speech: Its function and development*. New Haven: Yale University Press.
De Lemos, C. (1981). Interactional processes and the child's construction of language. In W. Deutsch (Ed.), *The child's construction of language*. London: Academic.
De Lemos, C. (1982). La specularità come processo costitutivo del dialogo nella acquisizione del linguaggio. In L. Camaioni (Ed.), *La teoria di Jean Piaget*. Firenze: Giunti-Barbera.
DeMatteo, A. (1977). Visual imagery and visual analogues in American Sign Language. In L. Friedman (Ed.), *On the other hand: New perspectives on American Sign Language*. New York: Academic.
Di Stefano, G., D'Odorico, L., Gobbo, C., & Levorato, M.C. (1985). Influenze dello stile interattivo della madre sull'attività esplorativa del bambino. *Psicologia Clinica, 2,* 169–197.
D'Odorico, L. (1984). Non segmental features in prelinguistic communications: an analysis of some types of infant cry and non-cry vocalizations. *Journal of Child Language, 11,* 17–24.
Dore, J.A. (1974). A pragmatic description of early language development. *Journal of Psycholinguistic Research, 3,* 343–350.
Dore, J.A. (1985). Holophrases revisited: Their "logical" development from dialogue. In M.D. Barrett (Ed.), *Children's single-word speech*. New York: Wiley.
Dore, J., Gearhart, M.S., & Newman, D. (1978). The structure of nursery school conversation. In K. Nelson (Ed.), *Children's language, Vol. 1*. New York: Gardner.
Eckerman, C.O. & Stein, M.R. (1982). The toddler's emerging interactive skills. In K.H. Rubin & H.S. Ross (Eds.), *Peer relationships and social skills in childhood*. New York: Springer.
Efron, D. (1941). *Gesture and environment*. New York: Kings Crown Press. (Republished 1972 as *Gesture, race, and culture*. The Hague: Mouton).
Ekman, P. (1972). Universal and cultural differences in facial expressions of emotion. In J.K. Cole (Ed.), *Nebraska Symposium on Motivation 1971*. Lincoln, NE: University of Nebraska Press.
Ekman, P. & Friesen, W. (1969). The repertoire of non-verbal behavior: Categories, origins, usage and coding. *Semiotica, 1,* 49–98.
Ekman, P. & Friesen, W. (1972). Hand movement. *Journal of Communication, 22,* 353–374.
Ekman, P. & Friesen, W. (1978). *Facial action coding system*. Palo Alto, CA: Consulting Psychologists.
Elder, J. & Pederson, D. (1978). Preschool children's use of objects in symbolic play. *Child Development, 49,* 500–504.
Erting, C. (1981). An anthropological approach to the study of the communicative competence of deaf children. *Sign Language Studies, 32,* 221–238.
Ervin-Tripp, S. (1972). On sociolinguistic rules: Alternation and co-occurrence. In J.J. Gumperz & D. Hymes (Eds.), *Directions in sociolinguistics: The ethnography of communication*. New York: Holt, Rinehart and Winston.
Escalona, S. (1973, October). *On precursors of language*. Paper presented at Teacher's College, Columbia University, New York.
Ewing, A. & Ewing, E.C. (1964). *Teaching deaf children to talk*. Manchester: Manchester University Press.
Exline, R.V. & Fehr, B.J. (1982). The assessment of gaze and mutual gaze. In K.R. Scherer & P. Ekman (Eds.), *Handbook of methods in nonverbal behavior research*. Cambridge: Cambridge University Press.
Facchini, M., Guidicini, G., Volterra, V., Beronesi, S., & Massoni, P. (1981). Il bambino sordo nei primissimi anni di vita. *Età Evolutiva, 10,* 46–57.
Fagan, J.F. (1976). Infants' recognition of invariant features of faces. *Child Development, 47,* 627–638.
Fant, L.J. (1972). *Ameslan: An introduction to American Sign Language*. Silver Spring, Md: National Association of the Deaf.

Fantz, R.L. (1966). Pattern discrimination and selective attention as determinants of perceptual development from birth. In L. Kidd & G. Rivoire (Eds.), *Perceptual development in children*. New York: International University Press.

Fein, G.G. (1975). A transformational analysis of pretending. *Developmental Psychology, 11*, 291–296.

Feldman, H. (1975). *The development of a lexicon by deaf children of hearing parents, or There's more to language than meets the ear*. Unpublished doctoral dissertation, University of Pennsylvania, PA.

Feldman, H., Goldin-Meadow, S., & Gleitman, L. (1978). Beyond Herodotus: The creation of language by linguistically deprived deaf children. In A. Lock (Ed.), *Action, gesture and symbol*. London: Academic.

Fenson, L. & Ramsay, D. (1980). Decentration and integration of the child's play in the second year. *Child Development, 51*, 171–178.

Ferguson, C. (1977). Baby talk as a simplified register. In C. Snow & C. Ferguson (Eds.), *Talking to children*. New York: Cambridge University Press.

Ferguson, C. & Farwell, C. (1975). Words and sounds in early language acquisition. *Language, 51*, 419–439.

Fernald, A. (1987, April). *Form and function in mothers' speech to preverbal infants*. Paper presented at the Meeting of the Society for Research in Child Development, Baltimore, MD.

Field, T.M. & Fogel, A. (1982). *Emotion and early interaction*. Hillsdale, NJ: Erlbaum.

Field, T.M., Sostek, A.M., Vietze, P., & Leiderman, P.H. (1981). *Culture and early interactions*. Hillsdale, NJ: Lawrence Erlbaum.

Fillmore, C.J. (1968). The case for case. In E. Bach & R.T. Harms (Eds.), *Universals of linguistic theory*. New York: Holt, Rinehart and Winston.

Fischer, S. (1973). Two processes of reduplication in American Sign Language. *Foundations of Language, 9*, 469–480.

Fischer, S. (1975). Influences on word order change in ASL. In C. Li (Ed.), *Word order and word order change*. Austin: University of Texas Press.

Fleishman, E.A. & Rich, S. (1963). The role of kinesthetic and spatial-visual abilities in perceptual motor learning. *Journal of Experimental Psychology, 66*, 6–11.

Fleiss, G. (1973). *Statistical methods for rates and proportions*. New York: Wiley.

Flory, C.D. (1935). Osseous development in the hand as an index of skeletal development. *Monographs of the Society for Research in Child Development, 1*.

Fogel, A. (1981). The ontogeny of gestural communication: The first six months. In R.E. Stark (Ed.), *Language behavior in infancy and early childhood*. New York: Elsevier, North Holland.

Fok, Y.Y. & Bellugi, U. (1986). The acquisition of visuospatial script. In H. Kao (Ed.), *Graphonomics: Contemporary research in handwriting*. Amsterdam: North Holland.

Folven, R.J. & Bonvillian, J.D. (1987). *The onset of referential signing in children*. Paper presented at the Biennial Meeting of the Society for Research in Child Development, Baltimore, MD.

Folven, R.J. Bonvillian, J.D., & Orlansky, M.D. (1984/85). Communicative gestures and early sign language acquisition. *First Language, 5*, 129–144.

Freedle, R. & Lewis, M. (1977). Prelinguistic conversations. In M. Lewis & L. Rosenblum (Eds.), *Interaction, conversation, and the development of language*. New York: Wiley.

Freedman, N. & Grand, S. (1977). *Communicative structure and psychic structures: A psychoanalytic approach*. New York: Plenum.

Friedman, L.A. (1977). Formational properties of American Sign Language. In L.A. Friedman (Ed.), *On the other hand: New perspectives on American Sign Language*. New York: Academic.

Friedman, S. (1972). Habituation and recovery of visual response in the alert human newborn. *Journal of Experimental Child Psychology, 13*, 339–349.

Frishberg, N. (1975). Arbitrariness and iconicity: Historical change in American Sign Language. *Language, 51*, 696–719.

Furrow, D. & Nelson, K. (1986). A further look at the motherese hypothesis: A reply to Gleitman, Newport, & Gleitman. *Journal of Child Language, 13*, 163–176.

Gardner, J. & Zorfass, J. (1983). From sign to speech: the language development of a hearing-impaired child. *American Annals of the Deaf, 128*, 20–24.

Gerard, A. (1984). *Imitation and sequencing in early childhood*. Unpublished doctoral dissertation, University of California, San Diego.

Gesell, A. & Halverson, H.M. (1936). The development of thumb opposition in the human infant. *Journal of Genetic Psychology, 48,* 339-361.

Gesell, A. & Thompson, H., assisted by Amatruda C.S. (1934). *Infant behavior: Its genesis and growth.* New York: McGrawHill.

Gleitman, L., Newport, E., & Gleitman, H. (1984). The current status of the motherese hypothesis. *Journal of Child Language, 11,* 43-79.

Goldin-Meadow, S. (1975). *The representation of semantic relations in a manual language created by deaf children of hearing parents.* Unpublished doctoral dissertation, University of Pennsylvania, PA.

Goldin-Meadow, S. (1979). Structure in a manual communication system developed without a conventional language model: Language without a helping hand. In H. Whitaker & H. Whitaker (Eds.), *Studies in neurolinguistics, Vol. 4.* New York: Academic.

Goldin-Meadow, S. (1982). The resilience of recursion: A study of a communicative system developed without a conventional language model. In L.R. Gleitman & E. Wanner (Eds.), *Language acquisition: The state of the art.* New York: Cambridge University Press.

Goldin-Meadow, S. (1985). Language development under atypical learning conditions: Replication and implications of a study of deaf children of hearing parents. In K. Nelson (Ed.), *Children's language, Vol. 5.* Hillsdale, NJ: Erlbaum (Children's Language ser.).

Goldin-Meadow, S. (1986). Sentential redundancy in a language developed without a language model: The importance of conventional linguistic input. In B. Lust (Ed.), *Studies in the acquisition of anaphora, Vol. 1.* Dorolrecht: Reidel.

Goldin-Meadow, S. & Feldman, H. (1975). The creation of a communication system: A study of deaf children of hearing parents. *Sign Language Studies, 8,* 225-234.

Goldin-Meadow, S. & Feldman, H. (1977). The development of language-like communication without a language model. *Science, 197,* 401-403.

Goldin-Meadow, S. & Morford, M. (1985). Gesture in early child language: Studies of deaf and hearing children. *Merrill Palmer Quarterly, 31,* 145-176.

Goldin-Meadow, S. & Mylander, C. (1983). Gestural communication in deaf children: The non-effects of parental input on language development. *Science, 221,* 372-374.

Goldin-Meadow, S. & Mylander, C. (1984a). The development of morphology without a conventional language model. *Chicago Linguistic Society, 20.*

Goldin-Meadow, S. & Mylander, C. (1984b). Gestural communication in deaf children: The effects and non-effects of parental input on early language development. *Monographs of the Society for Research in Child Development,* (Serial No. 207), vol. 49, Nos. 3,4.

Goodglass, H. & Kaplan, E. (1983). *The assessment of aphasia and related disorders* (rev. ed.). Philadelphia: Lea and Febiger.

Gopnik, A. (1981). Development of non-nominal expressions in 1-2-year-olds. In P.S. Dale & D. Ingram (Eds.), *Child language. An international perspective.* Baltimore, MD: University Park Press.

Greenfield, P., Reilly, J., Leaper, C., & Baker, N. (1985). The transition from one- to two-word speech. In M. Barrett (Ed.), *Children's single word speech.* New York: Wiley.

Greenfield, P.M. & Smith, J.H. (1976). *The structure of communication in early language development.* New York: Academic.

Gregory, S. & Bishop, J. (1982). *The language development of deaf children during their first term at school.* Paper presented at the Child Language Seminar, Birkbeck College, London.

Gregory, S. & Mogford, K. (1981). The early language development of deaf children. In J. Kyle, B. Woll, & M. Deuchar (Eds.), *Perspectives on sign language and deafness.* Bristol: Croom Helm.

Griffiths, P. (1985). The communicative functions of children's single-word speech. In M.D. Barrett (Ed.), *Children's single-word speech.* New York: Wiley.

Gruber, J. (1973). Correlations between the syntactic constructions of the child and of the adult. In C. Ferguson & D. Slobin (Eds.), *Studies of child language development.* New York: Holt, Rinehart and Winston.

Gutmann, A.J. & Turnure, J.E. (1979). Mothers' production of hand gestures while communicating with their preschool children under various task conditions. *Developmental Psychology, 15*(2), 197-203.

Hainline, L. (1978). Developmental changes in visual scanning of face and non-face patterns by infants. *Journal of Experimental Child Psychology, 25,* 90–115.

Halliday, M.A.K. (1975). *Learning how to mean: Explorations in the development of language.* London: Arnold.

Halverson, H.M. (1933). The acquisition of skill in infancy. *Journal of Genetic Psychology. 42,* 3–48.

Halverson, H.M. (1937). Studies on the grasping response of early infancy. *Journal of Genetic Psychology, 51,* 393–424.

Halverson, H.M. (1940). Motor development. In A. Gesell (Ed.), *The first five years of life* (chap. 6). New York: Harper.

Harding, C.G. & Golinkoff, R.M. (1979). The origins of intentional vocalizations in prelinguistic infants. *Child Development, 50,* 33–40.

Harris, M., Jones, D., & Grant, J. (1983). The nonverbal context of mothers' speech to infants. *First Language, 4,* 21–30.

Harris, M., Jones, D., & Grant, J. (1984). The social-interactional context of maternal speech to infants: an explanation for the event-bound nature of early word use? *First Language, 5,* 89–100.

Harris, M., Clibbens, J., Tibbitts, R., & Chasin, J. (1987). *Communication between deaf mothers and their deaf infants.* Paper presented at the Child Language Seminar, York, England.

Hatch, E. (1978). *Second language acquisitions: A book of readings.* Rowley, MA: Newbury House.

Heath, S.B. (1983). *Ways with words: Language, life, and work in communities and classrooms.* Cambridge: Cambridge University Press.

Heider, F. & Heider, G.M. (1941). Studies in the psychology of the deaf, No. 2. *Psychological Monographs, 53,* 1–157.

Herscherson, M. (1964). Visual discrimination in the human newborn. *Journal of Comparative and Physiological Psychology, 85,* 270–276.

Hiatt, S., Campos, J., & Emde, R. (1979). Facial patterning and infant emotional expression: Happiness, surprise, and fear. *Child Development, 50,* 1020–1035.

Hittelman, J.H. & Dikes, R. (1979). Sex differences in neonatal eye contact time. *Merrill Palmer Quarterly, 25,* 170–184.

Hoffmeister, R.J. (1978a). *The development of the demonstrative pronouns, locatives and personal pronouns in the acquisition of American Sign Language by deaf children of deaf parents.* Unpublished doctoral dissertation, University of Minnesota, Minneapolis.

Hoffmeister, R.J. (1978b). *The development of pluralization in deaf children of deaf parents.* Unpublished manuscript, Temple University, School of Education, Philadelphia, PA.

Hoffmeister, R.J. & Moores, D. (1973). *The acquisition of specific reference in the linguistic system of a deaf child of deaf parents* (Research Rep. No. 53). University of Minnesota, Development, and Demonstration Center in Education of the Handicapped.

Hoffmeister, R.J. & Wilbur, R. (1980). Developmental: The acquisition of sign language. In H. Lane & F. Grosjean (Eds.), *Recent perspectives on American Sign Language.* Hillsdale, NJ: Erlbaum.

Holmes, K.M. & Holmes, D.W. (1980). Signed and spoken language development in a hearing child of hearing parents. *Sign Language Studies, 28,* 239–254.

Hooper, H.E. (1980). *The Hooper visual organization test.* Los Angeles: Western Psychological Services.

Huxley, R. (1970). The development of the correct use of subject person pronouns in two children. In G.B. Flores D'Arcais & W.J.M. Levelt (Eds.), *Advances in psycholinguistics.* Amsterdam: North Holland.

Illingworth, R.S. (1966). *The development of the infant and young child.* Edinburgh: Churchill Livingstone.

Ingram, D. (1971). Toward a theory of person deixis. *Papers in Linguistics, 4,* 37–54.

Ingram, D. (1981). The transition from early symbols to syntax. In R. Schiefelbush & D.D. Bricker (Eds.), *Early language: Acquisition and intervention.* Baltimore: University Park Press.

Izard, C.R. (1971). *The face of emotion.* New York: Appleton-Century-Crofts.

Jackowitz, E.R. & Watson, M. (1980). Development of object transformations in early pretend play. *Developmental Psychology, 16,* 543–549.

Jaffe, J., Stern, D., & Peery, C. (1973). "Conversational" coupling of gaze behavior in prelinguistic human development. *Journal of Psycholinguistic Research, 2,* 321–329.

312   References

Jakobson, R. (1957). Shifters, verbal categories and the Russian verb. Cambridge, MA: Harvard University, Department of Slavic Languages and Literatures, Russian Language Project.

Jakobson, R. (1969). *The paths from infancy to language*. Heinz Werner Lectures. Worcester, MA: Clark University.

James, W. (1890). *The principles of psychology* (Vols. 1–2). New York: Holt.

Jespersen, O. (1924). *The philosophy of grammar*. New York: Norton.

Jones, C.P. & Adamson, L.B. (1987). Language use in mother-child and mother-child-sibling interactions. *Child Development, 58,* 356–366.

Jones, F.D. (1942). *The principles of anatomy as seen in the hand.* Baltimore: Williams and Wilkins.

Jones, M. & Quigley, S. (1979). The acquisition of question formation in spoken English and ASL by two hearing children of deaf parents. *Journal of Speech and Hearing Disorders, 44,* 196–208.

Kachru, B. (1978). Code-mixing as a communicative strategy in India. In A. Gurt (Ed.), *International dimensions of bilingual education*. Washington: Georgetown University Press.

Kagan, J. (1981). *The second year.* Cambridge, MA: Harvard University Press.

Kantor, R. (1980). The acquisition of classifiers in American Sign Language. *Sign Language Studies, 28,* 193–208.

Kantor, R. (1982a). *Communicative interaction in American Sign Language between deaf mothers and their children: A psycholinguistic analysis.* Unpublished doctoral dissertation, Boston University.

Kantor, R. (1982b). Communicative interaction: mother modification and child acquisition of American Sign Language. *Sign Language Studies, 36,* 233–282.

Kato, M. (1986). *No mundo da escrita.* Sao Paulo: Atica.

Kaye, K. (1982). *The mental and social life of babies.* Chicago: Chicago University Press.

Kegl, J.A. (1977). *ASL syntax: Research in progress and proposed research.* Unpublished manuscript, Massachusetts Institute of Technology, Cambridge, MA.

Kegl, J.A. & Wilbur, R. (1976). Where does structure stop and style begin? Syntax morphology, and phonology vs. stylistic variations in American Sign Language. *Chicago Linguistic Society, 12,* 376–396.

Kendon, A. (1980a). Gesticulation and speech. Two aspects of the process of utterance. In M. Key (Ed.), *The relationship of verbal and non-verbal communication*. The Hague: Mouton.

Kendon, A. (1980b). The sign language of the women of Yuendumu: A preliminary report of the structure of Warlpiri Sign Language. *Sign Language Studies, 27,* 101–112.

Kendon, A. (1980c). *Some uses of gesture.* Paper delivered to the New England Child Language Association, New London, CT.

Kinsbourne, M. & Warrington, E.K. (1963). The development of finger differentiation. *Quarterly Journal of Experimental Psychology, 15,* 132–137.

Klima, E. & Bellugi, U. (1979). *The signs of language.* Cambridge, MA: Harvard University Press.

Kozak Mayer, N. & Tronick, E.Z. (1985). Mothers' turn-giving signals and infant turn-taking in mother-infant interaction. In T. Field & N. Fox (Eds.), *Social perception in infants.* Norwood, NJ: Ablex.

Kricos, P.B. & Aungst, H.L. (1984). Cognitive and communicative development in hearing-impaired preschool children. *Sign Language Studies, 43,* 121–140.

Kuschel, R. (1973). The silent inventor: the creation of a sign language by the only deaf mute on a Polynesian island. *Sign Language Studies, 3,* 1–27.

Kyle J., & Ackerman, J. (1987). *Signing for infants: Deaf mothers using BSL in the early stages of development.* Unpublished manuscript, University of Bristol, Education Research Unit, Bristol, England.

Lack, R., Ling, D., Ling, A., & Ship, N. (1970). Early speech development in deaf infants. *American Annals of the Deaf, 115,* 522–526.

Laing, R. (1970). *Knots.* London: Tavistock.

Lane, H., Boyes-Braem, P., & Bellugi, U. (1976). Preliminaries to a distinctive feature analysis of handshapes in American Sign Language. *Cognitive Psychology, 8,* 263–289.

Launer, P. (1982a). *"A plane" is not "to fly": Acquiring the distinction between related nouns and verbs in American Sign Language.* Unpublished doctoral dissertation, City University of New York.

Launer, P. (1982b). *Early signs of motherhood: Motherese in American Sign Language.* Paper presented at the Meeting of the American Speech-Language-Hearing Association, Toronto, Canada.

Lempers, J.D. (1979). Young children's production and comprehension of nonverbal deictic behaviors. *Journal of Genetic Psychology, 135,* 93-102.

Lempers, J.D., Flavell, E.R., & Flavell, J.H. (1977). The development in very young children of tacit knowledge concerning visual perception. *Genetic Psychology Monographs, 95,* 3-53.

Lenneberg, E.H. (1964). The capacity for language acquisition. In J.A. Fodor & J.J. Katz (Eds.), *The structure of language: Readings in the philosophy of language.* Englewood Cliffs, NJ: Prentice Hall.

Lenneberg, E.H. (1967). *Biological foundations of language.* New York: Wiley.

Lenneberg, E.H., Rebelsky, F.G., & Nichols, I.A. (1965). The vocalizations of infants born to deaf and to hearing parents. *Human Development, 8,* 23-37.

Leopold, W.F. (1939-1949). *Speech development of a bilingual child* (4 Vols.). Evanston, IL: Northwestern University Press.

Leung, E.H.L. & Rheingold, H.L. (1981). Development of pointing as a social gesture. *Developmental Psychology, 17,* 215-220.

Lewis, M. & Michalson, L. (1983). *Children's emotions and moods: Developmental theory and measurement.* New York: Plenum.

Liddell, S. (1977). An investigation into the syntactic structure of American Sign Language. Unpublished doctoral dissertation, University of California, San Diego.

Liddell, S. (1980). *American Sign Language syntax.* The Hague: Mouton.

Lillo-Martin, D. (1985a). Null pronouns and verb agreement in American Sign Language. In S. Berman, J.W. Choe, & J. McDonough (Eds.), *Proceedings of the North Eastern Linguistic Society, 15.* Amherst: GLSA.

Lillo-Martin, D. (1985b). *Two kinds of null arguments in American Sign Language.* Working paper, The Salk Institute, La Jolla, CA.

Lillo-Martin, D. (1986a). Effects of the acquisition of morphology on syntactic parameter setting. In S. Berman, J.W. Choe, and J. McDonough (Eds.), *Proceedings of the North Eastern Linguistic Society, 16.* Amherst: GLSA.

Lillo-Martin, D. (1986b). *Parameter setting: Evidence from use, acquisition, and breakdown in American Sign Language.* Unpublished doctoral dissertation, University of California, San Diego.

Lillo-Martin, D. (1988). Children's new sign creations. In M. Strong (Ed.), *Language learning and deafness.* Cambridge: Cambridge University Press.

Lillo-Martin, D. & Klima, E. (in press). *Pointing out differences: ASL pronouns in syntactic theory.* In: P. Siple (Ed.), *Theoretical issues in sign language research.* Berlin, Heidelberg, New York: Springer.

Lillo-Martin, D., Bellugi, U., Struxness, L., & O'Grady, M. (1985). The acquisition of spatially organized syntax. *Papers and Reports on Child Language Development, 24,* 70-78.

Lock, A.J. (1978). *Action, gesture and symbols.* New York: Academic.

Lock, A.J. (1980). *The guided reinvention of language.* London: Academic.

Locke, J.L. (1983). *Phonological acquisition and change.* New York: Academic.

Loew, R. (1981). Learning sign language as a first language: Roles and reference. In F. Caccamise, M. Garretson, & U. Bellugi (Eds.), *Proceedings of the Third National Symposium on Sign Language Research and Teaching.* Silver Spring, MD: National Association of the Deaf.

Loew, R.C. (1983). *Roles and reference in American Sign Language: A developmental perspective.* Unpublished doctoral dissertation, University of Minnesota, MN.

Lombardino, L.J. & Sproul, C.J. (1984). Patterns of correspondence and non-correspondence between play and language in developmentally delayed preschoolers. *Education and Training of the Mentally Retarded, 19,* 5-14.

Lyons, J. (1968). *Introduction to theoretical linguistics.* Cambridge: Cambridge University Press.

Macnamara, J. (1977). From sign to language. In J. Macnamara (Ed.), *Language learning and thought.* New York: Academic.

Macnamara, J. (1982). *Names for things.* Cambridge, MA: Bradford.

MacWhinney, B. (1976). Hungarian research on the acquisition of morphology and syntax. *Journal of Child Language, 3,* 397-410.

MacWhinney, B. (1978). The acquisition of morphophonology. *Monographs of the Society for Research in Child Development, 43,* Nos. 1-2 (Serial No. 174).

Maestas y Moores, J. (1980). Early linguistic environment: Interactions of deaf parents with their infants. *Sign Language Studies, 26,* 1-13.

Mandel, M. (1977). Iconic devices in American Sign Language. In L. Friedman (Ed.), *On the other hand: New perspectives on American Sign Language.* New York: Academic.

Maratsos, M. (1973). Nonegocentric communicative abilities in preschool children. *Child Development, 44,* 697–700.

Marlborough, C. (1986). *The interaction of deaf mother/infant dyads: A unique linguistic environment.* Unpublished manuscript, Gallaudet University, Culture and Communication Studies Program, Washington, DC.

Marslen-Wilson, W., Levy, E., & Tyler, L.K. (1982). Producing interpretable discourse: The establishment and maintenance of reference. In R.J. Jarvella & W. Klein (Eds.), *Speech, place and action: Studies in deixis and related topics.* Chichester: Wiley.

Maskarinec, A.S., Cairns, G.F., Butterfield, E.C., & Weamer, D.K. (1981). Longitudinal observations of individual infants' vocalizations. *Journal of Speech and Hearing Disorders, 22,* 267–273.

Masur, E.F. (1980). The development of communicative gestures in mother-infant interactions. *Papers and Reports on Child Language Development, 19,* 121–128.

Masur, E.F. (1982). Mothers' responses to infants' object-related gestures: Influences on lexical development. *Journal of Child Language, 9,* 23–30.

Masur, E.F. (1983). Gestural development, dual-directional signaling, and the transition to words. *Journal of Psycholinguistic Research, 12,* 93–109.

Mayberry, R. (1976). An assessment of some oral and manual language skills of hearing children of deaf parents. *American Annals of the Deaf, 121,* 507–512.

McCall, R., Parke, E., & Kavanaugh, R. (1977). Imitation of live and televised models by children one to three years of age. *Monographs of the Society for Research in Child Development, 42*(5, Serial No. 173).

McClure, E. (1977). Aspects of code-switching in the discourse of bilingual Mexican-American children. In M. Saville-Troike (Ed.), *Linguistics and anthropology.* Washington: Georgetown University Press.

McCune-Nicolich, L. (1981). Toward symbolic functioning: Structure of early pretend games and potential parallels with language. *Child Development, 52,* 785–797.

McCune-Nicolich, L. & Bruskin, C. (1982). Combinatorial competency in play and language. In K. Rubin & D.J. Pepler (Eds.), *The play of children: Current theory and research.* New York: Karger.

McDonald, B. (1982). *Aspects of the American Sign Language predicate system.* Unpublished doctoral dissertation, University of Buffalo, NY.

McIntire, M.L. (1977). The acquisition of American Sign Language hand configurations. *Sign Language Studies, 16,* 247–266.

McIntire, M.L. & Reilly, J. (1988). *Nonmanual behaviors in L₁ and L₂ learners of American Sign Language. Sign Language Studies, 61,* 351–375.

McNeill, D. (1985). So you think gestures are nonverbal? *Psychological Review, 92,* 350–371.

McNeill, D. & Levy, E. (1982). Conceptual representations in language activity and gesture. In R.J. Jarvella & W. Klein (Eds.), *Speech, place, and action: Studies in deixis and related topics.* Chichester: Wiley.

McShane, J. (1979). The development of naming. *Linguistics, 17,* 879–905.

Mead, G.H. (1934). *Mind, self and society.* Chicago: University of Chicago Press.

Meadow, K. (1972). Sociolinguistics, sign language, and the deaf sub-culture. In T. O'Rourke (Ed.), *Psycholinguistics and total communication: The state of the art.* Silver Spring, MD: American Annals of the Deaf.

Meadow-Orlans, K., MacTurk, R., Prezioso, C., Erting, C., & Day, P. (1987). *Interactions of deaf and hearing mothers with three- and six-months-old infants.* Paper presented at the Meeting of the Society for Research in Child Development, Baltimore, MD.

Meier, R. (1981). Icons and morphemes: Models of the acquisition of verb agreement in ASL. *Papers and Reports on Child Language Development, 20,* 92–99.

Meier, R. (1982). Icons, analogues, and morphemes: The acquisition of verb agreement in American Sign Language. Unpublished doctoral dissertation, University of California, San Diego.

Meissner, M. & Philpott, S.B. (1975). The sign language of sawmill workers in British Columbia. *Sign Language Studies, 9,* 291–308.

Menig-Peterson, C. (1975). The modification of communicative behavior in preschool aged children. *Child Development, 46,* 1015–1018.

Millar, S. (1964). Visual and haptic cue utilization by preschool children: the recognition of visual and haptic stimuli presented separately and together. *Journal of Experimental Child Psychology, 12,* 88–94.

Mohay, H. (1982). A preliminary description of the communication systems evolved by two deaf children in the absence of a sign language model. *Sign Language Studies, 34,* 73–90.

Mohay, H. (1983). The effects of cued speech on the language development of three deaf children. *Sign Language Studies, 38,* 25–50.

Mohay, H. (1984). The relationship between the development of spoken and gestural communication in two profoundly deaf children. *Journal of the British Association of Teachers of the Deaf, 8,* (2), 35–47.

Mohay, H. (1986). *The development of spoken and gestural communication in young hearing-impaired children of hearing parents.* Unpublished doctoral dissertation, University of Queensland.

Moore, M.K. & Meltzoff, A.N. (1978). Object permanence, imitation, and language development in infancy: Toward a neo-Piagetian perspective on communicative and cognitive development. In F.D. Minifie & L.L. Lloyd (Eds.), *Communicative and cognitive abilities early behavioral assessment.* Baltimore: University Park Press.

Moores, D.F. (1974). Nonvocal systems of verbal behavior. In R.L. Schiefelbusch & L.L. Lloyd (Eds.), *Language perspectives: Acquisition, retardation, and intervention.* Baltimore: University Park Press.

Moores, D.F. (1979). *Educating the deaf: Psychology, principles and practices.* Boston: Houghton Mifflin.

Morkovin, B.U. (1960). An experiment in teaching deaf preschool children in the Soviet Union. *Volta Review, 62,* 260–265.

Murphy, C.M. (1978). Pointing in the context of a shared activity. *Child Development, 49,* 371–380.

Murphy, C.M. & Messer, D.J. (1977). Mothers, infants, and pointing: A study of gesture. In H.R. Schaffer (Ed.), *Studies in mother-infant interaction.* London: Academic.

Murray, L. & Trevarthen, C. (1985). Emotional regulation of interactions between two-month-olds and their mothers. In T. Field & N. Fox (Eds.), *Social perception in infants.* Norwood, NJ: Ablex.

Nelson, K. (1973). Structure and strategy in learning to talk. *Monographs of the Society for Research in Child Development, 38* (1–2, Serial No. 149).

Nelson, K. (1974). Concept, word and sentence: Interrelations in acquisition and development. *Psychological Review, 81,* 267–285.

Nelson, K. (1979). The role of language in infant development. In M. Bornstein & W. Kenne (Eds.), *Psychological development from infancy: Image to intention.* Hillsdale, NJ: Erlbaum.

Nelson, K. (1981). Individual differences in language development: Implications for development and language. *Developmental Psychology, 16,* 170–187.

Nelson, K. & Lucariello, J. (1985). The development of meaning in first words. In M.D. Barrett (Ed.), *Children's single-word speech.* New York: Wiley.

Neville, H.J. (1985). Effects of early sensory and language experience on the development of the human brain. In J. Mehler & R. Fox (Eds.), *Neonate cognition: Beyond the blooming, buzzing confusion.* Hillsdale, NJ: Erlbaum.

Neville, H.J. (1988). Cerebral organization for attention. In J. Stiles-Davis, M. Kritchevsky, & U. Bellugi (Eds.), *Spatial cognition: Brain bases and development.* Chicago, IL: University of Chicago.

Neville, H.J., Schmidt, A., & Kutas, M. (1983). Altered visual evoked potentials in congenitally deaf adults. *Brain Research, 266,* 127–132.

Newport, E.L. (1981). Constraints on structure: Evidence from American Sign Language and language learning. In W.A. Collins (Ed.), *Minnesota symposium of child psychology, Vol. 14.* Hillsdale, NJ: Erlbaum.

Newport, E.L. (1982). Task-specificity in language learning? Evidence from speech perception and American Sign Language. In E. Wanner & L.R. Gleitman (Eds.), *Language acquisition: The state of the art.* New York: Cambridge University Press.

Newport, E. (1984). Some constraints on learning. *Papers and Reports on Child Language Development, 23,* 1–9.

Newport, E. & Ashbrook, E. (1977). The emergence of semantic relations in American Sign Language. *Papers and Reports on Child Development., 13,* 16–21.

Newport, E. & Meier, R. (1985). Acquisition of American Sign Language. In D.I. Slobin (Ed.), *The crosslinguistic study of language acquisition*. Hillsdale, NJ: Erlbaum.

Newport, E. & Supalla, T. (1980). Clues from the acquisition of signed and spoken language. In U. Bellugi & M. Studdert-Kennedy (Eds.), *Signed and spoken Language. Biological constraints on linguistic-form*. Weinheim: Verlag Chemie.

Newson, J. (1978). Dialogue and development. In A. Lock (Ed.), *Action, gesture and symbol*. London: Academic.

Newson, J. & Newson, E. (1975). Intersubjectivity and the transmission of culture. *Bulletin of the British Psychological Society, 28*, 437–445.

Nicolich, L. (1975). *A longitudinal study of representational play in relation to spontaneous imitation and development of multiword utterances*. (ERIC Document No. PS007 854)

Nicolich, L. (1977). Beyond sensorimotor intelligence: Assessment of symbolic maturity through analysis of pretend play. *Merrill Palmer Quarterly, 23*, 89–99.

Nienhuys, T.G., Horsborough, K.M., & Cross T.G. (1985). A dialogic analysis of interaction between mothers and their deaf or hearing preschoolers. *Applied Psycholinguistics, 6*, 121–139.

Ninio, A. & Bruner, J. (1978). The achievement and antecedents of labeling. *Journal of Child Language, 5*, 1–15.

Nokony, A. (1978). Word and gesture usage by an Indian child. In A. Lock (Ed.), *Action, gesture and symbol: the emergence of language*. London: Academic.

Ochs, E. (1982). Talking to children in Western Samoa. *Language in Society, 11*, 77–104.

Ochs, E. & Schieffelin, B. (1984). Language acquisition and socialization: Three developmental stories and their implications. In R. Shweder & R. LeVine (Eds.), *Culture theory: Essays on mind, self, and emotion*. New York: Cambridge University Press.

O'Connell, B. (1984). *The development of sequential understanding revisited: The role of meaning and familiarity*. Unpublished doctoral dissertation, University of California, San Diego.

O'Connell, B. & Gerard, A. (1985). Scripts and scraps: the development of sequential understanding. *Child Development, 56*, 671–681.

O'Grady, L., Bellugi, U., O'Grady, M., Corina, D., & Lillo-Martin, D. (1986). *The link between hand and brain*. Unpublished manuscript, The Salk Institute, La Jolla, CA.

Orlansky, M.D. & Bonvillian, J.D. (1985). Sign language acquisition: Language development in children of deaf parents and implications for other populations. *Merrill Palmer Quarterly, 31*, 127–143.

Padden, C. (1981). Some arguments for syntactic patterning in American Sign Language. *Sign Language Studies, 32*, 237–259.

Padden, C. (1983). *Interaction of morphology and syntax in American Sign Language*. Unpublished doctoral dissertation, University of California, San Diego.

Papousek, M. (1987, April). *Models and messages in the maternal speech in tonal and nontonal languages*. Paper presented at the Meeting of the Society for Research in Child Development, Baltimore, MD.

Papousek, H. & Papousek, M. (1987). Intuitive pareting: A didactic counterpart to the infant's integrative competence. In J.D. Osofsky (Ed.), *Handbook of infant development* (2nd ed., pp. 669–720). New York: Wiley.

Papousek, M., Papousek, H., & Haekel, M. (1987). Didactic adjustments in fathers' and mothers' speech to their 3-months-old infants. *Journal of Psycholinguistic Research, 16* (5), 491–516.

Peery, J.C. & Stern, D.N. (1975). Mother-infant gazing during play, bottle-feeding and spoon feeding. *The Journal of Psychology, 91*, 207–213.

Penman, R., Cross, T., Milgrom-Friedman, J., & Meares, R. (1983). Mothers' speech to prelingual infants: a pragmatic analysis. *Journal of Child Language, 10*, 17–34.

Pereira, C. (1985). An interactional approach in the study of gestural communication in hearing-impaired children. In W. Stokoe & V. Volterra (Eds.), *Sign language research '83*. Silver Spring: Linstok; Rome: Psychology Institute, National Research Council.

Perez, B. (1911). Les trois premieres années de l'enfant. Paris: Alcan.

Peters, A.M. (1983). *The units of language acquisition*. New York: Cambridge University Press.

Petitto, L.A. (1977). *The acquisition of pronominal reference in ASL: Report on research in progress*. Working paper, The Salk Institute, La Jolla, CA.

Petitto, L.A. (1980). *Some preliminary observations of prelinguistic communicative behaviors in one deaf child.* Working paper, The Salk Institute, La Jolla, CA.

Petitto, L.A. (1981). *On the acquisition of anaphoric reference in American Sign Language.* Working paper, The Salk Institute, La Jolla, CA.

Petitto, L.A. (1983a). From gesture to symbol: The acquisition of personal pronouns in American Sign Language. *Papers and Reports on Child Language Development, 22,* 100-107.

Petitto, L.A. (1983b). *From gesture to symbol: The relationship between form and meaning in the acquisition of personal pronouns in American Sign Language.* Unpublished doctoral dissertation, Harvard University.

Petitto, L.A. (1986). *Language versus gesture: Why sign language are not acquired earlier than spoken languages.* Paper presented at the Theoretical Issues in Sign Language Research Conference, Rochester, NY.

Petitto, L.A. (1988). "Language" in the pre-linguistic child. In F. Kessel (Ed.), *The development of language and language research: Essays in honor of Roger Brown.* Hillsdale, NJ: Erlbaum, pp 187-221.

Petitto, L.A. & Bellugi, U. (1988). Spatial cognition and brain organization: Clues from the acquisition of a language in space. In J. Stiles-Davis, M. Kritchevsky, & U. Bellugi (Eds.), *Spatial cognition: Brain bases and development.* Chicago, IL: University of Chicago Press, pp 299-326.

Piaget, J. (1945). *La formation du symbole chez l'enfant.* Neuchatel: Dechaux et Niestlé.

Piaget, J. (1952). *The origins of intelligence in children.* New York: Norton.

Piaget, J. (1955). *The language and thought of the child.* Cleveland, OH: World Publishing.

Piaget, J. (1962). *Play, dreams, and imitation in childhood.* New York: Norton.

Pizzuto, E. (1978). *Notes on deixis and anaphora in spoken and signed languages.* Unpublished manuscript, Harvard University, Graduate School of Education, Cambridge, MA.

Pizzuto, E. (1980a). *The early development of the indexic reference system of ASL.* Working paper, The Salk Institute, La Jolla, CA.

Pizzuto, E. (1980b). The early development of pronouns in American Sign Language: From pointing gestures to pointing signs (Summary). *Handbook of the Fifth Annual Boston University Conference on Language Development.* Boston, MA: Boston University, School of Education.

Pizzuto, E. (1980c). *Indexes of various types in ASL acquisition.* Working paper, The Salk Institute, La Jolla, CA.

Pizzuto, E. (1982a). Untitled paper on the acquisition of deixis in a deaf child learning American Sign Language. University of Palermo, Istituto di Psicologia Sperimentale.

Pizzuto, E. (1982b). *What's the point in signed and spoken languages? Insights from the study of child-adult interaction in American Sign Language.* Paper presented at the European Meeting on Sign Language Research Brussels, Belgium.

Pizzuto, E. (1983). Dal gesto comunicativo al segno linguistico nella acquisizione di linguaggi dei segni. In G. Attili & P. Ricci-Bitti (Eds.), *I gesti e i segni.* Roma: Bulzoni.

Pizzuto, E. & Williams, M. (1980). The acquisition of the possessive forms of American Sign Language. In B. Frøkjaer-Jensen (Ed.), *Recent developments in language and cognition: Sign language research.* University of Copenhagen, Denmark.

Poggi, I. (1983). La mano a borsa: analisi semantica di un gesto emblematico olofrastico. In G. Attili & P. Ricci-Bitti (Eds.), *Comunicare senza parole.* Roma: Bulzoni.

Poizner, H. (1981). Visual and 'phonetic' codings of movement: Evidence from American Sign Language. *Science, 212,* 691-693.

Poizner, H., Bellugi, U., & Lutes-Driscoll, V. (1981). Perception of American Sign Language in dynamic point-light display. *Journal of Experimental Psychology: Human Perception and Performance, 7,* 430-440.

Poizner, H., Klima, E.S., & Bellugi, U. (1987). *What the hands reveal about the brain.* Cambridge, MA: MIT Press.

Posner, M.I. (1967). Characteristics of visual and kinesthetic memory codes. *Journal of Experimental Psychology, 75,* 103-107.

Prinz, P.M. & Prinz, E.A. (1979). Simultaneous acquisition of ASL and spoken English in a hearing child of deaf mother and hearing father: Phase I – Early lexical development. *Sign Language Studies, 25,* 283-296.

Prinz, P.M. & Prinz, E.A. (1981). Acquisition of ASL and spoken English in a hearing child of a deaf mother and hearing father: Phase II — Early combinatorial patterns. *Sign Language Studies, 30,* 78–88.

Pugh, B. (1946). The speech vocabulary of young deaf children. *Volta Review, 48,* 267–275.

Ratner, N. & Bruner, J. (1978). Games, social exchange, and the acquisition of language. *Journal of Child Language, 5,* 391–401.

Reilly, J., McIntire, M., & Bellugi, U. (1985) *Faces: The relationship between language and affect.* Paper presented at the Tenth Boston University Conference, Boston MA.

Reilly, J., McIntire, M., & Bellugi, U. (in press). Baby face: a new perspective on universals on language acquisition. In P. Siple (Ed.), *Theoretical issues in sign language research.* New York: Springer.

Robson, K. (1967). The role of eye to eye contact in maternal-infant attachment. *Journal of Child Psychology and Psychiatry, 8,* 13–25.

Sachs, J. & Devin, J. (1976). Young children's use of age-appropriate speech styles in social interaction and role playing. *Journal of Child Language, 3,* 81–88.

Sachs, J. & Johnson, M. (1976). Language development in a hearing child of deaf parents. In W. van Raffler-Engel & Y. Lebrun (Eds.), *Baby talk and infant speech.* Amsterdam: Swets and Zeitlinger.

Sachs, J., Bard, B., & Johnson, M. (1981). Language learning with restricted input: Case studies of two hearing children of deaf parents. *Applied Psycholinguistics, 2,* 33–54.

Samuels, C.A. (1985). Attention to eye-contact opportunity and facial motion by three-month-old infants. *Journal of Experimental Child Psychology, 40,* 105–114.

Schaeffer, B. (1978). Teaching spontaneous sign language to nonverbal children: Theory and method. *Sign Language Studies, 21,* 317–352.

Schaeffer, B. (1980). *Linguistic functions and language intervention.* Unpublished manuscript (Available from [Neurological Sciences Center, Good Samaritan Hospital, 1015 N.W./22nd Avenue, Portland, OR 97210]).

Schieffelin, B. (1979). Getting it together: An ethnographic approach to the study of the development of communicative competence. In E. Ochs & B. Schieffelin (Eds.), *Developmental pragmatics,* New York: Academic.

Schieffelin, B. & Ochs, E. (1986). Language socialization. *Annual Review of Anthropology, 15,* 163–191.

Schiff, N. (1979). The influence of deviant maternal input on the development of language during the preschool years. *Journal of Speech and Hearing Research, 22,* 581–603.

Schiff, N. & Ventry, I. (1976). Communication problems in hearing children of deaf parents. *Journal of Speech and Hearing Disorders, 41,* 348–358.

Schiff-Myers, N. (1982). Sign and oral language development of preschool hearing children of deaf parents. *American Annals of the Deaf, 127,* 322–329.

Schlesinger, H.S. & Meadow, K.P. (1972). *Sound and sign: Childhood deafness and mental health.* Berkeley: University of California Press.

Scollon, R. (1979). A real early stage: An unzippered condensation of a dissertation in child language. In E. Ochs-Keenan & B. Schieffelin (Eds.), *Developmental pragmatics.* New York: Academic.

Scollon, R. & Scollon, S. (1981). *Narrative, literacy, and face in interethnic communication.* Norwood, NJ: Ablex.

Scroggs, C.L. (1981). The use of gesturing and pantomime. The language of a nine-year-old deaf boy. *Sign Language Studies, 30,* 61–77.

Shatz, M. & Gelman, R. (1973). The development of communication: Modification in the speech of young children as a function of listener. *Monographs of the Society for Research in Child Development, 38* No. 5 (Serial No. 152).

Shore, C. (1986). Combinatorial play, conceptual development and early multiword speech. *Developmental Psychology, 22,* 184–190.

Shore, C. & Bauer, P. (1983). *Individual styles in language and symbolic play.* Paper presented at the American Psychological Association Annual Convention, Anaheim, CA.

Shore, C., O'Connell, B., & Bates, E. (1984). First sentences in language and symbolic play. *Developmental Psychology, 20*(5), 872–880.

Sinclair, H. (1971). Sensorimotor action patterns as a condition for the acquisition of syntax. In R. Huxley & E. Ingram (Eds.), *Language acquisition: Models and methods.* New York: Academic.

Sinclair-de Zwart, H. (1967). *Acquisition du langage et développement de la pensée.* Paris: Dunod.

Skarakis, E.A. & Prutting, C.A. (1977). Early communication: semantic functions and communicative intents in the communication of the preschool child with impaired hearing. *American Annals of the Deaf, 122,* 382–391.

Slama-Cazacu, T. (1976). Nonverbal components in message sequence "mixed syntax". In W.C. McCormack & S.A. Wurm (Eds.), *Language and man: Anthropological issues.* The Hague: Mouton.

Slobin, D.I. (1971). *Psycholinguistics.* Glenview, IL: Scott, Foresmann.

Slobin, D.I. (1982). Universal and particular in the acquisition of language. In E. Wanner & L. Gleitman (Eds.), *Language acquisition: The state of the art.* Cambridge: Cambridge University Press.

Slobin, D.I. (1985). Crosslinguistic evidence for the language-making capacity. In D.I. Slobin (Ed.), *The crosslinguistic study of language acquisition, Vol. 2.* Hillsdale, NJ: Erlbaum.

Smith, C.B., Adamson, L.B., & Bakeman, R. (1986). Interactional predictors of early language. Paper presented at the Biennial International Conference on Infant Studies, Los Angeles.

Smolak, L. (1982). Cognitive precursors of receptive versus expressive language. *Journal of Child Language, 9,* 13–22.

Snow, C.E. (1988). The last word: Questions about the emerging lexicon. In M.D. Smith & J.L. Locke (Eds.), *The Emergent lexicon.* New York: Academic.

Snow, C. & Ferguson, C. (1977). *Talking to children.* London: Cambridge University Press.

Stenberg, C., Campos, J., & Emde, R. (1983). The facial expression of anger in seven-month-old infants. *Child Development, 54,* 178–184.

Stern, D.N. (1971). A microanalysis of mother-infant interaction: behavior regulating social contact between mother and her 3,15 month old twins. *Journal of the American Academy of Child Psychiatry, 10,* 501–517.

Stern, D.N. (1974a). The goal and structure of mother-infant play. *Journal of the American Academy of Child Psychiatry, 13,* 402–421.

Stern, D.N. (1974b). Mother and infant at play: the dyadic interaction involving facial, vocal and gaze behaviors. In M. Lewis & L. Rosenblum (Eds.), *The effect of the infant on its caregiver.* London: Wiley.

Stern, D.N., Beebe, B., Jaffe, J., & Bennett, S.L. (1977). The infant's stimulus world during social interaction: A study of caregiver behaviors with particular reference to repetition and timing. In H.R. Schaffer (Ed.), *Studies of mother-infant interaction.* New York: Academic.

Stevenson, M.B., Ver Hoeve, J.N., Roach, M.A., & Leavitt, L.A. (1986). The beginning of conversation: early patterns of mother-infant vocal responsiveness. *Infant Behavior and Development, 9,* 423–440.

Stiles-Davis, J., Kritchevsky, M., & Bellugi, U. (Eds.). (1988). *Spatial cognition: Brain bases and development.* Hillsdale, NJ: Erlbaum.

Stokes, W. & Menyuk, P. (1975). *A proposal for the investigation of acquisition of ASL and signed English by deaf and hearing children.* Unpublished manuscript, Boston University.

Stokoe, W.C. (1960). Sign language structure: an outline of the visual communication system of the American deaf. *Studies in Linguistics. Occasional Papers 8.* University of Buffalo (Rev.ed. 1978, Silver Spring, MD: Linstok).

Stokoe, W.J., Casterline, D.C., & Croneberg, C.G. (Eds.). (1965). *A dictionary of American Sign Language on linguistic principles.* Washington, DC: Gallaudet College Press.

Strayer, J. (1977). *The development of personal reference in the language of two-year-olds.* Unpublished doctoral dissertation, Simon Fraser University, Port Moody, BC, Canada.

Sugarman, S. (1982a). Developmental change in early representational intelligence: Evidence from spatial classification strategies and related verbal expressions. *Cognitive Psychology, 14,* 410–449.

Sugarman, S. (1982b). Transition in early representational intelligence: changes over time in children's production of simple block structures. In G. Forman (Ed.), *Action and thought: From sensorimotor schemes to symbolic operations.* New York: Academic.

Sugarman-Bell, S. (1978). Some organizational aspects of preverbal communication. In J. Markova (Ed.), *The social context of language.* London: Wiley.

Supalla, T. (1982). *Structure and acquisition of verbs of motion and location in American Sign Language.* Unpublished doctoral dissertation, University of California, San Diego.

Swan, C. (1936). *Postural patterning of resting infant hands.* Unpublished master's thesis, Yale University New Haven.

Tervoort, B. (1961). Esoteric symbolism in the communicative behavior of young deaf children. *American Annals of the Deaf, 106,* 436–480.

Tervoort, B. & Verbeck, A. (1967). *Analysis of communicative structure patterns in deaf children.* Vocational Rehabilitation Administrative Project. Groningen: The Netherlands.

Todd, P. (1975) A case of structural interference across sensory modalities in second language learning. *Word,* 102–118.

Trevarthen, C. (1979). Communication and cooperation in early infancy: A description of primary inter-subjectivity. In M. Bullowa (Ed.), *Before speech.* New York: Cambridge University Press.

Trevarthen, C. (1980). The foundation of intersubjectivity: development of interpersonal and cooperative understanding in infants. In D.O. Olson (Ed.), *The social foundations of language and thought.* New York: Norton.

Trevarthen, C. & Hubley, P. (1978). Secondary intersubjectivity: Confidence, confiding, and acts of meaning in the first year. In A. Lock (Ed.), *Action, gesture and symbol.* London: Academic.

Trevarthen, C. & Marwick, H. (1986). Signs of motivation for speech in infants and the nature of a mother's support for the development of language. In B. Lindblom & R. Zetterstrom (Eds.), *Precursors of early speech.* (Wenner-Gren International Symposium Series, Vol. 44). New York: Stockton.

Tronick, E. (Ed.). (1982). *Social interchange in infancy: affect, cognition, and communication.* Baltimore: University Park Press.

Tronick, E., Als, H., & Adamson, L. (1979). Structure of early face to face communicative interactions. In M. Bullowa (Ed.), *Before speech: The beginning of interpersonal communication* (pp. 349–370). Cambridge: Cambridge University Press.

Ungerer, J. A., Zelazo, P.R., Kearsley, R.B., & O'Leary, K. (1981). Developmental changes in representations of objects in symbolic play from 18–34 months of age. *Child Development, 52,* 186–195.

Uzgiris, I. (1981). Two functions of imitation during infancy. *International Journal of Behavioral Development, 4,* 1–12.

Uzgiris, I.C. & Hunt, J.M. (1975). *Assessment of infancy: Ordinal scales of psychological development.* Urbana: University of Illinois Press.

Vaid, J., Schemenauer, D., Bellugi, U., & Poizner, H. (1984). *Hand dominance in a visual-gestural language.* Paper presented at Annual Meeting of the Body for the Advancement of Brain, Behavior, and Language Enterprises. Niagara Falls, Ontario.

Van der Veer, R. & van Ijzendoorn, M.H. (1985). Vygotsky's theory of the higher psychological processes: Some criticisms. *Human Development, 28,* 1–9.

Van Hoek, K., O'Grady, L., & Bellugi, U. (1987). Morphological innovation in the acquisition of American Sign Language. *Papers and Reports on Child Language Development, 26,* 116–123.

Vihman, M. & Miller R. (1988). Words and babble at the threshold of language acquisition. In M.D. Smith & J.L. Locke (Eds.), *The Emergent lexicon,* New York: Academic.

Volterra, V. (1981a). Gestures, signs, and words at two years: When does communication become language? *Sign Language Studies, 33,* 351–361.

Volterra, V. (Ed.). (1981b). *I segni come parole: la comunicazione dei sordi.* Torino: Boringhieri.

Volterra, V. (1987). From single communicative signal to linguistic combinations in hearing and deaf children. In J. Montangero, A. Tryphon, and S. Dionnet (Eds.), *Symbolism and knowledge* Geneva: Foundation Archives Jean Piaget, pp 115–132.

Volterra, V. & Antinucci, F. (1979). Negation in child language: a pragmatic study. In E. Ochs-Keenan & B. Schieffelin (Eds.), *Developmental pragmatics.* New York: Academic.

Volterra, V. & Bates, E. (1984). On the invention of language: An alternative view. Commentary on S. Goldin-Meadow and C. Mylander, Gestural communication in deaf children: The non-effects of parental input on language development. *Monographs of the Society for Research in Child Development, 49,* (3–4, Serial No. 207).

Volterra, V. & Caselli, C. (1985). From gestures and vocalizations to signs and words. In W. Stokoe & V. Volterra (Eds.), *Sign language research '83.* Silver Spring: Linstok; Rome: Psychology Institute, National Research Council.

Volterra, V. & Caselli, C. (1986). First stage of language acquisition through two modalities in deaf and hearing children. *The Italian Journal of Neurological Sciences, 2,* (Suppl. 5), 109–115.

Volterra, V. & Massoni, P. (1978). Un'esperienza di rieducazione con bambini sordi. *Giornale Italiano di Psicologia, 3,* 585–629.

Volterra, V. & Taeschner, T. (1978). The acquisition and development of language by bilingual children. *Journal of Child Language, 5,* 311–326.

Volterra, V., Bates, E., Benigni, L., Bretherton, I., & Camaioni, L. (1979). First words in language and action: a qualitative look. In E. Bates, L. Benigni, I. Bretherton, L. Camaioni, & V. Volterra. (Eds.), *The emergence of symbols.*. New York: Academic.

Volterra, V., Beronesi, S., & Massoni, P. (1983). Quando la comunicazione gestuale diventa linguaggio? In G. Attili & P. Ricci-Bitti (Eds.), *I gesti e i segni.* Roma: Bulzoni.

von Tetzchner S. (1984). First signs acquired by a Norwegian deaf child of deaf parents. *Sign Language Studies, 44,* 225–257.

Vygotsky, L.S. (1966). Development of the higher mental functions. In *Psychological Research in the USSR.* Moscow: Progress.

Vygotsky, L. (1978). *Mind in society.* Cambridge, MA: Harvard University Press.

Wechsler, D. (1974). *Wechsler intelligence scale for children — Revised.* The Psychological Corporation, San Diego CA.

Weeks, T. (1971). Speech registers in young children. *Child Development, 42,* 1119–1131.

Weir, R. (1962). *Language in the crib.* The Hague: Mouton.

Werner, H. & Kaplan, B. (1963). *Symbol formation.* New York: Wiley.

Whitney, W.D. (1867). *Language and the study of language: Twelve lectures on the principles of linguistic science.* New York: Scribner's Sons.

Wiener, M., Devoe, S., Rubinow, S., & Geller, J. (1972). Non-verbal behaviour and non-verbal communication. *Psychological Review 79,* 185–214.

Wilbur, R. (1979). *American Sign Language and sign language systems: research and applications.* Baltimore, MD: University Park Press.

Wilbur, R. & Jones, M. (1974). Some aspects of the bilingual, bimodal acquisition of sign and English by three hearing children of deaf parents. In M. La Galy, R. Fox, & A. Bruck (Eds.), *Papers from the Tenth Regional Meeting* of the Chicago Linguistic Society, Chicago: Chicago Linguistic Society.

Wilbur, R. & Petitto, L.A. (1983). How to know a conversation when you see one: Discourse structure in American Sign Language conversation. *Journal of the National Student Speech Language Hearing Association, 91,* 66–81.

Williams, J.S. (1976). Bilingual experience of a deaf child. *Sign Language Studies, 10,* 37–41.

Wolf, D. & Gardner, H. (1979). Style and sequence in early symbolic play. In M. Franklin & N. Smith (Eds.), *Symbolic functioning in childhood.* Hillsdale, NJ; Erlbaum.

Wolff, P. (1961). Observations on early development of smiling. In B.M. Foss (Ed.), *Determinants of infant behavior, Vol. 2. London: Methuen.*

Woodward, J. (1978, July). *Sign marking: "Stage" four handshapes.* Paper presented at the Summer Meeting of the Linguistic Society of America, Champaign-Urbana, Illinois.

Wundt, W. (1973). *The language of gestures.* The Hague: Mouton. (Original work published 1900).

Zinober, B. & Martlew, M. (1985a). Developmental changes in four types of gesture in relation to acts and vocalizations from 10 to 21 months. *British Journal of Developmental Psychology, 3,* 293–306.

Zinober, B. & Martlew, M. (1985b). The development of communicative gestures. In M.D. Barrett (Ed.), *Children's single-word speech.* New York: Wiley.

Subject Index